Sociology of Economic Innovation

This is the first comprehensive work on the sociology of innovation. It's an original contribution that shows the importance of social relations in the process of invention and innovation. Ramella provides an extremely useful tool for students and scholars from other disciplines that are interested in the sociological view of innovation.

Professor Carlo Trigilia, *University of Florence, Italy*

Francesco Ramella's book is an important and original contribution which helps to clarify how innovation emerges, pointing to its social and territorial embeddedness.

Professor Arnaldo Bagnasco, *University of Turin, Italy*

Sociology of Economic Innovation by Francesco Ramella offers a timely and innovative account of how economic innovation takes place. It shows what sociological analysis at its best can do when applied to understanding economic phenomena, while at the same time relying on an impressive amount of work from other disciplines. The analysis of the actors of innovation, of their relations and of the contexts in which they operate is supported by robust theoretical and conceptual frameworks and represents a very important contribution to our understanding of this key phenomenon. Ramella's book lucidly and insightfully fills in a longstanding gap in our knowledge of economic innovation and promises to change our thinking about it, thus renewing the best tradition of the 'Italian school' of economic sociology. It will be of great interest to social scientists as well as to students and policy-makers.

Professor Marino Regini, *University of Milan, Italy*

This book offers a sociological overview of the theories and research on economic innovation. Over the past few decades, the economics of innovation has given rise to a lively flow of studies, and Innovation Studies continues to develop as an interdisciplinary field of research. Sociology in general, and economic sociology in particular, have already made a significant contribution to innovation and continue to play a crucial role in this emerging field.

This book presents an integrated sociological approach to the study of economic innovation. It explores the key theories and sociological research on innovation, as well as other contributions to the field of Innovation Studies from economists, geographers and psychologists. Ramella argues that in order to understand the processes of innovation, it is necessary to look at the *actors* of innovation, at the *relations* that exist between them, and at the sectoral and territorial *contexts* in which they operate. For students, this book includes international case studies throughout, as well as further study questions at the end of each chapter.

Francesco Ramella is Professor of Economic Sociology at the University of Torino, Italy.

T0330486

Routledge Advances in Sociology

Sociology of Economic Innovation

Francesco Ramella

Routledge
Taylor & Francis Group

LONDON AND NEW YORK

First published 2016 by Routledge

2 Park Square, Milton Park, Abingdon, Oxfordshire OX14 4RN
52 Vanderbilt Avenue, New York, NY 10017

Routledge is an imprint of the Taylor & Francis Group, an informa business

First issued in paperback 2019

British Library Cataloguing in Publication Data
A catalogue record for this book is available from the British Library

Library of Congress Cataloging in Publication Data
Ramella, Francesco.
Sociology of economic innovation / Francesco Ramella.
    pages cm. – (Routledge advances in sociology ; 154)
    1. Technological innovations–Social aspects. 2. Economics–
Sociological aspects. I. Title.
    HC79.T4R357 2015
    306.3–dc23   2015005340

ISBN: 978-1-138-80373-2 (hbk)
ISBN: 978-0-367-35998-0 (pbk)

Typeset in Times New Roman
by Wearset Ltd, Boldon, Tyne and Wear

Contents

Figures

Tables

Acknowledgements

This book was first published in Italian under the name *Sociologia dell'innovazione economica* by Il Mulino, in 2013. This Routledge edition, translated by Stuart James Wilson in 2014–15, is an updated version of the Italian book.

Many of the ideas contained in this book were developed in the course of research carried out together with Carlo Trigilia, which prompted me to reflect on the theme of innovation in a more systematic manner. My warm thanks go out to him for this. I am also extremely grateful to Jan Fagerberg and Ben Martin for providing me with some of the data and information from their studies.

This book is dedicated to Anna: neither it, nor many other things, would have been possible without her support.

Introduction
Innovation Studies

In this Introduction, I discuss the possible contribution of Economic Sociology to Innovation Studies and provide some conceptual coordinates for reading the later chapters, starting from the definition of 'economic innovation' and different types of innovation. At an international level, Innovation Studies is an emerging field of research, one that tends to cross over the boundaries of traditional academic disciplines. A number of sociological studies, as well as sociological research, have provided a significant contribution to the development of this new scientific field.

I.1 A field of interdisciplinary research

This book offers an overview of the theories and research (both sociological and otherwise) regarding economic innovation. In economics, there is a large and well-established literature about this particular topic. Over the past few decades, the *economics of innovation* has given rise to a lively flow of studies, including textbooks, university courses and a great deal of empirical research. This has not, however, been the case with economic sociology. Few books exist that are devoted explicitly to innovation and there is also lack of reviews on the subject in the literature. For example, an entry for 'economic innovation' is entirely absent from the first edition of the *Handbook of Economic Sociology* (Smelser and Swedberg 1994), which takes stock of the discipline's issues and the state of the art. Only in the second edition does a chapter appear dedicated to the relationship between technology and the economy: its authorship, however, was assigned to three economists (Dosi, Orsenigo and Sylos Labini 2005). Even the *International Encyclopedia of Economic Sociology* (Beckert and Zafirovski 2006) lacks a specific entry.[1] Paraphrasing Robert Solow's well-known paradox concerning the new economy, it could be argued that innovation can be seen everywhere today except in books about economic sociology.[2]

This lack is not due to the absence of sociological reflection on the subject. On the contrary: starting with the classics, there is a long tradition of studies that address the issue of economic innovation by linking it to the dynamics of capitalist systems. In comparison, in economics the topic of innovation has been more controversial and, notwithstanding the hints in the work of Adam Smith, only more recently has it become a subject of research. The beginning of the twentieth century saw the pioneering contribution of heterodox economist Joseph Schumpeter – not, coincidentally, very open-minded towards other social sciences – where the question of innovation was treated systematically and correlated with economic development. Such original considerations were, however, only rediscovered in the late fifties and early sixties, when the first contributions by economists regarding the themes of innovation and scientific and technological research were brought together in a collective volume edited by Richard Nelson: *The Rate and Direction of Inventive Activity* (NBER 1962).

Later, in 1974, Christopher Freeman published a book that summarised the main results achieved in the previous decade, and which would go on to become a classic: *The Economics of Industrial Innovation*. Finally, Innovation Studies gained momentum in the eighties with the publication of *An Evolutionary Theory of Economic Change* (1982) by Richard Nelson and Sidney Winter. The book, which puts technological innovation at the centre of the debate about economic change, marks the foundation of an *evolutionary approach* to economics that provides an alternative to neoclassical theories of growth. The contribution of economists to Innovation Studies then progressively becomes prevalent. These economic approaches, however, are 'heterodox' in nature and tend to be located on the outer edges of the mainstream current. Nelson and Winter's book, despite being one of the most cited works on innovation, remains at the margins of 'orthodox' economic science.[3]

This is not accidental. Innovation is a subject that is difficult to understand using the conventional analytical categories of neoclassical economics. The latter is a discipline focused on choice maximisation by individual actors who have well-defined preferences and utility functions, and who compete with one another for the acquisition of scarce resources. Innovative behaviour, however, is marked by insights and choices made in conditions of deep uncertainty, which contrast with the probabilistic and maximising calculations of rational actors. It is also driven by motivations that are not exclusively economic-utilitarian and that follow a logic of interaction in which trust and cooperation often mingle with the customary market transactions. For these reasons the issue of innovation represents a borderline area open to contributions from a number of different disciplines.

At an international level, in fact, Innovation Studies (IS) is taking shape as an emerging field of research – one that tends to cross over the boundaries of traditional academic disciplines (Fagerberg 2013). It is a scientific field that:

- is defined by a shared cognitive focus, centred on the theme of economic innovation;
- hosts a large community of scholars from a wide range of different countries;
- possesses shared intellectual references, as well as specific research centres and meeting places.

A recent study shows a steady increase in articles devoted to innovation, starting from the sixties, with a particularly strong acceleration taking place in the last two decades (Fagerberg and Verspagen 2009, 220, fig. I.1; Fagerberg and Sapprasert 2010, fig. I.1). Researchers who deal with innovation and identify themselves with this field of study are estimated to number, on a global scale, around 4,000 (ibid., 229, note 33), and there are 136 research centres dedicated to the subject. Most of these scholars belong to economic disciplines (58 per cent), followed by engineering (9 per cent), geography (8 per cent), management (6 per cent) and sociology (5 per cent). The remaining 14 per cent come from other areas, ranging from political science to psychology to history, etc.

The field is composed of a multiplicity of small groups that interact closely with one another, but are linked to a wider scientific community. It is a community with a common literature of reference, a number of leading scholars,[4] scientific journals[5] and professional associations,[6] as well as meeting places and conferences (ibid., 228). The vast majority of scholars involved are European (71 per cent), and they, together with those from the United States (17 per cent), clearly dominate the field.[7] Europe, in fact, has a strong tradition in Innovation Studies. A major contribution was made in the mid-sixties with the foundation of the Science Policy Research Unit (SPRU) at the University of Sussex (initially directed by Christopher Freeman), which organised Masters and PhD courses of an interdisciplinary nature (involving economists, sociologists, psychologists, engineers, etc.) and conducted pioneering research on the role of innovation in economic and social changes (e.g. the Sappho project concerning factors of success and failure in innovation). This research centre was also responsible for the founding of the field's most prestigious journal, *Policy Research*, established in 1972 and directed in the beginning by Freeman himself (Fagerberg 2005).

Comparatively speaking, Innovation Studies in the United States has remained more heavily restricted to disciplinary contexts and this partially helps to explain the low proportion of scholars who 'identify' themselves with a scientific field which, as has been said, is highly interdisciplinary in character (Fagerberg and Verspagen 2009, 223).

I.2 The contribution of sociology

IS thus represents a new scientific field – one that is establishing itself at an international level and which focuses on a particular research topic (innovation) shared by researchers from a variety of disciplines. Judging by their numbers, the role played by sociologists seems rather limited. In fact, this is only partially true. A study by Ben Martin (2012) well illustrates the seminal contribution provided by sociology.[8] Martin analyses the scientific papers that have had the greatest impact (the most quoted articles) in what he calls – in a broad sense – Science Policy and Innovation Studies (SPIS).

In the group of so-called *precursors* of SPIS (works published before the end of the fifties), together with Schumpeter's works, there is also a study on social change carried out in the twenties by William Ogburn (1922) – a sociologist whose observations focused on technological transformation. There are, moreover, many sociological contributions among the *pioneering* works – those published from the late fifties on. First, the research conducted in 1954 by James Coleman, Elihu Katz and Herbert Menzel on the process of diffusion of new drugs in the medical field (1957, 1966). The study concerns the adoption of a new broad-spectrum antibiotic – tetracycline – by doctors in four small Illinois towns, and it highlights the importance of networks of interpersonal communication and the role of opinion leaders in the transmission of innovation. The authors show how the diffusion of innovation takes place according to processes of 'social contagion' arising from informal discussions within the medical profession; and how the dynamics of contagion (the timing of the adoption rate) depend to a large extent on the formal properties of the network of relationships. The work of Coleman, Katz and Menzel, although relevant to studies on the diffusion of innovation, has remained mostly confined to the field of sociology.

A rather different case is that of another pioneering contribution of a sociological nature, *Diffusion of Innovations*, the influential book by Everett Rogers which is still the benchmark work for 'diffusionist studies' and the first edition of which dates back to 1962. This work systematically reconstructs innovation adoption processes, demonstrating how these have well-defined actors and roles and follow a recurring pattern of diffusion: the logistic curve of adoption rates (S-curve). Rogers' book has gone through five different editions up to the present time – the last being in 2003, the year before his death – and is by far the most cited publication in the field of SPIS (Martin 2012).[9]

Other pioneering contributions hail from the world of industrial and organisational sociology, with two works in particular at the forefront. The first, by Joan Woodward (1965), highlights the close relationship between the type of technologies employed, the organisation of work and the economic performance of companies. The second contrasts two organisational models that will have a major influence on subsequent research. In a study of electronics companies, Burns and Stalker[10] (1961) developed two ideal-typical models: a 'mechanistic' organisation of work (of a hierarchical and centralised kind), and an 'organic' one (which is a more decentralised, horizontal and complex model). According to the two researchers, the second model allows for greater fluidity and flexibility in communication, both within and outside the organisation, and in doing so fosters creativity and innovation by ensuring more successful adaptation to technological and market changes.

Even in the period of *maturity* of the SPIS – works published after the eighties – there is no lack of sociological contributions. Ronald Burt's reappraisal (1987) of the study by Coleman, Katz and Menzel on medical breakthroughs – which criticises the idea of social contagion – is much cited. Burt's article, however – like the original work by Coleman and his colleagues – remains confined to the field of sociological literature. Mark Granovetter's essay 'Economic Action and Social Structure: The Problem of Embeddedness' (1985) has, on the other hand, enjoyed far wider circulation. This deals with the importance of social networks for the circulation of information, and has come to be considered as a kind of manifesto for the 'new economic sociology', an approach that gives preferential attention to social networks. While not explicitly addressing the topic of innovation, this work is among the most cited in IS, and the same goes for the book on 'structural holes' – also dedicated to social networks and the circulation of information – written by Ronald Burt a few years later (1992b). This attention devoted by IS to sociology that deals with social networks – even when it is not explicitly addressing the theme of innovation – should not surprise us.

Starting from the mid-nineties, in fact, IS showed growing interest in inter-organisational relations due to the exponential growth of collaborative relationships between companies (Meeus and Faber 2006). In particular, research and development (R&D) partnerships around world rose from a few dozen in the sixties and seventies, to several hundred in the eighties – reaching a peak of more than 700 examples of cooperation in the mid-nineties. From the early eighties, moreover, these partnerships were concentrated in the high technology sectors (pharmaceuticals, IT and telecommunications, aerospace, etc.).

The second reason why the new economic sociology receives attention is linked to the development of the literature concerning high technology innovation systems, which gives a prominent place to networks of collaboration. Not coincidentally, the research conducted by Walter Powell, Kenneth Koput and Laurel Smith-Doerr (1996) on biotechnology has had a wide resonance. The study shows that in an industry characterised by rapid scientific and technological change, one in which the knowledge base and required skills are complex and dispersed amongst a variety of subjects, *networks of learning* become the 'locus of innovation' *par excellence*. Innovative processes, in other words, pass beyond the boundaries of individual companies and put down roots in inter-organisational networks.

Other relevant sociological contributions to IS came from several studies with an organisational approach (Kimberly and Evanisko 1981; Ettlie *et al.* 1984; Dewar and Dutton 1986) and from neo-institutionalism – in particular from the work of DiMaggio and Powell (1991) on the mechanisms of institutional isomorphism that condition the processes of diffusion and adoption of organisational innovation.

A great deal of attention was also paid to Piore and Sabel's celebrated work (1984) on the issue of flexible specialisation, which shows the changes in the models of competition and organisation of companies in the new post-Fordist scenarios, with the shift from the production of mass standardised goods to diversified quality goods.

Finally, to conclude this brief look at the contributions of economic sociology to IS, two highly cited works come from adjacent areas. The first, which has its origins in the field of Science and Technology Studies (STS), is the book by Wiebe Bijker, Thomas Hughes and Trevor Pinch (1987) devoted to the social construction of technological systems. The second work is concerned with modes of knowledge production and is the result of an interdisciplinary collaboration that also saw the involvement of sociologists. The book, by Michael

Gibbons and others, and emblematically titled *The New Production of Knowledge* (1994), analyses the transition from Mode 1 to Mode 2 knowledge production. In the first mode, production is mainly academic and disciplinary, with marked scientific autonomy in relation to the demands and needs of society. In the second mode, disciplinary boundaries are looser and 'ivory towers' more accessible: research becomes more interdisciplinary and involves a variety of centres and institutions; borders between industry and society are blurred; and the scientific community becomes more responsive to social needs.

As can be seen both sociology in general, and economic sociology in particular, have made a significant contribution to IS. It should also be added, however, that their contribution has so far been sporadic and unsystematic, mostly confined to narrow disciplinary fields (e.g. organisational studies).

There is no justification for this state of affairs. Many scholars of innovation employ concepts and address issues (institutions, trust, collaboration networks, etc.) to which sociology can make a significant contribution at both macro and meso levels (national, regional and sectorial systems of innovation), and at micro level (learning networks and innovative partnerships). In recent years, moreover, the subject of innovation has also become increasingly present within economic sociology's two major approaches: the *comparative political economy* and the *new economic sociology*. Economic sociology has gained in vigour thanks to these two strands, though they themselves have remained separate (Regini 2007; Trigilia 2007a, 2009; Barbera and Negri 2008). IS provides an opportunity for dialogue between them in order to develop an analytical approach of an integrated kind. We will return to this point at the end of Chapter 1. First, however, we need to provide some conceptual coordinates to delineate the topic at hand.

I.3 A first definition

What is meant by 'innovation'? Derived originally from Latin, the verb *innovate* and noun *innovation*, as they are currently used, indicate *the transformation of an existing state of things, in order to introduce something new.*[11] The reference, therefore, is both to the action of change and to its result, implying a contextualisation and a diachronic comparison. Innovation needs to be collocated within the context in which it occurs, and its results can be understood only by making a comparison between *before* and *after*: the state of things prior to and successive to its introduction. These simple considerations give us a process-oriented and relational idea of the concept.

I.3.1 Innovation is processual

Innovation is a complex activity that comprises a series of interconnected phenomena. It involves a number of activities and transitions that scholars have often combined into phases. Everett Rogers (2003, 137ff.), for example, indicates six such phases:

1 the identification of a need or a problem that requires a solution;
2 the decision to carry out research (basic and/or applied) to find this solution;[12]
3 the development of innovation to give it a form and content that meet the needs of those who will use it;
4 the marketing, which is the production and distribution of the product/service that contains the innovation;
5 its adoption and diffusion;
6 the consequences of innovation, which relate to the changes associated with its adoption.

The steps mentioned by Rogers are designed for different kinds of innovation. In recent years, a procedural approach and a division into stages have also been developed for company innovations.

- *The input stage.* Starting off the whole process, a decision is taken to initiate research and innovation by investing human and financial resources in it.
- *The throughput stage.* The central section features the path that the company must take in order to transform input into output through company innovation.
- *The output stage.* At the end of the process, there are the results achieved: the fruits of innovation in terms of new products or services offered on the market. The European survey regarding company innovation (CIS) follows this pattern, with data collection for each of these three steps (Kemp *et al.* 2003).

To avoid misunderstanding, however, some clarification is required. The division of the innovation process into different stages has a purely analytical value: it is useful to define the ideal-typical categories and reference points for the analysis of specific cases. It does not imply that innovation should be thought of in strictly sequential terms, as an orderly and linear succession of stages, each one rigidly distinct from the other; nor that innovative activity necessarily includes the explicit employment of scientific research, from which innovation derives. While the innovative process is always concerned with the creation, diffusion and use of new knowledge, it is not always the case that this new knowledge derives from scientific research: it often comes from the experiences of suppliers, producers and the users of certain goods and services.

For a long period of time, studies on economic innovation were dominated by the so-called *linear model of innovation*, which defines a rigid sequence of stages. It starts with basic research, moves on to applied research, passes into the development stage of innovation, and concludes with production and diffusion.[13]

It is a sequence involving one single direction: upstream (basic research) to downstream (market). As an approach, this was severely criticised by Kline and Rosenberg (1986), who opposed the so-called *chain model*, highlighting how innovation is an uncertain, complex and untidy process, which in most cases does not start out with research activity. It is a process with a great deal of cross-feedback between the stages, so that much important input to the research comes from the developmental and market phases.

Innovation has a recursive, circular connotation, so it would be an error to limit the 'creative' dimension only to the first phase indicated above – the input stage. For example, with reference to companies, the transformation phase of input into output is not simply a moment where the invention packaged by the R&D department is implemented. This particular phase often produces the stimuli and ideas that then become the subject of systematic company research. Moreover, in the implementation phase, the inventions that come out of the laboratories are profoundly modified, with an ongoing interactive process taking place between research staff and production staff. The same applies to the downstream phase, which involves the economic valorisation of innovations. Market feedback, together with the needs of, and suggestions from, the company's most important customers, provide essential contributions for the generation and development of new products. The innovation process, therefore, cannot be represented as a *direct current*, as a continuous and fixed flow of electrons going in a single direction, but should be thought of rather as an *alternating current*, in which the flux of electrons varies over time, sometimes going forward and at other times going backward.

I.3.2 Innovation is relational

First of all, innovation is relative: it has to be considered in relation to a period and a context. It can be understood and defined only through a comparison between the state of things as they exist within an economic sector, a company, a geographical area, in terms of time T1, and the new state of things realised, in terms of time T2. In addition, innovation relies on the contribution – in an implicit or explicit form – of other actors, both in the generative phase (exchange of ideas, interpretations, etc.) and in the implementation phase. In order to have an impact on the context, it must also be accepted and diffused, and this occurs through the mediation of interpersonal relationships, as sociological studies on diffusion show (Rogers 2003).

I.3.3 Innovation is different from change

Change is a broader and more generic term, and refers to transformations that are not necessarily of an innovative kind. Innovation does bring change with it, but always in order to introduce something new; it involves 'the doing of new things or the doing of things that are already being done in a new way (innovation)' (Schumpeter 1947, 151).

I.3.4 Innovation should be distinguished from invention

Invention means to conceive a new product or process; innovation implies putting these new ideas into practice for the first time (Fagerberg 2005, 34). It was Schumpeter once again who suggested this distinction, drawing a line between the inventor and the innovator-entrepreneur: 'the inventor produces ideas, the entrepreneur gets things done' (Schumpeter 1947, 152; 1912 Eng. trans. 2012, 65). While the first activity remains confined within the context of knowledge advancement, the second assumes meaningful economic importance. As the Austrian economist observed, ' "getting new things done" is not only a distinct process but it is a process which produces consequences that are an essential part of capitalist reality' (Schumpeter 1947, 152). That said, the line between invention and innovation is not always easy to draw, since in some production sectors inventive and innovative activity tend to overlap (biotechnology, software, etc.). Moreover, as Schumpeter himself pointed out, inventors often tend to exploit their inventions entrepreneurially. This book will, therefore, also deal with inventors (industrial and academic), and inventions for the economy, and in this I take my lead from the suggestion of one of the major economic historians of technology who observes that 'invention and innovation are complements in the long run, technologically creative societies must be both inventive and innovative' (Mokyr 1990, 10). Since inventors and inventions have been neglected by economic sociology, a certain amount of attention will be dedicated to them in this work, considering them as examples of *generative mechanisms of innovation*: in other words, as one possible mode of initiating economic innovation (Hedström and Swedberg 1998; Barbera 2004).

I.3.5 Innovation does not always bring positive results

The term 'innovation' is freighted with a certain evocative power; a kind of bias that leads us to suppose that the changes brought about will always have a positive value. Innovation thus ends up becoming a synonym for 'progress'. This is the wrong way to look at things, since it generates the fusion of two analytical levels which instead must be kept quite distinct: that of the intentions of the innovators and their expectations for improvement, and that of the evaluation of the results produced. The introduction of something new is not necessarily positive; it does not always, at least, lead to the desired results. Innovation can, in fact, fail and/or generate unexpected consequences which are not necessarily beneficial to innovators and/or to the community of reference. The many harmful innovations that have been introduced in recent years in the financial world are a good illustration of this. Here, therefore, the term will be used with a neutral sense. This is for three reasons. The first is that this allows us to problematise – or place within an analytical context – the economic and social impact of innovation. The second is that this use is consistent with the indications provided by the *Oslo Manual*,[14] which gives standardised guidelines for data collection and the study of innovation at company level (OECD/Eurostat 2005). The third is that the activity of innovation is problematic precisely because it is a risky and uncertain one. It is subject to failures that can be technological (relating to the attempted technical solutions), social (relating to the resistance of the actors involved who are threatened by the new solution) or economic (relating to the market). The introduction of marginal change creates situations of risk (where the probability of success can be calculated based on past experience), while the introduction of fundamental innovation creates situations of radical uncertainty (where the calculation of probabilities is not possible because there is no previous experience to refer to).[15]

I.4 Economic innovation

This book is not concerned with the subject of innovation in general but with economic innovation. In the social sciences there are two different ways of perceiving the economy. The first, defined by Karl Polanyi as *formal*, applies the term to the nexus which unites the means to the ends of an economic action. It refers to a hypothetical situation of choice in which the actor follows rational criteria in assessing the benefits that derive from the allocation of the actor's (scarce) resources to alternative ends. The rationale, then, concerns not the means or the ends, but the relationship between them. The problem with this approach is that of falling into a sort of 'economistic fallacy' (Polanyi 1977). There is, in other words, a process of universalisation of the (utilitarian) motivations and logics of action (based on the assumption of scarcity of resources and the maximising rationality of behaviour) that are unique to a specific historical epoch: that of liberal capitalism, in which trade takes place within a system of markets that regulate prices. It is a definition of economics that is too narrow to investigate – in a historical-comparative perspective – the relationship between economy and society. For this reason, sociology uses a broader and more substantial concept of the term 'economy', which starts with the assumption that man depends on nature and on other people for his survival and the satisfaction of his needs. According to Polanyi (1968), the origin of the substantial concept lies within the concrete economic systems. These can be defined as an instituted process of interaction between man and his natural and social environment, which gives rise to a continuous flow of material means for the satisfaction of human needs.

What is, then, economic innovation? Based on the above, we can provide a first general definition. *Economic innovation* is a process of change that introduces new economic and regulatory elements: in the needs that are met, in the goods and services that are produced, and in the modes of production, distribution and use of these goods and services. The unit of reference varies depending on the analytical level selected: it might be a company, or the consumers, but it could also be the local, regional or national economies, etc.

Picking up on the suggestion of Schumpeter,[16] different authors have defined innovation as a problem-solving process of a combinatorial type: that is, oriented towards the search for new combinations with known elements as a starting point. Often these definitions refer to technological innovation (Fleming 2001; Fleming and Sorenson 2001). The search for new technical solutions, however, is only one aspect of the phenomenon we are dealing with – which is broader and more complex. Economic innovation is not limited to technological change.

Following Keith Pavitt's observation, we can think of it as a process that involves 'matching technological opportunities with market needs and organizational practices' (2005, 88). The role of the innovator (whether an individual or an organisational unit) is to activate and coordinate all the factors that are necessary to achieve this goal (Fagerberg 2005, 34).

With reference to economic sociology, however, these definitions require two specifications:

1   the needs and the actors that it considers are not only those of the market;
2   its purpose is to show that, in each of the phases of the innovation process, there are also social and institutional factors at work in addition to economic ones.

I.4.1 Types of innovation

But let's now try to give some more specific and operational definitions, ones useful for orientation in the study of these phenomena. Our starting point is innovation at company level. The reference point, in this case, is the *Oslo Manual*, which deals with the collection of data in the surveys conducted throughout the various countries of the European Union: 'an innovation is the implementation of a new or significantly improved product (good or service), or process, a new marketing method, or a new organisational method in business practices, workplace organisation or external relations' (OECD/Eurostat 2005, 46).[17] There are therefore four types of innovation.

1   *Product innovation* involves the production of goods or services that are entirely new, or modified in respect to the previous version.
2   *Process innovation* includes changes in the method of production or delivery of goods and services.
3   *Organisational innovation* refers to new forms of organisation of business operations.
4   *Marketing innovation* may relate to the design and/or packaging of the product, its mode of promotion and placement on the market, as well as methods for determining the selling prices of goods and services.

Every change in these activities must include a certain degree of newness. The degree, however, can vary a great deal. The literature mainly defines two types of innovation:

1   *Incremental innovation*, introducing minor changes – that is, limited modifications in the production or use of a particular good/service.
2   *Radical innovation*, which brings about a far more significant level of newness, reconfiguring the state of knowledge and expertise hitherto used in a given area, and which can, sometimes, create new markets.[18]

Examples of the first type of innovation are the constant changes introduced in the cars, TVs and computers that we use. These modifications are made by manufacturers to improve functionality and/or aesthetics, in order to attract new consumers and beat the competition. Examples of the second type, on the other hand, are the introduction to market of the *first* cars, television sets and computers designed for personal use. Incremental innovation, however, should not be underestimated, given that, in terms of quantity, it represents the largest part of economic innovation, and, in terms of quality, many incremental innovations of a cumulative kind can end up determining changes of great importance.

There is also a third type of innovation which concerns the relationship between products and components. Products are, in fact, composed of various elements assembled together, and innovation can sometimes relate to these individual components without this having an effect on their various relationships. When innovation involves the manner in which the components are integrated together, however, this produces *architectural innovation*, which brings about an overall reconfiguration of the product. An example given by the two scholars who first drew attention to this phenomenon is that of Xerox (Henderson and Clark 1990). At the end of the forties, the American company launched the first photocopying machine on to the market and quickly became the leader in this sector. In the mid-seventies, however, Xerox found itself in difficulty because of competition from a number of companies able to produce smaller and more reliable copiers. Despite the fact that there were no major technological innovations in these new machines, it took several years for Xerox to meet the challenge effectively, since this process involved changes in the architecture of its products.

Alongside individual innovations, broader technological changes must also be considered. *Shifts in technological systems* tend to be very wide-ranging changes that involve a number of economic sectors and bring about the introduction of a constellation of interrelated innovations – some radical, some incremental and some organisational. An example of this is the introduction of new techniques for the production of synthetic materials that, in the first half of the twentieth century, was accompanied by innovations in the petrochemical and machinery fields. *Shifts in techno-economic paradigms (technological revolutions)* involve even more extensive changes that can alter economic development as a whole. The most appropriate example in this case is the technological revolution that took place towards the end of the eighteenth century with the introduction of the steam engine (Freeman 1994, 734).

In this book we will deal with economic innovation in a sociological perspective.[19] The aim is twofold:

1   to stir the interest of students and scholars in the field of economic sociology, demonstrating that the subject of innovation provides room for reflections of a sociological nature;
2   to support the idea that the study of innovation requires an integrated approach, involving an interdisciplinary dialogue and explanations conducted

at a number of levels, both geographical and analytical. In order to understand the processes of innovation, it is necessary to look at the *actors* of innovation, at the *relations* that exist between them, and at the sectoral and territorial *contexts* in which they operate.

I will begin, in Chapter 1, by presenting various sociological contributions to the study of innovation, to be used as *focusing devices*[20] to frame and analyse the different dimensions of innovation. In Chapters 2 and 3 I will focus on a particular type of *innovation actor*: the inventor. Chapter 4 will look at a special configuration of *innovative relationships*: the small-world networks. Finally, the last three chapters will deal with three important *contexts of innovation*: the national, regional and local systems.

Box introduction Self-study prompts

1   What is Innovation Studies?
2   What is sociology's contribution to this particular field of study?
3   What is meant by 'innovation'?
4   Which are the basic traits of this concept?
5   How can 'economic innovation' be defined?
6   What are the main types of innovation?

Notes

1 There are, on the other hand, entries for both 'technological change' and 'organisational innovation'.
2 The original phrase, known as the Solow paradox, runs as follows: 'You can see the computer age everywhere but in the productivity statistics' (1987, 36). There are, fortunately, some notable exceptions, and a few recent sociological studies seem to bear witness to the emergence of new attention for these issues. To cite some of the most relevant studies we can mention Hage and Meeus (2006), Stark (2009) and Block and Keller (2011).
3 At the end of May 2015, the research engine Google Scholar reported almost 29,000 references to this book – an extraordinarily high number for the social sciences. For the most part, however, the references come from articles published in journals of organisational and management sciences and Innovation Studies (Fagerberg and Verspagen 2009, 229).
4 Such figures include Joseph Schumpeter, Richard Nelson, Christopher Freeman, Bengt-Åke Lundvall, Nathan Rosenberg, Keith Pavitt, Giovanni Dosi and others.
5 The most prestigious are *Research Policy, Industrial and Corporate Change* and the *Journal of Evolutionary Economics*.
6 For example, the International Schumpeter Society (ISS), the Danish Research Unit for Industrial Dynamics (DRUID) and several others.
7 In a subsequent study, conducted on the core literature on innovation (the most cited publications in leading handbooks), the United States emerges as having a greater role in both the production and use of this literature (*knowledge users*). Among the 20 most important contributions to IS, 11 are authored by North American scholars, eight by Europeans and one by a Japanese. Among knowledge users, however, 46 per cent

are European, 42 per cent American, and the remaining 12 per cent belong to other nationalities (Fagerberg and Sapprasert 2010).

8 Ben Martin teaches Science and Technology Policy Studies at the SPRU – one of the most important centres in the world for Innovation Studies – of which he was director from 1997–2004.

9 Even in Sapprasert and Fagerberg's research (2010) on core IS literature – which uses a different method of identification from that of Martin – Rogers' book receives the highest number of overall citations. It also appears in eighth place in the shortlist of the 20 contributions that have had the greatest impact (the ranking is obtained on the basis of the J-Index value: a normalised citation index that takes into account the various years of publication of the works).

10 Only the first of the two authors is a sociologist.

11 A fairly common definition, found in the best English, French and Italian dictionaries.

12 *Basic research* can be defined as a type of exploratory research, oriented primarily towards the advancement of scientific knowledge and the theoretical understanding of the phenomena studied. *Applied research*, instead, is a kind of research aimed at the practical application of knowledge to solve specific problems. Despite the apparent clarity of this distinction, it is not always obvious into which category a particular type of research falls, or what the relationship is between them. A hierarchical relationship is often assumed: basic research → applied research. In reality, things tend to be more complex, especially if a broad interpretation of applied research is employed which includes all the activities aimed at solving technical problems. *Technique* is a form of operational knowledge regarding 'knowing how' and it can be defined as the set of rules that are applied to the performance of a task, a job, a manufacturing process and the use of related tools and machinery. *Technology* is the body of knowledge related to technical matters. The boundaries that separate applied research and technological knowledge are blurred and the influential relationships between the latter and scientific knowledge are far from unidirectional. Historically, the search for a practical solution for production problems preceded (and drove) scientific understanding of such problems. Moreover, it is not uncommon that applied research and technical innovation are in fact the elements that enable progress in scientific research. On this point, see the remarks made by Nathan Rosenberg (1982).

13 For a detailed historical reconstruction of the acceptance of this particular model, see Godin (2005). Its origins are also linked to the first sociological reflections of Ogburn and Gilfillan, who, in the twenties, integrated the theme of invention with that of innovation (Godin 2008). We will discuss the contribution of these sociologists in Chapter 3.

14 The *Manual* is the result of the joint work of the Organization for Economic Cooperation and Development (OECD) and the European Union (EU).

15 The distinction between risk and uncertainty was introduced by economist Frank Knight (1921). Nelson and Katzenstein, writing about the recent financial crisis, referred to a 'world of risk' and a 'world of uncertainty' (Katzenstein and Nelson 2011; Nelson and Katzenstein 2014). The term radical uncertainty 'refers to the kind of uncertainty that cannot be transformed into calculable risk on a probabilistic basis, and cannot be subjected to evaluation of a statistical and mathematical kind' (Mutti 2009, 262).

16 Schumpeter (1912) talks about 'new combinations' of the means of production.

17 The last version of the *Oslo Manual* provides a very broad definition of 'innovation', which also covers areas neglected in the past. Previous versions (the first and second editions date back to 1992 and 1997 respectively) focused primarily on technological innovations relating to products and processes that interested companies active in the manufacturing sector. The new edition, however, also considers non-technological innovation – such as organisational innovations, and those relating to the marketing of products. In addition, greater importance is given to innovations in sectors less driven

by R&D, such as services, or low-tech manufacturing activities. Finally, the systemic and relational character of innovation is acknowledged, with more attention paid to the analysis of relationships with the other firms and institutions that interact in the innovation process (OECD/Eurostat 2005, 12).

18 A related concept is that of 'disruptive innovation', which focuses on the impact of innovation on markets (Christensen 1997). Disruptive innovation tends to reshape economic activities in a radical way, creating new markets.

19 Little, on the other hand, will be said about organisational, and science and technology studies, which have, over the years, developed a copious and interesting literature. This is, however, much more generally well-known, and its treatment would take up space not available in this book.

20 An expression used by Bengt-Åke Lundvall (one of the leading scholars in IS) with reference to 'national innovation systems', which will be discussed in Chapter 5.

1   Innovation and social change

This chapter provides an overview of sociology's theoretical contributions to economic innovation. After presenting Adam Smith's reflections on the division of labour (sections 1 and 2), the first part (sections 3 and 4) introduces the classics of sociology, showing how innovation is studied in close connection with social change. The second part starts with Schumpeter (section 5) and then focuses on contemporary sociologists, illustrating the contribution of comparative political economy and the structural approach of the new economic sociology (sections 6, 7 and 8). The former draws attention to the relationship between models of capitalism and innovative regimes; the latter to the role played by social networks in innovative partnerships.

1.1 Capitalism, society and innovation

Sociology was born in the nineteenth century and dealt essentially with social change and capitalist society. As has been observed, this new discipline 'is the daughter of a great historical rupture, one that saw the rise of modern industrial society', providing a strong thrust to the production process (Ferrarotti 1986, 11). A richly admiring awareness of the intrinsically innovative nature of capitalism finds one of its most impressive formulations in the book that offers the most radical critique of the capitalist mode of production: *The Communist Manifesto*:

> The bourgeoisie cannot exist without *constantly revolutionising the instruments of production*, and thereby the relations of production, and with them the whole relations of society. Conservation of the old modes of production in unaltered form, was, on the contrary, the first condition of existence for all earlier industrial classes. Constant revolutionising of production, uninterrupted disturbance of all social conditions, everlasting uncertainty and agitation distinguish the bourgeois epoch from all earlier ones.... The bourgeoisie, during its rule of scarce one hundred years, has created more massive and more colossal productive forces than have all preceding generations together.
>
> (Marx and Engels 1848, Eng. trans. 1969, 16–17, my italics)

The discontinuity brought about by capitalism in relation to 'economic traditionalism' is also underlined by another classic author of economic sociology – Max Weber – who sees the preeminent and more independent role of the cultural and religious dimensions behind the continuous pursuit of production, in the beginning at least. Specific considerations regarding economic innovation are not always found in the works of classical sociologists. However, even if the term does not appear explicitly, there is an awareness that the dynamism of capitalism is linked to changes introduced in modes of production and consumption. The engagement of classical sociologists with these issues tends to be primarily of a 'macro-sociological' kind – relating, that is, to the study of overall changes in the economy and capitalist society. However, 'micro' observations are also present, relating to the more specific dynamics of economic innovation: pages dedicated to technological change, to innovators (entrepreneurs, inventors, etc.) and to mechanisms of innovation (specialised division of labour, collective effervescence, marginality and social intermediation, personal charisma). There is also the perception that the introduction of new economic elements involves relationships of power and conflict. These are aspects that tend to elude the current debate on innovation, especially amongst economists. Having said that, economists are the first to speak about economic innovation in a specific manner, as will be seen from the fundamental contributions offered by Adam Smith and Joseph Schumpeter – scholars who are, not by chance, attentive to the topic of development. This is a characteristic that links them to sociologists concerned with social and economic change.

In recent decades, economic sociologists have further studied and researched the topic of innovation, with analyses at both a macro and micro level. This chapter, therefore, will show the analyses of both classical and contemporary authors from this discipline (with the addition of Smith and Schumpeter), in order to demonstrate the contribution that economic sociology can make to IS. The review offered will not pretend to be a comprehensive one, but rather illustrative, and it will focus selectively on the studies closest to the topic that interests us here: economic innovation.

1.2 Adam Smith and the division of labour

Where innovation is concerned, it is inevitable to begin with the pioneering contribution made by the founder of economics, Adam Smith, in his main work with the symbolic title *An Inquiry into the Nature and Causes of the Wealth of Nations* (published in 1776). For Smith, the wealth of a nation is nothing more than the work done in a year, i.e. the set of goods produced within the country or acquired externally through trade. Wealth will be greater or lesser depending on the relationship between the product and the people who consume it. The amount of goods produced – that is, the productive capacity of a nation – in turn depends on two parameters: (1) the proportion of people in the total population who carry out 'useful work', and (2) the productivity of the workers – namely the competence and dexterity with which they do their work. Smith has no doubt that the 'ultimate cause' of a nation's wealth is to be found in this second parameter.

But what determines worker productivity? The answer is simple: the *division of labour*. To explain this point, the Scottish economist uses the famous example of the *pin factory*. Smith writes:

> If all the parts of a pin were to be made by one man, he would hardly be able to produce one per day. In English factories, however, this 'simple' work is divided into 18 'special' steps, each of which is carried out by people with specific skills. In a factory of this kind, with 10 workers, the daily output of pins reaches an average of 48,000 units, which means 4,800 pins per head.
>
> (Smith 1776 (2005), 11)

The division of labour allows an exponential increase in productivity, generating three types of benefits: (1) increases the dexterity of workers, who, specialising in one activity are able to perform it with greater skill, (2) saves time because it is not necessary to switch from one task to another, and (3) facilitates the invention of new machines (ibid., 13–15). The factor of most interest to us here is the third. According to Smith, the majority of new machines used in manufacturing were created directly by the workers, concerned as they were to alleviate their own hardships. They are assisted in this by their total concentration on a specific task, which facilitates discovery aimed at improving the production techniques. Other inventions, meanwhile, derive from the ingenuity of those who build the machines, when this activity becomes a specific professional occupation. The simplest inventions originate from the users of the machines, i.e. from the workers; the more complex from the manufacturers. In both cases it is a matter of incremental innovation – of small, step-by-step improvements introduced in a cumulative and collective manner thanks to a process of 'learning by doing' (Smith 1997, 20; Eng. trans. 1965). With the increase in the ingenuity of the inventions, however, it is a different matter. Radical innovation, in fact, requires the use of more complex concepts, possessed by the so-called 'philosophers, or men of speculation'; that is, people 'whose trade is not to do any thing, but to observe every thing, and who, upon that account, are often capable of *combining together the powers of the most distant and dissimilar objects*' (Smith 1776 (2005), 15, my italics). Smith notes that with society's progress, these activities of philosophical speculation become, in turn, the employment of a particular class of citizens, and are subdivided into a number of different branches – and this specialised division of labour greatly increases their productivity.

From Smith's reflections, then, there emerge *two different generative mechanisms regarding innovation*. The first is an incremental process based on the division of labour: innovation resulting from gradual improvements introduced by persons employed directly in the activity of production. These incremental innovations are the result of strict specialisation. The second is a more discontinuous and radical process based on the use of theoretical knowledge: innovations are more far-reaching and come from 'intellectual workers' who combine extensive and diverse forms of knowledge. As Smith observes:

To apply in the most advantageous manner those powers, which are already known and which have already been applied to a particular purpose, does not exceed the capacity of an ingenious artist. But to think of the application of new powers, *which are altogether unknown*, and which have never before been applied to any similar purpose, belongs to those only *who have a greater range of thought and more extensive views of things* than naturally fall to the share of a mere artist.

(Smith 1763 (1937), 337–8, my italics)

The point I would like to draw attention to is that in the second mechanism, the process of specialisation does not seem to be the determining force behind innovation. It is rather the ability to combine different components, overcoming the rigid barriers of specialisation to bring together 'the most distant and dissimilar' knowledge and phenomena. This point – often overlooked in comments on Smith's work – anticipated (albeit in embryonic form) Schumpeter's conception of innovation, defined as a new combination of production factors that introduces a sharp discontinuity into the economy.

What is the original force behind the division of labour? According to Smith it is the natural tendency in men to 'truck, barter, and exchange one thing for another' (Smith 1776 (2005), 18). In 'civilised societies' men always require the cooperation and assistance of others. This 'interested cooperation' is the fundamental drive behind the division of labour and is also present in societies which preceded the commercial (capitalist) form of society.

That said, the natural tendency to 'trade' varies from society to society. The pursuit of one's interests is tempered by a search for the approval of others. It is, in other terms, socially regulated, and in this regulation institutions – both economic and otherwise – play an important role. The wealth of a nation, in fact, also depends on its socio-institutional structure: the presence of a competitive market; the efficiency of state administration; the manner in which wealth is distributed across social classes, ensuring low profits for entrepreneurs and high wages for workers, to stimulate the innovativeness of the former and the collaboration of the latter (Trigilia 2002, chapter 1.2).

Let's recap some of the most salient aspects of Smith's reflections.

First, there is no technological determinism in his conception of innovation and economic development. It is true that inventions and new machinery are essential to increase the productive capacity of a nation, but it is the social division of labour that creates the conditions that facilitate these discoveries. That is to say, everything depends on the social and economic organisation of the production process. Even the differences in personal ingenuity ultimately derive not so much from the 'natural talent' of the individual as from the different socio-professional roles and the division of labour between them (Smith 1763 (1937), 341). In this, paradoxically, Smith demonstrates greater sociological sensitivity than that present in the work of Durkheim, who – as we shall see – speaks of the innate qualities of people.

Second, the division of labour gradually consolidates itself alongside social development and market expansion. This development is, on the other hand,

linked once again to socio-institutional factors: to the transformation (in the capitalist sense) of the social and economic arrangements of nations, and to the efficiency and effectiveness of state regulations – for example, making safe the
routes of communication and commerce (Smith 1776 (2005) chapter III).

It is present in the work of the very founder of economic science, therefore, a
reading of innovation that is anything but 'economistic'. Innovation, in fact, ultimately depends on a complex social construction: on a socio-institutional context
that allows the expansion of the market; and on a specific organisation of the production process based on the division of labour. According to Smith, these conditions are realised to the fullest extent in commercial societies, where there is a
structure of a capitalistic kind based on competition amongst a number of manufacturers and the total mobility of all factors of production (land, labour and
capital). Smith, therefore, frames the issue of innovation within an analysis that
brings together economy and society, economic behaviour and institutional regulation – as will the economic sociology that comes to the fore in the following
years.

Unlike the classical sociologists, however, the Scottish economist does not
bring out the contradictory and adversarial nature of the process. For Smith, in
fact, the division of labour creates more wealth, and in developed societies –
despite the greater inequalities – this higher level of well-being also extends to
the lower classes (Smith 1763 (1937), 332). In short, *the division of labour produces innovation and economic development and, thanks to the distribution of
wealth, social consensus as well*. As shown in the next section, economic sociology offers a less 'pacified' reading of capitalism.

1.3 Between conflict and consensus: Marx and Durkheim

Smith's idea that division of labour inevitably tends to qualify work and create
greater well-being is challenged by two classical sociologists, Marx and Durkheim. They are considered the founders of two antagonistic sociological traditions based on conflict (Marx) and social order (Durkheim) (Collins 1985). Both,
however, devote great attention to the division of labour and, as has been per-
ceptively observed, are aware of its side based on cooperation and solidarity, and
its side based on conflict (Giovannini 1987, 11).

Let's start with Karl Marx's contribution. As previously mentioned, the
German scholar is deeply aware of the innovative nature of capitalism and is a
keen observer of technology. Not only because he is interested in understanding
its effects on the condition of the working class, but also because he realises that
the increase in the production capacity of capitalism is closely related to scientific and technological progress (Rosenberg 1982). Perhaps this explains why
Marx has been read in terms of technological determinism. Some passages of his
works, often cited by proponents of this view, do in fact leave the reader thinking that it is technological invention and change that, in the final instance, determines social and economic change. *The Poverty of Philosophy*, for example,
states:

In acquiring new productive forces men change their mode of production; and in changing their mode of production, in changing the way of earning their living, they change all their social relations. *The handmill gives you society with the feudal lord; the steam-mill, society with the industrial capitalist.*

(Marx 1847, Eng. trans. 1892, 109, my italics)

A similar interpretation may also be given to a passage from the famous introduction to *A Contribution to the Critique of Political Economy*, where Marx describes the materialistic conception of history and social change:

In the social production which men carry on they enter into definite relations that are indispensable and independent of their will; these relations of production correspond to a definite stage of development of their material powers of production. The sum total of these relations of production constitutes the economic structure of society – the real foundation, on which rise legal and political superstructures and to which correspond definite forms of social consciousness.... *At a certain stage of their development, the material forces of production in society come in conflict with the existing relations of production, or – what is but a legal expression for the same thing – with the property relations within which they had been at work before. From forms of development of the forces of production these relations turn into their fetters. Then comes the period of social revolution.*

(Marx 1859, Eng. trans. 1904, 11–12, my italics)

A more detailed analysis of Marx's texts, however, does not justify their interpretation in terms of technological determinism, and this for two reasons. The first is that forces of production do not correspond only with the technical tools employed in the production process, but also include the labour force (MacKenzie 1984, 476–7). The second is that technological change plays no role in the origin of capitalism and in its early stages (Rosenberg 1982).

For Marx, *labour is a productive force that creates use-values*: it is employed to produce useful goods to satisfy needs. In its general abstract form – that is, independent of the type of society in which it appears – labour is 'a process in which both man and Nature participate' (Marx 1867, Eng. trans. 1887, 124) and it is composed of three elements: (1) the conscious activity intended to achieve the goal, that is, the work itself; (2) the subject of the work; and (3) the instruments of the work. These last two elements represent the *means of production* (ibid., 124–5). Technical instruments, then, are the *means* which man uses intentionally in order to achieve his goals:

Technology discloses man's mode of dealing with Nature, the process of production by which he sustains his life, and thereby also lays bare the mode of formation of his social relations, and of the mental conceptions that flow from them.

(Ibid., 326, fn 4)

It is man, then, who makes use of technology to change the course of his history. These initial observations are already enough to raise some doubt in relation to a reading of Marx in terms of technological determinism. In addition to this, technical change played no role in the early stages of capitalism.[1] Let's have a closer look at this second point.

The labour process takes different forms depending on the historical era and, with the advent of capitalism, cannot be separated from the process of valorisation of capital. This new mode of production began when capitalists started to employ large numbers of workers in the same place under their control (ibid., 223). This took place at first through the *manufacture*, but – as Marx himself states – this simply represented a quantitative extension of the handicraft industry of the medieval guilds. Manufacturing, in other words, involved only an enlargement of the workshop of the master craftsman. *The technical basis of the work remained identical* to that of the stage previous to industrial development – referred to as 'artisanal' – even though there were changes in the mode of division of labour (ibid., 234).

The increase in production capacity that took place in the manufacturing phase was due to *organisational innovation*: a revolution in 'the conditions of production', which assumed a cooperative form (ibid., 217). A large number of workers were forced to work together by the capitalist according to a plan, and this increased output. Work, however, did not lose its artisanal connotation, depending as it did on the strength and ability of individual workers in handling their work tools. Use of machinery was still quite limited and the increase in productivity was due to the concentration and the coordination of the workers and their *increasing unilateral specialisation*. Meanwhile, legions of unskilled workers were formed alongside those with skills. In both cases, training costs were reduced.

Thus began a process of *devaluation of the labour force* that went hand-in-hand with the increasing *valorisation of capital*, which appropriated a larger share of surplus labour. Progressively, productive intelligence – once the possession of the artisan or farmer, became separated from the worker and concentrated in the capital. This process was brought to completion with the introduction of machinery and the application of science to the production process, which characterises the next stage of the development of capitalism: that of *the modern industry*.

This separation begins in simple cooperation, where the capitalist represents to the single workman the oneness and the will of the associated labour. It is developed in manufacture which cuts down the labourer into a detail labourer. It is completed in modern industry, which makes science a productive force distinct from labour and presses it into the service of capital (ibid., 245).

It is only with the advent of large-scale industry that a radical process of alienation came to fruition, separating the worker from his work, impoverishing him economically and diminishing his professional status, reducing him to the role of a mere 'appendage of the machine' (ibid., 313) . In the manufacturing phase, the revolution in the mode of production started from the labour force; in large-scale industry, on the other hand, it started from the means of production. The craftsman's instrument of labour was replaced by the 'working machine' (ibid., 257–8), a device that mechanically performed the operations that were previously performed manually by the workers. To the working machine was then applied the driving force of the steam engine, thus generating a complex 'system of machinery', which was also used to 'construct machines by machines' (ibid., 263). In large factories, therefore, process innovations occurred due to the use of new technologies that radically changed the organisation of work: cooperation became a 'technical necessity dicatated by the instrument of labour itself' (ibid., 264).

With the arrival of a technological base of a mechanical kind, *science was transformed into a productive force of primary importance*. In the manufacturing phase, in fact, the subjectivity of artisanal skills rendered the production process uncertain. Mechanisation, however, made it more 'impersonal' and objective – analysable and calculable according to scientific criteria. Only with mechanisation, therefore, did the science applied to production make it possible to exponentially increase the productivity of machinery and labour. This crucial transformation required the convergent action of three distinct elements: (1) the incentives provided by capitalist principles (competition and profit), which made capitalists sensitive to technological change; (2) the development of a body of scientific knowledge which, although linked to the needs of the economic sphere and the material needs of men, possessed a certain degree of autonomy from these factors; and (3) an adequate technical basis, which did not exist in the artisanal and manufacturing phase (Rosenberg 1974, 718).

The process of mechanisation, however, clashed with the resistance put up by the proletariat. This occurred even at an early stage because machines had the 'effect of the plague' on expert craftsmen, with whom they were in direct competition (Marx 1867, Eng. trans. 1887, 294). The workers' struggle marked the whole process of the affirmation of capitalism, but it was only with the phase of large-scale industry that the conflict became directed at the means of production, which embodied 'the material basis of the capitalist mode of production' (ibid., 283). This battle, however, only served to stimulate further mechanisation. Indeed, in Marx's view, many of the technological inventions of those years were aimed specifically at reducing the power of skilled labour and neutralising the resistance of the workers. It took time and experience for the workers to learn to differentiate between the machines and their 'employment by capital' and, as a result, 'to direct their attacks, not against the material instruments of production, but against the mode in which they are used' (ibid., 284). The strategic use that the bourgeoisie made of inventions led Marx to interpret technological innovation within the context of class conflict. The introduction of new machinery made it possible to increase the extraction of surplus value from the workers and to beat the other competing capitalists. And yet, according to Marx, what was rational for the individual capitalist, in the long run produced disastrous consequences for capitalists as a class – consequences that were both unexpected and unintended. Increasing mechanisation tended to create unemployment, fuelling proletarian hardship and class conflict. It also reduced the share of variable capital (wages given to workers), from which capitalists extracted surplus value, while increasing that of constant capital (machinery and tools), from which no surplus value was extracted. The resulting trend was a fall in the rate of profit, which weakened the capitalists. In brief, technological innovation and mechanisation of the production process tended to create the conditions that facilitated the advent of socialism.[2]

Apart from the fact that such predictions were never fulfilled, what needs to be emphasised here are some points of Marx's analysis.

> Economic innovation is not the same as, and is not limited to, technological change.

- The origins of capitalism are not determined by technical innovation, but by a more comprehensive transformation of relations of production (MacKenzie 1984, 482). It is only within these social relations that science and technology applied to the production process deploy their effects.
- Inventions and innovation are not the result of individual ingenuity, but should be seen as complex social processes framed within a specific socio-historical context.[3]
- There is a process of mutual interaction between economy and technology, as well as a number of feedback effects (Rosenberg 1982).
- Technological and economic innovation is situated within a nexus of power relationships that can trigger conflictual dynamics.
- In capitalism, the division of labour in society, and that of a technical nature within industry, triggered a radical process of deskilling of artisans/workers, creating alienation and hindering the development of their creative skills. For Marx, in fact, overcoming capitalism would also require overcoming division of labour, particularly in relation to that between manual and intellectual work.

From this point, it is possible to engage with the observations of Emile Durkheim, who devoted an entire book to the matter: *The Division of Labour in Society*. For the French sociologist, the division of labour had, in theory, a positive value for social cohesion. In ancient society, there was a *mechanical solidarity*, based on the similarity of members of a group and on a pervasive 'collective conscience' that, together with common values, prescribed detailed rules of behaviour. In modern society, however, where division of labour is established, there is an *organic solidarity* based on the differentiation of individuals who, specialising in different activities, make them indispensable to one another. In this case, collective consciousness is less strong and pervasive and, because of this, individuals are free to choose their own preferences and rules of action. The imperative, in this case, is not to conform to the values and behaviour of the group, but to emphasise individuality, with each person striving to make the most of their own particular abilities and inclinations. This does not mean that social cohesion is completely absent. Everyone, in fact, each with their own specialisation, 'joins with others in maintening general life' (Durkheim 1902, Eng. trans. 1947, 354).

Durkheim, therefore, outlined two distinct forms of social cohesion that derived from two sources: the uniformity of conscience and the division of social labour. In modern society, collective morality – which ensured the cohesion of the group – developed, strengthening the individual personality and leaving ample margin to individual initiative. Division of labour, on the other hand, generated a form of cooperation based on trade and on norms of reciprocity, which were expressed through contracts, and these presupposed normative regulation, not only of a legal, but also of a moral kind.[4] The French sociologist, in other words, recognised that the division of labour increased the productivity of labour by providing resources in greater number and of better quality. From this, economists deduced that the origin of the division of labour lay in the desire of men to constantly increase their material well-being and happiness (ibid., 233). However, Durkheim did not find such a utilitarian and economistic reading convincing.

In the division of labour economists saw 'the supreme law of human society and the condition of their progress' (ibid., 39). Durkheim argues, however, that change does not always coincide with progress, and that increase in pleasure does not necessarily lead to greater happiness: there is 'no relation between the variations of happiness and the advances of the division of labor' (ibid., 250). Years later, in his study of suicide, he showed that the production of social integration requires, in contrast, an equilibrium between individual desire and the ability to satisfy it: a social regulation of desire, in other words, and of the (legitimate) means of satisfying it. Division of labour and economic competition do not produce greater well-being through material consumption and do not inevitably generate social progress and solidarity. They are not, in themselves, cohesive forces: division of labour leaves personal interest 'distinct and opposite' (ibid., 213), while competition exercises a 'dispersive influence': that means that 'when competition places isolated and estranged individuals in opposition, it can only separate them more' (ibid., 275). Durkheim derived from this a need for moral cohesion and collective regulation that was instead wholly lacking in the industrial society of his own time. The last part of *The Division of Labour in Society* is, in fact, devoted to an analysis of the abnormal forms of division of labour, which, rather than producing solidarity, generate conflict and separation.[5] What are the implications, then, of these observations for economic innovation? There are two main points to consider.

1   In order to produce positive effects (progress), division of labour must go hand-in-hand with solidarity and social justice. In other words, specialisation can achieve positive results – in terms of innovation as well – only if it is associated with an adequate consensual base. It is precisely the abnormal forms of division of labour that – in contrast – indicate the conditions required to generate progress. The coercive division of labour (the second abnormal form mentioned by Durkheim) is pathological – that is,

divisive – since it binds individuals to perform activities below their capabilities. Individuals, in fact, are obliged to carry out a specific type of work solely on the basis of their social origins. This method of dividing labour does not generate social solidarity because it violates a principle of equity – based on individual merit – and brings about a waste of resources and (innovative) capabilities, disengaging the allocation of social functions from the 'distribution of natural talents' (ibid., 375).

2   In order to produce positive effects (progress), division of labour must go hand-in-hand with the appropriate qualification, coordination and motivation of the workers. With regard to the third abnormal form, Durkheim notes that this particular pathology relating to division of labour occurs when there is excessive dequalification of labour in terms of tasks which do not 'offer sufficient material for individual activity'. In other words, we are in the presence of a functional impoverishment that does not satisfy the individual's need for work. This means that the functions flag, and are badly coordinated, since workers 'incompletely feel their mutual dependence' (ibid., 390).

Something similar occurs in the first abnormal form: the anomic. Durkheim, discussing the antagonism between capital and labour in large industries, shows that in this case as well, conflict arises from a deficiency of regulation that induces excessive deskilling of labour. In fact, if the worker becomes a mere appendage to the machine, the work carried out becomes monotonous and fragmented, with no clear sense. The final aim of division of labour – the moral aim – which is to enable the 'perfection of the individual', is thus lost. This objective requires that the individual is not exclusively devoted to his task but remains in contact with the other operations close at hand, collaborating with other skilled workers. The worker, in other words, must not become a 'machine who repeats his movements without knowing their meaning': he should, rather, be aware that 'they tend, in some way, towards an end that he conceives more or less distinctly'. Only in this way 'He feels that he is serving something' (ibid., 372).

These observations of Durkheim's highlight two points. First, that in order for division of labour to foster cooperation and, potentially, the innovative capacity of workers, it is necessary that: (1) the work is not excessively impoverished, otherwise this generates deskilling; and (2) that there is also a subjective involvement in the work's goals and in teamwork. This second point suggests a stimulating line of reflection with regard to the theme of innovation. The latter, in fact, is not only the result of specialisation and differentiation, but requires: (1) subjective involvement (social psychologists speak of 'intrinsic motivation'); (2) the exploration and combination of different elements; and (3) often, coordination and teamwork. This line of reasoning was developed by Durkheim in a book dedicated to religions, in which he speaks about rites and moments of '*collective effervescence*'. The ritual moments of celebration serve not only to revitalise the old group belief, but also to create new ones (Giddens 1978). In certain situations, in fact, the intensification of social relations can generate states of collective exaltation that strengthen the capacity of individuals, enabling them to produce new religions, collective values or otherwise enhance their actions.[6] This innovative mode, fusional in nature, thus serves to enrich the set of conceptual tools that can be used in the analysis of innovation.

To sum up, both Marx and Durkheim engage with the ideas put forward by Smith, that is to say:

- Both hold that in a capitalist society, the division of labour does not (necessarily) determine an increase in individual and collective well-being: either because not all social classes benefit to the same extent (Marx) or because material wealth is not concomitant with individual happiness (Durkheim).
- Both Marx and Durkheim also see the 'dark side' of division of labour which, under capitalism, tends to generate conflict rather than consensus.
- Finally, they are in agreement on the fact that excessive specialisation of labour tends to impoverish rather than enrich professional skill, reducing the subjective availability and innovative capacity of the workers. From here on, these two great sociologists went down different paths: Durkheim believed that division of labour – properly regulated – created solidarity and was an unsuppressible feature of modernity. In Marx's view, however, capitalist division of labour was not 'reformable' and must be overcome in the communist society of the future.

1.4 The innov-actors: Simmel, Sombart and Weber

If in Marx and Durkheim attention is focused mainly on the – largely impersonal – structural and procedural dimensions of innovation, other economic sociologists, members of the 'German school', concentrate above all on the actors. Georg Simmel, Werner Sombart and Max Weber examine the historical and social origins of a new figure, the entrepreneur – one taken rather for granted by classical economists. Before focusing our attention on Weber, we will briefly look at some ideas offered by Simmel and Sombart, who highlight a mechanism for economic innovation based on *social marginality*. Along with the historical and institutional conditions that facilitate the emergence of capitalism, these two authors study the social groups that promote the use of money, the accumulation of capital, and the spread of commerce and trade, making them bearers of a new economic mentality: the 'spirit of capitalism'.[7]

Simmel was the first to draw attention to individuals and groups who are marginal (1907, Eng. trans. 2004, 221). These include social, ethnic and religious groups that, demeaned and downtrodden, are relegated (or relegate themselves) to the margins of society and are excluded from full enjoyment of the rights of citizenship.[8] Not being able to obtain recognition and prestige through legitimate career paths that are socially recognised and valued, these individuals engage in activities that are considered morally dubious: business, foreign trade, loans at interest. The possession of money, in fact, makes them sought after and essential, allowing them to gain the power and influence which confers upon them the social recognition that would otherwise be precluded. In fact, even in societies where extremely strict restrictions apply towards certain professions (e.g. money-lending), money '*is accepted by everyone from everyone*' (ibid., 223, my italics).

Jews and *foreigners* embody the ideal-type of this kind of social figure, willing to carry out these 'morally dubious' activities because other avenues of work and social recognition are closed to them.[9] They cannot gain access to public offices and other opportunities related to the full possession of civil rights; nor can they break into the more usual occupations – such as agriculture and craftsmanship – which are already in the hands of the (native) components of the community. They must *innovate*, therefore, in order to find a specific position for themselves. And since they are not bound by the rules of the group and its prohibitions, they are able to undertake financial and commercial activities that others are not willing to carry out, given that these are negatively sanctioned within the community. In so doing, however, they progressively contribute to their own entrenchment, favouring the spread of the monetary economy, a phenomenon that Simmel studies in *The Philosophy of Money*.[10]

The figure of the stranger deserves further examination, since Simmel's reflections on the subject have exercised a certain influence on studies dedicated to the diffusion of innovation (Rogers 2003, 42). The formal position of the stranger is a 'synthesis of nearness and distance' (Simmel 1908, Eng. trans. 1950, 404): he is not a wayfarer, since he makes the decision to settle in the community, but at the same time, due to his origins and the relationships that link him to other distant subjects external to the community, he does not wholly belong there. 'In the relationship to him, the distance means that he, who is close by, is far, and strangeness means that he, who also is far, is actually near' (ibid., 402). This special social position confers particular propensities upon the foreigner: for example, greater freedom from the rules of the group, which allows them, in terms of their actions, to be less constrained 'by habit, piety, and precedent' (ibid., 405) – potentially more innovative, in other words. In this they are also helped by their collocation, both cultural and relational, on the border between different worlds. Commercial activity makes it possible for them to come into contact with different ideas, to experiment with fertile cultural blends, to try out 'new combinations' precluded to other members of the community:

> For in trade, which alone makes possible unlimited combinations, intelligence always finds expansion and new territories, an achievement which is very difficult to attain for the original producer with his lesser mobility and his dedpendence upon a circle of customers that can be increased only slowly.
>
> (Ibid., 403)

These insights are enriched by Sombart's reflections on the subject of 'migrants', where he notes that those who decide to migrate are usually the most bold,

capable and strong-willed of the community of origin – those who project themselves towards the new.

> Emigration breaks all ties with the old homeland's customs and traditions,
> while those of the group in which the migrants settle are foreign. The for-
> eigner is therefore not limited by any constraint in the development of his
> entrepreneurial spirit.... No tradition! No old company! Everything has to
> be created anew and at the same time from nothing.
> (Sombart 1916, Eng. trans. from the Italian version 1967, 282)[11]

Observations regarding the social profile of the foreigner/migrant provide two
ideas relevant to Innovation Studies. The first evokes a *socio-normative dimension*: that is, it alludes to the distancing that renders the social and cultural norms
of both the community of origin and that of arrival less prescriptive and binding.
For the foreigner/migrant, communities and social relationships are less closed
and boundaries less impassable and, because of this, socio-regulatory control
mechanisms, which require compliance with the group, are more tenuous. The
second point, on the other hand, refers to a *socio-cognitive dimension*: the for-
eigner/migrant's collocation on the border between different worlds allows him
to build bridges between them. It allows him – to use Burt's terminology, which
will be presented later – to obtain 'non-redundant' information and knowledge:
to create communication between different ideas that can be combined in a
variety of new ways.

These ideas also clarify two distinct mechanisms of economic innovation.
The *first mechanism is based on marginality*: in an economic sector that offers
opportunities for innovation (e.g. related to technological change) it is more
likely that they will be seized by new, marginal (perhaps small) firms rather than
large, incumbent (dominant) firms, given that the latter are subject to factors of
inertia and constraints of various kinds. The second mechanism is based on *bro-
kering*: being situated at the boundary of distinct social and economic circles
multiplies the chances of introducing new combinations through the exploitation
of ideas from 'different worlds'.[12] As will be seen in the following sections and
chapters, these 'mechanisms' have been widely used and developed in contemporary studies on innovation.

Let us, therefore, move on to Weber, who provides us with another kind of
explanation for the birth of bourgeois entrepreneurship. His definition of capitalism is the starting point. Capitalism exists where the satisfaction of the needs
of a human group takes place through a firm. This latter is of a rational kind
when its profitability is checked by calculating the capital[13] (Weber 1958, Eng.
trans. 1987). Different forms of capitalism, according to Weber, have existed in
various historical periods. But only in the West – from the second half of the
nineteenth century – was there witnessed a full satisfaction of 'daily needs'
through rational firms producing for the market.

This *modern form of capitalism* is based on certain socio-institutional conditions:
(1) a rational calculation of capital, made possible by the rational organisation of

formally free labour and the rational organisation of industry oriented according to the circumstances of the market; (2) a 'predictable' institutional organisation (rational-legal state, rational-formal law, etc.); (3) the perennial renewal of technology and the use of science as a production factor:

> Now the peculiar modern Western form of capitalism has been, at first sight, strongly influenced by the development of technical possibilities. Its rationality is today essentially dependent on the calculability of the most important technical factors. But this means fundamentally that it is dependent on the peculiarities of modern science, especially the natural sciences based on mathematics and exact and rational experiment. On the other hand, the development of these sciences and of the technique resting upon them now receives important stimulation from these capitalistic interests in its practical economic application. It is true that the origin of Western science cannot be attributed to such interests.
>
> (Weber 1922a, Eng. trans. 2005, xxxvii)

Weber observes that there was a remarkable flowering of capitalism in the ancient Greek and Roman societies without there being any corresponding technological progress. In modern societies, however, these two phenomena go hand-in-hand (Weber 2005, 27–8). This scientific-technological development was able to flourish thanks to the 'disenchantment of the world' connected to the West's religious and cultural rationalisation, which allowed a free application of reason to the understanding of natural phenomena and then to the activity of production.

The Western city also played a role in this process. It was the breeding ground not only of an entrepreneurial middle class oriented towards acquisition, but also, from ancient times, of modern science (Weber 1958, Eng. trans. 1987). The application of science and technology to the economy had a dual effect: (1) it emancipated the production of goods from any link with tradition and bound it closely to rational free thought (ibid.); and (2) it made a systematic lowering of production costs possible by promoting 'a feverish hunt for inventions' from the seventeenth century on, which, in England, gave birth to the first rational law on patents (ibid.). For Weber, as for Marx, this represented a turning point in the history of Western capitalism: the democratisation of luxury – made possible by cost reduction – gave a major boost to 'mass marketing' and capitalist industrialisation based on price competition (ibid.). Only the West was familiar with this form of rational market-oriented capitalism, and Weber observed that the more rational it is, the more it is connected to mass demand and the satisfaction of mass needs (ibid.). Technological innovation, therefore, played a major role in the development of Western capitalism. Weber, however, suggests the avoidance of any form of technological determinism and the application of a bidirectional analytical approach, following the chain of causal links in both directions, from technology to economics, to politics and to religion (Weber 2005, 31).

And this brings us to the point that interests us the most. What Weber sees as making Western capitalism stand out so distinctly is the presence of a rational economic ethic focused on innovation. The German sociologist paid particular attention to the formation of an entrepreneurial bourgeoisie for which profit orientation and the indefinite accumulation of capital became a kind of professional duty: a 'social ethic' that legitimised gain and encouraged acquisitive behaviour, innovative in nature and distant from tradition – that is, from the routines of production and consumption established in the past. In the next few pages, two specific aspects of Weber's ideas will be looked at:

1   the ascetic-religious origins of this economic ethic; and
2   the rupture it represents in terms of economic traditionalism.

1.4.1 Ascetic-religious origins

Weber connects modern capitalism to specific features of Western civilisation – in particular the process of rationalisation, in the formal sense, that expands into a plurality of spheres of life (Rossi 1981, 154). In Weber's view, only the West created the rational organisation of labour, the modern state of a legal-rational type, the formal-rational law, the city and its citizens and science and rational technology. Above all, however, Western culture is distinguished from every other by the presence of men with a *rational ethos for the conduct of life* (Weber 1958, Eng. trans. 1987). This form of capitalism, then, arises from a complex constellation of socio-institutional factors to which, integrating with it, is added a *'rational economic ethos'* (ibid.). Weber goes more deeply into the original 'religious foundation' of this rational conduct of life, exploring the relationship between the Protestant ethic and the spirit of capitalism. The thesis is well-known and can be summarised in a few points.

•   The dogmas and precepts of ascetic Protestantism (Calvinism above all) lead the faithful to a constant ethical rationalisation of their conduct of life.
•   The faithful carry out a methodical supervision of their 'state of grace' through active engagement in professional activity.
•   Success in business provides them with the confirmation of their 'state of election': namely, the certainty of belonging to the ranks of those who are predestined by God for eternal salvation.

Let's look at these points in a little more detail. Worldly asceticism, typical of Calvinism, endows their behaviour with a profoundly innovative character. The sole aim of the earthly world is to serve the glorification of God and the 'elect' are nothing more than tools of this divine plan: their 'worldly' commitment is to increase the glory of God. This is also true for professional work, which is at the service of the community.

> The social activity of the Christian in the world is solely activity *in majorem gloriam Dei.* This character is hence shared by labour in a calling which serves the mundane life of the community. Even in Luther we found specialized labour in callings justified in terms of brotherly love. But what for him

remained an uncertain, purely intellectual suggestion became for the Calvinists a characteristic element in their ethical system. Brotherly love … is expressed in the first place in the fulfilment of the daily tasks given by the *lex naturæ* and in the process this fulfilment assumes a peculiarly objective and impersonal character, that of service in the interest of the rational organization of our social environment.

(Weber 1922a; Eng. trans. 2005, p. 64)

The dogma of predestination, however, arouses a constant state of anxiety in the faithful regarding their eternal destiny, even if they are encouraged to reject these doubts and, through tireless professional work, 'to attain certainty of one's own election and justification in the daily struggle of life' (ibid., 67). To subjectively achieve security in relation to their 'state of grace', they must therefore perform ascetic action in the world and feel themselves to be 'an *instrument* of divine power': their faith must, indeed, be an 'effective' one (*fides efficax*) (ibid., 68)

This then is the trigger for a powerful psycho-social syllogism that has profound economic impact: only an elect is able to increase the glory of God through 'good works'; but given that the elect are mere tools in the hands of God, 'effective work' (e.g. professional success for the 'greater glory of God') becomes an unequivocal sign of belonging to the ranks of the elect. The need to prove their faith in secular professional life creates, therefore, an aristocracy of saints *in the world*, predestined by God, which is also expressed through the creation of sects. The point to emphasise is that this ascetic conduct no longer takes place, as in the monastic communities of the Middle Ages, out of the world, but within it. Their discipline thus begins to permeate the profane life of everyday, and transform it into a rational life *in* the world, and yet not *of*, or *for*, this world:

The religious life of the saints … no longer lived outside the world in monastic communities, but within the world and its institutions. This rationalization of conduct within this world, but for the sake of the world beyond, was the consequence of the concept of calling of ascetic Protestantism.

(Ibid., 100)

It is here that Weber identifies the religious origins of the 'spirit of capitalism', which manifests itself in a sense of professional duty towards the indefinite accumulation of capital. A utilitarian social ethic that has no hedonistic objective – it is not designed, in other words, to meet material needs – but which is at the service of earning money as an end in itself. For Weber, this sense of moral obligation, this sense of professional duty, has therefore an irrational and even transcendent foundation, which originates in Protestant asceticism.

1.4.2 The rupture with economic traditionalism

The second point, as noted above, concerns the rupture with economic traditionalism and the ascetic and charismatic foundation of economic innovation. As already mentioned, modern capitalism is based on rational economic behaviour and conduct of life. But this was long hampered by the prevalence of traditionalism. Traditional economic action means that the satisfaction of needs is based on 'traditional acceptance of inherited techniques and customary social relationships' (Weber 1922b, Eng. trans. 1947, 166). In Weber's view, at the start of each economic ethic there is a form of traditionalism – that is, the sacralisation of the past and of habit, which dictates that economic activity must be carried out in one way only, and that is the way that has been inherited from previous generations. Opposed to breaking with tradition are both the material interests of the classes that benefit from the status quo and the magical elements present in the visions of the world and in the practical attitudes of action. These magical elements hinder the breaking of habit because people fear the negative effects due to the reaction of the spirits. Weber states, therefore, that the domination of magic was one of the most serious impediments to the rationalisation of economic life. 'Magic involves a stereotyping of technology and economic relations' (Weber 1958, Eng. trans. 1987, 361). In other words, economic traditionalism, especially when it is reinforced by elements of magic, is opposed to all forms of economic innovation.

The break with magic is the result of the rationalisation process triggered by the major world religions and the great ethical prophecies of charismatic religious leaders (Cavalli 1981a). As has been observed, the description of the charismatic prophets who break with traditional routine closely resembles that of Schumpeter's 'dynamic innovator', a figure that we will discuss in the next section (Ferrarotti 1985, 103–5). This process of anti-traditional rationalisation finds its fulfilment within the Western Jewish–Christian civilisation, in Protestant asceticism and in the ethics of Beruf (vocation-profession), which nourishes a 'specifically bourgeois economic ethic' (Weber 1922a, Eng. trans. 2005, 120). In other words, a professional vocation experienced as a rational commitment to work that expresses itself in acquisitive capitalist activity as the fulfilment of a task willed by God (Weber 1958; Eng. trans. 2003). This worldly asceticism breaks with all forms of economic traditionalism: with the traditional conduct of life, with the traditional standards of profit and work, with the traditional habits of business and of relationships with workers, customers, etc. (Weber 1922a). This does not, however, occur without resistance: 'Its entry on the scene was not generally peaceful. A flood of mistrust, sometimes of hatred, above all of moral indignation, regularly opposed itself to the first innovator' (ibid., 31).

An 'extraordinarily resolute' character was therefore required to stand up for innovation – personal qualities and motivation that could provide the innovator with the 'ability to free oneself from the common tradition' (ibid., 32). The new bourgeois entrepreneurs, in other words, had to have a great deal of charisma, together with great skills of personal leadership,

> along with clarity of vision and ability to act, it is only by virtue of very definite and highly developed ethical qualities that it has been possible for him to command the absolutely indispensable confidence of his customers and

workmen. Nothing else could have given him the strength to overcome the innumerable obstacles, above all the infinitely more intensive work which is demanded of the modern entrepreneur. But these are ethical qualities of quite a different sort from those adapted to the traditionalism of the past.

(Ibid., 31)

This also had an impact on technological innovation. Even though modern science was not born with the Reformation, the fact that it put science at the service of technology and the economy is a specific development of Protestant-ism (Weber 1958, Eng. trans. 1987). These, then, are the ascetic-religious foundations of the innovative dynamism that from its origins distinguished the entrepreneurial bourgeoisie. However, the progress of rationalisation, with the growing secularisation of economic behaviour, altered the picture. For Weber, the desiccation of the 'religious roots' of modern economic man tended to create problems for capitalism. First, because it freed the conflict of the under-privileged classes, their protest no longer curbed by the expectation of other-worldly rewards. Second, because it dried up the ethical and motivational well-springs of bourgeois entrepreneurship (Weber 1922a, Eng. trans. 2005, 119). Weber feared that secularised and radicalised Western rationalisation would mean the prevalence – both in the economic and political sphere – of a bureaucratic mentality averse to risk and innovation, reducing the space for indi-vidual action and personal charisma (Cavalli 1981a; 1981b, 165). In the 'polit-ical writings' of his later years, in fact, he voiced serious concerns regarding the spread of a spirit of discipline that weakened the personal responsibility and leadership skills that private entrepreneurs and 'political leaders' brought to the table (Weber 2008). These were concerns that, as we shall see in the next section, also found an echo in Schumpeter's work. To conclude and summarise, then, Weber offers us two readings related to the formation of capitalist entre-preneurship oriented towards innovation. The first, 'macro' in nature, stresses the importance of a set of institutional, social and cultural factors that created a professional-rational ethos which spurred on innovative behaviour and broke with economic traditionalism. The second, at a 'micro' level, focuses on a *char-ismatic mechanism of innovation*: that is, the ethico-personal qualities of Puritan entrepreneurs who, to escape the influence of tradition and overcome resistance to innovation, had to deploy charismatic traits in order to exert their leadership.

1.5 Schumpeter and the economy of innovation

Joseph Schumpeter is a special economist. Although he evolved as a thinker as part of the 'Austrian School' of economics and shared many of the assumptions of neoclassical analysis, he was also influenced by the ideas of the 'historical school' of economics – quite widespread in Germany at the time – as well as by the Marxist and sociological approaches.[14] This multiplicity of influences made him very attentive to the study of development's 'non-economic' factors. The importance of these socio-institutional elements is already to be found in *The*

Theory of Economic Development (1912), the most famous work of his early years. It is a book that addresses the issue of development by placing the entrepreneurial role at the centre of the explanation and sees Schumpeter clearly distancing himself from traditional (neoclassical) economic analysis. This he shows to be substantially static and incapable of explaining the central element of capitalist development: innovation.

The essay opens with a description of the 'circular flow of economic life', a situation characterised by a market equilibrium that determines the quantity and price of the goods produced, based on established routines and customs. The phenomena of *growth* experienced in this context are continuous, marginal and incremental in nature, and occur without substantially altering the framework of given conditions. This static theory is, however, unable to encompass the phenomena of *development*:

> is not only unable to predict the consequences of discontinuous changes in the traditional way of making things; it can neither explain the occurrence of such productive revolutions nor the phenomena which accompany them.... Development in our sense is a distinct phenomenon, entirely foreign to what may be observed in the circular flow or in the tendency towards equilibrium. It is spontaneous and discontinuous change in the channels of the flow, disturbance of equilibrium, which forever alters and displaces the equilibrium state previously existing.
>
> (Schumpeter 1912, Eng. trans. 2012, 62–4)[15]

Traditional economic analysis, then, fails to account for the radical changes that are at the basis of the development processes and cyclical evolutions of the capitalist economy. In order for these phenomena to come into being, *innovation* is required in the ways of combining 'materials and forces' of production – that is, 'new combinations of productive means have to be introduced' (ibid., 66). These innovations may involve: (1) the production of new goods, not familiar to consumers; (2) a new method of production or marketing; (3) the opening of new markets; (4) the acquisition of new sources of supply of raw materials and semi-finished products; and (5) the reorganisation of an industry, such as the creation or destruction of a monopoly (ibid.). It is the entrepreneurs who come up with these innovations, providing a 'creative response' for the situations that they are facing (Schumpeter 1947, 150).

Schumpeter reads innovation as a social phenomenon that shapes economic development (Fagerberg 2003, 135). Unlike the (so-called neoclassical) economists of his time, he does not consider change in the states of equilibrium as due to factors external to the economy. Capitalism, in fact, has an essentially dynamic character that should be explained – as Marx had done – with endogenous factors: the new economic elements that are introduced by 'new men' through 'new firms' (Schumpeter 1939, 92–4). This dynamism, moreover, is not based on price competition between companies, but on technological and organisational competition: on 'doing things differently', in other words, in the realm of economic life (ibid., 80). Development takes place through industrial change that *incessantly* revolutionises the economic structure from within, *incessantly* destroying the old one and *incessantly* creating a new one. It is this process of 'creative destruction' that characterises capitalism in such a specific way (Schumpeter 1942, Chapter VII).

Successful innovation ensures economic profit for the entrepreneurs, but this is transient in nature since the new element will soon be imitated by competitors. Other aspects of innovation which Schumpeter draws attention to are the following: (1) it is not present everywhere in the economy, but is concentrated in particular areas; (2) it tends to appear in clusters, nourishing other innovation in connection with it (Schumpeter 1939, 98); (3) it is cyclical in nature; (4) it is mostly related to the creation of new businesses, or to the advent of new men at the helm of old businesses, since the latter generally demonstrate 'symptoms of what is euphemistically called conservatism' (ibid., 94).

Schumpeter makes a clear distinction between *innovator-entrepreneurs* and those who, in the running of enterprises, engage solely in administrative tasks and management, exploiting already-acquired knowledge and established routines. Entrepreneurs are not even the owners of the means of production or financial capital. To ensure that they are provided with the necessary resources, the action of the financial credit system is crucial so that – through the use of deposits – additional purchasing power is created in order to finance innovation. Entrepreneurs are also different from inventors, since their role is not so much to discover new things, but to introduce innovation into the economic sphere, thwarting the social and psychological resistance that it can arouse.[16] To overcome this type of opposition a particular kind of personality is required – one endowed with energy, determination and intuition. The ability to lead others is another important trait, creating consensus around a project, the results of which may be shrouded in a great deal of uncertainty.

The logic of entrepreneurial action is very different from the utilitarian and maximising logic employed by conventional theory to describe 'economic man'. Entrepreneurs, in fact, lack the information required to apply a rational assessment of the costs and benefits of their behaviour, since the latter is unconstricted by established routine. The motivation that urges him to act, moreover, is neither rational nor hedonistic in nature:

> First of all, there is the dream and the will to found a private kingdom, usually, though not necessarily, also a dynasty.... Then there is the will to conquer: the impulse to fight.... Finally there is the joy of creating, of getting things done, or simply of excercising one's energy and ingenuity.
>
> (Schumpeter 1912, Eng. trans. 2012, 93)

If in delineating the profile of the entrepreneur Schumpeter places strong emphasis on the individual and psychological characteristics that are typical of such a figure, he also gives equal importance to the historical context within which the entrepreneur comes to the fore. The socio-institutional context and the actors are set in a relationship of mutual interdependence. Schumpeter is also aware that development will alter the institutional framework upon which capitalism is based, modifying the very logic of competition and innovation. He distinguishes, in fact, *competitive capitalism* from *trustified capitalism* (Schumpeter 1939, 93). In the first model, innovation is introduced by individual entrepreneurs – new men who place themselves at the head of new business. The typical industrial entrepreneur of the nineteenth century was a man who innovated by placing himself at the head of an enterprise that he led personally and of which he was the owner. In the second model, on the other hand, innovation is produced by the R&D labs of large oligopolistic companies that, especially in the United States, dominated capitalism from the beginning of the twentieth century.[17] In this second scenario, competition becomes more restricted: it takes place between a few giant firms, where ownership is separated from management (given over to managers) and the entrepreneurial role loses those personal traits that characterised the previous phase (Fagerberg 2003, 133).

That said, what is the relationship that links the bourgeoisie and capitalism to the entrepreneurial role? Entrepreneurs do not constitute a specific social class and should not therefore be confused with the bourgeoisie, a class from which they do not necessarily hail. Because being an entrepreneur is not a profession and not, as a rule, a lasting condition 'entrepreneurs do not form a social class in the technical sense, as, for example, landowners or capitalists or workmen do' (Schumpeter 1912, Eng. trans. 2012, 78). However, a close relationship does exist between the bourgeoisie and the entrepreneurial role, since the former tends to absorb the entrepreneurs and their families into their own ranks, drawing new strength from them. The innovative role and economic dynamism ensured by the entrepreneur confer upon the bourgeoisie the prestige and social legitimacy that is at the foundation of their class position: 'Economically and sociologically, directly and indirectly, the bourgeoisie therefore depends on the entrepreneur and, as a class, lives and will die with him' (Schumpeter 1942, 134). This quote also helps us to clarify the causes which, according to Schumpeter, lead to the crisis of capitalism and its ruling class – an issue at the heart of his most famous book, *Capitalism, Socialism and Democracy*. The originality of Schumpeter, which sets him apart from Marx, is to identify some of the 'socio-cultural contradictions' that can lead to the crisis of capitalism, since its own success (development) 'undermines the social institutions which protect it' (ibid., 61). From a strictly economic point of view, capitalism is still capable of providing an increase in well-being. The large oligopolistic companies possess organisational structures capable of promoting – on an extensive and ongoing scale – the introduction of new combinations of productive factors.

Innovation, indeed, is to some extent routinised, ensured by a team of specialists working as employees. Economic progress tends therefore to become depersonalised and automated (ibid., 134). This bureaucratisation of innovation, however, takes away space from the entrepreneur, reducing the scope for leadership based on individual strength of will, intuition and personal responsibility (ibid.; Schumpeter 1947, 157–8). As this occurs, the ruling class loses much of its social legitimacy, which was linked to the exercise of this social function.

If capitalist evolution – 'progress' – either ceases or becomes completely automatic, the economic basis of the industrial bourgeoisie will be reduced eventually to wages such as are paid for current administrative work.... The perfectly bureaucratised giant industrialised unit not only ousts the small or medium-sized firm and 'expropriates' its owners, but in the end it also ousts the entrepreneur and expropriates the bourgeoisie as a class which in the process stands to lose not only its income but also, what is infinitely more important, its function.

(Schumpeter 1942, 130)

Schumpeter's reflections on innovation are of great interest. In the first place, because they show an interdisciplinary approach to study, one in which the institutional-historical analysis of capitalist development is combined with a microfoundation based on the innovative behaviour of entrepreneurs. Second, because his works have had a profound impact on the contemporary economics of innovation. Schumpeter's contribution was long-ignored by the dominant economic theories, which tended to consider technological progress as an exogenous factor in relation to the economy (Freeman 1994, 732; Helpman 2004). In recent decades, however, there has been a strong revival of attention given to innovation, which has gradually been 'endogenised' within the new theories of economic growth (Helpman 2004, Chapter IV). A rediscovery of Schumpeter's ideas has thus taken place, especially due to so-called 'evolutionary economics', which sees innovation and technological competition between companies as the driving force of capitalist development.[18]

1.6 Models of capitalism

This brings us to contemporary economic sociology. In this context, we will deal exclusively with two analytical approaches: that of *comparative political economy* and that of *new economic sociology*, but, as already seen in the preceding pages, only with reference to the subject of innovation. The first approach, prevalently macro in nature, is to be covered in this section, while the second approach, to be discussed in the next section, is characterised by a micro perspective. Political economy represents a line of study that analyses the relationships of reciprocal influence between economic, social and political phenomena and their modes of regulation in different institutional contexts.[19] In relation to this line, we are interested in a specific topic that, starting from the end of the eighties, has mainly attracted the attention of sociologists and political scientists: the study of the various institutional forms of advanced economies – that is, the debate on *varieties of capitalism*.

Comparative analysis highlights the existence of different models of capitalism which differ from each other in the way they regulate a wide range of economically important activities: for example, the financing and management of firms, relationships with suppliers and customers, the training of human capital, and systems of industrial relations and social protection. These differences depend on the institutional, political and social factors that have historically been formed in various countries and which influence economic performance at national, regional and sectoral levels: in terms of growth, employment, social inequality and innovation capacity (Dore 1987, 2000; Albert 1991; Hollingsworth *et al.* 1994; Hollingsworth and Boyer 1997; Soskice 1999; Hall and Soskice 2001).

This literature has produced two ideal-typical models of contemporary capitalism: on the one hand, the *Anglo-Saxon model of liberal market economies*; on the other, the *Rhine model of coordinated market economies*. The first type (which includes countries such as the United States and the UK) is characterised by the greater importance accorded to the market in regulating the economy.[20] In contrast, in coordinated economies (which in addition to Germany and Japan include many central and northern European countries), the joint action of political and economic institutions and interest organisations tends to limit market mechanisms and to produce more extensive and inclusive social protection systems.

Various studies have analysed the different economic performances offered by these two models. With reference to the eighties, emphasis was placed on the advantage of the Rhine model in terms of promoting employment stability and the dynamism of businesses. In the following decade, however, the strong revival of the Anglo-Saxon economies led to the re-evaluation of some of the strengths of the other model. In a context of rapid technological change and growth in international competition, the greater flexibility of liberal economies not only made for a better employment performance – especially in the service sector – but also a high level of specialisation in the most dynamic sectors of high technology.[21]

One specific point of this literature is of particular interest: *the nexus between the two models of capitalism and the relative innovation regimes*. Hall and Soskice (2001), for example, argue that the two models generate specific institutional advantages that steer the innovative initiatives of companies in different directions. The two authors put forward a relational view of companies, which are perceived as actors who need to develop their dynamic and innovative capabilities in order to compete effectively in the market (ibid., 6). This depends on the quality of the relationships that they establish internally with employees and externally with a number of other stakeholders: customers, suppliers, financial organisations and public institutions.

These relationships are used to solve 'problems of coordination' in five spheres of activity that are crucial for company competitiveness:

1   the industrial relations sphere, to handle matters related to wages and labour productivity;
2   the education and professional training sphere, to provide human capital equipped with the necessary professional skills;
3   the corporate governance and financing sphere, to support innovation;
4   the external relationships sphere, to deal with other firms, subcontractors and customers;

5   the internal relationships sphere, to ensure the cooperation of employees in the achievement of corporate objectives.

The thesis advanced by Hall and Soskice is that to solve these problems of coordination 'firms will gravitate towards the mode of coordination for which there is institutional support' (ibid., 9). The two models of capitalism have a high level of 'institutional complementarity', i.e. a congruence of logic in the various spheres of activity, which tends to reinforce the overall performance of the institutions and to promote a certain type of action.[22] In each of the five spheres mentioned above, therefore, companies in liberal economies will rely on internal hierarchy and market competition. Conversely, those in coordinated economies will rely more on 'non-market' relationships – in other words, on more collaborative forms of interaction with the other actors.

The incentives provided by the institutional framework steer companies to produce certain goods, to specialise in certain areas, and to innovate in a certain way. In particular, coordinated economies facilitate incremental innovations which lead to small improvements to existing products and production processes. This kind of innovation is typical of productive sectors where technological change is not too fast (slow-tech), such as mechanical engineering, transport and consumer durables (domestic appliances, etc.). In other words, Rhine capitalism sustains *a regime of incremental innovation* consistent with its institutional structure. Coordinated economies, in fact, have a funding system based on banks – on a 'patient capital' that knows how to evaluate company results over time; a form of industrial relations that encourages collaboration and wage moderation; a well-trained workforce provided with employment guarantees; and stable and cooperative relations with suppliers and customers. All these elements support a long-term management strategy as well as productive specialisation and gradual innovation requiring appropriate skills and medium-/long-term development.

The opposite is the case for liberal economies, which are characterised by an 'impatient capital' (based on the stock market and venture capital) and market relationships that do not ensure stability in either contractual (between companies) or occupational (for employees) terms. This model therefore shortens management time horizons, but also provides flexibility, agility and a willingness to take risks that may be useful for projects featuring a high level of uncertainty. This set of attitudes sustains, therefore, *a regime of radical innovation* and specialisation in areas characterised by rapid technological change (fasttech), such as high technology (biotechnology, semiconductors, computers and telecommunications), or in areas which require ongoing innovation, such as entertainment and advertising. Analysing the productive specialisation of their most representative countries, Germany and the United States, Hall and Soskice found confirmation of these different vocations of the 'two capitalisms' (ibid., 41ff.).

More recently, this line of reasoning has been adapted to interpret some economic developments that represent anomalies with regard to the internal logic of the two models outlined above, such as the spread of innovative start-up companies in high-tech sectors in European coordinated economies. The policies introduced to develop sectors of the new economy (from biotechnology to software to telecommunications) have highlighted some unexpected results: for example, successful experiences in Germany in the field of biotechnology and, along with Sweden, in the software industry for the internet; in Britain, however, experiences in biotechnology were more disappointing (Casper and Soskice 2004, 349).

These results are surprising in light of the debate on varieties of capitalism, given the coordinated economies of the first two countries and the liberal economy of the third. In theory, in fact, it should be the UK that has an institutional framework more favourable to the highly dynamic and innovative sector of advanced technology. The problem is solved by 'contaminating' the literature on institutional models of capitalism with that on sectoral systems of innovation (which will be discussed in detail in Chapter 5). This strand of literature highlights how innovative dynamics vary from sector to sector, because of the different opportunities for innovation and the cumulative effect of the knowledge present in their technological regimes. The puzzle dissolves when it is observed that the *new* policies implemented in coordinated economies have created incentives for the emergence of high-tech companies, but these are directed towards sub-sectors more compatible with the institutional framework of the Rhine model.

Technological companies have to face certain organisational and coordination dilemmas: for example, they must be equipped with adequate resources of knowledge through cooperation with universities; they need to recruit highly motivated scientists and technicians and hold on to them in an industry that, from the employment point of view, is very unstable; and they must obtain financial resources for their innovation projects, etc. (Casper 2006, 488ff.; 2010). A solution to these dilemmas varies depending on the institutional context in which the companies work, since this influences the mode of regulation of the research system, the labour market, the banking and financial system, and so on. The thesis developed is therefore as follows: (1) A mix of policies aimed at creating an institutional environment more conducive to the emergence of technological companies has been quite successful in some European coordinated economies, such as Germany.[23] (2) Analysis carried out on the sub-sectors of these companies' activity, however, shows that the institutional structure of the Rhine model played a role in their choice of specialisations.

In the case of biotechnology in Germany, the incentives and collective goods provided, along with other characteristics of the institutional system, directed businesses towards specialisation sub-sectors with technological systems featuring a high degree of cumulativity in terms of knowledge. These are, therefore, subject to incremental innovation: examples include platform technologies sold to research laboratories to perform certain routine tasks such as the purification of DNA and other molecules, or applications designed for the automation of certain discovery processes (the screening of therapeutic components, etc.). Subsectors, in other words, that are most compatible with the stability and long-term orientation typical of the German industrial system.

Institutional characteristics also help to explain the British case: the country has a strong presence in biotechnology, especially in specialisations involving a high level of uncertainty, but since the end of the nineties results there have been rather disappointing. In comparison with the similar case of the United States – which also specialises in highly advanced sub-sectors with a high level of risk – the UK presents two problems of scale: (1) the inadequate size of the scientific-educational system, not up to the task of providing the managerial and research staff necessary for the field to really take off, and (2) the shortcomings of the labour market, which does not provide adequate opportunities for star-scientists in the biotechnology sector: this meant they either opted for safer jobs in the big pharmaceutical companies or for exit strategies in the direction of the United States (Casper and Soskice 2004, 380). A check carried out on companies listed on the new technology stock markets confirms the thesis of compatibility between the two European countries' institutional arrangements and their specialisations in the new economy, with 88 per cent of German companies gravitating towards sub-sectors deploying incremental innovation and the same percentage of UK companies working in those featuring more radical innovation (Casper and Whitley 2004).

A comparative institutional approach has also been used to examine the role of the state in promoting innovation. It is a theme that is coming back to the centre of attention, including that of public opinion, thanks to the book by economist Mariana Mazzucato (2013) which advocates abandoning 'market-centered' conceptions of development and innovation and a reconsideration of the state's entrepreneurial role. To argue her thesis, the Italian-English scholar refers to the well-known distinction between risk and uncertainty introduced by American economist Frank Knight (1921). *Risk situations* are those in which the results of actions, although unknown, can still be predicted to a certain extent, based on a probability distribution familiar to the actors. The latter can therefore apply decision rules based on expected utility maximisation. With *uncertainty situations*, on the contrary, the unknown factors include not only the result of actions but also the probability of occurrence of one particular event or another.

Private entrepreneurs tend to shy away from situations of uncertainty such as those, for example, typical of projects at the frontiers of scientific research. These kinds of project – capital intensive and involving incommensurable risk – are, however, essential for long-term development and form the basis of almost all the new 'general purpose technologies' discovered in the second half of the twentieth century: from the internet, to biotechnology, to the nanotechnology and renewable energy of today.

And this, therefore, is where the entrepreneurial function of the state comes in: funding forward-looking and uncertain research projects from their inception up to the marketing of results. Mainstream economic theory justifies government intervention only in certain specific situations, to remedy so-called 'market failures'. According to Mazzucato, however, this position does not do full justice to the visionary and anticipatory role of the state in the context of technological change, where it performs two unique tasks: providing innovators with 'patient capital', something that is in short supply in the market economy; and promoting innovative partnerships between researchers, universities, government laboratories and companies, guiding them in directions consistent with the public good. In other words, the *entrepreneurial state* explores the 'risk landscape', creating new markets, especially where high capital investment is required in situations of radical uncertainty, and playing a leading role as *risk taker* and *market-shaper*.

Mazzuccato's book didn't simply drop unheralded from the skies. We only have to consider the institutional turn that has taken place in recent decades in the field of development economics (Evans 2005); or the literature on the developmental state (Block and Evans 2005) and national innovation systems (see Chapter 5); or even the recent rediscovery of the 'invisible hand of government' in the technological progress of the United States (Block 2011). All these contributions underline the importance of the institutional context in explaining both innovation and the trajectories of development followed by countries (Rodrik 2007; Acemoglu and Robinson 2012).

In particular, I would like to draw your attention here to a line of studies – those regarding the *new developmental state* – which has analysed the development of emerging economies in technologically cutting-edge productive sectors. It is a line that originates in certain research in the field of comparative political economy carried out in the eighties on the processes of 'late industrialisation' followed by Japan and other Asian economies after World War Two. As one researcher has observed, 'all late industrializers have in common industrialization on the basis of learning .... These countries industrialized by borrowing foreign technology rather than by generating new products or processes, the hallmark of earlier industrializing nations' (Amsden 1989, v). In these early studies, the economic success of the Asian countries is attributed to the presence of a *developmental state* that on the one hand protects infant industries from foreign competition, and on the other stimulates the competitiveness and exports of strategic companies, 'setting stringent performance standards' for groups receiving public support (ibid., 145).

But what are the essential features of the developmental state? The first element regards *development strategy*. State action is aimed at promoting economic growth through a long-term, structural, industrial policy which, while recognising the role of the private sector, tends to guide and direct it towards international markets. It is, therefore, a strategy based on high levels of productive investment, the strategic allocation of capital resources, and selective exposure of domestic industry to international competition (Wade 1990).

The second element relates to *state structure*. Industrialisation is led by a political élite equipped with broad powers and relatively insulated from the pressures of social groups. Moreover, thanks to the legacy of the Confucian tradition, the government can take advantage of a robust and efficient bureaucracy – one that is selected on a meritocratic basis, endowed with high prestige, devoted to the national interest and, thanks in part to the informal links forged during the period of studies, internally cohesive. The classic description of such a bureaucracy and its role in development is provided by Chalmers Johnson (1982) in relation to Japan's Ministry of International Trade and Industry (MITI). Although carrying on relationships with private companies, these political and bureaucratic élites are sufficiently insulated and competent to pursue policies that promote long-term economic growth (Johnson 1982; Onis 1991). In other words, East Asian developmental states were able not only to promote economic development but also to direct and coordinate industrialisation.

As has been noted, however, these early studies provide a reductive and simplified vision of relations between the public and private sectors, where 'the state prevails over civil society, and social groups are pacified agents of economic changes' (Moon and Prasad 1994, 363). This 'rigid binary demarcation of state-society relations through the "dominance/insulation" hypothesis' has therefore come under fire on two fronts (ibid., 370): on the one hand, for the overvaluation of the unitary and cohesive character of Asian states and the degree of success achieved in the various productive sectors; on the other, for the underestimation of the ties linking public agencies to their economic and social constituencies.

A new study approach therefore emerges from these criticisms – that of the *new developmental state* (Evans 1995; Ó Riain 2004; Breznitz 2007; Block 2011) – which places greater emphasis on the embeddedness of the state in society and focuses on the most dynamic and innovative high technology sectors. The first major contribution came from Peter Evans (1995) on the birth of the information technology sector in certain newly industrialising countries (Korea, Brazil and India). Evans develops two ideal-types of state: *predatory states* (e.g. Mobutu's patrimonial regime in Zaire), with corrupt and particularistic politico-bureaucratic élites that extract resources from society and undermine development capabilities; and *developmental states* (such as Korea), where the élites have a more universalistic orientation, focused on national interests.

This second type of state can play an active role in development thanks to: (1) its internal structure, and (2) its relations with society. Where the former is concerned, the organisation of the state approximates Weber's description of a modern and independent public bureaucracy: 'Highly selective meritocratic recruitment and long-term career rewards create commitment and a sense of corporate coherence' (ibid., 12). With regard to external relations, politico-bureaucratic élites are far from isolated: 'To the contrary, they are embedded in a concrete set of social ties that binds the state to society and provides institutionalized channels for the continual negotiation and renegotiation of goals and policies' (ibid.).[24]

The developmental state is based, therefore, on a subtle alchemy involving two seemingly contradictory characteristics. On the one hand, *autonomy* – its ability to preserve a certain independence from private élites – which allows it to formulate medium- to long-term development goals, passing over the immediate interests of the most powerful lobbies; on the other, *embeddedness* – its ability to build alliances with certain social groups (especially industrialists) 'with whom the state shares a joint project of transformation' (ibid., 59). Only when both of these aspects are combined, as in the case of Korea, are the conditions created for what Evans calls an *embedded autonomy* that 'provides the underlying structural basis for successful state involvement in industrial transformation' (ibid.).

Following this approach, other emerging countries (Ireland, Israel and Taiwan) with a leading position in high-tech sectors have also recently been studied. These 'success stories' should be understood against the background of the birth of 'global production networks': an increasingly fragmented and geographically dispersed production process that allows emerging countries to specialise in a specific stage of production and compete on an international scale (Breznitz 2007).

The strategies followed by the first developmental states are ill-adapted to these new scenarios, particularly in market sectors subject to rapid technological change that require more flexibility on the part of both the state and companies. For this reason, Seán Ó Riain (2000, 2004, 2014), studying the development of the software industry in Ireland, contrasts the old model of the *bureaucratic developmental state* (typical, for example, of Japan) with a new model of the *developmental network state*. The latter 'is defined by its ability to nurture post-Fordist networks of production and innovation, to attract international investment, and to link these local and global technology and business networks together in ways that promote development' (2000, 158). Ó Riain shows that this new form of state assumes a more flexible and decentralised 'networked organizational structure', based on the 'multiple embeddedness of state agencies in professional-led networks of innovation and in international capital' (2004, Kindle digital edition, position 146).

While starting from assumptions very similar to those of Ó Riain, Dan Breznitz's study of Ireland, Israel and Taiwan tends to underline that these new development strategies are not, however, connected to a single form of state. Since the 1960s, all three of these countries have taken steps to create their own high-tech industry by following some common policies, such as strengthening education and communication infrastructure and supporting SMEs. But the similarities end there. The states involved, in fact, have very different bureaucratic structures, which followed different industrial and research policies – and as a result generated very different forms of technological skills and production specialisation. The methods of embeddedness are also dissimilar, with the relationship between the state and private enterprises established differently, both in the domestic and international market.

These three cases clearly show the usefulness of a *comparative political economy* perspective to explain how institutional contexts and differing political choices shape differentiated development trajectories. It should also be added that the emphasis placed on embeddedness tends to create a space for dialogue with the new economic sociology approach which will be looked at in the next section. That said, perhaps the most significant suggestion that arises from these neo-developmentalist studies is that of not exaggerating the 'demiurgic' potential of the state – its ability, in other words, to manage and plan economic and technological development.

To clarify this point I would like to refer to Peter Block's reconstruction of the evolution of the innovation system in the United States over the last few decades. Since technological innovation cannot be directed from above, the US federal government has promoted a 'coordinated decentralization' of innovation policy, based on public-private partnerships (Block 2011). In this system, public agencies do not appear able to define, ex-ante, a precise strategy of technological change. In addition to financial support they carry out an essential role in terms of socio-institutional brokerage, promoting the conditions for the cooperation of all those who can make a significant contribution. In this way they create 'collaborative public spaces' (Lester and Piore 2004) where stakeholders can discuss and exchange information useful for development and innovation (Block and Keller 2009; Block 2011). In other words, public agencies resolve situations of *network failure* that occur through the opportunism of the actors involved and/or the lack of adequate incentives, information and expertise (Schrank and Whitford 2011).

In this process of change, strategy is not defined, a priori. It is rather the emerging product – more or less intentional according to the various programmes – of organisational interactions and modalities involving a plurality of players. The role of the state is not, therefore, hypostasised. Block, analysing the influence of the US government, talks about an effect of 'social resonance', with specific reference to the catalytic role performed by a peripheral intervention programme: the Small Business Innovation Research Program (SBIR), which multiplied the creation of innovative SMEs. Two significant points emerge from Block's account: (1) The change in the US innovation system is not the result of a 'unified plan', as described by Chalmers Johnson (1982) with regard to Japanese industrialisation. In fact, behind the changes that have occurred over the past 30 years, there is no deliberate strategy visible that is aimed at augmenting the role of the public actor and reshaping the relationship between the state and the economy, given that all this happened in an era of 'market fundamentalism' (Block and Keller 2009, 475–7). (2) The SBIR programme triggered critical consequences only in resonance with other social, economic and political changes that were already in place, enhancing the overall effect (Keller and Block 2013, 21).

In conclusion, what can we learn from the comparative political economy studies examined in this section? Essentially, three lessons. First, the institutional analysis of capitalism is useful for the study of national innovation systems, both in advanced and emerging countries. The ideal-typical models mentioned earlier, however, require further elaboration: (1) to take account of innovation systems pertaining to other models of capitalism (e.g. the countries of Mediterranean Europe and emerging economies); (2) to analyse the territorial and sectoral variations of innovation systems (more about this in Chapters 5, 6 and 7).

The second lesson is that institutional arrangements should not be considered unmodifiable and therefore the dynamics of institutional change must also be taken into account.[25]

The third lesson is that the emphasis placed on the institutional structures of the economy and the systemic aspect of innovation should not over-restrict the space attributed to *agency factors* – in other words, the intentional action of public and private actors. As has recently been pointed out, a common error in various institutional and systemic approaches is to read the behaviour of the actors – the companies, for instance – only through the characteristics of the contexts in which they operate (Gertler 2010, 5).[26]

But companies have a certain strategic autonomy with regard to the institutional contexts to which they pertain: they are not exclusively *rule-takers* but also *rule-makers* (Crouch *et al.* 2009). They derive a substantial degree of freedom from the reflexive re-elaboration of the repertoire of skills and experience they have inherited from their own past. And this in a way that is partly independent of the industry and the country in which they operate. Susan Berger, together with a group of MIT researchers (2005), described this approach as the 'dynamic legacies model' and applied it to an empirical study of 500 North American, European and Asian companies, showing that their behaviour and strategy in the face of globalisation (e.g. with regard to choices of outsourcing and offshoring) could not be explained either by their productive sector or by their pertaining to one of the models of capitalism that we have looked at. More recently, the MIT research group on 'Production in Innovation Economy' also studied a wide variety of American companies in order to analyse the relationship between innovation and manufacturing production (Berger 2013; Locke and Wellhausen 2014). The conclusions reached are that innovation is not linked only to R&D activity and high-tech sectors, occurring not just in the initial phases of product development but 'throughout the value chain' (Locke and Wellhausen 2014, Kindle digital edition, position 94). This happens because 'much learning takes place as companies move their ideas beyond prototypes and demonstration and through the stages of commercialization' (Berger 2013, 5).[27] These scholars, therefore, emphasise the risk that the offshoring of production to emerging countries, implemented by many American companies, may in the long run weaken the basis of the US economy's innovative capacity and development. This is due to the fact that 'manufacturing firms have a critical role both as sites of innovation and as enablers of scaling up to commercialization the strong flow of innovations from America's research laboratories, universities, public laboratories, and industrial R&D facilities' (ibid., 26).

The study of innovation cannot, therefore, leave the choices made by companies, and their competitive and organisational strategies, out of consideration. With regard to the latter, for example, certain studies link the innovative capacity of companies to the specific organisational solutions that they adopted. Research carried out by Lester and Piore (2004) on case studies in the fields of mobile phones, medical appliances and clothing, shows that the most important innovations derive from an organisational and management approach of an 'interpretive' type. The authors contrast two different procedural approaches to problem-solving: analytical and interpretive. *Analytical processes* are those that can be applied when the problems to be solved and the possible results are well-known. *Interpretive processes*, however, are more appropriate when neither the decision alternatives nor the possible outcomes are known in advance. Solutions, therefore, must be sought by exploring the frontier of innovation.

In the latter case, the activity of discovering new solutions proceeds through *interpretive conversations* between people that pertain to different organisational areas and workgroups. The outcome is neither predictable nor obvious, a priori. Managerial activity, therefore, is aimed at promoting the open exchange of communication and integrating a variety of resources in order to cross predetermined cognitive and organisational boundaries. The results of the study shed light on how the creation of these 'interpretive spaces' – open to the contribution of a plurality of subjects – produce the best results: 'The key innovations in each of the case studies grew out of an integration: in every case different domains of knowledge were brought together to form something new and original' (ibid., 10). The three case studies analysed by David Stark (2009) – through ethnographic research on the media and on finance in the United States, and on the machine tool sector in Hungary – also bring out this interpretive aspect in relation to innovation. This is especially true when organisations find themselves operating in competitive environments characterised by scenarios of radical uncertainty. In these contexts the best performance is obtained by *heterarchical organisations*, which are able to take advantage of the uncertainty, nurturing an ongoing capacity for innovation.[28] These organisations tend to systematically and intentionally generate problematic situations within themselves. They constantly question organisational routine and foster co-presence and dialogue between different evaluative criteria, deriving from different units and skills.

Heterarchy, therefore, represents a strategy that tends to 'organise dissonance', exploiting the intelligence dispersed within an organisation and coordinating it, without suppressing the presence of different principles of evaluation and valorisation. These, in fact, serve rather to create new productive combinations: in other words, to innovate. This implies: (1) the involvement of a plurality of units in the innovation process; (2) the strengthening of their operative interdependence through ongoing reciprocal monitoring; (3) the decentralisation of decision-making and the development of alternative forms of non-hierarchical coordination, based on 'collateral responsibility' between the working groups; and (4) greater simultaneity with respect to the design and implementation phases of innovation.

As Stark points out, with the assumption of this analytical perspective, the entrepreneurial role is not a matter of the attributes of an individual (as in Schumpeter) or his relationships, but is a property of the organisation itself. The entrepreneurial ability to generate innovation lies in the borderline and overlapping areas between networks and working groups, which possess distinct forms of knowledge and evaluatory criteria. The interactive coexistence of dissonant elements, not allowing the consolidation of predictable routine, generates 'creative frictions' and these foster the innovative recombination of resources.[29]

If, on the one hand, this perspective on business complicates the institutional analysis of capitalism, on the other it enriches our understanding of innovation processes. Reclaiming the analytical independence of 'agency factors' does not mean isolating the economic actors from the institutional context in which they operate. It is to see how they exploit the opportunities or compensate for obstacles through their strategies and interpersonal skills. And this is a theme that brings us to the next section, which deals with socio-economic networks and their influence on innovation.

1.7 Innovative networks

As we mentioned in the Introduction, over the last few decades there has been an increase in collaborative relationships between economic actors. The rapidity of technological change, the uncertainty of its evolutionary trajectories, growing international competition, and the pluralisation of knowledge sources have made companies more dependent on external resources. Inter-organisational partnerships (strategic alliances between companies, research consortia, collaboration with universities, etc.) have therefore multiplied, especially in the field of research and innovation. And this has focused the attention of scholars on the social and economic networks that support them. In the context of new economic sociology, this type of analysis has been developed through the so-called 'structural approach', which has applied the network analysis to the study of socio-economic phenomena. The starting assumption is that economic activity is *embedded* within the social relationships between individual or collective actors (Granovetter 1985). These relationships – and the social structures that they generate – influence economic activity, as they allow access to resources and information of various kinds, create trust and discourage opportunism in transactions.[30]

The networks are not, however, all the same. They are configured differently depending on the type of relationships that exist between the actors. These relationships can be: (1) informal (based on acquaintanceship of a personal kind, membership of the same professional community, etc.) or formal (based on contractual relationships such as alliances between companies, research consortia, etc.); (2) long- or short-term; (3) focused on individual (managers, researchers) or collective actors (companies, research organisations); (4) directed toward specific or more indefinite goals, etc.

Networks can also: (1) be purely *transactional* (such as in trade relations) or *relational* (personal and social relationships); (2) possess different modes of governance (more or less hierarchical, more or less regulated); (3) present a configuration that is more or less closed and dense.

Many studies have been devoted to analysing the impact of networks on innovation.[31] Research has mostly dealt with *innovative partnerships* (inter-organisational collaborations), showing that they foster the circulation of information, the sharing of project risks, access to resources that are different and complementary to those of the company, and also reciprocal learning regarding solutions and organisational practices. The results show that, especially in areas of high technology, learning networks become the 'locus of innovation' (Powell et al. 1996). This, however, should not lead us to think that innovative networks and partnerships play no role in traditional manufacturing sectors (as, on the contrary, is shown by the Italian industrial districts) or in the world of finance.[32] Two important results emerge from all these studies.

1   There is a positive relationship between collaboration and innovation networks, proven by numerous empirical studies in various productive sectors.[33] A kind of virtuous circle is created in which the relationships that companies form with other external actors improve their innovative performance and this tends in turn to foster further collaborations (Powell and Grodal 2005, 67).
2   There does not, however, emerge a univocal link between the type of relationship, the position in the network, and the innovative performance of the actors analysed.

To understand the lack of this nexus, let us examine some theoretical contributions and research on the topic, which to some extent have become classic points of reference in this field, beginning with the studies of Mark Granovetter. Granovetter became famous for his thesis on the 'strength of weak ties', developed from research into the labour market of technicians, professionals and managers in the Boston suburbs (Granovetter 1974). The American scholar distinguishes between two types of relationship: '*strong ties*', referring to subjects with whom there exists a relationship of familiarity and trust (friends, family, relatives), and '*weak ties*', referring to relationships that feature less communicative and affective intensity.[34] The survey results highlight a fact that is apparently counterintuitive: the greater importance of the second type of tie in terms of gathering information that is useful in the search for a new job. The explanation is simple and brilliant at the same time.

Weak ties (e.g. acquaintanceships struck up in the workplace) allow the subject to obtain new information that was not available to him and which he could not obtain through strong ties. Relatives and friends, in fact, belong to the same 'information area' as the subject and are therefore unlikely to be able to provide significant new information. It is a thesis that has been the subject of a great deal of debate. Subsequent research has shown that the type of relationship useful in searching for work varies across countries, productive areas and professional sectors. Granovetter has also dealt with the importance of social networks for innovation, for example in the creation of the electricity industry in the United States in the late nineteenth century. To explain the predominance of the solution backed by Thomas Edison, which envisaged the construction of large hydroelectric power stations, Granovetter draws attention to the inventor's social networks. Edison's solution ended up winning through not so much because of more *efficient technology* with regard to the other solutions possible at the time (maintenance of gas lighting, construction of local generators), since this was a difficult parameter to assess, especially in relation to its long-term effect: what proved decisive, rather, was Edison's *relational effectiveness* in promoting, and achieving the acceptance of, a solution that was then highly innovative (and problematic). This effectiveness is explained by the structure of his social relationships, which enabled him to mobilise his personal contacts with international financiers, entrepreneurs in the electricity sector and many other inventors and researchers whose opinion affected the decisions taken regarding the lighting system of the major American cities (Granovetter and McGuire 1998). Granovetter has also applied his weak ties thesis to the matter of innovation. At the time of its first formulation in the early seventies, he had already stressed the importance of these kinds of ties in the diffusion of innovation, advancing the hypothesis (previously proposed by Simmel and Sombart) that social marginality favoured the latter's adoption (Granovetter 1973, 1366–7).[35]

These ideas were later taken up and developed in a more recent essay that shows the (variable) importance of social marginality, but also the (potentially) conflictual character of innovation when it challenges power structures and positions of dominance. The argument put forward is that, especially in scientific fields, 'new information and ideas are more efficiently diffused through weak ties', thus facilitating the flow of non-redundant information (Granovetter 2005, 34).[36] In contrast, strong ties and extremely dense social networks, while on the one hand strengthening trust, on the other circulate ideas that are already familiar. These stabilise to become 'normative ideas' – shared ideas about the 'proper behavior' to follow. This type of pattern thus makes deviance from group norms more difficult and non-compliant behaviour easier to sanction (ibid.). In other words, it hinders highly innovative behaviour. This does not mean that it cannot foster the institutionalisation of innovation.

Granovetter exemplifies this point of view through reference to certain studies on the formation of new high-risk financial products, initially perceived as simple 'gambling'. In some cases, these became institutionalised as respectable financial instruments. In others, they were opposed and then prohibited by the financial élite. A study by MacKenzie and Millo (2003) regarding the introduction and legitimisation of so-called 'financial derivatives'[37] on the Chicago Stock Exchange well illustrates the role played by social networks in the process of the institutionalisation of innovation. Chicago financial circles were highly structured by personal relationships that distinguished between *insiders* and *outsiders*. The institutionalisation of this financial innovation was possible only through the mobilisation of cohesive groups of *insiders*: these were, however, supported by actors from different institutional spheres (economists and politicians).

Granovetter, however, also shows that the most radical innovation is produced by marginal individuals who are more easily able to distance themselves from conformist behaviour. The example given is that of *junk bonds*: risky but highly profitable financial products. During the seventies, these instruments were widely used and publicised by a young American trader (Michael Milken) who worked for a small finance company. Junk bonds soon became a sort of symbol for medium-sized companies excluded from the circuits of the financial élite, and a tool to promote hostile takeovers towards the latter. *Insider* companies however, members of the financial élite, were able to mobilise the support of their political allies who, in a number of states, introduced rules restricting the use of junk bonds. These subsequently led to Milken's judicial prosecution and his disqualification from financial activity.

This research – according to Granovetter – highlights how innovation involves the breaking of established routine (as indicated by Weber) and the combination of previously unconnected resources to attain a new economic purpose (Schumpeter). The creation of new institutional forms, as the case of venture capital shows,[38] also involves overcoming conventional boundaries. Thus, the actor collocated astride different networks, separate circuits of exchange, and distinct institutional spheres 'is well placed to innovate' (Granovetter 2005, 46).

Here Granovetter refers explicitly to the argument made by Ronald Burt (1992) regarding 'structural holes'. Social relationships tend to agglomerate around clusters of individuals between whom interaction is frequent and intense. These relational clusters constitute 'islands of opinion and behavior' that can 'create barriers to information inconsistent with prevailing beliefs and practice' (Burt 2005, 15). There may also be disconnections in the social structure: in other words, a lack of relation between clusters, which are isolated one from the other. These relational gaps form structural holes, spaces in the social structure, which impede the flow of information but also create entrepreneurial opportunities. Their potential value is due to the fact that 'they separate nonredundant sources of information' (ibid., 16). Individuals who collocate themselves within these spaces thus create a bridge between different circuits of communication and derive benefits therefrom: they obtain a greater variety of (non-redundant) information; gain access to important information before others; and control the flow of information between the various clusters. These figures constitute the entrepreneurs of the networks, true brokers, playing a mediating role between the various relational circuits and in this way achieving competitive advantages, for example in terms of innovation and creativity (Figure 1.1).

Burt considers this aspect through an examination of the 'social origin of good ideas'. In his analysis, he shifts the focus from the production of the idea to the value that this produces when it is imported into different environments: its 'valorisation' is the function of a transaction between information deriving from distinct and separate groups. In other words, creativity is presented as information brokerage, as a sort of import-export activity: '*creativity by brokerage*' implies the movement of 'an idea mundane in one group to another group where the idea is new and valued' (ibid., 64). To demonstrate this thesis, Burt examined the suggestions made by 673 managers of the supply network of a large American electronics company to improve the network itself. The ideas that received the best evaluations from top management came from managers who could take advantage of less redundant information sources (ibid., 69ff.).[39]

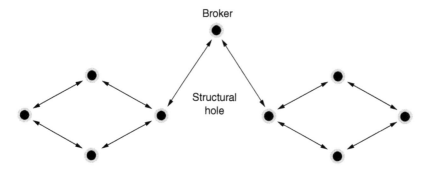

Figure 1.1 Structural holes and relational brokerage.

Another line of research involving the role of networks in innovation is that by Walter Powell and his colleagues in the field of biotechnology. Studies in this field show that *inter-organisational partnerships give companies a significant advantage in terms of innovation.* Two elements emerge as crucial:

1   The effectiveness of the partnership depends very much on trust and the ability to learn new knowledge. Relationship building – that is, the ability to build and make use of external collaborations – therefore assumes strategic importance. A central position in the network and experience in managing these partnerships have a positive influence on innovative performance (Powell *et al.* 1996; Powell and Owen-Smith 1999).

2   The ability to learn from external relations is conditioned by internal company resources, in terms of knowledge and technical skills.

An interesting aspect of these studies is that they use a diachronic and contextual approach. In fact, the configuration of the network changes over time, both at the individual level (in the history of a single company) and at the industrial level: the biotechnology sector, for example, shows increased connectivity between businesses and other organisations as the sector develops. In addition, the networks are studied within a specific production sector and the importance of contextual factors is recognised. To explain the tendency of biotechnology companies towards territorial agglomeration, the complex economic and institutional infrastructure that sustains the transfer and commercialisation of scientific knowledge is brought into play: universities of excellence, technical and legal consultancy firms, venture capital businesses, and so on (Powell *et al.* 2002). Recently, finally, John Padgett and Walter Powell (2012) have dealt with organisational innovation through combining the analysis of social networks with models of autocatalysis drawn from biochemistry. Through various case studies – taken from history, post-socialist economies, and sectors of biotechnology – the two authors explain the emergence of organisational innovation as the result of spillover deriving from interconnected social networks: in other words, through the interaction of autocatalytic mechanisms within different networks.[40]

Another line of research that refers to social relations is that dealing with the diffusion of innovation. These studies show that the adoption of innovation and its diffusion depends on interpersonal relationships and the conformation of the social structure.[41] Diffusion is defined by Everett Rogers (2003, 11) as 'the process by which (1) an *innovation* (2) is *communicated* through certain *channels* (3) *over time* (4) among the members of a *social system*'. One of the best-known results of this particular line of research concerns the speed of innovation adoption. Much research, in fact, identifies a distribution of the rate of adoption that assumes a characteristic S-shaped form, even if there are differences from case to case in the grade of the curve (Figure 1.2). This phenomenon is easily explained: in the beginning, innovation is adopted only by a handful, but after a while – thanks to word of mouth from those who have tried it out – the rate increases more rapidly (so the curve rises) and then decelerates as the number of individuals who have not yet adopted it gradually reduces.

Other studies have focused on the diffusion of information and knowledge useful for innovation, and the role played by the various kinds of social ties: strong ties being considered more reliable and suitable for conveying tacit, complex and interdependent knowledge;[42] weak ties instead for codified knowledge and non-redundant information (Hansen 1999; Van Wijk *et al.* 2003; Powell and Grodal 2005).

These should not be imagined as automatic, however: no necessary correspondence always exists, in fact, between weak ties and non-redundancy of information. In the analyses, therefore, the form and content of the ties must be kept distinct, as must the socio-cognitive (variety of knowledge conveyed) and

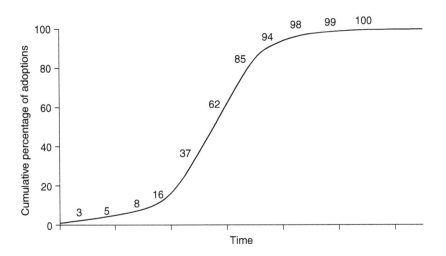

Figure 1.2 The process of innovation diffusion: the S-curve of the adoption rate.

socio-normative (role of trust and frequency of contact) aspects (McEvily and Zaheer 1999, 1153; Ramella and Trigilia 2010b, 107–8).

Variability also exists in relation to production specialisation: in traditional and slow-tech sectors, for example, strong ties play a more important role; while weak ties are more important in high-tech sectors. Some studies, however, have shown that the type of ties activated by employers varies greatly with the functions and activities carried out (Ramella 2005; Ramella and Trigilia 2006). As far as innovation is concerned, for example, emphasis has been given to the fact that companies need to balance strong and weak ties, internal cohesion and variety in external relations: in other words, the necessity of using complementary relationships and resources for innovation (Ramella 2011; Ruef 2002).[43] To conclude, what studies about social networks show is the importance of interpersonal and inter-organisational relationships for innovative performance. However, it should also be added that the relevance of networks takes on a highly contingent and contextual value: their presence, effectiveness and conformation depends on a plurality of social and institutional factors.

1.8 The economic sociology of innovation

This short review of the contributions of economic sociology to the subject of innovation is not intended to be exhaustive, but rather show (selectively) their relevance for Innovation Studies. As will be seen in the rest of the book, many of the topics covered in this chapter demonstrate a clear connection with contemporary research. There is an increasing awareness, in fact, that innovation takes the form of a complex process in which institutional and socio-relational factors occupy a prominent place.

Sociology can make an important contribution on both these fronts, thanks to the tradition of studies which it has developed. First of all, there is the contribution of the classic sociologists, for whom innovation does not correspond to 'simple' technological change but also brings the overall structures of capitalism into play. Their observations are closely related to the theme of social change, and raise questions regarding the relations of power, legitimisation and conflict involved in the innovation process.[44] This macro-sociological focus does not mean, however, that the classics did not also present more specific reflections on the social aspects of technological change,[45] the actors and the micro-mechanisms of innovation.[46] As already mentioned, many of the insights provided by the classics of sociology are echoed in contemporary research. And yet, reviewing the latter, the feeling aroused is that today's thinking about innovation – especially in the economic sphere – has in a certain sense been 'sterilised'. In fact, although the importance of socio-relational and institutional aspects has been recognised, some of the constitutive elements of the innovation process (power, legitimisation and conflict) are neglected, and the same applies to their interdependence with social change.

In recent years, however, innovation has been the subject of fresh attention in economic sociology. For example, the 'macro' tradition regarding the relationship between capitalism and innovation has been revitalised by the studies of *comparative political economy* on models of capitalism. The tradition regarding 'micro' mechanisms, meanwhile, has found a place in the *new economic sociology*, and in particular in the structural approach's reflections on networks.[47] Economic sociology has gained in vigour in recent decades, thanks to the contribution of both these analytical strands. However, comparative political economy and new economic sociology have remained separate (Trigilia 2007a, 2009; Regini 2007; Barbera and Negri 2008). Innovation Studies offers the opportunity for a dialogue between them, in order to develop – within a specific field of research – an integrated approach. A theoretical perspective that Randal Collins would define as *meso* in nature, which sees the analysis of social networks as a connecting link between structures and actors.

As we will see in the following chapters, in fact, innovation is based on interaction processes that involve a plurality of actors and institutions, including non-economic elements: companies, universities, research centres, advanced services, local government, foundations, etc. It is this multiplicity of actors and interaction that requires an integrated analytical approach that takes into account both *the dimensions of the economic and socio-institutional context*, which constitute a structure of opportunity more or less conducive to innovation; as well as the *individual and relational dimensions*, which condition the ability of economic actors to exploit the potentialities that they are presented with.

Box 1 Self-study prompts

1   What, according to Adam Smith, is the relationship between division of labour and innovation?

2   In Marx's work, what role does technological change play in historical transformation?

3   For Durkheim, what are the conditions for division of labour to create solidarity? What implications can be drawn from this for innovation?

4   Who are the actors of innovation for Simmel, Sombart and Weber, and which traits characterise them?

5   What, according to Schumpeter, is the function of the entrepreneur in the development of capitalism?

6   What is the relationship between models of capitalism and systems of innovation?

7   What role is played by social networks in innovation processes?

Notes

1   According to Marx, capitalism began to develop in Europe with the expansion of markets linked to the geographical discoveries of the fifteenth century (Rosenberg 1982).

2   For a more detailed explanation of these mechanisms, see Trigilia (2002, Chapter 1.5) and Aron (1965).

3 In a note in *Capital*, Marx writes: 'A critical history of technology would show how little any of the inventions of the 18th century are the work of a single individual' (Marx 1867, Eng. trans. 1887, 326, fn 4).

4 Indeed, 'everything in the contract is not contractual'. In order for it to function, social regulation is required, and that is the result of society rather than of individuals and their interests (Durkheim 1902, Eng. trans. 1947, 211). Personal interest, in fact, is too weak and unstable a bulwark to curb individual egoism and cement the social bond.

5 As is known, the remedy proposed by Durkheim was that of a new regulation through professional corporations.

6 In the second book of *The Elementary Forms of Religious Life* (1897, Eng. trans. 1965, vol. II, Chapter VII), Durkheim speaks of periods in history where – due to some collective shock – social interaction becomes more frequent and active, and this general effervescence results in revolutionary or creative epochs. The intensity of social interaction stimulates individual strengths, producing changes of a major kind. As Durkheim observed, this individual empowerment through social interaction does not manifest itself only in extraordinary situations, but also in ordinary activities.

7 Sombart defines this new economic mentality as a combination of 'entrepreneurial spirit' and 'bourgeois spirit'. On this point, see Trigilia (2002, Chapter 2.2.2).

8 The German sociologist provides many historical examples: Roman freedmen, certain Athenian slaves, the Armenians in Turkey, the Pariah and Chetty castes in India, the Huguenots in France, the Quakers in England, and so on.

9 Sombart also adds 'heretics' – those who do not belong to a country's dominant religion.

10 As noted by Simmel, in the sixteenth century the prosperity of Lyon and Antwerp's international stock exchanges was closely linked to the activity of strangers, thanks to the 'almost unlimited freedom of trade which the alien merchant enjoyed' in these markets (1907, Eng. trans. 2004, 226).

11 We'll come back to Sombart in Chapter 3 with a discussion of his reflections on technology and inventors. For reasons of space, however, it is not possible to discuss here certain parts of his work that would be interesting for studies on innovation: in particular those relating to the rationalisation, scientification and depersonalisation of work and business that occurs in mature capitalism, which is accompanied by the standardisation of products and uniformation of needs. For these aspects, see Chapters XLV to LII in Sombart (1916).

12 As we will see later on, both of these ideas have been taken up in the structural approach of the new economic sociology.

13 The concept of rationality in Weber refers to a procedure of control of reality within and external to man. It refers to practical behaviour – not to the understanding of objective social laws – and implies calculability, predictability and generalisability of means with respect to the objective of control of the world (Rusconi 1981, 189). Weber, with reference to economic action, distinguishes two forms of rationality: 'formal rationality', which indicates 'the extent of quantitative calculation or accounting which is technically possible and which is actually applied'; and 'substantive rationality', which indicates 'the degree in which a given groups of persons … is or could be adequately provided with goods by means of an economically oriented course of social action … interpreted in terms of a given set of ultimate values' (Weber 1922b; Eng. trans. 1947, 184–5). In the first case, *a form of rational action with respect to the objective* is evoked, which implies a rational calculation of means in relation to ends; in the second case, however, *rational action with respect to value* also comes into play – that is, an orientation and evaluation of economic behaviour in the light of particular values which are intended to be implemented.

14 For an intellectual biography of Schumpeter, see Swedberg (1991).

15 In note 1 at page 64 Schumpeter writes: 'Add successively as many mail coaches as you please, you will never get a railway thereby.'

16 In *Business Cycles*, Schumpeter offers a detailed historical account of the – sometimes violent – economic, social and political resistance put up by the classes threatened by innovation. His reconstruction of the development of the cotton industry in England is paradigmatic in this sense. In order to make innovation a reality, entrepreneurs have to influence not only the production sector but also the aspect of demand, transforming the consumption habits of the population (McCraw 2007, 258).

17 These two models of innovation are known amongst economists as Schumpeter Mark I and Schumpeter Mark II (Freeman 1994, 741). Sidney Winter (1984) has placed them in relation to two different technological regimes with a distinct role, as sources of innovation, played by *new firms* (entrants) or *established firms*. These two models will be seen again in Chapter 5, in the context of sectoral systems of innovation.

18 It is not possible here to describe the various strands of theory and research of the economics of innovation. For a comparison between the approach of neoclassical economics and that of evolutionary economics, see Malerba (2000, especially chapters I–IV). For a detailed reconstruction of the neo-Schumpeterian approaches, and for the differences with respect to new theories of growth, see Fagerberg (2003).

19 For a reconstruction of this line of study, see Ballarino and Regini (2008); Ramella (2007); Regini (2006a); Trigilia (2006; 2009, Chapter III). Its consolidation is well evidenced by the recent publication of a handbook dedicated to comparative institutional analysis. The objective of the latter – very similar to that of comparative political economy – is to understand 'how the forms, outcomes, and dynamics of economic organization (firm, networks, markets) are influenced and shaped by other social institutions (e.g. training systems, legal systems, political systems, educational systems, etc.) and with what consequences for economic growth' (Morgan *et al.* 2010a, 2).

20 The concept of *regulation* refers to the 'various modes by which that set of activities and inter-actor relationships associated with the production and distribution of economic resources is coordinated, these resources are allocated and the related conflicts, real or potential, are structured – that is, prevented or settled' (Regini 2006b, 4–5).

21 These models have attracted a great deal of criticism and, especially in recent years, have undergone numerous revisions. For a reconstruction of the debate, see Hancke (2009); Streeck (2009, 2010).

22 The concept of institutional complementarity has been interpreted throughout the literature in quite different ways. On this point, see Crouch (2010).

23 Germany is one of the leading countries in Europe in the field of biotechnology because of the launch, in the mid-nineties, of a public initiative – the BioRegio programme – which promoted a closer relationship between biotechnological research and its industrial application. In Germany today there are 25 bioregions, with over 500 active companies. This programme has led to the creation of technology parks, public offices for the support of biotech start-ups, and university spin-offs. Various forms of venture capital were also promoted and the emergence was fostered of a new stock exchange oriented towards advanced technologies (Neuer Markt).

24 As Evans observes, with reference to Japan, this focus on external links 'is a necessary complement to descriptions, like Johnson's, that stress MITI's ability to act authoritatively rather than emphasizing its ability to facilitate the exchange of information and build consensus'. Internal structure and external ties, however, are strictly interconnected: '[I]nternal bureaucratic coherence should be seen as an essential precondition for the state's effective participation in external networks' (1995, 50).

25 In recent years, sociological and political science studies have shown great interest in the topic of institutional change, with marked attention for the dynamic analysis of innovation systems as well (as will be seen in Chapter 5). For a reconstruction of the debate on this point, see Thelen (2010) and Campbell (2010). In a perspective of sociological neo-institutionalism, with particular reference to the case of China, see the innovation theory developed in Nee *et al.* (2010).

26 For a reconstruction of the relationship between institutional analysis and the role of the actors, see Jackson (2010).

27 The study also highlights the importance for companies to be collocated in a local context rich in collective goods and production activity (Berger 2013, 21).

> One of the key findings of this research project is the importance of local eco-systems and their role in providing firms with complementary resources and capabilities that they could not (or no longer) maintain on their own. By eco-system we do not mean simply the geographic proximity of R&D labs and manufacturing plants but also the existence of a critical mass of other firms – competitors, suppliers, financial intermediaries, lead customers – as well as skilled laborers and the schools that produce them. Together these different actors form a local ecosystem that promotes rapid prototyping of new products and processes as well as the support needed to move innovative ideas into the market place.
> (Locke and Wellhausen 2014, Kindle digital edition, position 127)

The importance of local contexts and 'forces of agglomeration' was also highlighted in a recent (and successful) book by Enrico Moretti (2012) to explain the change in economic geography and work in the United States. Moretti speaks of a 'Great Divergence' that is distancing 'innovation hubs' (the rapidly growing cities that attract the most skilled and creative workers) from other cities that are in a period of decline. These issues will be dealt with in an organic way in Chapter 7, where the theme of innovation and local development will be addressed.

28 These are organisations characterised by decentralisation of authority and a pluralisation of decision-making centres and evaluatory criteria.

29 Recently, Mathijs de Vaan, Balazs Vedres and David Stark (2014) have also applied this approach to explain the creativity and success of teams working in the field of video games, drawing attention to what they define as 'structural folding': 'the network property of a cohesive group whose membership overlaps with that of another cohesive group'. The hypothesis advanced by these scholars is that the effects of structural folding on creativity and success are especially strong when overlapping groups are cognitively distant.

30 According to Mark Granovetter (2005, 33), the structures of social relations influence economic outcomes for three reasons. First, they affect the flow and quality of information they make available to the actors, who acquire it through relationships with others they deem reliable. Second, they are a source of positive or negative incentives: rewards and punishments are, in fact, most effective when they are connected to personal ties. Third, because they generate trust between the actors. For Ronald Burt, too (1992, 13), networks produce advantages of information and of control relating to access to new information, to the speed with which the information is obtained, and to the quality and reliability of this information.

31 For an excellent review, see Powell and Grodal (2005). For networks of collaboration between inventors, refer to Chapter 3.

32 We will return at length to the importance of social networks, especially at local and regional levels, in Chapters 6 and 7.

33 For a review – as well as Powell and Grodal (2005) – see also Meeus and Faber (2006). For the chemical industry, see Ahuja (2000); for the biotechnology sector, Baum *et al.* (2000); for the mechanical engineering and high technology fields in Italy, see Ramella and Trigilia (2010a) and Ramella (2011).

34 In Granovetter's study (1974) a very simple indicator is used to measure the 'strength of ties': the amount of time spent together by two people. However, in a previously published essay, the American scholar provided a more complex definition: 'the strength of a tie is a (probably linear) combination of the amount of time, the emotional

intensity, the intimacy (mutual confiding), and the reciprocal services which characterize the tie' (Granovetter 1973, 1361).

35 In studies on the dissemination of information, partly contradictory research results emerge concerning the social centrality-marginality of innovators. The first rural sociology studies carried out in the early decades of the twentieth century showed that farmers with the best connections (more socially central) were the first to adopt innovation, agreeing to use the new hybrid seeds and pesticides (Rogers 2003). Coleman and his colleagues too (1966), in their study on the diffusion of new drugs among physicians, emphasise the key centrality of relationships to those who adopt them first. Becker (1970), however, with regard to innovation in health programmes, introduces an interesting distinction, noting that early innovators are socially central figures in cases where innovation is perceived as not particularly risky or controversial, and marginal figures when innovation is perceived as more controversial. Rogers as well (2003, 42), referring to Simmel, emphasises the aspect of social distance with regard to circles of affiliation, stating that innovators, like foreigners, are those who deviate from the norms of the social system. In relation to the diffusion of innovation, Rogers highlights two figures: *innovators*, who introduce change and who, due to their interest in new ideas, tend to gravitate away from 'a local circle of peer networks' and establish 'more cosmopolitan social relationships'; and *early adopters*, those who are first to adopt innovation and are more integrated into the local social system (ibid., 282–3).

36 In communication theory, the concept of redundancy indicates an overabundance of information of the same kind.

37 These are securities that are contingent on the value of other assets (stocks, currencies, interest rates, commodities, etc.). These 'derivatives' are designed to hedge the risks associated with changes in the prices of the goods to which they refer, but they can also be used to highly speculative ends.

38 These are forms of financing for extremely innovative high-risk projects, guaranteed by individuals/companies that combine a high level of technical and entrepreneurial skills with availability of financial resources.

39 Burt also offers some historical examples of this 'creativity by brokerage' – one being Eugene Stoner, inventor of the M-16 lightweight assault rifle. This invention derived from his previous military experience in the marines and his work as an engineer in the aircraft industry, which had made him familiar with the use of plastic and aluminium in the construction of airplanes (Burt 2005, 73).

40 'Autocatalysis' is defined as '*a set of nodes and transformations in which all nodes are reconstructed through transformations among nodes in the set*' (Padgett and Powell 2012, Chapter I, position 714).

41 For a review of 'diffusionist studies' see Rogers (2003) and Hall (2005). Some interesting insights regarding these issues are also provided by the new economic sociology's 'neo-institutional' perspective, which emphasises the importance of cultural factors and the cognitive and cultural embeddedness of economic action. Studies of organisational sociology pertaining to this line show the presence of isomorphic phenomena that tend to align organisations to the organisational patterns deemed appropriate according to the prevailing models in a specific field of activity. These studies offer stimulating perspectives not only on understanding factors of inertia and resistance to innovation, but also the diffusion mechanisms of legitimate and 'normatively accredited' innovation. For a review of this strand, see Trigilia (2002, Chapter 9.3.2).

42 The subject of tacit knowledge will be dealt with extensively in the second section of Chapter 6.

43 In relation to the economic performance of companies in the clothing and finance industries, Brian Uzzi (1997, 1999) has also emphasised the role of network complementarity and the 'contingent' value of social ties. Uzzi, however, refers to the need to mix socially embedded economic relations (*embedded ties*) together with market

relations (*arm's-length ties*) within the company network. This makes it possible to balance the ability of the former to prevent opportunistic behaviour and channel rich and reliable resources and knowledge, with that of the latter to facilitate the acquisition of new information and adaption to innovation, thus avoiding isolation from the stimuli offered by the market and the environment.

44 The theme of the social legitimisation of economic innovation would be better explored in two directions: that of consumption and the construction of meanings connected thereto, and that of the processes of institutional regulation. The importance of both these aspects emerges very clearly from the story of genetically modified foods. This case well exemplifies the socio-institutional variability in the legitimisation of radical innovation, and shows the different kinds of acceptance that GMOs have received in the United States and Europe (Jolivet and Maurice 2006).

45 With regard to technological change, the studies carried out as part of the so-called SCOT (Social Construction of Technology) approach are of great interest nowadays. In addition to the famous book by Wiebe Bijker, Thomas Hughes and Trevor Pinch (1987) for a review of studies in the sociology of science and technology see Bucchi (2010); Klein and Kleinman (2002); Parini and Pellegrino (2009); Sismondo (2007); Williams and Edge (1996). Regarding, instead, the advent of a new form of society – the network society – connected to the revolution in information technology and communication, see Castells (2010).

46 On the existence of different theoretical models of actor in the literature on innovation, see Perulli's interesting observations (1989, 14ff.).

47 There are also contributions that tackle the issue of innovation using a systemic-evolutionary approach (Addario 2009).

2 Inventors and creativity

This chapter discusses the generative phase of innovation, analysing certain issues relating to inventors and creativity. The first part outlines various historical modes of organisation and regulation of the inventive process, with particular reference to the USA: the 'golden age' of independent inventors in the phase of liberal capitalism; the birth of the great industrial research laboratories in the Fordist phase; and the development of social and territorial systems of innovation in the post-Fordist phase. The second part presents the observations of social psychologists regarding individual and collective creativity.

2.1 Genius or puppet?

As we saw in the previous chapter, the theme of innovation has returned in recent years to the centre of reflection on economic development. Studies, however, have focused mainly on its economic valorisation while little has been said about the actors and *generative mechanisms* that underlie it. In the wake of Schumpeter's observations, innovative entrepreneurs have received the lion's share of the attention, and the inventors far less.

Who are the protagonists of invention and innovation? In answering this question, the approaches present in the social sciences oscillate between two opposing visions: an *individualistic perspective*, which tends to attribute a prominent role to particularly creative subjects with specific personal characteristics, and a *holistic conception*, which assigns almost exclusive importance to the conditions of the context that determine the emergence of innovation (the functional requirements of the market or society; the cultural, territorial and organisational features of specific environments).

The first view has deep roots in Western culture, which has so often celebrated great innovators and creative genius. For example, to limit ourselves to the modern era, such figures occupy a special place in the social representations that accompany the first industrial revolution, when technological change started to affect economic growth in a more systematic way. In the writings of the time, in fact, the pioneers of technological innovation, such as James Watt, inventor of the steam engine, are celebrated as heroic characters, representative of an emerging industrious middle class (MacLeod 2007).

The importance attributed to particularly creative individuals has also been fully consecrated through the so-called 'Lotka law'. In 1926, while working for the Metropolitan Life Insurance Company in New York, the statistician Alfred Lotka made the discovery that most scientific production depended on a small number of men. Starting from an analysis of publications in the field of chemistry and physics, Lotka developed a generalisation according to which scientific productivity follows a distribution based on the inverse of the square. Two results emerge from the analysis: the number of scholars who publish n articles is approximately $1/n^2$ of those who publish only one; and the share of the latter is around 60 per cent of the total (Lotka 1926). In other words, taking 100 as the number of scientists who publish in a given field, 60 publish only one article, 15 publish two (equal to a quarter of the first 60: $60/2^2$), seven publish three (equal to a ninth: $60/3^2$), 4 publish four ($60/4^2$), and so on down the scale. The *inverse square law of scientific productivity* was subsequently tested and confirmed in several creative fields: humanistic sciences publications (Murphy 1973; Coile 1977); the patents of a sample of American inventors (Carr 1932); the inventive productivity of the researchers of some American semiconductor companies (Narin and Breitzman 1995) and of a number of German companies in the electric, chemical and mechanical engineering sectors (Ernst *et al.* 2000). Historiometric research (the quantitative study of historical phenomena), relaunched by Dean Simonton in the seventies, shows that half the innovation in every field is generated by 10 per cent of its practitioners (Simonton 1999).

All these studies show, therefore, a highly asymmetric distribution of scientific productivity and creative capacity. This tends to give credence to the idea that invention and innovation can be attributed to individuals endowed with exceptional qualities and gives rise to the tendency to study inventor creativity as a kind of personal trait. Certain personality aspects surely play a role in the creative process but these must be properly contextualised. This does not mean committing the opposite error, however – typical of holistic approaches and the functionalist variety especially – which explain the emergence of invention and innovation as a predictable (necessary and automatic) answer to market and society requirements or to the characteristics of particular contexts. As we shall see in the next chapter, with reference to the sociology of inventions that developed in the thirties, such precepts come to assume a deterministic approach that deprives social actors of all space and relevance. What is needed, instead, is an integrated analysis approach, which in addition to the individual aspects (the social attributes and personal characteristics of the inventors) also takes into account the relational (social networks) and contextual (territorial, sectoral and organisational factors) aspects that structure the inventive processes. This chapter will deal primarily with the historical process of the *professionalisation of inventive activity* and the research carried out by psychologists on creativity. The subsequent chapter will discuss sociological approaches and the latest research regarding inventors.

2.2 On the shoulders of giants

There are few systematic studies dealing with inventive activity. Above all it has been psychologists who have analysed creativity, and for a long time they tried to measure it at an individual level, using tests similar to those used to assess intelligence. Economists have focused mainly on innovation in companies, and inventors and inventions have been rather neglected. This underestimation is partly related to the 'decline of independent inventors' (Lamoreaux and Sokoloff 2005) that characterised the Fordist model of development, and the great socialisation and formalisation of innovative processes that followed: collective research teams, an increase in education and codified knowledge, standardised procedures for the evaluation of project costs and benefits, and routinisation of research. Although with national, sectoral and territorial variations – often neglected – during the twentieth century the growth of corporate research (i.e. the laboratories of large industrial companies), universities and public funding led to a downsizing of the role played by individual inventors on the one hand and of the technological innovation 'market' on the other.

In fact, the social and professional figure of the inventor came to the fore during the nineteenth century, following the advent of the industrial revolution and the institutionalisation of a market for technological discoveries. A large part of the increase in productivity seen in England in the late eighteenth century is linked to the progressive improvement of technology applied to the production process. Historian David Landes (1969) describes the industrial revolution as a complex mix of innovation that transformed an economy based on agriculture and artisanship into one dominated by industry and the machine. Those were years that witnessed the introduction of the factory system and the invention of new materials that made it possible to expand the range of products available: iron, for example, gradually took the place of wood. Two aspects deserve to be highlighted. Machines were employed in the activity of production, increasingly replacing artisanal skills. In addition, the toil of men and animals was alleviated by the use of inanimate energy sources: fossil fuels and the steam engine. Technological innovation, in other words – that is, the growing use of new knowledge in the production process – was one of the most distinctive features of the new industrial society.

The invention of the steam engine well embodies one of the founding myths of this 'industrial modernity': faith in limitless progress driven along by science and technology – the idea that human creativity would pave the way for a growing dominance over nature and a decisive improvement in human living conditions. Although intellectual curiosity and the creative effort of gifted individuals can be detected behind the invention of the steam engine, it is difficult to ignore the constellation of interests and the collective commitment that formed the background to each stage of the discovery process. The introduction of the steam engine was, in fact, linked to the need to solve a practical problem that was hindering Britain's further development – that of pumping water out of coal mines. Towards the end of the seventeenth century there emerged a huge demand for fossil fuels. Due to the massive deforestation caused by the use of wood for both private heating and productive activity, coal became one of the biggest alternative energy sources for the nascent British industry. This entailed the need to dig deeper mine shafts and solve the problem of draining the water that formed therein.

In the second half of the seventeenth century, several inventors had already started using steam energy to build mechanical systems to extract water from wells. The first pump for domestic purposes, based on steam pressure, was invented by Thomas Savery and patented by him in 1698. Subsequently, in 1712, Thomas Newcomen developed the first engine designed for use in mines. Only 50 years later, in 1765, did James Watt make a fundamental improvement – a separate steam condenser – that made it possible to reduce the cost of steam engine use by three-quarters. The new system – patented in 1769 – was the origin of the famous firm Boulton & Watt, which, founded a few years later, continued to operate until the early nineteenth century. In 1783 Watt built a new version of the engine based on a rotary rather than a reciprocating motion, which allowed steam power to be used far more extensively. It was an immediately popular solution. Of the approximately 500 examples produced by Boulton & Watt, over 60 per cent were of the rotary type, and most of them were absorbed by the textile industry, which in those years was the beating heart of the industrial revolution (Furfery 1944, 148). Later, in the early decades of the nineteenth century, other inventors applied the steam engine to land transport, building the first locomotive and laying the foundations for a modern railway system.

The history of the steam engine is a good illustration of two elements: its discovery is linked to a complex socio-economic dynamic; and James Watt's invention follows a socio-cognitive development of a supra-individual kind. His steam engine was the latest in a long series of other inventions, developed over more than a century by a number of particularly creative and industrious figures. In other words, *invention does not take place everywhere*, but rather in specific areas and contexts, and is not produced as the work of an isolated individual. But *it is not created by just anyone* either: it requires the knowledge, passion and determination of specific figures. Many of the technological breakthroughs that have altered the contours of our modern age derive from the work of men of great talent; yet these men have been making good use of *already available* knowledge and mechanisms, often by improving upon existing designs (ibid., 152). In doing so, however, they have sometimes produced innovation of a fundamental kind. The best discoveries – as Isaac Newton stated[1] – take place on the 'shoulders of giants': many inventions, although produced by one individual (or a few individuals), are the result of a collective, and not merely an individual, endeavour.

2.3 The 'discovery' of inventors

But who were the main figures involved in the technological innovation that accompanied Britain's industrialisation process? As the chronicles of the time make clear, most invention came from *operatives*, i.e. people belonging to the working class (MacLeod 1999). These were mainly artisans and skilled workers, or foremen, supervisors and managers employed by a company. Some of these inventors were able to achieve substantial improvements in their conditions of employment: wage increases, profit sharing, even shares in the company. Most of the time, however, patenting costs and lack of adequate funds did not allow workers to adequately exploit their discoveries.

Although many of the 'first' inventors were employees, the era that started with the first industrial revolution and continued until the beginning of the twentieth century has rightly been portrayed as the '*golden age*' *of the independent inventor* (Hughes 2004). The emergence of inventors as an independent social group which followed an auto-entrepreneurial logic, was based on the institutionalisation of a real market for technological innovation and is intertwined with the history of patent systems. British patent legislation is the oldest in the world: its origins are rooted in the grants of rights on the part of the Crown. They were first established in 1624 with the *Statute of Monopolies* (Dutton 1984; MacLeod 1988). In the first half of the nineteenth century, in the UK, a market was already established for the purchase of technological innovation that had been developed by independent inventors (Dutton 1984, 122–49). However, it was only in the second half of the century – alongside the explosion of an intense debate concerning the patent system (the so-called *patent controversy*) – that a process of patent simplification and cost reduction was started in order to facilitate their use by elements of the working class, and to strengthen the contractual capacity of 'ingenious workmen' (MacLeod 1999).

In fact, uncertainty about the possibility of enjoying the benefits of their inventions made employee workers and artisans unwilling to reveal their findings. They feared their inventions would benefit their employers rather than themselves, given that it was the employers who possessed the means to develop and patent innovations. The reform of the British patent system was also inspired by the American example. In the US in the first half of the nineteenth century, a large market of technological knowledge had been established. Since the drafting of the constitution, and through several successive reforms, the US had created a particularly effective mechanism for protecting intellectual property. The American patent system also had very low access costs in comparison to Europe (Kanh and Sokoloff 2004). It was, moreover, based on more transparent procedures that guaranteed the ownership of the patent exclusively to those who were actually responsible for an innovative discovery (i.e. the *first and true inventors*). Furthermore, its provisions covered inventions from anywhere in the world. The invention was certified by the prior examination of a technical committee, which ascertained its innovativeness and lawfulness. The vast majority of European countries, in contrast, employed a registration system that only required formal verification of the correctness of administrative procedures.

The American system worked well and considerably reduced the transaction costs of technological innovation. Rigorous verification of the invention's originality, together with effective protection of the rights related to intellectual property, greatly reduced uncertainty regarding a patent's value. This in turn facilitated funding for the inventor's research and, above all, the commercialisation of their discoveries. Despite the delay in the process of industrialisation, the number of patents per capita in the United States in the early years of the nineteenth century exceeded that of Great Britain, and trade in technology patents reached far greater levels than in European countries (Lamoreaux and Sokoloff 2007, 5). The system also encompassed the working classes. Studies carried out on samples of patents granted at the beginning of the nineteenth century show that the social background of inventors was quite varied in the United States, and the percentage of those from the socio-economic élite much lower than in Britain (Khan and Sokoloff 1998). Even the typical profile of the 'great inventor' – a figure responsible for the most significant discoveries – is marked by his lack of formal education and modest social background (Khan and Sokoloff 1993, 2004).

With the increase in technology transactions, the number of specialised professionals operating in the field of patents grew rapidly. These professions expanded to include journalists and publications dedicated to the subject; lawyers specialising in the protection of intellectual property; and consulting agencies and intermediaries to assist inventors with the submission of their applications and the marketing of their licences, etc. In the US, therefore, the increasing mechanisation of production and the creation of a modern patent system encouraged the institutionalisation of a real market for technological innovation and, alongside this, the emergence of a *social group of independent inventors*: that is, professionals specialised in research who, through patenting their discoveries, could earn an income and often create a path of upwards social mobility for themselves.

The number of patents surged from the 1840s on, and continued to increase until the end of the century. At the same time there were a growing number of inventors who specialised exclusively in research and patenting. The number of inventors who managed to take out ten or more patents during the course of their careers (i.e. specialised inventors) rose from 3.5 per cent at the beginning of the nineteenth century to 35.9 per cent by the end of it. By contrast, those who took out only one patent (i.e. occasional inventors) fell from 51 per cent to 19.5 per cent (Lamoreaux and Sokoloff 2007, 10, Table I.1). The way in which inventions were used also changed. In the early years of the nineteenth century inventors often exploited their discoveries directly, by founding new companies. In some cases – and as a complementary activity – they marketed their patents on a limited scale, licencing them in regions other than those in which their own businesses operated.

The second half of the century, however, witnessed the growing *professionalisation* of the figure of the inventor. There was not only an increase in the number of those who specialised in inventive activity, there was also a rise in the commercialisation of patents. On the one hand, inventors became more skilled at mobilising ex ante funding for their research in exchange for the granting of rights to future discoveries; while on the other they became more willing to sell rights to companies with which they did not have a stable relationship (ibid., 6–7). So, in the nineteenth century – and especially in the US – a professional group of independent inventors began to take shape. These were figures who specialised in research and 'discoveries', entrepreneurially deft in the technology marketplace, and showing – especially the most productive of them – a high level of geographical and contractual mobility thanks to the legal protection obtained for the results of their ingenuity. There was a dense agglomeration of such activities in the more economically developed regions of the north-central Atlantic coast (ibid.), with the great inventors tending to operate mainly in the southern part of New England and New York State (Khan and Sokoloff 1993).

But the beginning of the twentieth century saw the golden age of independent inventors fall into decline, in the United States as well as elsewhere. Their autonomy became rapidly reduced as they began to establish long-term and exclusive relationships with certain companies, to whom their ideas would be 'sold'. This was a very varied kind of process, however: in the north-east inventors accepted employment in large companies, while in the Midwest they tended to create their own enterprises or, more frequently, go into partnership with companies that made use of their discoveries. This territorial variability was related to differences in the institutional context of the various states, particularly with regard to local financial market conditions. In the north-east there was a vigorous hierarchisation of access to venture capital, with the main stock market in New York favouring larger, more established companies. In contrast, in some smaller Midwestern cities, such as Cleveland, the presence of a vibrant local market of venture capital, with local investors willing to support new technology companies, conferred a greater slice of entrepreneurial autonomy to persons endowed with inventive talent (Lamoreaux and Sokoloff 2005, 27–30; 2007, 15–18).

Besides these regional variations, however, the fact remained that from the early years of the twentieth century the number of independent inventors was shrinking, and with them the number of patents (Schmookler 1957; Lamoreaux and Sokoloff 2005). In parallel, the role of the *employee inventor* expanded, with an increasing amount of research being carried out by highly educated staff working for large private or public organisations. This is not to say that independent inventors vanished altogether – far from it. In the early fifties in the US they still made up an estimated one-third of the total (Schmookler 1957, 325, Table 2). The first decades of the twentieth century, however, saw a substantial change in the social organisation of invention. Science and technology played a more important role in development and became more receptive to economic requirements. The production of new knowledge became more directly connected to decisions made by actors responding to market stimuli (Rosenberg 2007, 80). Companies, especially the larger ones, began investing in research, creating *large industrial laboratories*. This new organisational set-up saw its first applications in the German chemical industry of the late nineteenth century, but the model was subsequently applied extensively in the US. In part this was also the result of particularly strict antitrust legislation, which pushed US companies to merge and intensify their innovative efforts to beat the competition.[2] Large diversified companies such as General Electric and DuPont in the chemistry field, IBM in data processing systems, Westinghouse in the electricity sector, and General Motors in the automobile industry, are the best-known examples of companies that became leaders in their respective industries through a process of massive investment in R&D. Their laboratories were used to test a wide range of innovations, using large amounts of capital raised from private investors (Lamoreaux and Sokoloff 2007, 19).

The emergence of industrial research had important consequences not only for new technology, but also for the scientific advances that, in some cases, resulted from these activities. The best-known example is provided by Bell Labs. From 1925 Bell Telephone Laboratories (Bell Labs) – owned by the American Telephone and Telegraph Company (AT&T) and Western Electric (the manufacturing arm of AT&T) – was actively involved in research that achieved considerable success. Bell Labs' primary task was to produce systems and equipment for telecommunications, which would then be marketed by AT&T – but it was also engaged in basic and applied research. These activities resulted in many technological innovations (e.g. the fax, sound film, long-distance transmissions, and so on). A number of truly revolutionary discoveries were made (in the fields of radio astronomy, laser technology, information theory, software operating systems, etc.), bringing a total of seven Nobel prizes to company employees. Bell Labs became best-known for its invention of the transistor, a device which opened the way for the miniaturisation of electronic circuitry. In years to come this would revolutionise the world of electronic devices and computers. The invention was developed in 1947 by three researchers at Bell Labs – John Bardeen, William Bradford Shockley and Walter Houser Brattain, who were awarded the 1956 Nobel Prize for Physics.

But industrial laboratories not only carried out research, they also provided companies with the necessary skills to explore the knowledge being produced by the scientific community, and to monitor any possible repercussion on the market. Scientific and technological research was also carried out in universities and research centres funded by the government or other private philanthropic institutions (the Rockefeller, Guggenheim and Carnegie foundations in the USA, for example). Public and private-social funding was another major force that influenced the direction and intensity of inventive activity in the post-war period. This was especially so in areas where public benefit heavily outweighed any possible private gain. In the United States in the early fifties, for example, the federal government reached the point where it was financing more than half of the national investment in R&D (Lamoreaux and Sokoloff 2007, 19; see also Chapter 5 on this point).

The emergence of large private and public research techno-structures cast a shadow over the social figure of the inventor and the generative mechanisms of invention. Studies focused on large research organisations and on economic and organisational aspects: funding, the division of labour, knowledge specialisation and the economies of scale of the research – in other words, on the 'visible hand' of the organisation and the pre-eminence of the large public and private techno-structures in scientific and technological innovation.

From a theoretical point of view, moreover, 'knowledge' was conceptualised by economists as a pure 'public good', characterised by high costs of production and low costs of reproduction and circulation: i.e. a good that would be difficult to be regulated through market rules and incentives. This aspect, it was believed, disincentivised private actors – especially smaller ones – from investing in research, due to the low appropriability of its results.[3] An emblematic case of 'market failure', then, that justified intervention in research activity, first, by public institutions (Arrow 1962) and, second, by large diversified firms (Nelson 1959), with a clear distinction between 'public' and 'private' knowledge: the 'scientific community' – based mainly in universities and driven by reputational incentives – promoted open knowledge and the free circulation of research results; while the 'technological community' – based in private companies and driven by economic incentives – promoted proprietary knowledge, through secrecy and patent protection of inventions (Dasgupta and David 1994).

Other authors have pointed out different reasons for the spread of the great industrial laboratories. David Mowery, for example, notes that it was not the lack of private appropriability of results that led to a push towards the corporatisation of research. The reasons must rather be sought in the special characteristics of industrial know-how and the difficulties encountered in the negotiation and implementation of market contracts (Mowery 1983, 351). First, Mowery draws attention to the high specificity of industrial research which, to be useful, must be closely integrated with productive activity and adapted to the specific needs of individual companies. Second, he emphasises the need for the latter to have a high provision of human capital to monitor and exploit knowledge arriving from the outside. And third, he indicates difficulties relating to the definition and enforcement of research contracts awarded to third parties in order to ensure the confidentiality of the results. In short, the need to provide adequate internal *absorptive capacity* (Cohen and Levinthal 1990) – together with the high transaction costs associated with the use of the market – induced companies to internalise much of their strategically valuable research. This did not completely rule out the use of external agencies, but rendered their use more limited.

Mowery, in fact, detects the presence of a dualistic structure in American industrial research throughout the first half of the twentieth century. In addition to the companies' internal laboratories, numerous private research institutes sprang up (about 350 in total) which came to employ up to 5,000 researchers and engineers (Mowery 1983, 353). A relationship of great complementarity was formed between these two sectors. The research institutes specialised in routine, standardised activities (such as materials testing), exploiting the economies of scale to be had. These institutions catered to a wide range of industries, offering generic services that did not require cognitive input tailored to individual companies. In contrast, company in-house laboratories specialised in more complex and strategic projects that were tuned to their own particular needs – *firm-specific*, in other words. The difficulty and idiosyncratic nature of such projects made it difficult to use external institutions or to determine appropriate contracts under which they might be carried out: the activities required to achieve the outcome of the projects presented a high level of uncertainty in terms of success and were (in formal contractual terms and conditions) difficult to define *ex ante*. Given the specialised nature of these services, the supply structure was far from competitive and, in the event of counterparty default, objective difficulties arose in enforcing agreements. As the economic theory of transaction costs showed, all these factors made the use of the market difficult, since they exposed both parties to the high risk of opportunism – in other words, to non-compliance with established agreements.

Other research carried out by economic historians, however, seriously challenged the idea that the corporatisation of research, at least in the initial phase, could be attributed to these factors. The studies of Lamoreaux and Sokoloff (1997), for example, show that during the nineteenth century companies were perfectly able to use the market for these kinds of transactions. That said, they did for a long time have problems in regulating relations with their staff with regard to the discoveries that they made – as is evidenced by the many disputes that arose between the two parties concerning patents. To ensure that inventions made during working hours were assigned to the company, they resorted to specific employment contracts that contained detailed provisions. Prior to this, however, they had to legitimise the idea that discoveries made in the workplace were the exclusive property of the company. This involved a huge set of difficulties: overcoming worker resistance; limiting the mobility of 'ingenious' employees; obtaining their cooperation in the event of discoveries (e.g. informing the company), and so on.

In short, then, even the in-company (*intramuros*) organisation of inventive activity and research required a complicated process of negotiation and regulation. Contrary to the argument put forward in much of the economic literature, 'Economic actors at that time had a great deal of experience with contracting for new technological ideas in the market; what they did not know how to do, and had to spend a great deal of time and energy learning, was *managing creative individuals within the firm*' (ibid., 51, my italics). These difficulties in regulating *intramuros* inventions – related to the organisational costs and conflict over intellectual property rights – were not only present in the American case, but also in the British one, where the external technology market was developed on a much smaller scale (MacLeod 1999).

In brief, entrepreneurs had to convince *independent inventors* and *employee inventors* that cooperation with the company would carry less risk and healthy economic opportunities. The basis for this organisational breakthrough developed between the late nineteenth and early twentieth centuries at the precise moment when technological innovation was becoming central to certain sectors (e.g. communications, transport, electricity, iron and steel, the chemical industry etc.); and at a time when its economic and organisational costs were starting to grow. The increase in resources required and the uncertain outcome of projects at the frontier of technology thus tended to redirect the preferences of all those involved in innovation activity, i.e. the *entrepreneurs*, the *financiers* and the *inventors* themselves.

Technological innovation was becoming increasingly *capital intensive*. This provided a competitive advantage to those large companies that were beginning to organise and diversify their own research, and to embark upon a number of projects entrusted to their own in-house technical staff. This created the socio-organisational structure that, in the private sector, led to the *institutionalisation of the employee inventor*. In this way, large companies became privileged collectors of both the human and economic capital required for innovation. They were able to attract independent inventors (who saw an opportunity to continue their research in what were often well-funded industrial laboratories), and to create a job market for the technico-scientific figures produced by the university system. But they also attracted financiers, who felt better protected in this environment than in investing in high-risk individual projects carried out by small companies or independent inventors.

The growth of these huge industrial techno-structures was not, however, without its drawbacks. Research found itself hampered by *a process of bureaucratisation* that in many cases limited the ability to make truly innovative discoveries or failed to exploit them to their full potential. One classic example was Xerox PARC in Palo Alto, a research centre located at Stanford University and funded by Xerox, a leading manufacturer of office machines (photocopiers in particular). Founded in 1970 and endowed with great human and financial resources, in its first five years the centre produced a number of high-impact discoveries: the first prototype personal computer; the mouse; icons and drop-down menus; local area networks; and the laser printer. Xerox, however, only commercialised this last innovation, leaving the rest to be exploited by other companies. The whole story is told in a book with a highly significant title: *Fumbling the Future: How Xerox Invented, and Then Ignored, the First Personal Computer* (Smith and Alexander 1988).

As has been noted, the geographical and cultural distance of the Californian laboratory from its parent company (which had its headquarters in Connecticut) meant that many revolutionary innovations were undervalued by Xerox's management, who saw the company as one that dealt exclusively with photocopiers. The hierarchical model of the management team also clashed head-on with the informal and horizontal organisational set-up at PARC. The west coast style of life and work of the creative staff served to hinder the transfer of technology to the parent company on the east coast (Rogers 2005, 155). However, Steve Jobs of Apple Computer – who visited Xerox at the end of 1979 – was very impressed by the potential he saw in the PARC research team, and hired several of them himself. In 1985, after five years of further research, Apple launched the Macintosh – an innovative personal computer for business purposes – on to the market. It was a huge success.

Most of the time, however, the problems that arose in industrial laboratories were of a different type. Routinisation of research, management imposition of greater constraints and financial controls (including making cost-benefit assessments of the various projects under study) progressively tended to reduce the ability of corporations to carry out truly cutting-edge projects. This is the argument put forward by William Baumol, who says that most of the key innovations produced during the twentieth century were the work of independent inventors or of small- and medium-sized companies.[4] There did exist, however, a strong complementarity with the large companies. With a few rare exceptions, the large companies were not responsible for fundamental innovation; rather they carried out the subsequent (significant and indispensable) work of developing and fine-tuning products to make them commercially viable (Baumol 2002, 2004).

Most research conducted in the US is carried out by large companies. In early 2000, private companies accounted for almost 70 per cent of the expenditure on R&D, with 46 per cent of these funds coming from just 167 huge companies (those with 25,000 employees or more). This rises to 80 per cent with the addition of the approximately 2,000 companies who employ more than 1,000 workers (Baumol 2004, 10–11). According to Baumol, however, most of the big laboratories are responsible for routine activities and incremental innovation. Post-World War Two studies show that about 80 per cent of the funds for industrial research are used to *improve* existing products (Rosenberg 2007, 84). Such figures enable the conclusion that although the majority of R&D is carried out by large companies, most of the truly innovative activity is the prerogative of medium- and small-sized firms (Baumol 2004, 14).

Baumol cites studies conducted by the US Small Business Administration into the most important innovations introduced by small businesses over the course of the twentieth century. These include the aeroplane, FM radio, the helicopter, the pacemaker and the personal computer. The studies also highlight the high patent productivity and greater innovative impact of small- and medium-sized companies (up to 500 employees) compared to larger ones: the probability that the former will take out highly innovative patents (1 per cent of the most-cited patents) is twice that of the latter (ibid., 15–16).

These studies, however, must be placed in context, and against a background of transformations that have affected the most advanced economies and specific productive sectors. With the advent of post-Fordism and the knowledge economy (Snellman 2004; Rullani 2004) the role of small- and medium-sized companies regained momentum – first in traditional sectors (involving incremental innovation), and then in high-tech sectors and the field of more radical innovation. Examples include development in the areas of telecommunications, IT, personal computers and biotechnology.

The number of venture capitalists who have been willing to support highly innovative companies has grown in more recent times. Independent inventors and the innovation market have thus, once again, begun to attract scholarly attention. In many areas large research laboratories have been downsized, while small firms specialising in research in cutting-edge activities (notably the so-called technological start-ups) have mushroomed. Such companies have gone on to sell the rights related to the intellectual property of their discoveries.[5] And so patenting activity, and market transactions involving technological breakthroughs, have taken off once again (Lamoreaux and Sokoloff 2007, 35).

This evolution brought about a reorientation of studies on innovation, which today focus more on its relational dimensions, with interest tending to concentrate on the flow of information and territorial agglomeration of innovative companies. The creation and learning of new knowledge are seen as collective processes based on interaction between companies and institutions in specific geographical areas (Silicon Valley being the classic example[6]).

From a theoretical perspective, highlighting tacit aspects of knowledge, information asymmetries, and the complexity of innovation processes tend to reduce the emphasis previously placed on the low appropriability of research results. There is now more stress on the fact that knowledge, including public knowledge, requires a capability of use that encourages private actors to invest in R&D, to enhance the 'absorptive capacity' of knowledge and of the information produced outside individual companies (Cohen and Levinthal 1990). In addition, changes occurring in the cognitive bases of some sectors – especially those related to information technology, life sciences and biotechnology – involve increasing integration between different types of knowledge, as well as between companies and universities. The boundaries that once separated the scientific community from the technological community, and 'academic inventors' from 'company inventors', have thus tended to become less rigid.[7]

After the transformation inspired by Schumpeter in the middle of the last century, we now have another – both factual and analytical – sea change in Innovation Studies. The *locus of innovation* alters once again, passing from the innovative entrepreneur, through the great innovative companies, to the *social and territorial systems of innovation*. The importance of the relationship between economic enterprises and 'non-economic' institutions is thus brought to light. The role of the inventors, however, remains in the shadow. Inventors, who became invisible during Fordism, only partially emerge as subjects to be studied in the subsequent phase of post-Fordism.

As we shall see in the next section and in Chapter 3, creative individuals and inventors have been the subject of several studies, not always with very satisfactory results. The literature has contrasted individualistic and holistic approaches, projecting an 'undersocialised' and 'oversocialised' vision of inventors. They have been studied as 'creative individuals' and 'men of genius', with reconstructions of their biographical journeys and personal and social characteristics. Conversely, they have been analysed as the mature and inessential fruit of historical circumstances. They have also been seen as 'actors of an innovation system', in order to understand how modes of governance, organisational culture and incentives provided by universities and host companies influenced their inventive activity and capacity to patent. The social dimension that permeates discovery processes has, however, often been overlooked. Even when networks of collaboration have been analysed, the processual dynamics that link inventors to their research groups, and to the contexts in which they operate, have been little investigated.

The analysis of inventive activity, on the other hand, requires an integrated perspective of analysis that is capable of seeing invention as the outcome of a complex process of social construction.[8] The paths that lead to the discovery of something new are, in fact, highly socialised. They are the result of effort not only by single individuals or companies, but of effort that is collective in nature – effort that varies according to technology sectors, territories and different forms of *social embeddedness*. The analysis of the generative mechanisms of innovation requires, then, an interdisciplinary approach. In the remainder of this chapter, and in the chapter that follows, the focus will therefore be on the topics of creativity and invention, reviewing contributions from a variety of disciplines. To start with, the next section presents some studies from the field of social psychology.

2.4 The psychology of creativity

What is meant by creativity? In social psychology studies, reference is made to a specific skill: *the ability to generate new and appropriate products or ideas* (Sternberg and Lubart 1999, 3; Hennessey and Amabile 2010, 570). In other words, it is the ability – individually or in groups – to develop original solutions that are proven to be useful, or at least influential (Mayer 1999). The presidential speech given in 1950 by Joy Paul Guilford (1950) at the American Psychological Association (APA), marks the official start of a specific line of research on this subject – one that had hitherto been neglected by the theoretical approaches prevalent in academic psychology, in particular those of a behaviourist kind.

In reality, some ideas had already been developed, but in the context of non-mainstream approaches. The psychology of form (*Gestaltpsychologie*), for example, had devoted some attention to certain aspects of creativity, such as *insight* (intuition/illumination), considering it as an adaptive response to situations perceived as unusual. In particular, *Gestalt* psychologists identified two styles of thinking employed in different conditions. When faced with routine problems, *reproductive thinking* prevails: a way of thinking that applies solution procedures that have already been tried in the past. Conversely, when unusual problems emerge, for which no ready-made solutions exist, *productive thinking* – a form of creative reasoning – can take over (Mayer 1995). On the basis of experiments conducted on the perceptions and responses provided for practical or mathematico-geometrical dilemmas, *Gestaltists* defined insight as a phenomenon of sudden and discontinuous learning, resulting in a restructuring of the cognitive field in the face of situations perceived as problematic. In short, creativity involves the ability to analyse data deriving from external reality in an original way, reorganising the properties of phenomena in order to provide a more appropriate behavioural response to the problematic situation (Rossi and Travaglini 1997, 18–21).

In the psychoanalytic approach, on the other hand, creativity is attributed to impulses with a strong emotional value for the subject (Sternberg and Lubart 1999, 6). Creative thinking is a way of expressing unconscious desires in socially acceptable forms through an activity of sublimation that finds its most obvious manifestations in artistic phenomena or in the work of great inventors and artists such as Leonardo da Vinci – to whom Sigmund Freud devoted a famous essay (1910). At base, there is the ability of certain individuals to exploit the regressive tendencies of the ego in functional forms, allowing desires and the deepest kind of psychic energy to flow freely at a conscious level. This makes it possible to satisfy latent impulses by reconciling the two principles of reality and pleasure (Rossi and Travaglini 1997, 59–62).

It is only from the fifties on – after the official legitimisation bestowed by Guilford's speech – that research on creativity began to develop in a more organic way. This took place at the height of the Cold War. It is no coincidence that a book containing the proceedings of three conferences held between 1955–59, and dedicated to the question of the 'identification of creative talent in the scientific field', opens with an essay written by a White House advisor. The essay in question explicitly links studies on creativity to economic, technological and military competition with the Soviet Union – a competition, according to the essay, that in the long run will be decided by the supremacy of scientific knowledge and the ability to use the greater number of its citizens in applying the creative work of science (Golovin 1963, 22).

At first, psychologists sought to study creativity as an aspect of individual personality, measuring it with tests used for intelligence. In the early sixties, however, it was shown that intelligence and creativity traits were – to a large extent – independent. Creativity presupposes a certain level of intelligence (*threshold theory*), but this in itself is not enough (Sawyer 2006, 44). Guilford had in fact, in his first essay (1950, 447), already pointed out that the usual systems used to measure individual IQ did not identify creative abilities. Intelligence tests measured, above all, what academics would later define as *convergent thinking*, a mode of reasoning that exploits the logico-rational capabilities of the human mind to find the correct answers to the questions put by the researchers. At the basis of creativity, however, lay *divergent thinking*, which seeks to determine not the *one right answer* to a question, but rather the *number of potentially viable solutions* (Guilford 1967).

Indicating the mental abilities that recur in creative subjects, Guilford specifically refers to 'the scientist and the technologist, including the inventor', assuming that different types of creativity exist and that the underlying cognitive abilities might be different for various fields of activity (Guilford 1950, 451). Subsequent research identified the main dimensions of divergent thinking (Mumford 2001, 267–9): (1): *fluency*, the ability to generate a large number of ideas quickly; (2) *originality*, the ability to provide new answers – unusual perhaps, yet still acceptable – in situations where one single answer is not possible, and; (3) *flexibility*, the ability not to become embroiled in a single pattern of reasoning and instead to be able to take alternative models into consideration.

That said, Guilford also takes into account other issues that influence the various stages of the creative process: the 'upstream phase', for example, is affected by individual sensitivity towards the discovery of problems – the variable capacity to perceive dilemmatic situations worthy of further investigation; the 'ideation phase', the ability to analyse situations and synthesise various solutions and the degree of complexity of the conceptual structure that the subject is able to elaborate; and, finally, the 'downstream phase', the ability to evaluate and refine the solutions generated, subjecting them to the selective evaluation of critical reasoning.

Guilford proposes appropriate tests for each of these aspects, with the aim of measuring divergent thinking. The novelty introduced by the American scholar is in fact the idea that creativity can be studied in ordinary people – and not exclusively in so-called 'geniuses' – using a psychometric approach (Sternberg and Lubart 1999, 7). Guilford also believed that intellectual and creative abilities could be improved through special training processes (Rossi and Travaglini 1997, 36–7). This led to the design of a number of tests and scales for the comparative assessment of individual creativity. The best known are the *Torrance Tests of Creative Thinking*, which were used for over 40 years to assess divergent thinking ability among individuals (Hennessey and Amabile 2010, 570). Despite their success, and the popularity gained from educational creative thinking programmes, this type of study also attracted a great deal of criticism. Mental abilities indicated by Guilford were deemed unsuitable for defining and delimiting the concept of creativity. It was also claimed that, given their sectoral specificities, the tests proposed to evaluate them were inadequate (Amabile 1983; Baer 2008; Mumford *et al.* 2008). This first wave of psychometric studies and, more generally, the personality studies that were so very fashionable during the sixties, lost momentum over the following decades as other approaches gradually came into favour.

From the seventies on, cognitive psychologists – winning out over the old schools of behaviourism and psychology of the personality – opened a new phase of studies. This involved in particular the analysis – through both research on people, and using computer simulations – of the mental representations and cognitive processes underlying creative thinking. One argument put forward was that creativity emerged from the normal mental procedures used in everyday activities. Studies by Weisberg (1993), for example – based on laboratory experiments and research carried out on highly creative people – showed that insight is derived from the use of conventional cognitive processes that exploit knowledge already stored in the memory. Creativity, in other words, involves 'ordinary' cognitive processes that lead to 'extraordinary' results (Sternberg and Lubart 1999, 8).

The first studies on creative processes provided some noteworthy results that brought such phenomena more clearly into focus (Sawyer 2006). Creativity: (1) is not a special mental process, rather it involves cognitive activities of an ordinary kind; (2) is not a distinct personality trait but derives from a combination of basic mental abilities; (3) is the result of hard work; (4) is specific to a field, and – contrary to the often held idea that equates genius with a sense of wild indiscipline – is associated with those who are well-balanced and successful in their own particular area. Research into personality also made it possible to define certain recurring traits possessed by creative individuals:

high valuation of esthetic qualities in experience, broad interests, attraction to complexity, high energy, independence of judgment, autonomy, intuition, self-confidence, ability to resolve antinomies or to accommodate apparently opposite or conflicting traits in one's self-concept, and, finally, a firm sense of self as 'creative'.

(Barron and Harrington 1981, 453)

These early studies, however, also served to focus on how psychology provides only *part* of the explanation; and how individualistic approaches, concentrating on personality traits, are insufficient for an understanding of creative processes (Sawyer 2006, 74).

Over the last three decades, studies regarding creativity have become highly institutionalised in the psychology field, and there has been a proliferation of journals and research topics. Until the eighties, studies tended mainly to focus on a few major issues – in particular on the relationship between personality, creativity and intelligence. In subsequent years, however, topics, methods of enquiry, and theoretical perspectives mushroomed, accompanied by a marked division of labour with compartmentalisation in specialised sub-sectors.[9] Some authors, however, attempted to build integrated analytical approaches that were open to interdisciplinary collaboration. This created more than a few opportunities for dialogue with sociology. In fact, psychologists began to study the social and cultural contexts of creativity, connecting them both with personal and motivational traits and with the processual aspects of these phenomena. Awareness gradually emerged that previous studies had tended to decontextualise and desocialise creativity; whereas creative individuals, even when working alone, are always in some relation of influence with others (Hennessey 2003, 181). Social dynamics, in fact, permeate the rules, motivations, knowledge and skills that – at both an individual and group level – condition creativity (Paulus and Nijstad 2003, 6).

The work of academic Teresa Amabile (1983) is emblematic of this new approach, starting with her simple definition of what being creative is: a product is creative when experts in a particular sector judge it to be so. Emphasis of the consensual and *domain-specific* nature of creativity opens up the possibility of a sociological perspective of analysis. In order for a 'creative intersection' to exist it is necessary to determine the convergence of a plurality of factors. The subject must possess: (1) specialised knowledge and abilities (*domain skills*); (2) specific abilities to generate new ideas, and to deal with complex situations and problems (*creativity skills*); and (3) appropriate motivations with regard to the objective being pursued (*task motivations*) (Hennessey 2003, 182). Several studies emphasised the centrality of the third factor, highlighting the variability of the motivations and their 'situational contingency'. The level of involvement and personal interest in the problem at hand represents an essential ingredient to explain the performance and the individual creative ability deployed in the execution of a task. These motivational aspects, however, are not only influenced by the individual's subjective characteristics and the objective nature of the task, but also by the socio-organisational context and the type of incentives provided.

Amabile (1983, 1996) identifies two types of motivation. *Extrinsic motivation* is linked to the achievement of some objective or external benefit other than that deriving from the work itself. This type of motivation is often related to sanctions or benefits distributed by an outside authority or organisational body (the market, an employer, an examination committee, a jury) and depends on an evaluation of the efforts or performance of an individual in executing a task.

In contrast, *intrinsic motivation* is connected to the interest and specific rewards that result from performing a certain task – it originates within the individual, therefore, and from the activity itself, rather than from the external environment. If a person feels interest in an activity and finds it stimulating because of the challenges it presents, then the probability of creative performance is increased. This type of motivation cannot be adequately replaced by economic incentives, sanctions or hierarchical control. Hence the idea develops that organisations must form an environment that is capable of engaging its members, offering tasks that interest them, and minimising control from above. In contrast, external pressures – such as rewards and objectives that are defined by superiors – tend to be associated with low intrinsic motivation. These will tend to limit creative performance. More recent studies, however, have shown that in the presence of strong subjective motivation, and in very specific contexts, incentives that are geared towards providing recognition of effort made and skills attained can increase extrinsic motivation without limiting intrinsic motivation, thus producing a positive influence on creativity (Amabile 1996; Hennessey 2003, 197).

These early studies analysed the motivational impact of the socio-organisational context in 'impersonal' terms. However, the various social environments influence the creativity and motivation of their components above all through the interpersonal relationships that are established therein (ibid.), giving rise to the recent trend of paying attention to the socio-relational dynamics that develop from the family, school and work experiences of the subjects. All this, however, without neglecting the influence of socio-cultural factors that act at a more impersonal level – such as different national and corporate cultures, etc. In these new approaches, therefore, the creative process is studied by linking individual characteristics to the various contexts of interaction, while also taking into consideration the social and cultural factors that shape them (ibid.). Frameworks such as these have therefore led psychological studies regarding creativity to increasingly assume a systemic perspective that is open to contributions from other disciplines (Hennessey and Amabile 2010, 571).

What has been defined as the 'socio-cultural approach' to creativity, for example, moves in this direction – aiming as it does to study creative people against the background of the different contexts in which they operate (Sawyer 2006). This is informed by the awareness that creativity incorporates a variability related to culture, society and historical epoch. Studies and definitions relating to creativity tend to oscillate between two different conceptions. On the one hand, there is what is commonly labelled as the 'big C': that rare and august kind of creativity that has a strong social and economic impact. On the other, there is the 'small c': that widespread form of creativity which is possessed to varying degrees by all individuals, and which is employed in everyday life to solve ordinary problems (Gardner 1993, 29). The socio-cultural approach refers to the former kind of creativity, which is conceived as 'a novel product that attains some level of social recognition' (Sawyer 2006, 27). To be innovative, an idea must not only be original but also appropriate – recognised, in other words, as socially valid within a community of reference.

Mihaly Csikszentmihalyi's systemic approach (1988, 1996) has made a fundamental contribution to this perspective. An academic of Hungarian descent, Csikszentmihalyi sees creativity not just as a psychological event, but as a social and cultural one as well. The creativity of a new product depends not so much on its intrinsic qualities as on the effect it has on others. In other words it requires public recognition, based on interaction between producer and audience: 'Creativity is not the product of single individuals, but of social systems making judgments about individual's products (Csikszentmihalyi 1999, 313). To understand creativity, therefore, one must also analyse the environment in which the individual operates, and this is composed of two elements: a symbolic-cultural aspect (*domain*) and a social aspect (*field*). More precisely, the creative process derives from the interaction of three elements (Figure 2.1): the person (source of innovation), the field (composed of experts of a creative field who select the ideas that are considered original and appropriate), and the domain (the area into which innovation, once it is recognised as such, enters and is diffused).

The domain consists of all products created in the past and all the rules and conventions accepted in a specific sector of activity. Creativity, in fact, without the sharing of certain specific conventions, is impossible. Innovation consists of the transformation of cultural practices in an appropriate manner with respect to the criteria recognised in a particular sector. Culture is composed of several domains (music, maths, religion, technological fields, etc.), each with its own

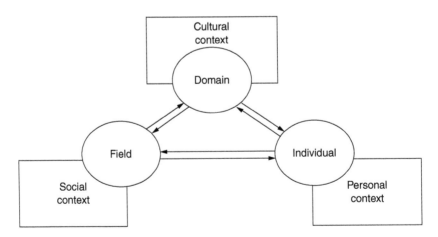

Figure 2.1 Systemic approach to creativity (source: adapted from Csikszentmihalyi (1999, 315)).

own rules, objects, representations and shared notation systems. The level of integration and of separation of the domains varies depending on the society and the historical epoch. Innovation takes place within each of the domains, thanks to the work of individuals who possess specific creative abilities.

Creative individuals make use of the information and knowledge in a particular field, introducing new ideas through the use of cognitive processes, personality traits and motivations that derive from both their own talent and their personal background (family, the social and territorial context in which they were educated and in which they work, etc.). The experts who make up the field – teachers, critics, the owners and editors of specialised journals, directors of theatres, museums, foundations that provide funding, etc. – represent the '*gatekeepers*' of a specific sector. They constitute a network of experts who have internalised the conventions of a domain and thus possess the shared criteria to evaluate and certify the creativity of a new product. In other words, they confer the recognition of novelty to a certain product and allow its diffusion throughout the relevant industry. After selection by the experts, the final acceptance test of the new idea comes from a wider audience, stratified according to a decreasing level of competence (Sawyer 2006, 126–7).

The levels of creativity present in a given area depend not only on the quantity of individuals possessing originality, but also on the characteristics of the domain and the field in which they operate. There are various ways in which the structuring of the sector affects the creative process: with regard to the domain, the clarity of its internal structure (i.e. the level of codification and integration of its constituent elements), its centrality within the culture of reference, and its openness and accessibility, are all important. As regards the field, it is essential to mention the level of institutionalisation and autonomy from other sectors, as well as its ability to attract social resources and to stimulate and implement the innovation proposed by the individuals who work within it. As we have seen, the first psychological studies analysed creativity as an aspect of the personality of particular individuals, neglecting the social dimension. Yet the latter permeates creative phenomena, both in the generative phase of new ideas and in the subsequent stages of their development – which pass through the dynamics of evaluation, elaboration and communication that take place within a specific sector. The socio-cultural approach goes beyond these limits, surpassing the individualist perspective and considering the social context in which the creative process takes place. This social dimension emerges even in a creation's most crucial and apparently individual stage, i.e. during *insight*: the moment when, quite suddenly, something new is discovered/created, when the solution appears to a long-considered problem. In this phase, a specific mental state is generated, involving a swift restructuring of the cognitive frame, with the emergence of an idea that is perceived as being able to provide a new understanding of a problem or phenomenon that has kept the subject busy for a long time.

Intuition has been predominantly studied in isolation, and as a cognitive process that takes place in solitude. Mihaly Csikszentmihalyi and Keith Sawyer (1995, 331), on the other hand, making use of research carried out on a variety of creative subjects, analyse it within a sequence of stages that structure the creative process, integrating the *intra-psychic* and *contextual dimension*: 'When we look at the complete "life span" of a creative insight in our subjects' experience, the moment of insight appears as but one short flash in a complex, time-consuming, fundamentally social process.' It is true that from the interviews the crucial moment of discovery emerges as a solitary moment, but these moments are inserted into a narrative that depicts the effort and dynamics that precede and follow the insight, and the overall significance of these *narratives of discovery* tends to emphasise the salience of social and interactional factors. The creative process is divided into four stages:

1　the discovery *preparation* phase, which involves intensive study and research into a problematic issue;
2　the discovery *incubation* stage, which develops during a period of inactivity when the individual is momentarily detached from work on that specific issue;
3　the *insight* stage, during which time the new idea emerges;
4　the *development* phase, which follows the discovery and involves hard work elaborating and evaluating the new idea in order to develop and fine-tune it.

This division into stages refers to the models developed in social psychology with regard to the processes of *problem-solving* (for a critical review see Lubart 2001). The sequence of stages, however, should not be thought of as linear: the creative process is composed of multiple loops and involves continuous feedback (Csikszentmihalyi and Sawyer 1995, 344).

The work upstream and downstream of the discovery is profoundly influenced by social dynamics. The preparatory phase is stimulated by external pressure and/or internal motivation formed in a specific domain. There is in fact no 'creativity quotient' as there is an intelligence quotient. Creative people are not creative in general, but are so in particular spheres of activity; creativity, as we have said, is *domain-specific*. *Preparation* thus entails a long phase of learning specific knowledge related to a particular domain, and learning what knowledge has already been produced on the topic on which the person is working. Creativity often, after all, consists of a new combination of *already-known elements*. Precisely because it is necessary to know what already exists, formal education does not hinder creative work – although it is often possible to note an inverted 'U' relationship: both a deficit and an excess of formal education may be detrimental, since they generate a shortage or a surplus of socialisation with the domain, thereby rendering individual thinking, conventional (Sawyer 2006, 60).

The *incubation* phase is also important. Many creative figures recount that their best ideas occur to them during periods of inactivity and idleness, when they are involved in doing something else. At these moments, the gestation work is, more or less unconsciously, carried out for the discovery that takes place in the central phase of the creative process: the insight stage. The 'discovery' however, is often preceded by a series of minor insights, related to the work being performed. In this respect – as Sawyer has observed (ibid., 71) – the crucial moment of insight is overvalued. The interviews reveal two generative models of discovery. The shorter *presented problem-solving process* occurs when the problem faced is already known within the domain; it is thus a matter of finding and organising the correct solution. The longer *discovered problem-finding process* is deployed when faced with problems that are less known and which may even become problematic thanks to the insight itself. This second mode is associated with paradigm shifts and the more significant kinds of discovery (Csikszentmihalyi and Sawyer 1995, 337).

As we have said, innovation is the ability to combine various types of ideas and information in an original manner. Thus, eminently cognitive and more or less conscious processes come into play. Analogical thinking is very important in scientific discoveries. New conceptual combinations often use metaphors and analogies that hail from different sectors and activities (Sawyer 2006, 266). Following a variety of projects therefore increases the possibility of *cross-fertilisation*. Creative people often work on a variety of partially overlapping projects. Particularly revolutionary discoveries (and insights) are based on the 'casual' convergence of ideas coming from different domains, usually facilitated by interaction with individuals working in different fields (Csikszentmihalyi and Sawyer 1995, 337). Subjects capable of radical innovation, therefore, frequently occupy a position on the boundary between different disciplines. This does not make them marginal figures, however: rather they are *field-switchers*, exploiting analogies and knowledge from different domains, since a greater number of ideas and basic concepts makes innovative combinations easier.

The ability to work and productivity also play an important role. Creativity requires a great many ideas that are then selected and combined with each other and for this reason the more productive subjects – i.e. those capable of generating a high volume of work – are in general also more creative (ibid., 161). Peaks of creativity vary according to discipline, but there is evidence that creativity tends to be continuous throughout life. Finally, the last phase – the development of ideas generated during insight – is a period of intense, fully conscious work that relies upon the specialised knowledge of the domain (Sawyer 2006, 68). The development and evaluation of the original idea always require modifications, adjustments and critical reconsideration. The social dimension emerges even more clearly in the *collective kind of creative dynamics* that are gaining a prominent place in this field of study. Nowadays, in fact, the most important forms of creativity are related to cooperative activities that involve complex networks of highly qualified experts. Creativity requires distributed knowledge – the integration of many creative workers specialised in different fields. The most creative groups have specific features. They are composed of individuals who have worked together for a while, who share knowledge and conventions, but who also possess complementary skills. Studies also show a certain variability related to the type of tasks they are faced with: the variety of knowledge present in the group is more effective when it is a matter of dealing with unfamiliar problems. In contrast, integration and shared knowledge are better suited to solving more conventional problems.

It is evident that, in order to analyse these forms of *collective creativity*, the individualistic approaches of traditional psychology are not very appropriate. For this reason, psychological studies dedicated to 'creative group' (John-Steiner 2000; Paulus and Nijstad 2003; Sawyer 2003), and 'work team' (West 2003) collaborations focus to a large extent on the socio-interactional dynamics and organisational aspects that favour or hinder collective creativity (King and Anderson 2002; for a review of recent studies, see Hennessey and Amabile 2010, 581–5). These areas of study represent fertile ground for interdisciplinary collaboration in which the sociology and psychology of organisations, the new economic sociology (which pays attention to social networks), and the psychology of creative groups can be integrated to explain the collective and *open source* innovative dynamics (which will be discussed in the next chapter): not only in artistic fields, but also in research teams and industry and service workplaces.

Box 2 Self-study prompts

1　What is meant by the 'golden age' of independent inventors?
2　Why did the figure of the independent inventor decline in the early years of the twentieth century and why did large industrial research laboratories become more prominent?
3　Why, nowadays, do we speak of social and territorial systems of innovation?
4　What is creativity and how can it be 'measured'?
5　What are convergent and divergent thinking?
6　What is the difference between intrinsic and extrinsic motivation?
7　What are the essential features of the socio-cultural approach to creativity?
8　What is meant by insight and what are the four stages of the creative process?

Notes

1　The actual remark attributed to Newton was: 'If I have seen further, it is only by standing on the shoulders of giants'. For a reconstruction regarding the origins and complex history of this aphorism, see Merton (1965).
2　The impact of US antitrust laws on the innovation system is explained in section three of Chapter 5.
3　For a definition of the concept of 'appropriability', see Chapter 5, section 4.
4　As will be seen in the next chapter, this is quite a controversial viewpoint. A number of studies have tried to estimate the level of 'innovativeness' of discoveries made by inventors working as part of a team, as against individually.
5　Even the famous Bell Labs – now owned by Lucent Technologies and Alcatel – has undergone drastic restructuring and downsizing in recent years.
6　Silicon Valley is a highly innovative area of the US, located in the southern part of the San Francisco Bay area. The area corresponds mostly with the Santa Clara Valley and has over four million residents in the metropolitan area of the city of San José. Its nickname derives from the intense concentration of industries related to computers and silicon-based semiconductors.
7　All these issues will be taken up and looked at in detail with the analysis of innovation systems in Chapters 5, 6 and 7.

8 Regarding the 'social construction' of innovation, see Trigilia (2007b). For an example of sociological analysis of the activity of 'genius' – through the study of a brilliant figure such as Mozart – see Elias (1991).
9 For a survey of the most recent developments, see Runco (2004), and Hennessey and Amabile (2010).

3 The sociology of economic inventions

This chapter deals with inventors and inventions. The first part introduces the observations of three classical sociologists who propose different ways of perceiving the role of the inventor: Sombart reflects on technology and inventors by placing them in different 'economic epochs'; Tarde sees them as creative and ingenious individuals; while Ogburn views them as mere 'extras' in the world of social change. The chapter then discusses the advent of a new socio-professional class – the creative class – which, according to Florida, provides the vital thrust for economic development. The central part of the chapter continues first with a look at research on the relevance of different types of inventors (autonomous, solitary, as part of a team) and then certain contributions focused on the opening out and democratisation of innovation processes. Finally, there is a review of organisational studies on innovation and of empirical studies on European and Italian inventors.

3.1 Sombart, Tarde, Ogburn: 100,000 inventors, one, or none?

Following World War Two, and for several decades thereafter, the analysis of the generative mechanisms of innovation was overshadowed on the one hand by studies on creativity in a psychological perspective and, on the other, by those on the technical and organisational characteristics of innovation from economic and sociological perspectives. The social figure of the inventor was rather neglected and the same fate was reserved for the inventive process.

It was a theme, however, that was certainly known to some of the classical figures of sociology. An early (and little-known) contribution was offered by Werner Sombart as part of his reflections on modern capitalism. As is well-known, for the German academic the economy is 'human activity directed towards securing the means of subsistence' (Sombart 1916; Eng. trans. from the Italian version 1967, 110). The distinctive characteristics of the various economic systems can be grasped by analysing three elements:

1 *economic mentality* – the set of spiritual elements that guide economic activity;
2 *technology* – the set of processes that economic actors employ to achieve their goals;

3   *organisation of work* – the rules to which economic transactions are subject (ibid., 110).

The question of the inventor is developed in relation to technology, which Sombart defines in two ways: one wide-ranging, the other more restrictive. The first refers to all the processes used to achieve certain goals; while the second, more specific, definition refers to what Sombart calls 'material or economic technology', defined as 'all the proceedings that serve for the production of goods' (ibid., 101). This definition consists of two strictly interrelated elements: on the one hand there is the *knowledge* necessary to act on materials and forces of nature; and on the other, *skill* deployed in the execution of work and the development of production tools.

Technology assumes very different forms in different historical periods and can be classified as: (1) *empirical*, when based on methods handed down and passively accepted; (2) *rational*, when based on a systematic review of the adequacy of the means in relation to ends; or (3) *scientific*, when the rationality of procedures is based on a causal explanation of the natural phenomena to which it is applied (ibid., 112).

The type of technology used in different historical periods is associated with different modes of social organisation of work and innovation (Table 3.1). In the artisanal economic system, which dominated the European Middle Ages and preceded the advent of the capitalist system, technology was 'empirical-organic' in nature: *empirical* because it was based exclusively on practical experience; *organic* because the procedures made use of humans, animals and plants as energy sources (and as materials). In addition, the resulting products were the result of creative acts through which humans expressed their personal skill. As a form of organisation of work, it was closely tied to tradition and left little room for innovation and the search for the new: the technology of the Middle Ages can therefore be described as stationary (Cavalli 1967, 34).

At the dawn of the new economic system – during the period of early capitalism which stretched until around the middle of the eighteenth century – this technological immobility was transformed as a whole series of inventions and discoveries of decisive importance took place. And yet, in technological terms, this era retained elements of continuity with the previous one since a solid anchoring of inventions in scientific knowledge was still lacking. The inventive process to a large extent still preserved an element of art and magic. Inventors included 'representatives of all walks of life and all professions': often they were *outsiders* gifted with great imagination and curiosity, and hailing from a variety of social situations; or *skilled experts*, craftsmen who invented within their own professional field; or *practical technologists*, who brought together theory and practice (such as court architects and military engineers). Yet alongside these non-specialist types there began to appear those figures that Sombart called *week-day inventors* (in contrast to *Sunday inventors*) whom he considered typical of early capitalism. Having the 'gift of the invention ... they sell their skills for a high price', carrying out inventive activity at a quasi-professional level, dedicating 'their entire life to invention, without limiting their activity to a specific area, but inventing tirelessly in all areas'(Sombart 1916; Eng. trans. from the Italian version 1967, 193). These 'inventors of any thing' compensated for their lack of scientific training with extraordinary creativity, and they animated early capitalism with intense creative fecundity.

Unlike the static conservatism that dominated the Middle Ages, the next epoch was in fact pervaded by a 'strong and tenacious will to innovate', which served to pack it with pioneers inspired by a *'determined desire for technical progress'*. Technological innovation increased significantly from the Renaissance onwards (ibid., 196). Sombart identifies three sources of change. The first kind, ideal in nature, was a general urge to know the world, *the Faustian trait of the time* – this urge manifested itself in inventions as well as in geographical discoveries and a 'yearning' for new forms of the state. The other two kinds were material ones, based on pecuniary or war interests (the *thirst for gold* or *the development of military apparatus*, respectively). Thanks to these changes, early capitalism established itself as the *era of rational technology*, oriented towards a conscious search for the most appropriate means to achieve specific ends, while still continuing to be based on an empirical and organic foundation.

A further turning point occurred with *mature capitalism*. At this point, modern technology was based on *scientific knowledge*, since its basis had become *inorganic* and *mechanical* and the production process was increasingly liberated from the creative power of the individual and human participation (ibid., 572). To explain the 'superabundance of invention' so typical of this era, Sombart refers to the changes that took place in the objective and subjective conditions of inventive activity (ibid., 577).

The *objective conditions* include three sets of factors. The first involves the anchoring of technology to a *scientific foundation* which constantly provides invention with nourishment. The second factor is change in the economic and cultural context. Mature capitalism, in fact, created a climate conducive to technical progress, ensuring a positive reception to invention and rewarding inventors with honour and success. A direct stimulus to invention came from its

Table 3.1 Technology in various economic systems

Economic system	Feudal-artisanal	Early capitalism	Mature capitalism
Epoch	Middle Ages	Renaissance-Baroque	Second half of the eighteenth century, onwards
Technology type and basis	Traditionalist Empirical-organic	Rationalist Empirical-organic	Scientific-rationalist Inorganic-mechanical
Actors	Artisans (1) masters (2) apprentices	Inventors (1) amateur (2) professional	Inventors (1) inventive geniuses (2) lay (3) specialised professionals

productive use by entrepreneurs as a way of outstripping the competition, establishing new businesses or generating extra profit. The commercial exploitation of invention was also fostered by the legal system, with the granting of patents that protected the rights to new discoveries. The materialistic culture that grew more widespread alongside capitalism also stimulated the demand for inventions to meet changing requirements, thus triggering an escalating spiral. Finally, the third factor was the *promotion* of inventive activity ensured by public and private bodies through:

- the creation of technical institutes equipped with special laboratories;
- the establishment of research departments in large companies;
- the subsidising of the inventor's freedom to invent (with the purchase of patents, financial assistance, contests and prizes).

Subjective conditions also contributed to the proliferation of inventions. The great increase in the number of inventors was a particular characteristic of mature capitalism. There were three types:

1 *inventive geniuses lacking professional specialisation*, figures similar to those present in early capitalism;
2 *lay inventors*, who came up with occasional inventions, discovering a wide variety of things, but of secondary importance;
3 *specialised, professional inventors* whose mission and work it was to invent.

This third type specifically represents modern inventive activity and explains the exponential increase of inventions. The figure of this typology is sometimes presented in the guise of the 'private inventor', carrying out his work in conditions of complete independence. The exemplary case is that of Thomas Edison, who created most of his inventions in the research laboratory he established in Menlo Park, New Jersey. However, the most widespread and representative figure is that of the specialised technician employed by large companies – such as the chemist or the engineer.

Sombart also deals with the motivations of inventors, and the needs that the latter tend to satisfy. The motivations are related to: (1) the joy of inventing; (2) the pursuit of success (defined variously as the common good, love for their fellow man, ambition and a passion for progress); (3) the desire for gain, which under capitalism is the most important motivational impulse. The needs to which innovation responds are also inextricably linked to gain and the logic of profit that dominates this economic system: 'The single need that in our economic system is rationally satisfied in as much as it constitutes the motive for invention, precedes it, arouses it, is the tendency to profit of the capitalistic entrepreneur' (ibid., 588). As can be seen, Sombart's observations on technological development and the proliferation of inventors are closely connected with the historico-comparative analysis of capitalism, which leads him to distinguish different forms depending on the economic era.

In the opposite corner, however, stands another classical sociologist – Gabriel Tarde – who puts forward a clearly scientific-positivist perspective in relation to inventors and inventions, with the aim of discovering general laws applicable to all societies (1890; Eng. trans. 1903, ix–x). Tarde was a French academic with a very individualist conception of sociology (Ferrarotti 2002, 157–8). He confers an important role upon 'creative individuals', to the point that in several of his writings he says that individuals are the basic unit of analysis in sociology – in clear contradiction to his contemporary, Emile Durkheim. For Tarde, therefore, society is nothing more than the sum of the individuals who compose it[1] (Clark 2010, 17).

More precisely, however, Tarde's approach (1898) is based on a relational sociology with a psychological backdrop: society consists of a network of mental states of interacting individuals; and social relations are nothing more than forms of influence that modify states of consciousness (Barry and Thrift 2007, 514; Hughes 1961, 555). The sociologist, then, must study the interpersonal relationships that are the basis of the regularities of behaviour that underpin all societies and which are governed by laws of imitation. For this reason, 'imitation ... is the elementary and characteristic social fact' with which sociology deals (Tarde 1898, Eng. trans. 2010, 96).

Besides imitation, however, there is another 'elementary social fact' that represents its antithesis: invention. The latter is defined as 'any kind of an innovation or improvement, however slight, which is made in any previous innovation throughout the range of social phenomena' (Tarde 1890; Eng. trans. 1903, 2). The source of these new elements is the association of (new) ideas emanating from individuals who are particularly gifted with creative talent, i.e those who introduce variation into the identical repetition of models already created in the past.

The great inventors are described by Tarde as figures of genius, oriented towards problem-solving, and who act intentionally to achieve specific goals.[2] Yet there are also other components related to physiological, emotional and even unconscious aspects: age, intense passion and dedication to a cause (an *idée fixe*), alongside other emotional elements, come together as part of a process of inventive inspiration. A particularly 'undersocialised' conception of inventive activity, then, emerges from these ideas.

Moreover in the second preface to the *Laws of Imitation*, Tarde writes that invention – from which all that is social derives – is not 'a purely social fact in its origin': it is rather the result of 'the intersection of an individual genius ... with the currents and radiations of imitation which one day happened to cross each other in a more or less exceptional brain'[3] (Tarde 1890; Eng. trans. 1903, xxii).

And yet the *social dimensions* of the inventive process are not completely neglected, as implied by the references to previous inventions and the recognition that the inventive process takes form as an encounter between an *interior purpose* and a favourable *exterior opportunity* (Tarde 1902b, Eng. trans. 2010). Furthermore, when speaking of the various levels of endowment in relation to inventive ability (of both the individual and society), Tarde makes explicit reference to socio-institutional factors. For example:

- Social inequalities make the upper classes more inventive, since they can benefit from a greater amount of leisure time, social interaction and exchange of ideas.
- Barriers of status stimulate the creativity of the élite, distancing them from mass conformism.
- Academic institutions guarantee freedom of thought and research.
- Geographical and social isolation hinders the inventive ability of society, groups and individuals.
- Cultural norms influence and guide inventive ability.

Tarde, moreover, is especially interested in 'successful inventions', i.e. those which – having been adopted – become socially diffuse and an origin of social change:

> When I say that social transformations are explained by the individual initiatives which are imitated, I do not say that invention, successful initiative, is the only acting force, nor do I say that it is actually the strongest force, but I say that is the directing, determining, and explaining force.
>
> (Tarde 1902a, 561)

This dynamic action is exerted in all spheres of society, including the economic sphere.[4] Tarde, in fact, criticises economists for having underestimated the role of ideas and creativity in economic life since the primary cause of wealth iself is invention (1895). There are two types of invention, which perform different economic functions. The first introduces new combinations of sensations and images, which then generate *new desires*.

The second (almost all industrial) are used to produce well-known objects that satisfy, at lower prices, desires that already exist – thus making them available to a wider range of consumers. The inventions also act on two levels: the level of desire and the level of trust. On the one hand, as has been said, they create new needs; while on the other, they respond to the need for certainty and reassurance that finds satisfaction not only through scientific and industrial discoveries, but also through innovation that today would be defined as institutional, i.e. that which occurs in the fields of legislation, administration and justice (ibid.).

It is for all these reasons that invention, in Tarde's view, must be added to other productive factors and play a crucial role in the explanation of economic development. But economists, forgetting the idea of invention, cut the head from their science (ibid.). In particular, Tarde criticises classical economists for the centrality they attribute to labour and capital (Lepinay 2007, 527). Work, as a simple duplicative act, is nothing more than mere imitative repetition, and cannot therefore be the ultimate source of wealth and development.[5] And the same goes for the accumulation of capital, which is, first of all, accumulated invention: a repetition of already-provided models. In other words, the emphasis placed on accumulation obscures the germinal and dynamic stage of the creation of new capital through innovation.

That said, not all inventions cause social change and economic development. There are many innovations, but only a few are successful in the sense that they are adopted and diffused. Why – Tarde asks – of the 100 innovations conceived at the same time, are only ten diffused while the others are forgotten? How is it possible to explain this phenomenon? To provide an answer we need to study the social influences that facilitate (or do not facilitate) expansion. These are the so-called *laws of imitation*, the most famous part of Tarde's work, and which are at the origin of studies on the diffusion of innovation that developed in the second half of the twentieth century (Kinnunen 1996; Rogers 2003, 41).

In the diffusion process, both logical and illogical kinds of social causes come into play (Tarde 1890; Eng. trans. 1903, 141). The former encourages the adoption of innovations for logical and rational reasons, because it is thought that they are more useful or more authentic than others in accordance with the already-established principles of that society. The latter, on the other hand, facilitate diffusion by acting on other, psycho-social, levers.[6] The phenomena of innovation and its diffusion, are, therefore, influenced by social factors. Tarde does not, however, allow for any historico-social determinism; rather, he leaves ample room in his concept of change for subjectivity and accidentalism (Taymans 1950, 614). Innovation occurs in a discontinuous way: it is unexpected and unintended, and occurs partly by chance (Tarde 1902a). Although the result of the deliberate action of specific individuals, there is an element of unpredictability that makes it indeterminable: 'only imitation and not invention is subject to law in the true sense of the word'[7] (Tarde 1890; Eng. trans. 1903, 142). Tarde, then, offers a non-deterministic reading of invention, which leaves plenty of space for the single individual's 'acts of genius' – the unique and imponderable qualities, in other words, of inventors. Great inventors, in fact, make an original and irreplaceable contribution and do not automatically emerge from social circumstances and requirements.[8] If in Sombart's view mature capitalism generated an exponential proliferation of professional inventors, for Tarde individuals of genius are unique and irreplaceable.

An almost completely opposite approach, however, is put forward in American sociology through the work of William Fielding Ogburn, who was, in some parts of his work, also influenced by Tarde (Clark 2010, 67). In the US during the twenties and thirties there developed a sociology of invention which was then rediscovered in the fifties and sixties (McGee 1995, 773). It was an orientation characterised by a holistic and deterministic analytical approach, which attributed a vital centrality to technology in social change, depriving individual inventors and their discoveries of any hint of relevance.

Ogburn (1922) highlights the profound difference between the slow rhythms that characterise the biological evolution of human nature and, in contrast, the rapid movements found in the cultural sphere. However, a marked imbalance is visible within the latter: while *material culture* (artefacts, technology, etc.) changes very quickly, immaterial culture (laws, values, social mores) proceeds more slowly and must adapt to the changes of the former. Ogburn therefore defines immaterial culture as an *adaptive culture*. Scientific and technological inventions are the mainspring of social change and the civilising process, especially in the West. Society adapts to innovation in the material sphere with resistance and at a slow pace, resulting in a systematic *cultural lag*.

But where does invention emerge from? Ogburn offers two explanatory models that he only partly succeeds in reconciling. On the one hand, he puts forward a reading of change in terms of cultural determinism, claiming that invention is dependent on the cultural conditions of the context; while on the other, he offers a reading similar to Tarde's, singling out the innate talent of inventors and their 'high degree of mental ability' (McGee 1995, 777).

In fact, if men are generally driven by habitual forms of behaviour, then the inventor stands forth as the 'great man', i.e. one in possession of above average natural abilities. The social construction of invention vanishes completely in this second explanation – in other words, the socio-relational conditions that allow certain individuals, in certain contexts, to achieve certain discoveries, are obscured. Ogburn, however, puts such an interpretation – i.e. the one that attributes a crucial role to the discoveries made by great men – into perspective. Invention is, in fact, mostly incremental. To explain new discoveries Ogburn refers to the accumulation-combination model that was widely used by the social sciences of the day. This model has invention resulting from a combination of principles and components that are already known within the cultural sphere. The incremental nature of invention tends to emphasise the collective aspect of the inventive process, thus downsizing the role of the 'great inventor'. The presence in history of a recurring multiplicity of simultaneous invention demonstrates, in his view, the final and determining influence of cultural conditions. The differences present in the inventive levels of various societies also depend on socio-institutional factors: economic demand and resources invested; the size and diversity of population (which facilitate innovative recombinations of cultural elements); the provision of communication networks and socio-territorial collocation (which can facilitate, or hinder, the diffusion of innovation from one sector or from one social group to another) (Del Sesto 1983).

Ogburn returns to the question of socio-cultural influence on innovative processes in a later essay emblematically entitled *The Great Man versus Social Forces* (1926), which addresses the question of the role of the individual in social change. The essay presents an oversocialised and functionalist conception of the inventive process, one that reflects the prevailing behaviourist psychology of the time: men are conceived of as 'mechanisms' that respond to social stimuli. Individual personality, in Ogburn's view, is influenced by two types of force: *social conditions* (tangible and intangible) and *social evaluations* (the values of a group). In situations of change, an imbalance is created between the first and the second that makes habitual patterns of behaviour inadequate. This generates a situation of tension that exerts pressure to reduce the distance between social conditions and social evaluations. This is where the inventor comes into play: the frustration created by this state of affairs leads certain individuals to produce inventions that are able to restore equilibrium within the social group (ibid., 228).

To sum up, Ogburn offers a functionalist and oversocialised reading of invention, alongside which co-exists (in more embryonic form) an undersocialised vision of the inventor. In the 'sociological school', which came to the fore in the twenties and thirties, it was the first of these two perspectives – the oversocialised idea – which prevailed. In 1935, a member of this school, Colum Gilfillan, published *The Sociology of Invention*, a book which rounds up many of the ideas that emerged from the debates of the time. Invention is seen as an incremental, evolutionary process, shaped by impersonal social forces. Although inventors play a role in progress, they appear as mere mediators of social forces that act through them. Invention is determined by the contextual conditions that render them mature and inevitable: 'the social causes of invention all come from the world outside the inventor and act through him and consist of changes in the outside world' (Gilfillan 1935, 44).

After World War Two this 'sociological reductionism' of the inventive process was accompanied by a symmetrical 'psychological reductionism' that neglected the social dimension. After this, the routinisation of inventive activity in the pay of large organisations (companies, universities, research centres) obscured the figure of the inventor, thereby discouraging studies about the generative mechanisms of invention. In recent years, however, there have been signs of a turnaround. A good example is the work of Richard Florida, who, while not dealing exclusively with inventors, attributes a crucial role in contemporary economies to creativity and inventiveness.

3.2 The creative class

Florida addresses the issue against the background of the transformation of contemporary capitalism. According to the American scholar, advanced economies have entered a new phase of development which he defines as a *'creative age'*. This new era presents many new features which will affect – in addition to the economy – culture and daily life. There is a widespread creative ethos in society, so naturally people will attach greater importance to the creative aspects of their existence than was the case in the past. Hence the preference for residential locations that provide rich and stimulating experiences, and workplaces that valorise *knowledge working*.[9]

The economy is also undergoing profound change, which constitutes a new 'social structure of creativity' (Florida 2002, 48ff.). With the emergence of the knowledge economy, the production of new ideas and innovation becomes central and permeates every sector. Although creativity fuelled economic progress in the past, what characterises this new phase is the speed and intensity of the growth of creative work, which gives rise to a new social class with a clear economic foundation: 'The *Creative Class* consists of people who add economic value through their creativity' (ibid., 68). Although these subjects do not see themselves as belonging to the same class, a growing coherence emerges between them, based on shared preferences, cultural tastes and values.[10] Florida indicates two components within this new class:

1   The *super-creative core*, composed of scientists, engineers, university professors, poets, artists, actors, etc., who are fully engaged in inventive and creative work, producing useful and transferable innovation.
2   The *creative professionals*, who work in knowledge-intensive sectors – high-tech areas, financial, legal and health services, etc. Additionally, professionals (doctors, lawyers, managers, etc.) are engaged in a creative kind of problem-solving, relying on complex structures of knowledge to deal with specific situations.

In the US this range of occupations, which at the beginning of the twentieth century made up just 10 per cent of the labour force, now constitutes around 30 per cent (ibid., 74; 2005b). The rest of the workforce is part of the working class and service class (unskilled and low-wage workers) that bring together those who carry out the more routine kinds of activity. These classes have a weak creative contribution.

According to Florida, in the new scenarios of the creative era, the magic formula for economic growth is the '3T' solution: technology, talent and tolerance. If the first two assets are the key ingredients of innovation, the third represents the key factor in mobilising it. Creative workers, in fact, move easily from one location to another, and the competition for talent is nowadays played out on a global scale[11] (Florida 2005a). The geography of development, therefore, particularly rewards the territories that attract those in possession of 'creative capital'. Such individuals prefer places that are 'diverse, tolerant and open to new ideas' (Florida 2002, 223). To identify these contexts, Florida makes use of various indices that measure the openness and tolerance of the local community, demonstrating that they are able to explain the localisation of creative workers and the more innovative companies.[12] He also puts together a general creativity index[13] which, he believes, is able to predict the ability of an area to sustain long-term development (Florida 2002, xx)

'Quality of place' thus becomes 'power of place' (ibid., 231–2). Places can attract creative workers if they are able to offer them what they value most: a high quality environment with a vibrant lifestyle and a wide variety of amenities. The presence of creative capital, in turn, becomes an economically attractive factor since investment and innovative companies follow creative workers. In brief, Florida's thesis is that 'regional economic growth is driven by the location choices of creative people' (ibid., 223). In particular, he draws attention to two important points:

1   the quality of life in urban centres may affect the location choices of the highly qualified part of the workforce that is willing to travel for reasons of work;

2   these contextual factors (tangible and intangible) are a key ingredient for economic development.

It is a thesis that has not been without its critics. Some studies show, for example, that an explanation based on the 'creative class' adds very little to the traditional analysis in terms of human capital. The economic performance of metropolitan urban areas of the US (growth of income and employment) is explained in the same way, or even more successfully, by traditional indicators relating to human capital and the composition of productive structure (Donegan *et al.* 2008; Hoyman and Faricy 2009). Florida's thesis has also been questioned by other academics. It is hard to believe that the mobility choices of creative workers are connected solely – or even primarily – to the amenities of a particular place; or that the presence of these workers is in itself sufficient to generate innovation and development regardless of the historico-productive context of such locations (Storper and Scott 2009, 156). On the contrary, it is the spatial dislocation of production, with its tendencies towards agglomeration, that explains both worker location choice and urban development.[14]

To this it must be added that the willingness of creative workers to relocate – with respect to mobility – is highly variable and influenced by socio-institutional factors. For example, research conducted in Italy and Europe on a particular component of this class, inventors,[15] shows high residential and employment stability – which is obviously linked to the different normative and cultural context of the 'old continent'. Even with reference to the value profile of the 'creative class', Florida's ideas are only partially confirmed in the Italian case – a great deal depends on the productive sector in question, and on the social and cultural contexts in which the inventors operate (Ramella and Trigilia 2010b). The last few points introduce the topic that will be discussed in the next section, which deals with inventors and their productivity.

3.3 Better alone or in good company?

Inventors have been the subject of several empirical studies in recent years.[16] One aspect that is analysed is the relevance and effectiveness of individuals involved in inventive activities – a much-debated issue, as we have seen, by the classics of sociology. Recently, scholars from different disciplines (sociologists, engineers, economists, economic historians, etc.) have been mulling over a similar question, wondering who produces the most significant inventions: independent inventors (who work for themselves), solitary inventors (who work alone) or team inventors (who work in groups for an organisation)? This question has been answered through empirical tests carried out across large databases of patented inventions and patent citations.[17]

Singh and Fleming (2010), for example, used a sample of more than half a million patents granted in the US over the period of a decade. The starting point is a theory of the inventive process, defined as a 'recombinant search over technology landscapes' (Fleming and Sorenson 2001, 1019). In other words, an invention consists of a *new combination of technological components* (whether already-existing or new), or of an improvement over previous combinations. The inventive process, moreover, is divided into three phases. In the *variation phase*, inventors try different combinations and generate new ideas. In the *selection phase*, these new ideas first undergo a process of evaluation and then those deemed unpromising are discarded. Both of these phases, unlike the next one, directly involve both the *solitary inventors* (working completely on their own, even if they are employees) and *team inventors* (working in a group). Finally, during the *retention phase*, ideas that passed through the first filter are evaluated by members of the scientific-professional community; and those that are deemed valid are taken up. This third, eminently social, phase is the one that determines the success of an invention in terms of the influence exerted on the community of inventors.

To investigate the different impact of the two groups of inventors, Singh and Fleming focused on patents that received a significantly different number of citations from the average – either positive (radical innovation) or negative (modest innovation). The results show that solitary inventors – especially if they do not belong to any organisation – are less likely to produce radical innovations. They do, however, tend to generate many modest inventions. Conversely, inventors working in teams are less likely to patent disappointing ideas and are more likely to produce important discoveries.

These results are explained by two distinct social mechanisms. The first involves the variation phase: in this phase, inventors working in a group – where a plurality of different experiences converge – have access to a greater number of ideas and sources of inspiration compared to the solitary inventors. This facilitates both the search for new combinations as well as the chance of making truly innovative discoveries. The second mechanism takes place in the selection phase, where solitary inventors evaluate their 'new ideas' by themselves, while the ideas of team inventors are subjected to the criticism of their colleagues. The latter process provides more rigorous scrutiny and this explains why team inventors generate fewer modest inventions (which can be discarded before being made public) as compared to solitary inventors. To sum up, team inventors benefit from a greater amount of generative stimuli and combinatorial opportunities during the variation phase, and more severe screening during the selection phase. They make use, in other words, of the informative and evaluative advantages embedded within social relations.[18] An autonomous influence is then exerted by the *variety resources* available to researchers. This variety of experience and technological knowledge reduces the probability of obtaining modest innovation; the extent of the network of external collaborations increases the likelihood of radical invention.

Using data from a wide-ranging survey involving several thousand European inventors, other academics have evaluated the influence of the individual inventor's experience on the chance of making fundamental discoveries[19] (Conti *et al.* 2010). The research in question highlights a learning process related to the 'career of inventors', so that increased experience and the development of inventive heuristics and routines augment patent productivity and the possibility of making breakthrough discoveries. Given the highly unpredictable nature of the latter, where chance plays such a significant part, the greater the number of inventions, the greater the likelihood of 'stumbling' on something radically new.

Other research of interest looked at those *independent inventors* who continue to operate, even in advanced economies. A study conducted in Canada in the mid-eighties emphasised the importance of this sector, and especially the variety of figures present within this category. Over half were occasional inventors, with only one patent to their name; the activity of others was more continuous, and with the aim of economic exploitation of their inventions. As in the case discussed above, experience gained in the past significantly influenced both their inventive productivity and their ability to commercialise their discoveries (Amesse and Desranleau 1991, 24).

The differentiation between independent inventors emerges from another investigation into patented inventions in the US during the eighties – in the tennis racket sector (Dahlin *et al.* 2004). In this case also, the significance and heterogeneity of independent inventors is highlighted. A large proportion of them were not habitual inventors (44 per cent had a single patent to their name), and these introduced low-impact inventions – the so-called *hobbyists*. Others, however, had a significant amount of technical and professional experience that allowed them to generate a high incidence of radical invention.[20] These are the *heroes of invention*, and are reminiscent of the legendary Thomas Edison. The study showed that independent inventors were over-represented at both ends of the invention scale: i.e. in the category of the decidedly modest inventions (hobbyist inventors), and in that of the breakthrough invention (inventor heroes). The latter phenomenon also occurs in the field of medical equipment (Lettl *et al.* 2009). On average, independent inventors were demonstrated to produce inventions of lesser impact than inventors employed by a company. However, if they possessed a high level of specialist skill within a specific technological area, they were able to achieve results comparable (or even superior) to inventors in different categories. Expertise and specialisation, therefore, are the elements that distinguish an inventor from a simple hobbyist.

These studies are of some interest since they show that in advanced economies there is still room for dispersed inventive processes – i.e. ones not concentrated solely within large organisations. However, they also have certain limitations. First of all, they do not analyse the variable roles that independent inventors and team inventors occupy in the various economies. These roles depend not only on the technological specificities of the various economic sectors, but also on the different ways in which these are regulated at a national and regional level. Second, the explanatory variables taken into account to explain the different results obtained by the inventors are almost exclusively cognitive (level of knowledge, experience, specialisation, plurality of evaluations). On the other hand, socio-normative variables – such as aspects relating to the social capital of the inventors and the organisation and cohesion of the project teams – are neglected. An integrated analysis of these aspects would in fact require a more complex and demanding approach, one that is based on surveys, case studies, relational data, etc. These are points that we will return to later when we present the results of a study on Italian inventors and innovative Italian companies.[21] First of all, however, we must address two other aspects: the pluralisation of the sources of inventions/innovations and their organisational configurations.

3.4 Pluralisation and decentralisation

Several scholars have noted that nowadays the generative mechanisms of innovation tend to involve a multiplicity of actors operating in different contexts. A *pluralisation and decentralisation of innovation sources* comes to the fore, highlighting two distinct points:

1   Inventions/innovations are in some cases the product of a joint effort in which it is difficult to distinguish individual contribution.
2   Both inventive and innovative processes are becoming more open and collaborative.

A plurality of diverse phenomena is collocated within these coordinates:

- *collective invention* – a particular type of inventive process;
- '*open innovation*' *communities* – innovative partnerships which adopt the form of a 'community' and are not motivated by economic incentives;
- the *democratisation of innovation*, which indicates a different division of innovative labour between users and manufacturers;
- '*open innovation*' *strategy* – a new innovative paradigm followed by companies.

Let's look at these briefly, one by one.

3.4.1 Collective invention

This phenomenon refers to a way of implementing and regulating the inventive process that is different from both the *collective public* and *private market* kinds. Collective invention is based on the free exchange of information between companies in a productive sector: faced with a common technical problem, they cooperate in order to find a solution, with each making a small cumulative contribution. The final invention is collective because all the incremental improvements introduced by individual firms have contributed to the solution of the technical problem and it is therefore impossible to attribute the discovery to a single inventor. Robert Allen (1983), who identified this model, cites the historical example of the iron industry in the English district of Cleveland. Between 1850–75, a number of improvements were made here in the construction of blast furnaces (increases in furnace height and combustion temperatures), which reduced costs and increased company efficiency. In the absence of appropriate theoretical knowledge, building higher furnaces and increasing temperatures was a very risky business. The solution to this technical problem was brought about through incremental changes contributed by several companies: slight changes made in the height and temperature of the furnaces, together with the sharing of information about the new developments, made innovation less risky and reduced the cost of failure (collapses, etc.). The reasons for this collaborative approach, alongside those of a technical-economic kind, were linked to the difficulty of keeping information secret within the local community and the emulative nature of competition present in the district: reputational reasons, in other words, related to the professional prestige bestowed upon successful innovators.[22]

Other more recent examples of collective invention are illustrated by Osterloh and Rota (2007, 161–2). These shed light on how, in the exploratory phase of a new technology, economic actors might decide to work together through the action of three factors:

1   the huge potential of learning: knowledge sharing increases the benefits for everyone;
2   low 'opportunity costs' – the absence of substantial losses resulting from information-sharing in the pre-commercial phase;
3   the presence of selective benefits, thanks to acquired reputation – the ability to guide the technological trajectory in directions favourable to their own interests, the opportunity to develop complementary goods, and so on.

When the technological trajectory is stable and a dominant design emerges (a successful technological architecture), these collaboration-favourable conditions cease and the actors go back to economic (profit-driven) strategies – unless other mechanisms come into operation, as happens in innovative communities.

3.4.2 Open innovation communities

During the last few decades the computer industry has seen the emergence of a 'struggle' between two forms of software: *proprietary* (protected by private patents and paid-for licences to use) and *open source* (available free of charge and based on free licences). In the latter case, the software authors make the 'source code' public so that others cannot only use it but also make their own constructive changes.[23]

Unlike the example discussed by Allen, in this case we are dealing with collaboration phenomena not motivated by economic incentives and not geared to producing goods for the market.[24] The development of open source software is based on voluntarily given, free-of-charge contributions that constitute a model of 'private collective' innovation, on the basis of which private actors invest their resources and expertise to produce a public good (Von Hippel and von Krogh 2003). A different model, therefore, from both the kind based on 'private investment' (inspired by the exclusive appropriation of private benefits in the market), and that based on 'collective action' (which – in the case of market failure – leaves it up to certain institutions to solve the problem of incentives that hinder collaboration for a public good).

These cooperative dynamics can create an open innovation community – that is, ' a group of unpaid volunteers who work informally, attempt to keep their processes of innovation public and available to any qualified contributor, and seek to distribute their work at no charge' (Fleming and Waguespack 2007, 166). Collaboration within these communities is maintained through a number of factors:

- institutional conditions (free licences);
- intrinsic motivations (love of problem-solving, technological-professional interest);
- extrinsic motivations (social and professional reputation);
- presence of 'prosocial' actors who enforce the rules of the community (Osterloh and Rota 2007, 161–2).

In some cases, due to the technical competence and social capital that can develop, some of these actors assume a leadership role in helping to keep the community united (Fleming and Waguespack 2007). Due to the absence of economic motives, this community form is distinct from the two cases that we discuss below – which do not exclude the search for economic benefits.

3.4.3 The democratisation of innovation

In a book published in the late eighties, Von Hippel (1988) drew attention to sectoral variability in innovation sources. What had already emerged from that study was the strong role of product users – in three areas (scientific instruments, semiconductors and printed circuit boards, and pultrusion process) the percentage of innovations introduced by users ranged between 67 per cent and 90 per cent (ibid., 4). With reference to this phenomenon, the author talks in a recent book about a real revolution being under way in innovation methods (von Hippel 2005) – a democratisation process seeing 'advanced users' of goods and services autonomously introduce modifications and novelties that they deem necessary. In other words, a model of *user-centred* innovation is increasingly developing alongside the *manufacturer-centric* kind dominant in the past.

Innovation is mainly introduced by *lead users* – i.e. cutting-edge actors in a specific field of activity who modify a product in order to better satisfy their own particular needs.[25] They engage in this kind of innovative activity because they

- can't find what they are seeking on the market;
- have needs, knowledge and sophisticated skills in that field of activity;
- are able – for the preceding reason – to innovate the product better than the manufacturers who act on the market.

Thanks to these information asymmetries, a sort of division of innovative labour is created. Users specialise in innovation that requires high-level information about the product's context of use and user needs, while manufacturers specialise in innovation related to more standardised and familiar requirements.

Often, users freely reveal information about the latest innovation, obtaining reputational and other benefits in exchange. At other times they can become an integral part of corporate strategy. An experiment carried out by US multi-national 3M, for example, clearly showed that innovation introduced with user collaboration produced more radical, and also commercially more profitable innovation compared to other kinds.[26] This last example brings us to a new company approach to innovation.

3.4.4 The open innovation strategy

This is a business model that embodies a new innovative paradigm in opposition to the *closed model of innovation* typical of vertically integrated companies (Chesbrough 2003; 2006; De Baker *et al*. 2008; OECD 2008). In the latter, research conducted exclusively in company laboratories led to the internal development of products which were then marketed through its distribution network. With the *open model of innovation*, in contrast, management promotes incoming and outgoing knowledge flow in order to accelerate innovative activity and expand the market for its own products. In other words, companies open up to external ideas and collaboration both to create and develop their own innovations, and to commercialise them. It is therefore a market-oriented model of innovation – creating value for the company, which starts off from the assumption that the knowledge useful for these ends is now dispersed among a plurality of different actors. This implies an opening up of borders and the development of external partnerships. These are phenomena that will be discussed again in later chapters. For the moment, however, they bring us immediately to the topic of the next section, which deals with the organisational architecture that supports this more flexible and open concept of innovation.

3.5 Organising innovation

One aspect that lacks comprehensive coverage in previous studies concerns the organisational dimension of inventive and innovative processes. Individual or collective invention, corporate innovation or open innovation, involve very different organisational methods. This section therefore will discuss not the innovation of organisations – which has an extensive specialised literature devoted to it – but rather the impact that certain organisational configurations have on the performance of inventive/innovative companies and other research institutions. Organisational studies highlight two important aspects in this regard: (1) organisational choices affect innovative capacity, and; (2) the *single best way* (or an organisational design that represents the best possible general solution) does not exist.

For many years classical organisation theory tended to identify universally valid solutions: the best-known examples are the bureaucratic organisation outlined by Max Weber and the multi-divisional version developed by Alfred Chandler with reference to large companies (Fenton and Pettigrew 2000, 10–12). Starting in the sixties and seventies, however, and with the emergence of the so-called 'contingency theory', this approach was set aside, with the recognition that there existed a variety of organisational forms related to the diversity of contexts. The most appropriate organisational structure, in consequence, is one that is best suited to a particular operational contingency, whether this is due to the size of the company, the type of technology employed, or the environment in which it operates (Lam 2005, 117).

After this 'turning point', investigations into *organisational design* have proliferated and ended up being integrated with those into technological innovation. In this case too, with reference to innovative companies, the variability of organisational configurations is acknowledged, with change depending on the production sector and the operational environment (Lazonick 2005).[27] In recent years there has been a growing emphasis on the procedural, informal and relational aspects related to innovative management strategies. It is not exclusively the *organisation* as a structure that is studied, but also *organisational activity*.

Once the wide variability and contingency of organisational solutions is acknowledged, is it then possible to identify the trends that characterise the studies and organisations involved with innovation? Two main points stand out. First, there is agreement on the fact that increased international competition and rapid technological change expose enterprises to a far greater amount of instability than in the past, forcing them to adopt a continuous learning process and more extensive organisational flexibility (Fenton and Pettigrew 2000). Second, certain underlying trends have been identified. Certain scholars have reconstructed an ideal-typical succession of 'organizational eras' that shows a transition 'in management thinking from vertical to horizontal organizing to open bounderies via outsourcing and partnering' (Anand and Daft 2007, 329). The eras elaborated by Anand and Daft concern organisational design, but also implicitly invoke a different configuration of innovative processes.

In the *first era* (*self-contained organisations*) – which lasted until the 1970s – hierarchical self-contained organisations were the norm: these were highly formalised and based on a division of labour for sectional functions or departments. The innovative process was prevalently confined within companies, with large companies making use of huge industrial research laboratories.

The *second era* (*horizontal organisations*) – beginning in the eighties – was characterised by a new emphasis on the horizontal coordination of functions, processes and teamwork, with the promotion of horizontal communication flows and a greater openness towards suppliers and customers. For innovation, this translated into project-directed work, the reduction of internal hierarchies, and a lessening of distance between innovators and other company stakeholders (production workers, but also suppliers and customers). Group work and the development of a 'community of practice' (a sense of shared identity based on the practice of working together) facilitated knowledge-sharing, the cross-fertilisation of ideas, and innovation (Lave and Wenger 1991; Brown and Duguid 1991; Wenger 1998, 2001; Gherardi 2010).

The *third era* (*open organisations*) began to develop in the mid-nineties and saw a far greater opening up of companies to the outside. New organisational forms took shape:

- *networked organisations,* combining units with a certain level of operational autonomy;
- *Networks of organisations,* connecting autonomous actors in cooperation with each other[28] (Catino 2012, 57ff.).

A *networked firm* such as Benetton is a good example of the first type – making use of production and sales units operating as franchises under the supervision and coordination of the parent company. An example of the second type are *networks of firms* such as those that unite small- and medium-sized companies operating in industrial districts, dividing the work between them. These kinds of organisational forms also modify innovation activity, which increasingly adopts a network structure: companies multiply their partnerships with external actors (companies, universities, etc.) and innovation systems develop within territorial areas through the collaboration of a number of actors (both in the economic field and others). In some high-tech sectors, external learning networks are increasingly being seen as the main *locus of innovation* (Powell *et al.* 1996).

This succession of organisational eras outlines ideal-typical configurations and general trends that should not, however, be taken as absolute – as has already been discussed, there exists great sectoral, strategic and contextual variety. In addition, the evolution described should not be thought of as rigid and unilinear – not just because the second and third eras tend to partially overlap, but also because there are exceptions and counter-tendencies that led some companies to rediscover self-contained and integrated forms of organisation (Berger 2005).

But what are the organisational choices that are deemed best suited to stimulating the creativity of inventors and the innovative capacity of companies? Research carried out during the nineties into organisational change in companies confirms many of the features already highlighted in the discussion of the typology of Anand and Daft. Innovative firms show a reduction of hierarchical levels, decentralisation of decision-making, widespread use of project teams, proliferation of forms of horizontal coordination, and external partnerships (Fenton and Pettigrew 2000, 37ff.).[29] Other elements that facilitate innovation also emerge from the literature: the presence of dedicated resources; frequency of internal communication; cohesive work groups; low staff turnover; flexible structures; an internal environment that encourages and appreciates newness; and mechanisms that focus attention on the external environment (Catino 2012, 213).

These results are also confirmed in studies on organisations at the cutting-edge of scientific research (Hollingsworth 2006; Hollingsworth *et al.* 2008). A survey of 250 institutions that achieved major breakthroughs in biomedical sciences shows the importance of the following organisational aspects:

- *moderately high scientific diversity* – the presence of a variety of scientific expertise within the same organisation;
- *communication and social integration between scientists* – the presence of frequent collaboration and exchanges of ideas (even in informal social contexts) among specialists from different disciplines;
- *organisational leadership* – the presence of coordinators who have both a strategic overview of the research being carried out, and the ability to guide and integrate the various existing skills;
- *recruitment* – the ability to hire individuals capable of bringing a mix of scientific skills to the table;
- *organisational flexibility and autonomy* of the research institution with respect to the external environment and/or of the research team in relation to the organisation to which it pertains (Hollingsworth 2006, 431).

3.6 Who are the inventors?

After analysing many aspects of inventive activity, but before concluding, there remains the task of delineating the socio-professional profile of the contemporary inventor. The best way to deal with this is to start with a large survey involving approximately 9,000 inventors from six European countries: France, Germany, Great Britain, Italy, the Netherlands and Spain (PatVal-EU 2005; Giuri *et al.* 2007). Who, then, are the inventors, and in which contexts do they operate? To a great extent they are middle-aged men with higher levels of education – in most cases working as employees, mainly for large companies.[30] Contrary to what has been said about 'creative workers' by Richard Florida, European inventors show a marked stability of employment, with 77 per cent never changing job during their career.[31]

In terms of the motivations and incentives that stimulate inventive activity, the industrial inventor turns out to be not very different from the academic inventor. Personal and social motivations dominate: the satisfaction of proving that something is technically possible; the individual gratification obtained from the improved performance of the organisation for which they work; the professional and scientific prestige and reputation arising from their discoveries. Material motives (linked to finance or career) – in contrast – come second. In other words, the motivations that prevail are those which social psychologists call 'intrinsic'. The survey also probed into the question of how new knowledge is produced. Only one-third of inventions derive from individual/solitary work – most are the result of collective work carried out within a research team. In 20 per cent of cases, partners outside their own organisation are involved. Having said that, the collaborations deemed most important by inventors were those that involved members of the same organisation, who worked close by.[32]

A specific survey of Italian inventors took place in 2009. This looked at the production sectors of high and medium-high technology (Ramella and Trigilia 2010b). The survey involved 739 inventors whose names were drawn from a sample of patents granted by the European Patent Office (EPO) between 1995–2004 in the pharmaceutical, medical appliance and mechanical engineering sectors.

Three 'social worlds' of invention emerge from the study: in each, the main players, areas of specialisation, territorial bases, organisational methods, research content, and even the ways in which discoveries come about, are all quite different from one another. The first world is that of *pharmaceuticals* and *medical appliances* – high-tech sectors that produce 13 per cent of Italian patents. In this world the inventive process is highly institutionalised, involving specialist players (researchers) with high academic qualifications, who are specifically devoted to the development of new inventions in suitably equipped structures, and who have the explicit aim of turning these inventions into patents. The careers of these inventors play out mainly within large companies, most of them located in the north-west of Italy, especially Milan. The spread in the centre and south of the country is much smaller, the significant exception being Rome. The other worlds of invention pertain to the very varied mechanical sector: its intense patenting activity (producing approximately one-third of Italian patents) is what most distinguishes Italy from other advanced economies.

The second world is that of *highly institutionalised research in the mechanical sector*. In this case, too, the inventive process involves specialised players and facilities, although generally at a level of formalisation inferior to that of the pharmaceutical sector. The career of the inventor plays out in medium- to large-sized companies, and is mainly concentrated in the industrial districts of the north and the centre.

The third and final world is that of *low-level institutionalisation in the mechanical sector*, which is present (though not exclusively) in the centre of the country, and in the south. In this last case, inventive activity is much less formalised, with organised research providing a very weak contribution. The inventor in this category is often self-employed, a small business owner, or an employee in a small company. Solitary inventors are also present, therefore, and inventions here can arise not from specifically targeted research but as the (sometimes unexpected) result of other activities such as the need to solve production problems or meet consumer needs. This research into Italian inventors offers various points of theoretical relevance.

- It once again emphasises the importance of the *social construction of invention*.[33] Inventive activity is in fact highly socialised in several respects. First, because the greatest number of patents are the result of a collective effort: 82 per cent of the inventors indicate that they are produced through the work of a collective research team. Second, because social relations – i.e. discussions between researchers and their constant exchange of ideas both during and outside work – profoundly permeate the 'dialectic of discovery' and have an influence on the results.[34] This investigation too, therefore, indicates that the golden age of the 'heroic and solitary' inventor (if it ever existed) is now a thing of the past. This does not imply, however, the disappearance or the irrelevance of either the independent inventor (who is not an employee, and represents 14 per cent of the total) or the solitary inventor (who carries out the research that gives rise to the patent itself, and who represents 18 per cent of the total). In this regard the research provides a less than predictable result: the persistence of a thread of individual creativity, which nourishes discoveries of a certain significance[35] – especially in the large and varied field of mechanical engineering (64 per cent of solitary inventors are concentrated in this sector).

- This last point highlights the *importance of an integrated study approach* that is capable of combining the contributions of different analytical strands. For example, the role of independent and isolated inventors – as it emerges from the research – must be properly framed within a perspective of political economy. In other words, it must be seen in relation to the importance of the mechanical sector in Italy, and its particular organisational and territorial configuration. In addition, the contribution of the new economic sociology allows us to avoid any 'psychological reductionism', emphasising instead the importance that social relationships play even in the case of individual inventions. To be a solitary inventor does not imply the absence of relationships with others. On the contrary: the greater the use they make of external knowledge sources, the more significant the patents of such inventors. These sources might include *informal* exchanges of ideas with their own colleagues or with workers from other organisations, personal relationships with universities, or access to scientific literature, and so on.

- Another aspect that emerges from the research is the *importance of the socio-organisational dimension*. An organisation that supports its research teams with the appropriate means and allows them full independence, creating cohesive working groups based on flexible coordination methods and a good mix of research integration and researcher autonomy, will significantly enhance inventive performance. This last, therefore, does not depend exclusively on the characteristics of individual inventors and not even on the simple sum of those of the research team. Rather, it manifests as an emergent property of (often informal) group interactions that are facilitated by an appropriate organisational structure. Such observations are in line with Robert Merton's reflections on the sociology of science: Merton emphasises the need to overcome an exclusively psychological perspective in order to understand the phenomena of *serendipity*, or the emergence of an 'unexpected scientific finding ... i.e., the discovery by chance or sagacity of valid results that were not sought for' (Merton 2002, 236).[36] Merton notes that this type of discovery – significant, yet unexpected – is fostered by particular organisational contexts: *socio-cognitive micro-environments* where a sort of 'institutionalised serendipity' is created thanks to unrestricted freedom of inquiry and frequent opportunities for informal interaction between researchers operating in different disciplines (ibid., 393–403). Internal organisational flexibility gives of its best when enriched by a plurality of knowledge. And this is true both for isolated inventors and for research groups. One key aspect for the success of inventive activity is the ability to make use of different skills – different in terms of both type and origin – and balancing *resources of cohesion and variety*. This leads to the last item worth considering here.

• What emerges from the research into inventors is the complementarity of resources useful for innovation:

> between the internal and external assets and relations of the organisation, between short (local/regional) and long (extra-regional) networks of collaboration, and between variety of knowledge and the cohesion of relationships.

While external relations increase an organisation's *requisite variety* (Ashby 1956), internal human capital and relations are known to potentiate its absorptive capacity (Cohen and Levinthal 1990). The same reasoning applies to long and short social networks. In fact, the success of the research team, and that of the innovative company, often depends on the ability to combine the 'nearby' resources of the local territory with those from further away. And this is all the more necessary when the context in which they operate lacks the appropriate skills and collective goods.[37] Last, the strict

---

Box 3 Self-study prompts

1   What is technology, according to Sombart? What different kinds of technology and inventor are found in the various economic eras?
2   How does Tarde define imitation and what importance does he attribute to inventions in economic development?
3   What role, according to Ogburn, do inventors play in social change?
4   Which social groups are part of the 'creative class' and why does Florida consider them important?
5   What are the '3T's' of growth and what relationship do they have with regional development?
6   What are the main results of the research regarding independent inventors, solitary inventors and team inventors?
7   What are collective inventions?
8   What does the term 'democratisation of innovation' refer to?
9   What is the difference between open innovation communities and open innovation strategies?
10   What is meant by 'organisational eras' and what are their distinguishing features?
11   Nowadays what are the organisational configurations considered most suitable to stimulate the creativity of inventors and the innovative capacity of companies?

interconnection is shown which, in the inventive process, links the assortment of cognitive resources (the plurality of skills) that facilitate the search for innovative combinations, with the presence of socio-normative resources (trust and social capital) that facilitate the exchange of ideas and the learning of new knowledge. In conclusion, research on inventors highlights therefore the *logic of complementarity* that governs inventive activity and innovation processes – a logic that operates at the individual, organisational and territorial level, balancing *generative mechanisms of variety and cohesion*. This is a point which will be returned to in the last chapter.

Notes

1 Actually, even Tarde conceives of society as a supra-individual entity, but unlike Durkheim believes that it should not be reified – not be seen, that is, as an autonomous body that acts on individuals from the outside, determining their behaviour. According to Tarde, in other words, society does not exist beyond the individuals who compose it and cannot act except through them (Ferrarotti 2002, pp. 165–6).

2 Imitative behaviour also contains elements – albeit extremely slight – of innovation, because 'the individual often innovates unconsciously, and, as a matter of fact, the most imitative man is an innovator on some side or other' (Tarde 1890; Eng. trans. 1903, xiv).

3 In *La logique sociale*, Tarde (1895) defines the question more clearly: What is an invention? The happy convergence of different imitations in a brain, that is, an ingenious idea that consists of establishing a link between two preceding inventions as a means to arrive at a new objective – inventions which until that time, independent and unrelated one to another, circulated separately in public, but which can now present themselves linked together and provide, through this link, a new impulse.

4 Tarde makes a distinction between theoretical and practical inventions, the latter including industrial innovation. In this respect, 'successful economic inventions' are very similar to what Schumpeter defines as innovations (contrasting them with inventions). The two authors are alike in how they define innovation as the introduction of 'new combinations' (Taymans 1950, 618).

5 While 'very different is the effort that tends toward the *unknown*. Searching for something new is not working' (Tarde 1902b; cited in Taymans 1950, 620).

6 There are three types of 'extra-logical' influences: (1) those that push from the interior to the exterior of a person (so that interior ideas are imitated first, and then external things); (2) those that move from high to low (so that it is easier to imitate ideas that come from higher social models and classes); (3) those that come from custom and fashion (sometimes from the past and sometimes from the present – in other words, depending on whether the era is one that favours tradition, or one that favours a taste for the new and exotic).

7 This does not prevent him from devoting Chapter IV of *La logique sociale* to the 'laws of invention'.

8 Tarde observes: 'Eliminate, in mathematics, Archimedes, Descartes, Leibniz, Lagrange (not to mention the living), and what would be left? Others, you say, would have taken their place. Are you sure? Others would have discovered other things, and the mathematical river would have followed another course, would have been nourished in other ways: individuals of genius charted its flow' (1902a, 563).

9 The number of knowledge workers – made up of scientists, managers, professionals and skilled technicians with a high level of education – has increased enormously in recent decades. For an analysis of their substantial presence in certain advanced economies, see Butera *et al.* (2008).

10 Florida (2002, 77–9) indicates four core values: a strong appreciation of individuality, meritocracy, diversity and openness.

11 Regarding the international mobility of skilled human capital and its impact on territorial development, see also Saxenian (2006).

12 Florida (2002, xx) constructs a Tolerance Index based on four indicators: (1) a *Gay Index* (measuring the presence of homosexuals); (2) a *Bohemian Index* (the presence of musicians, actors, writers and other artists); (3) a *Melting Pot Index* (the presence of foreigners); and (4) a *Racial Integration Index* (which detects the degree of separation/integration in the community).

13 This index is assembled on the basis of four factors: (1) the quota of the creative class in the labour force; (2) innovation (measured as the number of patents per capita); (3) the quota of high-tech industry; (4) the gay presence index.

14 Very similar conclusions were also reached by a study carried out in Italy on high-tech cities (Burroni and Trigilia 2011).

15 This will be discussed later in the fifth section.

16 It is impossible to give an exhaustive account of all the studies that have appeared, so here is a brief summary of the main lines of research. Some studies have been dedicated to the career patterns of inventors, analysing such things as: contextual and relational aspects of the activities of successful inventors and scientists (Simonton, 1992); the productivity of inventors throughout their lives and in different historical periods (Jones 2005a, 2005b); their productivity based on company size and other individual attributes (Kim *et al.* 2004; Mariani and Romanelli 2007); the effects of occupational mobility on patent productivity (Hoisl 2007) and patent citations (Breschi and Lissoni 2006); the type of incentives relevant to industrial inventors (Sauermann and Cohen 2010). Much research has also been devoted to academic inventors, focusing on their socio-biographical profile and the factors that influence their propensity to invent and patent their discoveries (Balconi *et al.*, 2004; Göktepe 2006, 2008a, 2008b; Ding *et al.* 2006; Göktepe and Edquist 2006; Baldini *et al.* 2007; Malva *et al.* 2007; Göktepe and Mahagaonkar 2008). Other issues studied were academic entrepreneurship and the involvement of star-scientists in the activities of private companies (Zucker *et al.* 1998; Murray, 2004; Lissoni, 2011).

17 Patents are legal instruments used to protect an invention. Citations obtained by a patent (from other subsequent patents) are often used as an indicator of its relevance and innovativeness (on this point see also fn 7 in Chapter 6).

18 The importance of the social dimension in scientific discoveries is also clear from ethnographic studies. Kevin Dunbar (1995) made an in-depth analysis of the social micro-mechanisms that drive the generation of new hypotheses, carrying out year-long observations of four molecular biology laboratories. The results of the study highlighted the importance of conversations between researchers at weekly laboratory meetings, when unexpected research results were analysed, alternative hypotheses suggested, or interest stimulated into looking for new explanations. These exchanges of opinion gave rise to most of the innovative ideas used by the researchers, who then forgot this 'collective origin'.

19 The authors speak of 'breakthrough' inventions, i.e discoveries capable of opening up new technological trajectories that have the possibility of providing a basis for subsequent inventions. To identify members of this category, the authors refer to patents that are at the top of the patent citation classifications (5 per cent higher in the frequency distribution of citations).

20 A radical invention is defined on the basis of its technological content, and must comply with three conditions: (1) it must be new (different from previous inventions); (2) it must be unique (different from other contemporary inventions); (3) it must have a strong impact (be adopted by other inventors). This third parameter is determined on the basis of citations obtained in subsequent patents (Dahlin and Behrens 2005).

21 This will be discussed later in this chapter (section 5), and again in Chapter 7 (section 4).

22 These dynamics will be dealt with again in Chapter 7, where the subject is innovation in industrial districts.

23 The development of the Linux operating system – originally designed by a computer science student at the University of Helsinki, Linus Torvalds – is an example of this, based on open cooperation carried out through the internet.

24 Although today many companies are resorting to forms of open source collaboration that have commercial ends.

25 There are numerous examples, ranging from leisure (surfboards, tennis rackets, etc.) to professional needs (medical equipment, detection tools, etc.).

26 For the role of users in the introduction of radical innovation in the medical technology field, see also Lettl (2005).

27 A point that will be discussed at length later on, in Chapter 5 – which deals with the systems of innovation.

28 Joel Podolny and Karen Page (1998, 59) define the 'network form of organization as any collection of actors ($N \geq 2$) that pursue repeated, enduring exchange relations with one another and, at the same time, lack a legitimate organizational authority to arbitrate and resolve disputes that may arise during the exchange.' Examples of this type are joint ventures, strategic alliances, business groups, etc..

29 Secondary analysis carried out on the data from many studies also confirms a positive association between innovation and internal and external communication, and a negative association with centralised decision-making (Damanpour 1991, 569).

30 The highest number of inventors working for large companies was in Germany (80 per cent), while the highest number working in small- and medium-sized enterprises was in Spain (36 per cent) and Italy (30 per cent).

31 The only country that partially deviates from this model is Great Britain (where the percentage drops to 63 per cent). Not coincidentally, this is a country where there are fewer restrictions on labour mobility and which adheres to the so-called Anglo-Saxon model of capitalism.

32 On the importance of proximity in relation to the quality of collaboration in teams engaged in innovative projects, see Hoegl and Proserpio (2004).

33 In sociological studies of science and technology, the social dimension of the inventive process has been emphatically underlined by the so-called SCOT (Social Construction of Technology) approach. Authors gravitating towards this line of study tend to emphasise the role played by negotiation between 'relevant social groups' of various types in the evolution of a 'technological artifact'. The studies carried out by the founders of this approach on the invention of the bicycle and Bakelite (the first synthetic plastic material to be produced) are emblematic in this regard (Pinch and Bijker 1987; Bijker 1987, 1995).

34 As we saw in Chapter 1, the importance of this dialogic component – in relation to 'conversations' – was particularly emphasised by Lester and Piore (2004).

35 Although in a minority, their role is far from marginal: they are in fact responsible for about a quarter of the most important inventions.

36 The list of 'famous inventions' that came about by chance, or through research and studies initially carried out for other purposes, is a long one. To cite just a few of the most sensational: the discovery of penicillin by Alexander Fleming; X-rays by Wilhelm Conrad Röntgen; the conditioned reflexes of dogs by Pavlov; the psychedelic effects of LSD by Albert Hofmann, etc.. A minor, but indicative, example is the invention of the much-used Post-It. Researchers at the US multinational 3M discovered a new adhesive agent that was rejected because it did not allow paper to stick to surfaces very strongly. Six years later, a researcher at the same company had the idea of creating small, easily removable Post-Its, which could be used as bookmarks or to pin down loose pages. The idea came to him while he was trying to solve a

practical problem when attending a religious function: how to find the right page in his hymn book without the paper bookmarks fluttering to the ground. The idea was commercialised, not without resistance, in the 1980s – and soon became one of the company's most successful inventions.

37 On this point, see the interesting research on innovative firms operating in a difficult environment such as Sicily (Ace and Trigilia 2010).

4 The small worlds of creativity and innovation

This chapter deals with the 'small-world' phenomenon. It starts by presenting the first experiments conducted by social psychologist Stanley Milgram on the transmission of information through chains of acquaintances, and then moves on to small-world and scale-free networks. The second part discusses the application of these models to the themes of innovation, analysing certain examples of empirical research regarding: affiliation networks in scientific collaboration and company boards of directors; the 'small worlds' of creativity and innovation in Broadway musicals and businesses partnerships; and the Silicon Valley hub.

4.1 Six degrees of separation

The expression 'six degrees of separation' has become popular both in everyday language and in scientific literature to indicate that each person can be reached through a limited chain of acquaintances. It is a good representation of the concept that 'the world is shrinking' – in the sense that it requires just a handful of intermediaries for us to get in touch with all the people we are interested in, no matter how geographically or socially distant they may be. This image, so familiar nowadays in the age of globalisation, is not of particularly recent origin. In fact, it appeared for the first time in 1929 in a short story, not coincidentally entitled *Chains*, by the Hungarian writer Frigyes Karinthy (2006). The story describes a little experiment carried out by a group of friends in order to demonstrate that the population of the planet is more accessible and closer than it had ever been in the past. Each of the participants had to select a random person in the world and show that it was possible to reach them through their network of personal acquaintances. Two of the friends immediately demonstrated that they could easily contact a Swedish Nobel Prize winner for literature and an ordinary American worker employed in a Ford factory – two complete strangers who could be reached via short 'acquaintance chains'. The game went on to try to demonstrate the plausibility of the assumption that 'nobody from the group needed more than five links in the chain to reach, just by using the method of acquaintance, any inhabitant of our Planet' (ibid., 23). Through this story Karinthy gives credence to the idea that *anyone, anywhere* in the world, can reach any other person through five intermediaries, only the first of whom is a person they know directly.[1]

Why should this literary idea be of interest here? First, because it influenced initial thinking about social networks; and second, because it received empirical confirmation from the small-world experiments, which then gave rise to less evocative and more scientifically rigorous theoretical formulations in the field of network studies. Third, because the phenomena described – the 'small worlds' and the ties that bind them – have important implications for Innovation Studies.

To start with the first point: towards the end of the fifties, two American scientists at the Massachusetts Institute of Technology in Boston (MIT) circulated a manuscript that marks the origin of scientific research into the 'small-world' phenomenon. The manuscript was published only 20 years later as, appropriately, the opening article of the first issue of a new journal – *Social Networks* – dedicated to the theoretical and empirical analysis of social networks. This text, devised by political scientist Ithiel de Sola Pool and mathematician Manfred Kochen, contains some of the basic questions that have guided subsequent research (Pool and Kochen 1978). The two scholars were interested in developing the first steps of a theory of (social and political) influence as a function of social relationships – the ability, in other words, to reach the 'right' people through the appropriate channels. With this in mind, they considered the morphology of social structure: the volume and distribution of social acquaintance present within a given population. The questions they asked are apparently simple: what is the probability that a pair of randomly selected individuals know each other? What is the chance that they have a friend in common? What is the probability that the shortest acquaintance chain to put them in contact is made up of two intermediaries – the friend of a friend, in other words? Or, perhaps, 3, 4, 5, 6 ... *n* intermediaries? The answer to these questions does not involve a simple calculation of probabilities, but rather a profound understanding of the society in question.

Acquaintance networks are not in fact randomly distributed amongst people: they are *socially structured*. This significantly lessens the distance between *certain*, apparently far-flung, individuals, while extending the distance between *certain others*. People and acquaintance networks tend, in varying degrees, to accumulate around certain dimensions of social structure: territory, with relationships of geographical proximity; occupations, through professional relationships; the family, within kinship relations; and leisure time, through elective relationships. Companies and organisations, in other words, can be thought of as social groups or clusters, within which the individuals collected together know each other well.[2] The problem is to understand to what extent these relationship clusters are self-contained, and to what extent they are connected to – or disconnected from – one another. The likelihood of reciprocal acquaintance between two people, therefore, is highly dependent on the relationship structure that links the various social clusters.

The two MIT academics address these issues by developing a *mathematical model* of acquaintance networks: a model that depends essentially on three parameters: the total number of persons (N) that make up the population studied; the average number of acquaintances (n) of each individual; the level of structuration (*k*) of social relationships (what others would, subsequently, call the *clustering coefficient*).

If the level of social structuration was equal to zero (i.e. if no relationship clusters existed) the likelihood of reciprocal acquaintance between two people would be known. It would be determined solely by the first two parameters (*N*, *n*). Taking the UK population as the total number of persons studied (amounting to about 64 million people), and assuming that on average each citizen has 1,000 acquaintances, the probability that two people know each other is equal to *n/N*, or 1/64,000.[3] To this very low probability, however, must be added an extremely low level of social distance. In this hypothetical society, with no structure, where each one of a person's acquaintances do not know each other, and where there are no isolated individuals, the relationship chain that makes it possible for one person to reach another is very short. Each of our acquaintances is, in turn, in contact with 1,000 people. Through our primary acquaintance network alone, then, we can easily reach a million people (1,000²). Through two intermediaries, we can contact a billion people (1,000³). With three intermediaries the scale of potential acquaintances widens to a trillion contacts: a million billion people (1,000⁴). In theory, therefore, one or two intermediaries are sufficient to establish contact with any other UK citizen. And if we want to contact another person on the planet, the chain does not have to be unduly lengthened: all we have to do is activate an acquaintance of an acquaintance of an *acquaintance of ours*.[4]

This case, however, is purely hypothetical. Real societies are different. Friends often live in the same city, have similar jobs, similar leisure tastes and habits, etc. They move within the same circuits of social relationships, so it is an easy matter for them to know one another. This means that the number of new acquaintances with whom a friend can put us in touch is more limited and this tends to extend – and complicate – the social 'chains'. In other words, it is the parameter *k* – the level of social structuration – that determines how many intermediaries are required to connect two people. And it is the distribution of relational capital (social capital) between the various groups and individuals that conditions their social opportunities.

Therefore, to understand how many steps are required to contact a specific person, probability calculation is of no help. We do need to know, however, the *relational structure present in the population studied*. Aware of this fact, and to estimate the unknown parameters of their equation, Pool and Kochen took advantage of research carried out on a limited sample of US citizens from a range of social backgrounds: blue and white collar workers, professionals and housewives.[5] Starting from the *contacts* registered by 27 'real individuals' in a time period of 100 days, they calculated the average number of acquaintances (*n*) of a typical citizen. Furthermore, based on the percentage of people who in turn knew one another amongst those included on the lists of sample contacts, they produced an estimate of the level of structuration (*k*) of social relations (Pool and Kochen 1978, 29). Finally, they defined a stylised model of the empirical situation, which they then applied to the US: from this, it appeared that the modal number of intermediaries required to connect any two people was equal to 2.

The two MIT scholars ended the article by conjecturing the following: if American society *was not structured* and the average number of acquaintances for each individual was equivalent to 1,000, then it would take fewer than two intermediaries to connect any two people chosen at random.

'In a structured population', said the article, this result 'is less likely, but still seems probable. And perhaps for the whole world's population probably only one more bridging individual should be needed' (ibid., 42).

To sum up, although the chance of direct acquaintance between two US citizens was – then – just 1/200,000, the addition of one or two intermediaries dramatically increased the likelihood of *indirect acquaintance*.

4.2 It's a small world

But the mathematical model developed by the MIT group, however interesting from a theoretical viewpoint, rested on rather fragile empirical grounds. The problem of structure and social connectivity was not resolved in a satisfactory manner. This stimulated a variety of different paths. In 1967, in *Psychology Today*, social psychologist Stanley Milgram published the results obtained using an experimental method: the so-called 'Harvard approach' to the small-world phenomenon. Milgram and his associates addressed the study of social structure and acquaintance networks via two ingenious empirical experiments. Certain 'randomly chosen' people (*starting-persons*) were equipped with basic information regarding a resident of another state (the *target-person*): they were then asked to send a letter provided by the researchers to this target-person. The only constraint was that if they did not know the person directly, exclusive use had to be made of chains of acquaintance: the letter had to be forwarded to a relative, friend or mere acquaintance (someone personally known, however).

In the first study, the starting-persons were chosen from among the residents of Wichita, Kansas. The target-person was Alice, the wife of a student who lived in Cambridge, Massachusetts. In the second study, the chains stretched out from Nebraska (for a detailed account of this experiment see section 4.2.1 below). Initially, the Harvard researchers were sceptical about the experiment's chances of success: they entertained serious doubts that any of the messages would ever reach their destination. The results were surprising. The first message reached Alice after only four days. At the end of the two experiments the 'transmission chain' count ranged from a minimum of two to a maximum of ten intermediaries, with a median value of 5 and a modal value equal to 6.[6] The number of messages that reached the goal, however, was limited. This induced the researchers to speculate that the length of the chains was slightly underestimated, assuming that the interrupted chains were also the longest. However, the experiment provided some interesting insights. First, that it was social rather than physical distance that limited the transmission of information. Second, that there existed relational hubs:[7] many different chains, in fact, converged towards a limited number of people who then delivered messages to the recipient.

Third, that these hubs are highly specialised: some were the terminals of *professional chains* (those who, to deliver the message, followed the professional tracks of the target-person), and others of *territorial chains* (those who followed the residential tracks).

Fourth, the chains revealed strong gender segregation (often men and women forwarded messages to friends of the same sex), and the tendency to use chains of acquaintances and friends rather than relatives. As the researchers observed, these social traits were specific to the US at that time and might vary from society to society. In brief, the experiment provided interesting indications regarding the modality of social integration and, more importantly, the social mechanisms that 'govern' the circulation of information.

4.2.1 How small is the world? The small-world experiments in greater detail

4.2.1.1 The sixties' experiment with traditional mail

At the end of the sixties, Stanley Milgram and Jeffrey Travers at Harvard University (Boston) carried out experimental research into the small-world problem (Milgram 1967; Travers and Milgram 1969). The question they asked was very similar to the one that had inspired Pool and Kochen: what was the probability that any two people, arbitrarily chosen from a large population such as that of the US, would know each other? And assuming that they did not know each other, how many intermediaries would be required to put them in touch? To answer these questions, the two scholars organised an experiment that was quite simple, yet at the same time ingenious. They randomly selected a target-person and a group of starting-persons with the aim of bringing them into contact through 'acquaintances chains' (Figure 4.1).

Each starter received a document containing the description and purpose of the study and the rules to follow to help it reach its objective. The document contained some basic information about the target-person: name and address, profession, the city in which he worked and the town he came from, age, his wife's name, etc. The rules regarding sending the document were as follows: if the starter was personally acquainted with the target (*on a first name basis*) then they must send the document directly to the person. Otherwise, it must be sent to an intermediary (a friend, relative or other personal acquaintance) who the starter believed capable of reaching – whether directly or indirectly – the target. At each step of the chain, a system of postcards sent to the research group made it possible to track the path of the document. This could end in two ways: by interrupting the chain of transmission, or with the attainment of the objective. In addition, on the postcard, each new intermediary had to write down some biographical information about themselves and about the person to whom they were forwarding the document. In this way the research team could, through comparison,

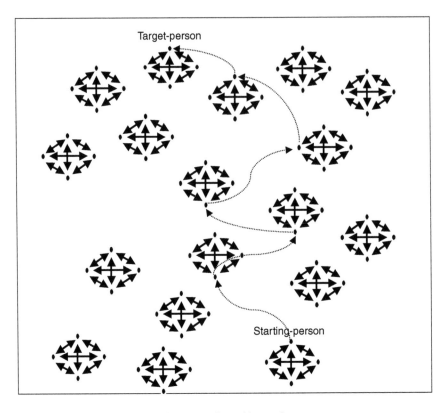

Figure 4.1 The Travers and Milgram small-world experiment.

accurately determine the characteristics of both the interrupted and the successful chains and, in the case of the former, even identify the 'breaking point'.

The person chosen as the target was a financial broker who lived and worked in Boston. The other participants in the experiment – the starters – were divided into groups: 196 residing in Nebraska (a state considered to be sufficiently distant from the target) and 100 in the Boston area. The first group included 100 share-holders in large companies listed on the stock exchange (*Nebraska stockholders*), with the rest randomly selected from the state population (*Nebraska random*). The Boston group was selected from people who replied to an advertisement placed in a newspaper (*Boston random*). The aim was to see how the different social and geographical distances to the objective influenced the success rate and the length of the chains of transmission. Of the 296 people selected for the study, 217 agreed to participate in the experiment. Some 64 chains reached the Boston broker, 29 per cent of those initiated. As regards the broken chains, no particularly significant social characteristic came to the fore. As the researchers expected, geographical and social distance influenced the results of the experiment. The Boston random group registered the highest success rate in terms of the chains (35 per cent), with an average number of intermediaries of 4.4. The Nebraska stockholders reached the goal in 31 per cent of cases, through an average of 5.4 intermediaries. The Nebraska random group reached the broker in only 24 per cent of cases, with an average of 5.7 intermediaries. The results of the experiment gave rise to the 'six degrees of separation' formula made famous by John Guare. The experiment was subsequently repeated by Milgram, and it recorded similar results, despite changes being made to certain social and statistical characteristics with regard to starters and targets (race, for example) (Korte and Milgram 1970).

4.2.1.2 The millennium email experiment

Nearly 40 years later, a team of researchers at Columbia University (New York) repeated the test on a larger scale using the internet. Peter Sheridan Dodds, Roby Muhamad, and Duncan J. Watts (2003) organised a social search experiment with several thousand participants of different nationalities. The targets to be reached were 18 people of different social backgrounds living in 13 different countries. These target-persons included, for instance, an Ivy League university professor in the US, an archival inspector in Estonia, a technology consultant in India, a police officer in Australia and an army veterinarian in Norway. In this case, too, participants had to deliver the message via acquaintances whom they believed were closer to their final destination. In addition to providing the research team with the name and email address of the intermediary, participants had to explain why they had chosen that person, how they had come to know each other, the type of relationship that linked them (parental, friendship, professional) and the intensity of their relationship. In short, the intention was to replicate the small-world experiment on a global scale, monitoring the transmission chains and their social characteristics. The experiment, conducted between 2001–03, involved more than 61,000 people from 166 different nations and triggered 24,163 'message chains'. About two-thirds of the starting-persons initiated the chain by using friends: 41 per cent described the relationship as 'very close' and another 33 per cent as 'quite close'. The success rate was higher in the case of those chains that made use of relations originating in the professional workplace, or from a period of higher education. Although strong ties were predominantly used, networks employing less close acquaintances actually reached the target-persons in greater numbers: giving rise to the observation – in line with Granovetter's thesis – that 'weak' ties are disproportionately responsible for social connectivity' (Dodds et al. 2003, 827).

This was a rather imperfect connectivity, however, judging by the limited number of chains that reached their destination: only 384, each using an average of 4.05 intermediaries. The success rate, therefore, was extremely low – only about 1.6 per cent of the chains originally initiated. Another, later, experiment, involving 85,000 participants and 56,000 message chains, proved even more disappointing (Goel et al. 2009, 703–4). This was mainly attributed – in addition to its greater geographic scope than the Milgram and Travers test – to the lack of incentives or interest in the experiment. The results, therefore, suggested that in the absence of 'sufficient incentives to proceed, the small-world hypothesis will not appear to hold' (Dodds *et al.* 2003, 828). The researchers did add, however, that it would only take a modest increase in incentives (not necessarily financial) to raise the success rate of this type of *social search*. This seemingly trivial conclusion has theoretical relevance. It tells us that the structure of relationship networks does not exercise social influence in itself, but assumes meaning and significance only in the light of the strategies and motivations of the actors that are placed within it.

Figure 4.1, however, makes the exact meaning of the Harvard experiment immediately clear. Separation by five intermediaries does not mean that the person who initiates the search is socially close to the target person. As Milgram observed (1967, 67), any citizen was theoretically separated by only five intermediaries from the president of the United States or Nelson Rockefeller. This did not mean, however, that their lives were effectively integrated with those of the White House incumbent or the US billionaire. The separation was not only a matter of five people, but of five *circles of acquaintance*; and that is a huge social distance. And the meaning of the experiment, especially with regard to innovation, is precisely this: it lies in the idea that social distance can be reduced and that, through social networks, people can access information and knowledge which is different from that which they – and their inner circle of relatives, friends, acquaintances and colleagues – already possess. To use the terminology of the previous chapters, it is possible, through these networks, to acquire *non-redundant information*.

But as we shall see, two other important things also came out of the experiment. The first is that the small-world phenomenon must be conjugated in the plural. Society, the fields of scientific research, the sectors of technological innovation, all constitute a series of *small worlds*, highly integrated internally. It is precisely because of the strongly *clustered* aspect of societies that the number of steps required to reach an individual increases, when compared to how many would be needed if acquaintance networks were randomly distributed. The fact that Stephen knows John and John knows Mike greatly increases the likelihood that Stephen and Mike will, sooner or later, get to know one another. The 'closure' of acquaintance networks therefore tends to reduce and complicate the ability to acquire new information. The second thing is that close acquaintance *cliques* (family, relatives, friends, work colleagues, etc.) – who communicate via direct links – are also connected to the outside by a series of indirect links. This is what creates communication between their *small social worlds*, leading to the small-world phenomenon.

This is an aspect, however, that requires correct interpretation. The experiments discussed so far – both the original version using traditional mail and the subsequent experiment using email –tell a different story from the one that is often highlighted: and that is *the difficulty in terms of the search for, and transmission of, reliable information*. In the small-world experiments, in fact, only a very small percentage of chains reached the established target, and even those that were successful were of very different lengths. This highlights the trans-action problems and costs inherent in the use of networks.

The most obvious factor is motivational. While it is true that it does not cost a great deal to connect two acquaintances, it is also true that sufficient motivation must exist in order for them to be brought together. The ties that convey non-redundant information, therefore, must be weak – but *not so weak* as to interrupt the flow. Another problematic aspect is linked to the fact that the longer the chains, the greater the risk of their breaking or not conveying the expected advantages. As Ronald Burt has pointed out, networks generate two types of benefit, involving *information* and *control*. These advantages are mainly related to *accessing new information* that creates favourable opportunities and the *time-liness* with which this can be obtained with respect to possible competitors. It is evident that each additional step in the chain tends to diffuse (and disperse) new information amongst multiple subjects and, above all, it delays access – thus reducing the benefits related to *timing*. There is also another important aspect that concerns a third type of advantage indicated by Burt: one connected to *refer-rals*. The acquaintances that pass on information, in fact, perform a filtering function that legitimises both the information and the person from whom it comes, in the sense that this renders them credible and reliable. It is evident that the more this *function of accreditation* is dependent on a long chain of 'acquaint-ances of acquaintances', the more it tends to lose power. As we shall see, these are aspects of importance in the study of research teams and the transmission of complex and tacit knowledge in situations of high uncertainty.

4.3 Small-world networks

The small-world experiment was replicated several times in order to test the influence of certain variables: sex (Lin *et al.* 1977); ethnicity (Korte and Milgram 1970; Weimann 1983); organisational context (Lundberg 1975); the media employed, e.g. the telephone (Guiot 1976) and email (Dodds *et al.* 2003; Goel *et al.* 2009).[8] This type of experiment – based on the sending of messages (*letter referral studies*) – was, however, subjected to severe criticism. Several empirical and methodological flaws were discovered that cast more than one doubt over the adequacy of such methods to detect the structure of social relations and measure the distances between subjects. Several of the reported problems were already evident in the investigations of Milgram and Travers: the limited size and arbitrariness of selection criteria undermined the randomness and represent-ativeness of the samples used (Erickson 1979); the low rates of response and chain completion made them unreliable for detecting social networks and esti-mating the length of the paths (White 1970; Kleinfeld 2002); the inappropriate strategies in the selection of intermediaries – in other words, the errors of choice made by the subjects – tended to elongate the chains, compared to shorter paths theoretically available to reach the target (Killworth *et al.* 2006).

Although many of these problems can be solved, and certain best practices have been identified to render experiments more robust (Schnettler 2009a), the fact remains that these types of study are becoming less frequently employed for the analysis of the structure of 'real networks'. In addition, the increasing availability of empirical data regarding large-scale networks (often digital) makes it possible to study the small-world phenomenon using others methods. A resurgence of interest has taken place through the creation of mathematical models for the small-world networks present in social, biological and technological systems. At the end of the nineties, two Cornell University researchers – Duncan J. Watts and Steven Strogatz (1998) – published an article that echoed throughout a wide variety of disciplines. The article showed that, starting from an ordered model of local clusters – i.e. short-range relationships between contiguous points – and with the random addition of a few long-distance relationships, it is possible to significantly reduce the average distance between the points present in the model. In short, it creates the small-world effect: from small (local) worlds to a small (global) world.

The model, in fact, describes a scenario composed of many small local worlds – made up of close relationships, dense networks, redundant information – connected to each other by certain random links that make them all accessible through just a few intermediaries. To prove their case the two scholars built two polar models: a regular network and a random one. The first represents an ordered interaction, a condition of strong social *clusterisation* where the probability that the friends of a social actor know one other is very high. In the second model, however, there is no order at all to the interaction: personal relationships follow a completely random logic, so that there is just as much likelihood of a person knowing any other person, whether a stranger or a 'friend of a friend'. The hypothesis put forward by the two researchers is that many situations present in the real world are collocated in an intermediate position between these two extremes.

These models should be interpreted against the background of graph theory inaugurated in the first half of the eighteenth century by the Swiss mathematician Leonhard Euler. A graph is a set of points (also called vertices or nodes) joined together by a series of lines (also called arcs, edges, links, etc.).[9] This branch of mathematics shows that graphs possess structural properties that depend on the number of nodes and the way they are linked. With this reasoning transposed to social relations, the configuration of a network provides social actors with both opportunities and constraints of a 'structural' kind.

Watts and Strogatz take as their starting point the ordered situation, represented through the properties of a *regular graph* (Figure 4.2), composed of nodes that have the same degree – that is, the same number of links.[10]

In particular, beginning from a *regular lattice*[11] and connecting the opposite vertices (so as to form a ring), a *periodic lattice* is formed. Each point of the regular network shown in Figure 4.2 presents the same number of links. For example, point A has 4 *adjacent nodes* (connected to it by a link: a1, a2, a3, a4) that constitute its 'neighbourhood' (Scott 1991). These are in turn joined together by three links: nodes a1 and a2 are adjacent, as are nodes a1 and a3, and nodes a3 and a4. Moving to the opposite side of the network – in correspondence to

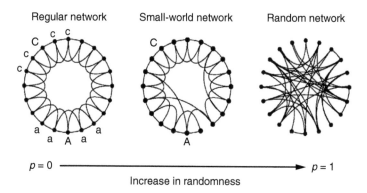

Figure 4.2 Small-world networks.

point C – the same arrangement of nodes is found. These are in fact the properties of the periodic network: that with any selected node, the relational structure is identical. And this is the reason why it is used to represent a situation of 'orderly interaction' (Watts 2004a, 84).

At the opposite extreme, however, we find the *random graph*, which represents the situation of interactions that lack any order. The two academics built this through a process of random reorientation of all the links between the nodes. In the first graph on the left (the regular example), each link has a zero probability ($p=0$) to be reoriented; while in the graph on the right (the random example), each link is randomly reoriented ($p=1$).

Before following Watts and Strogatz in their reasoning, it is useful to introduce some basic information regarding the *theory of random graphs*. The foundations of this theory were laid in 1959 by Hungarian mathematicians Paul Erdős and Alfred Renyi as part of their reflections on the formation of social networks. They proposed a model based on random connections, and decided that the simplest formation model for a network was to establish links between nodes using the throw of a dice. Connecting a set of isolated nodes in this manner initially results in the formation of dyads (pairs of nodes), and then, subsequently, some isolated clusters (groups of nodes separated from other groups of nodes).[12] When a certain threshold is reached there occurs what physicists call a 'phase transition' (a classic example is the freezing of water): the formation of a single complete cluster. All nodes will be part of a single network and will be accessible through direct links or paths of indirect links.[13]

Erdős and Renyi show that the minimum threshold for this change to be realised is for each node to have at least one tie. Once this critical threshold is reached, all the nodes become part of what mathematicians define as a 'giant component'. As links are gradually added, the theory of random networks shows that, with the critical threshold exceeded, the number of nodes excluded from the giant component decreases exponentially. As a pupil of Erdős will later demonstrate, for fairly extended networks all nodes also end up having on average the same number of links. In other words, randomly assigned links follow a 'Poisson distribution', gathering around a mean value, while decreasing rapidly in terms of both lower and higher than average values (Barabási 2002).

A random graph presents two main features. The first is that it has low levels of *clustering*: the nodes do not tend to agglomerate locally, according to highly integrated neighbourly relations. There is, in other words, a low local density: our friends do not know each other and the same goes for the friends of our friends. This means that the giant component – or society as a whole – is easily navigated through indirect links. The second characteristic of random graphs is that the distances between nodes are very short. As seen above, if each person has 100 or 1,000 acquaintances who do not know each other, any individual on earth can be reached through only three or four intermediaries.

Conversely, an ordered graph has properties of an opposite kind: there is a high level of local clustering in terms of links (friends of friends know each other), and limited explorability of the giant component. If we draw a graph loop consisting of 6.8 billion nodes (equal to the number of inhabitants of the earth), and imagine having to reach a point located exactly on the opposite side, using only the closest points – for example, in Figure 4.2, the two points a1 and a3 at the side of A – the chain becomes very long indeed.

Assuming that most of the networks in the real world fall in an intermediate position between these two poles, Watts and Strogatz show that just a few links added randomly (with probability $0 < p < 1$) will give rise to a situation that combines some properties of the regular network (the high clustering of local relations) with those of the random network (high reachability of all nodes). These are the so-called *small-world networks*. To make the kind of situation described by these networks more immediately comprehensible, it is worthwhile focusing your mind on the fact that most of us do not only have acquaintances who live in the same city but also, directly or indirectly (through our friends), ones located in other countries. There are, in other words, 'shortcuts' that drastically reduce the distance that – theoretically – separates us from any other person placed at the other end of the world. This plunges us back into the small-world phenomenon. The structural properties of each of the three types of graph are described by two parameters: *the path length* L (p) and the *clustering coefficient* C (p). The former is a global property of the graph and measures the average separation between any two nodes. The latter is a local property and measures the density level of a typical 'neighbourhood' of nodes.[14] The *regular network* $(p=0)$ is strongly clustered locally for which the value of C is close to 1 (the maximum possible density). The value of L, however, is also high: the average distance between nodes is very long. With the *random network* $(p=1)$, on the other hand, both the values are very low. The *small-world network* $(0 < p < 1)$ combines some features of the two previous types. Duncan and Strogatz show that in these networks the value of C remains very high, as in regular networks (the networks are highly *clustered*); but the value of L is very low, as in random networks. With the addition of just a few shortcuts – long-distance links – the world shrinks dramatically. The two academics also show that this type of network describes properties actually present in reality. To test their hypothesis they calculated the values of L and C for different kinds of real-world networks: the network of collaborations between Hollywood actors (an example of a social network); the network of electricity distribution in the western part of the US (an example of a technological network); the connection system of the 302 neurons that make up the *Caenorhabditis elegans* (better known as *C. elegans*, a small multicellular organism only 1 mm long, widely studied in developmental biology (an example of a neural network).

All three of these 'real networks' turned out to be small-world networks. Compared to a random network, with the same number of nodes (n) and average links (k), the three real networks demonstrate geodetic distances that are slightly higher than those present in the random simulation, but also far higher values in terms of clustering (Table 4.1). Two surprising elements came out of this experiment. The first is that the small-world phenomenon is not confined only to social networks. The second is that just a minimum number of local variations (a few long-range relationships) are required to generate highly consistent global effects (an exponential reduction in the average distance). The first randomly added five long-distance links reduce the average geodesic distance between all nodes by half, regardless of the size of the network. A logic of diminishing marginal returns is apparent, however: to reduce the average distances by another 50 per cent, another 50 long-distance links are required. And successive reductions require even more links to achieve a far smaller effect (Watt 2004a, 89–90).

This class of networks 'discovered' by the two academics meets the four conditions listed by Watts (1999, 495–6) to define the small-world phenomenon. In order for this label to be applied, in fact, it is necessary for the networks to be:

* numerically large;
* globally sparse (the number of links that connect the individual nodes to each other is on average much smaller in comparison to the total number of nodes);
* decentralised (there is no central node to which all others are directly connected);
* locally highly clustered (the links between adjacent nodes are very dense).

4.4 Scale-invariant networks

Subsequently, other studies have enriched the mathematical modelling of networks, providing a significant contribution to the understanding of their dynamic evolution. Almost at the same time as the analysis of small-world networks, Albert-László Barabási, a physicist at the University of Notre Dame, Indiana, together with two of his collaborators, Réka Albert and Hawoong Jeong, published two very influential articles in *Science* and *Nature* (Barabási and Albert 1999; Albert *et al.* 1999) highlighting the existence of other types of network – ones governed by different rules than those explored by Watts and Strogatz.[15]

Table. 4.1 Empirical examples of small-world networks

	n	k	Distance		Clustering	
			L (real network)	L (random network)	C (real network)	C (random network)
Actors	225,226	61	3.65	2.99	0.79	0.00027
Electricity network	4,941	2.67	18.7	12.4	0.08	0.005
C. elegans	282	14	2.65	2.25	0.28	0.05

Source: adapted from Watts and Strogatz (1998).

These researchers show that many real networks do not follow a normal distribution of links but rather a *power law*. With this type of distribution, cases peak at very low values and then tend to decline very slowly. The configuration then is a curve with a constant decrease, where *many small events* (nodes with few links) co-exist with *a few large events* (nodes with many links) (Barabási 2002). Applied to real-world networks, this means that a large number of nodes have a restricted number of links. As links increase, cases tend to rarefy. However, there are still nodes which possess extremely high numbers of links: these are the so-called *connectors*, or *hubs*. Power laws have a precise exponent, which is given by the ratio between the rarest and most frequent events. In random networks, all the nodes have, on average, the same number of links. In terms of connectivity, then, they have a *typical scale*, represented by the average node. For distributions that follow a power law, however, it does not make sense to indicate a mean value, since no 'representative' node exists that can summarise the characteristics. This type of network, not possessing a typical scale, is referred to as a *scale-invariant network* (ibid.).

Barabási and his collaborators used the world wide web as a starting point for their observations. Employing a specific software, they explored the pages (nodes) and the links that unite them.[16] Given the impossibility of exploring the network completely, they arrived at an inductive estimate of its diameter. Analysing increasingly large portions of the web, they showed the average distance between pairs of documents, and calculated the increment of the number of pages analysed. They thus derived a mathematical formula which was then applied to calculate the average distance between two documents chosen at random from the (then) estimated 800 million web pages.[17] The surprising result of this exploration was that the *vast world web* had a relatively limited diameter (equal to 18.6 links) – with all of its documents, in fact, lying at an average distance of just 19 clicks away from each other (Albert *et al.* 1999, 130). Furthermore, increasing the number of nodes had little influence on the extension of the diameter: the two authors estimated that even in the case of a 1,000 per cent increase, the average distance between nodes would increase only slightly, from 19 to 21.

In brief, as Barabási himself noted a general property of networks is that they are 'small worlds' (Barabási 2002). It is another aspect of the contribution from this group of physicists, however, which is the most significant and innovative. They show that global connectivity is not uniformly guaranteed by all the nodes – as is assumed in both random and 'small world' models – but above all by the hub. For example, by examining the 325,000 pages of the Notre Dame University domain, they discovered that 82 per cent of them had at most three links, while 42 (just 0.013 per cent) had more than 1,000. Expanding the exploration to 203 million web pages, the same phenomenon was observed: about 90 per cent of the nodes had a maximum of ten links, while two or three had about a million. Hence the conclusion that the web was based on a handful of highly connected nodes.

And, according to the group of physicists, the same goes for many other real-world networks. *The hubs are responsible for the small-world phenomenon*, their great connectivity holding together many nodes and ensuring reachability through fairly short paths. At base, there lay two generative mechanisms ignored by previous theories. Models based on random networks, for example, are static and egalitarian: the number of nodes is kept constant and each of them is considered equivalent. The scale-invariant model proposed by Barabási and Albert is based on two opposite hypotheses, explaining the generation of power laws on the basis of two simple mechanisms present in many complex systems, both social and otherwise:

1 *growth*, since networks tend to be in constant expansion, continually adding
2 *preferential connections*, since new nodes tend to enter into relationships by favouring nodes that are already well connected (Barabási and Albert 1999, 511; Barabási 2002).

Real-world networks are, in other words, often *dynamic systems*: the number of nodes grows and newcomer nodes, connecting to the existing network, tend to favour the hub.

From these initial reflections, and subsequent contributions from other physicists, mathematicians, sociologists, biologists and computer and information scientists, a field of study has taken shape regarding the evolution of networks, in which the scale-invariant model has become a special case. The topology of the networks and their different modes of transformation introduce greater variety into these models than Barabási originally imagined. For example, the different modes of ageing, disappearance and replacement of the nodes, the criteria for the generation of new links, and whether they are onerous (i.e. time-consuming) or not, considerably modify the number and size of hubs present in the real world. These developments led Barabási to admit that in the theory of network evolution the scale-invariant model is a particular case (ibid.). He also stated, however, that in complex networks, when growth and preferential connections are present, power laws and hubs will in any case emerge 'most of the time'.

While taking these clarifications on board, it should be added that the study of complex networks – especially social ones – would derive considerable benefit from empirical research into operating modes in different socio-institutional contexts: in other words, from a specifically sociological approach to the study. The resources required to foster social links, in fact, are very different from those needed to keep alive or generate web page links, and most importantly they vary with interactional context. Such elements make it quite clear that, in social worlds, the presence and role of the hub, as well as the degree of connectivity of the network, do not depend on the invariant properties of complex networks in their abstract sense. They are highly variable and contingent,[18] dependent as they are on the social and institutional contexts in which the links are deployed. And that is in a logic of complex, biunivocal interdependence, so networks both *condition* and are *conditioned by* the socio-institutional structure within which they develop interpersonal and inter-organisational relations.

To sum up, whereas Barabási characterises the new science of networks in a nomothetic sense, stating that certain 'simple and far-reaching *natural laws* govern the structure and evolution of all the complex networks that surround us' (2002, 6, my italics), a sociological approach tends instead to introduce more elements of variability and contingency. The effort to emancipate the study of complex networks from the *random* logic that had dominated the early stages – on the basis of the work of Erdős and Renyi – induced Barabási to focus on the transition from disorder to order, analysing the self-organisational mechanisms and laws that governed the phase transitions. This attempt to discover elements of uniformity should not, however, overlook the differences present in various scientific and phenomenal fields. It is not, in other words, possible to push forward to the formulation of universally valid natural laws. As Raymond Boudon taught (1984), when reflecting on the nomothetic and deterministic flaw present in many theories of social transformation, the new science of networks had to take into account the *place of disorder* in social phenomena.

However, a sociological approach to the study of complex networks does not appear to be in contradiction with the research agenda of the *new science of networks*. In what can be considered a sort of manifesto, Mark E. J. Newman, Albert-László Barabási and Duncan J. Watts (2006, 4) indicated the three characteristics that distinguished the new science of networks:

1   focus is on the properties of networks present in the real world and there is interest therefore in both theoretical and empirical issues;
2   networks are not assumed to be static: they evolve over time according to *various* dynamic rules;
3   the aim is to understand networks not as simple 'topological objects' but as structures on which dynamic distributed systems are built.

The authors of this 'new agenda' at the same time criticised both the *excessively abstract* nature of early graph theory – developed in the context of mathematics – and the *over-descriptive and empirical* nature of *social network analysis*, practised in the social science field.

This second criticism, however, seems less than appropriate, especially with regard to new economic sociology – a branch in which the use of network analysis has been accompanied by substantial theoretical elaboration, albeit in ways suitable to the social sciences (Boudon 1984). Its use, in fact, has allowed the development of *partial and local laws* – such as the law regarding the 'strength of weak ties' – which apply to specific historical and social situations: that is, within defined space-time coordinates. It has also developed *formal theories* with analytical purposes – specially constructed logico-formal models that are used to describe and explain certain empirical phenomena. This second category includes the 'theory' of small-world and complex networks.

The rehabilitation of the networks' 'social dimension', meanwhile, arose from the observations of the above-mentioned Duncan Watts, who, not coincidentally, taught sociology for several years at Columbia University. The sociological question was once again foregrounded in relation to the networks' 'issue of searchability', connected to the small-world experiments. The problem concerned the ability of individuals to identify the 'right tracks' through their relationships in order to reach to the individuals selected as their target. This question emerged as a result of certain of the writings published by Jon Kleinberg (2000a, 2000b), a computer scientist who analysed the phenomena of *direct research* such as those found in Milgram's small-world experiments. Kleinberg partially altered the procedure used in the experiments by Watts and Strogatz, introducing a provision regarding distance – randomly adding links to the nodes of an ordered graph, but with the condition that the probability that a link unites two nodes decreases according to their distance in the network. In brief, new connections are added at random *but are not, however, randomly distributed*, as they tend to favour the nodes adjacent to one other (a 'realistic' assumption). The question that Kleinberg wanted to answer was whether it was possible 'that individuals using local information are collectively very effective at actually *constructing* short paths between two points in a social network' (Kleinberg 2000b, 163). He showed that using *decentralised algorithms* – computer programs that operate exclusively through local information – it is not possible to find these paths (except under very restrictive conditions). As Watts points out, if the real world actually worked as the small-world network model did, as Strogatz and he described in the journal *Nature*, the *direct searches* observed in Milgram's experiments would be impossible.

Kleinberg showed that forcing the program to use only local information,[19] the short paths between two points in the network were difficult to find. The general conclusions that Kleinberg drew from his experiment are quite clear: the tracks present in the local structure, regarding the existence of long-distance connections, are those that provide crucial information for finding the right paths within the network (ibid., 167 and 170).

Should these tracks disappear, searching would be impossible: the actors would find themselves immersed in a huge throng of social relations, too homogeneous with one another to be distinguishable. This would lead to disorientation and the inability to identify which local acquaintances could point them in the right direction. The key factor in the whole argument was that the *various identities of the actors defined both the map and the compass required to navigate social networks.* They provided, for example, essential information about the distances present in interpersonal relationships, and the ability of some links to overcome the barriers that keep other social worlds separate. Two points should be emphasised:

1   The distances that separate these worlds – though very different from each other (it may be a matter of geography, income, professionalism, religion, education, race, etc.) – are however all intrinsically social: they are connected to relationships between individuals and the morphology of the social structure.
2   The identities of the nodes make social networks explorable, so that *searchability* is a specific property of these networks (Watts *et al.* 2002).

Banal as it may seem, the 'discovery' prompted by Kleinberg's observations is that *social networks* are composed of nodes equipped with *social identities*. The latter also structure their networks according to the sociological principle of homophily (Lazarsfeld and Merton 1954), which leads individuals to associate mainly with other people who share similar characteristics. As has been said, 'similarity generates connection', with the result that social networks tend to be homogeneous with respect to different characteristics (McPherson *et al.* 2001).[20] This principle of homophily restricts the individual's social world, limiting their interactions to a circle of 'similars', thus reducing the amount of information they can receive and the experiences they can encounter. That said, these small worlds of 'similars' are also layered and interconnected, allowing windows to open on different worlds. Identities and social interactions are indeed multi-dimensional and this makes it possible to navigate through a variety of contexts, exceeding even large distances. This dual profile of social identities, therefore, moulds the networks according to two principles which act in opposite directions: (1) *homophily* renders local worlds small, following a criterion of homogeneity; (2) *multi-dimensionality*, however, renders the global world small, making it possible to cross the boundaries of local worlds. In conclusion, *the distinctive feature of social networks is that they are composed of actors who deliberately use and manipulate their relationships and this feature conditions the properties that the social networks deploy.*

As Watts himself noted, in a scientific field increasingly dominated by physicists, mathematical simulations and computer algorithms, it is a significant step forward:

> [W]hile there's nothing wrong with simple models, for any complex reality there are many such models, and only by thinking deeply about the way the world works – only by thinking like sociologists *as well as* like mathematicians – can we pick the right one.
>
> (Watts, 2004a, 156)

It is precisely this return to sociological detail that gives these models – the small-world and scale-invariant networks – their interest for the social sciences.

Following the 'sociological track', it may be observed how studies based on the small-world approach are prevalently directed towards two main aspects: the phenomena of *diffusion* and *search* (Schnettler 2009b). The former relates to the events of infection (e.g. viruses and diseases) or the spread of phenomena of various kinds (e.g. innovation) through the relations between social actors. The second concerns the exploration of social networks through the use of intermediaries and research aimed at the transmission or retrieval of useful resources for those involved. In both cases these are matters of extreme importance for Innovation Studies. Many of Watts' observations on affiliation networks (applied to *interlock directorates* and scientific collaborations), on models of threshold decisions and cascade phenomena (applied to the phenomena of social contagion and diffusion of innovation), and the robustness of multi-scale organisational networks (applied to information exchange and problem-solving processes in situations of radical uncertainty requiring distributed innovative capacity),[21] indicate some of the possible applications to innovative processes. I will look at some of these in the following sections.

4.5 Affiliation networks

Affiliation networks – often referred to as bimodal or bipartite networks – consist of a set of nodes/actors and the events associated with them.[22] Applied to social phenomena, this means that they describe events associated with groups of actors, rather than simple links between pairs of individuals, and this makes it possible to analyse them from a dual perspective: that of the actors, and that of groups. Two social actors define themselves as affiliates when they belong to the same group. Two technicians working on an innovative project on behalf of a company; two inventors who patent a discovery together; two university researchers who publish an article as co-authors – these are all good examples of affiliation networks relevant for innovation processes.

These types of partnership, as suggested by research conducted by Mark Newman – a physicist at the University of Michigan – are often structured as small-world networks. Newman examined the collaborations between scientists, using co-authorships of articles and scientific papers as his basis. For the analysis he made use of a plurality of databases containing information about millions of articles and authors: an electronic archive of research contributions in the field of physics (LANL e-Print Archive); an archive on research in the field of biology and medicine (MEDLINE) and two minor archives relating to physics (SPIRES) and computer science (NCSTRL). The analysis of this huge amount of data confirmed the importance of small-world networks in scientific collaborations (Newman 2001a, 2001b, 2001c).

Despite the strong sectoral specialisation that characterises these particular professional areas – which might suggest the existence of researchers isolated from each other or otherwise segregated in small groups – the scientific communities show a high level of connectivity. Differences in the various scientific sectors do emerge from the study – with regard to the average number of collaborations, the clustering coefficient, and average distance – and yet the variations in the end are far from extensive. In all areas the vast majority of scientists are gathered into one 'giant component', within which distances are relatively limited. With regard to the two major archives (LANL and MEDLINE), it takes on average only four or five intermediaries to get in touch with any other component of the scientific community. In other words, each researcher can be reached by means of fairly short *chains of scientific collaboration*. Similar results were also achieved in the fields of mathematics and economics. In the former case, articles published jointly by more than 71,000 researchers between 1991–98 were analysed (Barabási 2002); while the latter involved articles co-published by more than 160,000 economists between 1970–2000 (Goyal *et al.* 2006). In all cases the various scientific communities present themselves as one small-world.

The same reasoning applies to a different type of affiliation network, one often studied in the field of economic sociology: *interlocking directorates*. The intersecting presence of managers on the boards of directors of different firms – something that has characterised American capitalism since the beginning of the twentieth century (Mizruchi 1982) – has been studied to analyse the coordinating modalities of economic activities in both manufacturing companies and financial and credit bodies. Cross-shareholding and positions, and mechanisms of co-optation and interpersonal relationships between corporate executives (managers or other representatives), constitute modes of regulation of company relationships – which go far beyond the rules of the market (Chiesi 1978, 1982; Burt 1979, 1983; Mintz and Schwartz 1985; Scott 1986; Mizruchi 1996).

Co-presence on the same board, for example, is a circulation channel of the changes introduced in organisational structures, managerial practices and business strategies – thus fostering innovation based both on contamination between different ideas and organisational isomorphism: the diffusion-imitation of the same innovations. In this respect, it represents a powerful coordination and transformation mechanism for large American companies. But how does this mechanism work? Is it an intentionally planned or spontaneous kind of phenomenon? Which actors and which institutions play a central role?

Studies conducted on the largest companies in the US across different historical periods – from the beginning of the twentieth century until the seventies – show a strong concentration and interconnection of business structures. Corporate board interlock networks rendered each component of the American managerial élite reachable in just a few steps: between four and five, depending on the study (Davis *et al.* 2003, 302ff.). Moreover, at least until the beginning of the eighties, the country's major commercial banks (such as J. P. Morgan and Chase Manhattan, which then merged in 2000) played a central role in the connectivity of this *corporate élite* (Mintz and Schwartz 1985). Given the need to monitor the companies they were financing, banks packed their own boards of directors with managers from the major companies dotted around the country. This tended to create reciprocal synergies: the banks obtained crucial knowledge about the strength and strategies of the companies (their clients), thus guaranteeing their investments; while managers were assured privileged access to the credit system and could influence decision-making. For several decades, there-fore, commercial banks represented the 'stable core of the interlock network' (Davis *et al.* 2003, 309).

After the eighties, however, this world of stability began to crumble: banks progressively lost their central role as the panorama of the major American com-panies went through changes. With the growth of internationalisation, the cri-teria for recruitment and management practices of the élite were also modified: mechanisms of corporate governance were increasingly directed towards share-holders. With the emergence of so-called *shareholder capitalism*, the boards of directors grew smaller in size (on average), thus becoming less interconnected with each other and comprising a smaller number of internal managers. Man-agers were paid in company shares and subjected to greater demands (including monitoring by institutional investors): the increased responsibilities associated with these tasks made it less possible for them to serve contemporaneously on an array of boards.

How, then, following these developments, did the integration of the American business élite, and the connectivity ensured by interlocking directorates, change? To answer these questions, three University of Michigan sociologists studied the composition of the boards of major American companies in the industrial, finan-cial, services and communications sectors, across three distinct phases: 1982, 1990 and 1999 (Davis *et al.* 2003). The hypothesis they intended to test – using the Watts and Strogatz method – was the presence of small-world networks: in other words, the presence of (1) small worlds highly integrated at a local level, but also (2) well-interconnected to each other. The results of the analysis showed that despite all the changes that had occurred in corporate governance, both at the beginning and at the end of the three periods analysed, the American business élite (which ranged from between 5,300 to 6,500 people) was in effect a small-world, combining high levels of local integration and low mutual distance.[23]

This was the case despite the great demographic change recorded during the three periods. In fact, less than one-third of the companies present in 1999 were also present in 1982. For managers, this presence fell to 5 per cent, and for rela-tionships between companies to 2 per cent. Even the ten central companies in the network were different.[24] In 1982, nine were commercial banks, but in the nine-ties their presence was reduced to three.

This data shows that the overall morphology of the network and its properties do not depend on specific managers or companies, or on the continuity of inter-organisational ties or the type of institutions that are at the centre (as, for instance, commercial banks). The high level of integration of the American busi-ness élite is an emergent property of the (small-world) network, which does not require any particular intentional design, or any centralised planning authority or group that facilitates coordination among the actors (ibid., 313). Network con-nectivity is especially stable over time, surviving even if certain principal nodes are lost. The authors, in fact, show that even by removing the central actors, the overall connectivity of the network is not weakened and the average distances do not grow to any great extent.

The same results also emerge in the analysis carried out by Bruce Kogut and Gordon Walker (2001) into shareholding and acquisitions by major German companies between 1993–97. The research highlights the particular stability (and German nationality) of the ownership structure, despite the ongoing processes of globalisation. Small-world networks, therefore, are particularly robust and resistant to change, and this attribute does not depend on the existence of specific hubs – as indicated in the scale-invariant networks highlighted by Barabási – but rather on the overall properties of the network. In this case, moreover, what is worth emphasising is that given the frequency of relations between the components of the business élite – many of whom meet at board meetings every month – interlocking directorates represent a particularly relevant mechanism of diffusion of innovation (Davis *et al.* 2003, 322).

4.6 The musicals industry

What is the relationship between small-world networks and innovative capacity? This is an issue addressed by Brian Uzzi and Jarrett Spiro (2005) in their study of the world of artistic creativity. The idea they take as their point of departure is that creativity and innovation are stimulated by a combination of different ideas, or by contamination between various artistic fields. Creative tension, moreover, derives not from the solitary efforts of lone individuals but from a system of social relations. The question that the two authors ask is whether the dual characteristic of small-world networks – that is, the fact of being highly clustered at a local level, but also strongly connected globally – does or does not influence creative performance. As they rightly point out, reflection on this kind of network is mostly limited to the classification of events, or to verify if it is traceable in the real world. Few studies correlate the structural properties of these networks with their performance.

Networks affect the behaviour of actors, influencing the connection and cohesion of their 'relational world'. In this respect, the high level of connectivity of small-world networks makes it possible to establish contact between a larger number of subjects, allowing information to circulate through the various clusters of relationships. Cohesion, however, creates a basis for trust and reputation, so that material coming from a particular cluster acquires credibility and value in different environments. Uzzi and Spiro tested these hypotheses starting with the Broadway musical industry. The data examined included information on more than 2,000 people who worked on 474 original musicals produced between 1945–89. The core team of a musical is made up of six figures: composer, lyricist, librettist (who writes the plot of the story), choreographer, director (who facilitates collaboration between the team members) and producer (who guarantees financial backing). Their collaboration begins when one or more of the artists create new material and involve others in the team. Intense group work is thus initiated – fusional in nature – which requires the sharing of ideas and the resolution of common problems. This teamwork generates great emotional and creative tension, which tends to cement strong collective ties (and here it is worth recalling Durkheim's remarks on 'collective effervescence', mentioned in Chapter 1). Once completed, if the musical manages to pass the test of the preview shows, then it is launched to market as a 'Broadway musical'. Commercial success is defined by takings at the box office, while artistic worth is determined by the judgement of the critics. Success is due in large measure to the originality of the new product, which, in turn, depends on two factors: the accessibility and diversity of the artistic material available to the team, and the perception that the new experimentations do not carry excessive risk. Both of these factors increase the creativity of artists and the chance of producing a 'hit' musical.

The creative material is rooted in conventions that provide the rules around which artists can fruitfully collaborate, while also allowing them to predict the reactions of the public and the critics. Original artists are able to tailor such conventions to their own requirements – creating a personal style and introducing innovations which, once they have become popular and imitated, themselves become part of the conventional artistic fabric. Innovation depends on the availability of the 'uncommon' creative materials that arise from collaborations with other artists. This new material expands the range of creative opportunities: it generates a reservoir of possible variations from which the team can draw to develop their own original product. A successful show is based on a combination of convention and innovative material. Without the first – shared standards – the product would be incomprehensible; while without the latter it would be boring and repetitive.

Groups of artists who collaborate closely and repeatedly with one another over time (local clusters) share the same artistic repertoire. In contrast, the bridge-links that are established between different clusters – by virtue of the relationships between certain artists – produce a double positive effect: on the one hand making it possible for a variety of conventions to come into contact, and on the other facilitating the validation of new material. The reputation of the new artists – made familiar through previous collaborations or through third parties – mitigates any risk associated with the testing of unfamiliar artistic material. Small-world networks constitute an ideal environment for this particularly felicitous union to be achieved: i.e. high levels of local cluster integration and low reciprocal distance. To illustrate the conformation of the Broadway musical network at different times, Uzzi and Spiro developed a *small-world quotient* (Q) whose values increased with the network's increasing connectivity and cohesion.[25] In bipartite affiliation networks – such as the musical team – the small-world effect influences actors through two distinct mechanisms: (1) *structurally*, through the relationships between the various clusters that facilitate the circulation of non-redundant information; and (2) *relationally*, through the cohesion-increasing links between actors. The effect induced by small-world networks, in fact, is not only to create bridge-links in order to overcome structural holes, but also to generate the necessary confidence so that innovators will take on the risks posed by new experimentations.

What Uzzi and Spiro succeeded in demonstrating empirically was that, as the mix of local cohesion and global connectivity changed, so creative performance changed as well. The relationship identified was not, however, a linear one: instead, it followed an inverted U function. Low values of Q (*small-world quotient*) were associated with poor performance, since weak network connectivity was not able to foster the circulation and validation of creative material. With higher Q values, the performance of the creative team and the success of the show improved, but only up to a certain threshold: above this, the performance tended to deteriorate again. Too high a level of global network connectivity and cohesion, in fact, tended to result in an excessive reduction of differences, thereby standardising conventions. In other words, Q values that were either too low or too high generated opposite problems: on the one hand an *excess of variety* in artistic products on the network (which did not circulate or were unusable); on the other, an *excess of homogeneity* (which reduced the range of variations available).

The best results, therefore, were at intermediate levels of the small-world quotient. A similar argument had already been made by Uzzi while analysing embeddedness effects on the performance of companies in the clothing and credit industries. Uzzi (1999, 500) placed particular emphasis on the importance of *network complementarity*: i.e. the need to mix socially rooted economic relations (*embedded ties*), with market relations (*arm's length ties*). This allowed companies to balance two types of benefit. The first type of tie prevented opportunistic behaviour and facilitated complex and reliable knowledge. The second type favoured the acquisition of new information and adaptation to stimuli coming from the market and the environment. For these reasons, companies that use a mix of both ties (*integrated networks*) perform better than those who only use market relationships (*under-embedded networks*) or economic relations that are overly influenced by personal ties (*over-embedded networks*) (Uzzi 1997, 59–60).

4.7 Strategic alliances and patent partnerships

In recent years, research on small-world networks has been extended to a number of economic phenomena. The presence of these networks has been reported in various areas of activity: agreements between investment banks (Baum *et al.* 2003); collaborations between companies in the fields of research and technology transfer (Verspagen and Duysters 2004; Schilling and Phelps 2007); and partnerships between inventors (Fleming *et al.* 2007). Several studies have emphasised their efficiency in terms of information flow, as well as the transfer and increase in level of knowledge (Cowan and Jonard 2003, 516 and 525; Verspagen and Duysters 2004, 570). In particular, small-world networks appear to positively influence the innovative capacity of companies through mechanisms similar to those identified for the artists of the Broadway musical. This is what emerges from a study conducted by Melissa Schilling and Corey Phelps (2007) on strategic alliances formed in the period 1990–2000 by more than 1,000 US firms operating in 11 high-tech sectors. Strategic alliances are widely regarded as an effective mechanism for knowledge-sharing between different organisations, and for facilitatating the production of innovative solutions (Freeman 1991; Gulati 1998; Powell, Koput and Smith-Doerr 1996). Schilling and Phelps conceptualise innovation as a recombinatory problem-solving process: the search for new solutions is often based on a creative combination of elements that are already partially known. In this respect, small-world networks delineate a favourable structure of innovative opportunity. High levels of local clustering do, in fact, improve the *capacity for information transmission* between companies, as well as generating the conditions of trust for knowledge-sharing and joint research into solutions. The presence, however, of *bridging ties* (which combine several local clusters), facilitates the circulation of non-redundant information between the various clusters, thus expanding the range of recombination possibilities available to the companies.

Research data confirms the hypothesis. First, strategic alliances are strongly clustered: companies tend to ally themselves with other companies which are in turn united by cooperation agreements. Moreover, in industrial areas where low distances exist between clusters – that is, where there is a small-world effect– the innovative capacity of the companies increases (when measured by the production of new patents in the years following the alliance).[26] In other words, Schilling and Phelps highlight the influence of the overall structure of the network present in various industrial sectors on the performance of individual companies.

The same effects are identified (by other scholars) in partnerships between inventors. Research work carried out in small teams fosters trust, as well as the sharing of ideas and a collective approach to problem-solving that enhances researcher creativity – especially in the development and diffusion phases of inventions. Excessive cohesion in such teams, on the other hand, hinders the circulation of non-redundant knowledge and the production of original ideas, and instead favours group conformity (*groupthink*).[27] Bridging ties avoid the problem, however – improving the inventors' *generative creativity* (Fleming *et al.* 2007, 458). At an individual level, therefore, small-world networks induce a 'virtuous and self-reinforcing cycle of creativity' (Fleming and Marx 2006, 11).

At a more aggregated, meso-style, level of analysis, the relationship is rather less evident. Lee Fleming, Charles King and Adam Juda (2007) find weak empirical support for the hypothesis of the positive influence of small-world networks on patent innovation at a regional level. The three academics analysed the collaborations between more than two million US inventors in the period 1975–2002, and from this data reconstructed the patent partnerships in 337 metropolitan areas.[28] The results of the analysis revealed a progressive 'narrowing' of the networks: a growing trend towards the aggregation of regional networks of inventors which increasingly took on a small-world configuration. As already mentioned, the inventors work in small, highly integrated research teams and this does not significantly change during the periods analysed in the study – the average level of local cluster cohesion remains fairly unaltered. Instead, what *does* change is global network connectivity: the average distances, in fact, decrease over time, and a growing percentage of inventors is included in the 'main component' of the regional network.[29] This is due to the growth of professional mobility and inter-organisational alliances, as well as the continuity of relationships between inventors who have worked together on the same patents. In particular, diachronic analysis shows the full development of a small-world network – first in Silicon Valley, and then in the Boston area (ibid.; Fleming *et al.* 2004). The analysis conducted in the 300 metropolitan areas, however, shows no statistically significant relationship between the small-world structure of collaborations between inventors and patent productivity at a regional level. What does tend to influence innovative activity is the network's degree of connectivity and the size of its main component: in other words, the reduction of the distances between the inventors, and their increasing integration into a fully connected regional network (Fleming *et al.* 2007, 949–51).

4.8 The Silicon Valley hubs

The new science of networks – often referred to as *complex network theory* – was also used by Michel Ferrary and Mark Granovetter (2009) to analyse a particularly well-known innovative cluster: Silicon Valley. The two scholars make a distinction between this type of cluster and the industrial type, characterised mainly by an incremental form of innovation within the prevalent specialisation. Innovative clusters, in contrast, are notable for their ability to radically reconfigure their value chain through *breakthrough innovation* that creates new industrial sectors (ibid., 328). In particular, the competitive advantage of these clusters lies in the continuous generation of cutting-edge start-ups. Innovation, however, is not produced by individual companies but by the entire local system: it derives from the interaction of a variety of actors rooted in a complex network of social relations. For these reasons, Ferrary and Granovetter believe that the new science of networks can make a significant contribution to the analysis of innovative clusters.

Complex networks possess certain distinctive features. First, they are composed of a plurality of nodes that interact without any form of hierarchical coordination. Second, the relational structure and the emerging modalities of coordination influence the efficiency of the actors. Their performance does not depend solely on individually possessed resources and skills but also on their modes of interaction with their surrounding environment. There exists, in other words, a systemic interdependence between the nodes and the network, and the survival capacity of both depends on the variety of the first and the connectivity of the second. Another distinctive feature of complex networks is their robustness – their resistance to external perturbations. Robustness does not mean the stability of the network, but rather its ability to reconfigure itself in the face of radical challenges that threaten its survival. This resistance comes from the *completeness* of the network, within which, in a decentralised manner, a plurality of heterogeneous actors interact: this makes it possible to integrate different modes of learning, stimulating the creativity and innovation of the system.

Ferrary and Granovetter present Silicon Valley as a paradigmatic case of an innovative cluster based on a complex network. It is a territory, in fact, where a wide range of socio-economic actors interact: not just businesses, universities and research laboratories, but also law and consultancy firms, investment and commercial banks, finance companies, service and recruitment agencies, and so forth. A dense network of relationships is formed, in which organisational and economic links are mixed with personal and social relations (*multiplex ties*). The innovative dynamism of this area also depends on the *completeness* of its network, which includes heterogeneous but complementary actors.

According to Ferrary and Granovetter, other areas with significant innovative resources under-perform due to the inferior completeness of their networks. Silicon Valley itself was formed historically through successive layers, with the addition of a variety of actors who have strengthened the relationship system. The presence of a prestigious university such as Stanford, the emergence of companies like Hewlett Packard, and the arrival of large external companies such as General Electric, IBM and Lockheed during the thirties, were not sufficient in themselves to render this area highly innovative. Only later, in fact, were other essential pieces of the puzzle added: private research laboratories (Stanford Research Institute in 1946 and Xerox PARC in 1970); the first investment banks in the late sixties; the birth of the large venture capital companies in the seventies; and the development of firms specialising in legal assistance to high-tech companies in the eighties. Only in the late fifties and early sixties, with the birth of the semiconductor industry, did Silicon Valley become an innovative cluster – something that would continue to evolve and grow with the completion of its network. The complexity of the network gives the system its special ability to alter organisational architecture and areas of specialisation through major innovation. The area, in fact, was given its initial boost through semiconductors (with companies such as Fairchild Semi-conductor, Intel etc.) but subsequently went on to specialise in personal computers (Apple), software (Oracle, Sun Microsystems, Symantec, etc.), telecommunication systems (Cisco System, Jupiter Networks, 3Com), and the internet (Netscape, Excite, eBay, Yahoo!, Google).

As we have seen, certain actors in complex networks can play the role of a hub (Barabási 2002). In Silicon Valley, venture capital firms (VCs) fulfil this function, investing venture capital in the most promising local start-ups. This strong VC presence distinguishes this area from many other technological districts. In 2006, 180 of the USA's 650 VCs had their headquarters in Silicon Valley. Between 1995–2005, investments directed towards the Californian VC cluster amounted to about one-third of the total of those made in the US and Europe.

The presence of these investment companies improves the innovative capacity and the overall robustness of Silicon Valley, and carries out five specific functions. The first, and most famous, is the *financing* of technological start-ups. The second is *selecting* them. The VCs fund a small part of the Valley's start-ups – about 9 per cent of the more than 2,000 new companies that are created every year. However, almost all of those that have been successful have received support from the VC: in 2006 as many as 28 of the 30 largest high-tech companies in the area fell within this category. The VCs' high level of competence in the leading sectors of the Californian cluster allows them to identify the most promising entrepreneurial projects, fostering their survival before market mechanisms come into operation. This links to the third function, which is that of *signalling* the best start-up: the fact of being funded by a VC, especially one of the more established ones, produces a ripple effect of accreditation in relation to other actors in the system – which in turn facilitates the subsequent development of new businesses. The fourth function is the *embedding* of new companies – the activation of the VCs' own relationships in order to facilitate the entry of start-ups into the network as a whole. From this point of view, the VCs – by performing activities of integration and coordination in the regional network – are one of the main hubs of Silicon Valley. The fifth function, finally, concerns *collective learning* – the accumulation of entrepreneurial knowledge and experience that is made available to new businesses.

Concluding, the use of the new science of networks allows Ferrary and Granovetter to focus on the interdependence between the performance of individual actors, and that of the overall network. As they point out, the theoretical contribution provided by their study is to highlight the relevance of the actors in the system. To explain the emergent properties of networks, complex network theory tends to focus on the structure of the links rather than on the nature of the nodes. As we have already observed, however, in social networks the identity of the actors is important. In Silicon Valley, for example, the specific characteristics of the VC determine their centrality in the network and condition the performance of the entire system. This, by implication, also draws attention to the role of the institutional and regulatory systems within which the actors operate. The modalities of the regulation of the financial market and of the contractual relations present in the US, together with the specific cultural climate of Silicon

---

Box 4 Self-study prompts

1 What is meant by the small-world phenomenon?
2 How were Stanley Milgram's experiments conducted and what did they show?
3 What are the essential characteristics of the small-world networks analysed by Watts and Strogatz?
4 What are scale-invariant networks and what role do the hubs play?
5 Is it possible to apply a sociological approach to the study of complex networks?
6 What is shown by empirical research on affiliation networks?
7 Do small worlds of creativity and innovation exist? What examples can be found in scientific research?
8 What role is played by venture capital firms in Silicon Valley?

Valley, are essential ingredients for an understanding not only of the identity of the actors but also of the modes in which they interact. This consideration therefore paves the way for the empirical and comparative analysis of complex networks, taking into greater account not only the actors and their ability to intentionally manipulate the networks, but also the role of institutions in shaping the context of interaction. While this research perspective inevitably introduces greater elements of contingency into the theory of complex networks, it also opens up more space to the contribution of the new economic sociology and comparative political economy.

Notes

1 This same idea – slightly modified – was divulged to a far larger audience by John Guare's play *Six Degrees of Separation*, which was then made into the eponymous film directed by Fred Schepisi. One of the play's characters comes out with the statement that has popularised the phenomenon: 'I read somewhere that everybody on this planet is separated by only six other people. Six degrees of separation. Between us and everybody else on this planet. The president of the United States. A gondolier in Venice. Fill in the names.... It's not just big names. It's anyone. A native in a rain forest. A Tierra del Fuegan. An Eskimo.... How every person is a new door, opening up into other worlds. Six degrees of separation between me and everyone else on this planet' (Guare 1994).
2 For a definition of the cluster concept in terms of graph theory, see note 11 below.
3 According to the classical definition of probability, the chance of an event, X, occurring (e.g. that two UK citizens chosen at random will know each other) is given by the ratio between the number of favourable cases (the average number of acquaintances, which we have arbitrarily set as 1,000) and the number of possible cases (64 million inhabitants) – provided that all the latter are equiprobable. With the number of favourable cases defined as n, and N the number of possible cases, the probability of X is the following: $P(X) = n/N = 1{,}000/64{,}000{,}000 = 1/64{,}000$.
4 Even drastically reducing the average number of acquaintances – to 100 units, for example – does not change the result much: three intermediaries are required to reach any UK citizen, rising to four to reach any inhabitant of the earth.
5 The data was collected by Michael Gurevitch as part of his PhD thesis (1961).
6 In statistics, the median represents the value that occupies the middle position in the orderly distribution of the values of a variable. In other words, it is the value that divides the frequency distribution in half. The mode, on the other hand, is the value with the maximum frequency of occurrence.
7 In computer networks, a hub is a device that operates as the sorting node of a data communication network. Think of the airport structure of a country or continent, where many small airports are linked to a few large airports (hubs) from which aircraft fly all over the world. Through simple local flights, from a small airport to a large regional hub, the inhabitants of any provincial city can move around on a global scale, with one or more simple changes.
8 Outside the experimental context, the small-world hypothesis has also recently been tested using Messenger, the instant messaging system from Microsoft. The dataset realised (30 billion conversations between 240 million people) made it possible to analyse a massive social network made up of 180 million nodes and 1.3 billion links. One of the results of the analysis was that the average length of paths between individual Messenger users was 6.6 (Leskovec and Horvitz 2007).
9 For an introduction to the concepts and terminology of graph theory and its applications to social networks, see Chiesi (1999) and Wasserman and Faust (1994).

10 In graph theory, the degree of node A is given by A's number of links with other nodes. In a graph composed, say, of a number of nodes (n) equal to 10, its value can fluctuate between 0, in the case of an isolated node – and 9 ($n-1$), in the case of a node connected to all the others.

11 This term is used as it is in physics (Watts 2004b, 244, note 1) – in other words, as a crystalline lattice whose constitutive components (atoms, etc.) possess a geometrically regular arrangement in all three spatial dimensions.

12 A cluster can be defined as an area of the graph with a relatively high density (Scott 1991). The density, in turn, is given by the proportion of effective links (k) with respect to the maximum number of links possible, given the numerosity (n) of the nodes. The number of possible links is calculated as follows: $n*(n-1)/2$. The formula for the calculation of density, therefore, is as follows: $k/(n*(n-1)/2)$. The values range between 0 (all nodes are isolated) and 1 (all nodes are linked).

13 A *walk* 'is a sequence of nodes and lines, starting and ending with nodes, in which each node is incident with the lines following and preceding it in the sequence'. Its length is given by the number of lines of which it is composed. A *path* 'is a walk in which all nodes and all lines are distinct'; that is, where the same nodes and lines can appear only once within a sequence. The geodesic distance is the shortest path between two nodes (Wasserman and Faust 1994, pos. 2976 ff.; Chiesi 1999, 87–8).

14 In formal terms, L (p) represents the average geodesic distance between all nodes, while the coefficient C (p) represents the average density of relationships between neighbouring nodes at each point of the graph.

15 According to Thomson Reuters' *Essential Science Indicators*, Barabási and Albert's article in *Science* was, in 2008, the fifth most cited in the field of physics. Between the year of its publication and 2009, the item received 4,363 citations (source: ISI Web of Science). The article in *Nature*, however, peaked at 1,076. By comparison, and in the same period, the article by Watts and Strogatz received 4,082 citations.

16 This is what computer scientists call a crawler (or 'spider' or robot/'bot'): a program that is able to perform automatic and recursive searches on the contents of a network. The software is similar to that used by search engines (Google, Yahoo!, Live Search, Ask.com, etc.) to explore the web.

17 The formula used is as follows: $d = 0.35 + 2.06 \log (N)$.

18 I use the term 'contingent' with reference to events whose occurrence does not depend on a fixed and necessary causal connection, but rather is related to certain situations and circumstances.

19 If the program could draw on the 'global knowledge' of all the connections present in the network, the shortest chain would very easily be discovered.

20 Duncan J. Watts recently carried out a survey on the principle of homophily from data collected on more than 30,000 students at a large American university and their email exchanges (Kossinets and Watts 2009). The study focuses on the formation of ties between students, with two factors kept distinct: the effects arising from 'choice homophily' – connected to individual preference – and those arising from 'induced homophily', which derives from the structural opportunity for interaction – connected simply to living in the same neighbourhood, working in the same organisation, attending the same school, etc. Regarding this distinction, see also McPherson and Smith-Lovin (1987, 371).

21 On this theme, from an organisational perspective, see the study carried out by Peter Sheridan Dodds, Duncan J. Watts and Charles F. Sabel (2003).

22 For an introduction to affiliation networks, see Wasserman and Faust (1994, Chapter 8).

23 The average geodesic distance remains stable across all three periods and is fairly limited: for companies, it is around 3.4, and for managers, 4.3.

24 These are the ten companies that in over the three periods demonstrate the highest values of 'betweenness centrality' – defined as the number of times a node appears in

the shortest geodesic distance between all possible pairs of network nodes (Wasserman and Faust 1997; Davis *et al.* 2003, 318).

25 Simplifying slightly, it can be said that the lower the geodesic distances between the actors, and the greater the density of the network, the more the small-world quotient increases. The latter takes the form of a ratio of ratios: CC_{ratio}/PL_{ratio}. The denominator shows the average length of the path (PL) or the average number of intermediaries between all the pairs of actors in the network. The numerator shows the clustering coefficient (CC), which measures the average fraction of the collaborators of an actor who in turn collaborate with one another. Following the model suggested by Watts (1999) – and as modified by Newman, Strogatz and Watts (2001) to adapt it to bipartite affiliation networks – the values of these two network parameters are compared to those of a random graph of the same size. PL_{ratio} values close to 1 indicate low levels of separation between the global network actors. CC_{ratio} values greater than 1 indicate two things: (1) that an increasing number of links connect the various teams to one another (*between-team clustering*); (2) that these cross-team links are increasingly composed of artists who have collaborated in the past or who have mutual acquaintances.

26 Patents are considered a strong indicator – albeit proxy in nature – of the generation of inventions and new knowledge (Basberg 1987; Trajtenberg 1987).

27 The term *groupthink* was used by social psychologist Irving Janis (1972, 9) with reference to the making of wrong collective decisions due to the presence of group dynamics that reduce individual capacity for reasoning and problem analysis. The term refers to the way of thinking prevalent within a strongly cohesive *ingroup*: a closed and homogeneous collective composed of subjects with the same background and isolated from outside opinions. In such a context the tendency to maintain consensus and avoid conflict with the other members of the group leads to the ignoring of differences of opinion and a lack of evaluation of alternative courses of action.

28 A unit of statistical measurement used in the US, which refers to metropolitan labour markets. The *metropolitan statistical areas* include high levels of population, distributed throughout several urban centres that revolve around a big city and have high levels of social and economic integration.

29 The main component of a disconnected graph indicates the largest sub-graph: the part of the overall graph that includes the greatest number of nodes connected to one another.

5   Innovation systems

This chapter examines a series of contributions that share a systemic-relational approach to the study of innovation: a perspective based on the relationships between a plurality of actors and institutions, both economic and otherwise. After a presentation of the conditions that lead to the emergence of the approach, the chapter reviews the features of different, but complementary, innovation systems – national, sectoral and technological. Finally, there is a discussion of the triple helix model, focused on the interactions between three distinct institutional spheres: university, industry and government.

5.1 An integrated approach

From the second half of the eighties, more integrated analytical perspectives began to appear in Innovation Studies. Despite substantial differences, certain basic elements are common to these 'new' approaches to innovation. First, the generalisation of the idea that knowledge is one of the key drivers of development (*knowledge economy*) and that learning processes are therefore essential to increase the competitiveness of companies, regions and nations (*learning economy*). Second, the definitive abandonment of a strictly economistic view of innovation, with the realisation that: (1) innovation requires the contribution of a heterogeneous plurality of actors, both economic and otherwise (companies, universities, governments, etc.); and (2) *institutions* play an important role in shaping the context in which these actors operate. Third, the recognition that these processes are inherently social and relational in character, and for this reason the production and dissemination of knowledge and innovation are embedded in networks of relationships between people and between organisations. Finally, all the approaches assume a *systemic perspective*: innovation, in other words, is interpreted as an emergent – only partially intentional – property of a system of elements and relations, with results that, for the actors involved, may be desired or involuntary, positive or negative. In brief, the idea that real *innovation systems* exist constitutes the lowest common denominator of the theoretical and empirical contributions that will be presented in this chapter.

5.2 Assumptions

The systemic approaches that have developed over the last 25 years have made use of much of the research work carried out in previous decades on innovation and factors of competitiveness at the micro (company), meso (sectoral and regional) and macro (national and international) levels. Their formulation is also a response to the emergence of certain economic phenomena, which demonstrate the increasingly complex and interactive character of innovation processes.

The *first of these phenomena* concerns the change which has occurred in the models of production (micro level) and regulation of the economy (meso and macro levels). With the crisis of Fordism, in fact, companies experiment with alternative models of production organisation that, on the one hand, show the increasingly relational character of the economy (Trigilia 2007b); and, on the other hand, the importance of the socio-institutional context and its territorial articulation. For example, studies on the industrial districts and regions of the 'Third Italy' (Becattini 1975, 2000; Bagnasco 1977, 1988; Paci 1980; Trigilia 1986) demonstrate the existence of an alternative development model to Fordism, one that is characterised by flexible specialisation (Piore and Sabel 1984) and is based on local systems of small- and medium-sized companies operating in traditional industries and linked to each other by specialised division of labour. The small business areas – and in particular the 'industrial districts'[1] – show how production efficiency and competitiveness are based on the social construction of the market. Studying them, therefore, requires a complex, interdisciplinary analytical approach, that takes into account the history of the territories as well as the existence of a plurality of actors and of modes of regulation. This approach, initially used to study the traditional manufacturing sectors, based on a diffuse, incremental kind of innovation (Bellandi 1989), subsequently also proved to be useful for understanding the processes of radical innovation, such as those taking place in Silicon Valley (Saxenian 1994).

The *second phenomenon* is the development of high-tech sectors, something that highlights a growing 'scientification' process in relation to technology (Carlsson and Stankiewicz 1991, 112). This is particularly evident in the so-called *science-based* sectors; that is, in the industries that make most use of knowledge coming from the scientific community (biotechnology, pharmaceuticals, etc.). In the US, for example, in just a few years there was an exponential growth in the number of patents that based their findings on scientific research financed with public funds. Patents citing publications of this type tripled in the space of five years, rising from 17,000 in 1987–88 to about 50,000 in 1993–94, and three-quarters of these refer to articles or papers produced by universities or other public research centres (Narin *et al.* 1997). This trend is concentrated in specific scientific-technological fields, especially in biomedical and clinical research: in 1988, scientific articles cited in American industrial patents from these disciplines accounted for about 54 per cent of the total, while in 1996 this figure rose to 73 per cent (OECD 1999, 16).

A *third phenomenon* is the growth of inter-company partnerships – especially in the field of R&D, due to the increasingly diverse and interdependent nature of the specialised knowledge necessary for innovation.[2] And, last, a *fourth phenomenon* is related to economic globalisation and the consequent reorientation of public policies. The emergence of new international competition from recently industrialised countries makes it clear that: (1) innovation is the winning strategy to compete with countries with low labour costs; (2) the role of public policies is crucial to support innovation; and (3) the policies must, however, be rethought within a more integrated and systemic framework (OECD 2005).

In short, all of these phenomena prompt a reconsideration of innovation in the light of the fact that the production of goods and services is becoming increasingly *knowledge-intensive* and involves a plurality of actors and institutions. The new approach of *innovation systems* is designed to respond to this requirement. The contributions presented in this chapter do not amount to a formal theory, in the sense of a shared, coherent set of concepts and propositions regarding precise relationships between variables. Rather, they develop an analytical and conceptual framework that guides the analysis towards one single object of research, albeit articulated on different levels. To employ an expression utilised by Lundvall (1992a, 1) in the introduction to his book on *National Systems of Innovation*, innovation systems represent a *focusing device* that places interactive learning and innovation at the centre of analysis. It is, in the words of Nelson and Winter (1982), an '*appreciative theorising*' that 'tends to be close to empirical work and provides both interpretation and guidance for further exploration' (Nelson 1998, 500). Analytical reasoning, in other words, which provides abstract causal models that are, however, empirically grounded and historically friendly; models which, to sociologists, will be reminiscent of Merton's middle-range theories and Weber's ideal-types.

As we shall see, there are certain shared assumptions that underlie these systemic approaches. But there are also differences that should not be overlooked, starting from those relating to the foundational dimensions of innovation systems. The latter, in fact, were defined by using *spatial/geographical criteria*, distinguishing between national, regional and local systems; or by using *industrial-technological criteria*, classifying them according to production or technological sectors; or, finally, by identifying them on the basis of the *types of actors and relationships* (as in the case of the triple helix model). In the next section, national systems and then other models will be analysed – with the exception of regional and local systems, which will be discussed in Chapter 6, which is dedicated to the territorial dimension of innovation.

5.3 National systems

The first formulations that refer to *national innovation systems (NIS)* appeared in the eighties in the work of some of the most important IS scholars. The term is used for the first time in an unpublished document written by Charles Freeman for the OECD, in which the English academic stresses the importance of an active role for governments in promoting technological infrastructure to support economic development (Johnson *et al.* 2003, 3). In the same period, other research groups underlined the need to take a variety of factors into account in order to understand innovation, while the idea of an innovation system appeared in an essay by Bengt-Åke Lundvall (1985). The term was then formalised in a study by Freeman (1987) on Japan, and a section was dedicated to NIS in a collective volume edited by some of the foremost experts on innovation (Dosi *et al.* 1988). Thereafter, in the nineties, certain important books came out that consecrated the relevance and centrality of the argument within IS (Lundvall 1992b; Nelson 1993; Edquist 1997).

In addition to the academic world, the concept became widespread throughout the political arena due to its use by certain international organisations. The OECD was the first to employ it in a series of studies and research that emphasised its potential to support innovation at both an analytical and political level. The concept was also accepted by the European Commission, the United Nations Conference on Trade and Development (UNCTAD), the Academy of Sciences of the United States and several other national governments (Lundvall *et al.* 2002). What can explain this success, amongst both scholars and policy-makers?

The first reason for such a positive reaction in the academic world is that it was an approach that developed a number of contributions made in previous years. These included the results of some important research, such as the Sappho investigation carried out by Freeman along with other SPRU (Science Policy Research Unit) colleagues – which highlighted the importance to innovation of long-term ties and relationships with actors external to the companies. Other research had emphasised the role of *non-market* relations in the transmission of knowledge and the role of the institutional context in regulating the economy, as was emerging from the first studies on Japan and on the 'variety of capitalisms' approach. In addition, the systemic approach was a confluence point for new reflections of a theoretical nature. A distancing was in fact taking place from neo-classical economics both at an analytical level, due to the lack of emphasis given to technological change in the explanation of economic growth, and at a political level, because of its neo-liberalist implications in terms of policy-making (Sharif 2006). The 'crisis' of the linear conception of innovation and the emergence of the evolutionary economy stimulated, therefore, the search for new conceptual coordinates. Innovation was placed at the centre of a new theory of development that integrated analysis of the *economic structure* and *institutional context*, both to explain the various trends and specialisations of advanced economies and to provide advice to national governments (Lundvall and Maskell 2000, 354).

This introduces the second reason for the rapid success of the new systemic approach. NIS established itself as a *policy concept*, as a useful idea to guide not only research but also public policies (Sharif 2006, 750). From the very beginning, in fact, NIS existed on the frontier between two communities – the scientific and the policy-making – by virtue of the role played by certain leading scholars in both fields (consider, for example, the involvement with the OECD of figures such as Freeman and Lundvall).

But what exactly are NIS? There are various definitions. For Nelson and Rosenberg the concept refers to 'a set of institutions whose interactions determine the innovative performance ... of national firms' (1993, 4; Nelson 1993, 349). Lundvall indicates the 'elements and relationships which interact in the production, diffusion and use of new, and economically useful, knowledge ... and are either located within or rooted inside the borders of a nation state' (1992a, 2). Edquist, finally, believes that NIS include 'all important economic, social, political, organizational, institutional and other factors that influence the development, diffusion and use of innovation' (1997, 14). These, as can be seen, are definitions that differ in part, yet behind which there lie certain shared theoretical assumptions (Johnson *et al.* 2003).

1   The first assumption is that national economies present a variety of specialisations which regard productive, commercial and also cognitive structures. These productive and cognitive specialisations are interdependent and co-evolve in a path-dependent manner: they follow trajectories shaped by history and previous experience, slowly transforming themselves as a result not only of economic change but also of learning processes developed by the actors.

2   The second assumption is that knowledge is *sticky*: it does not circulate easily from one place to another, is 'embodied' in the minds and bodies of people, in routine business, and in interpersonal and inter-organisational relationships.

3   The third assumption is that individuals, companies and other organisations never innovate in complete isolation; and to study their relations an 'interactionist' perspective is needed.

4   The fourth assumption is that the (heterogeneous) plurality of actors and institutions involved in innovation processes requires an analytical approach of a holistic, interdisciplinary and historico-evolutionary kind.

For all these reasons, scholars who follow this particular line take a systemic approach and focus on the social and political, as well as economic aspects, looking carefully at the origins and transformations of the institutional context in which innovation occurs (Edquist 2005). A qualifying concept for this approach is *system*, which is seen as an interconnected set of elements that work towards a common goal (Carlsson *et al.* 2002, 234). A system essentially consists of two parts – components and relationships – and possesses different and distinct properties from those of its constituent elements (Edquist 2005, 187).

The *components of the system* are organisations and institutions (Figure 5.1). The former refers to the set of actors who act and interact in the system, the latter to the rules – both formal and informal – that guide action and regulate interaction. Edquist and Johnson provide a precise definition of these two concepts: '*Organizations* are formal structures that are consciously created and have

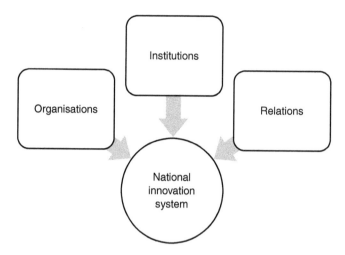

Figure 5.1 The national innovation system: a schematic representation.

an explicit purpose' (1997, 46). Examples are companies, universities, public and private research centres, credit agencies that finance innovation, government agencies that deal with research and innovation policies, and so on. '*Institutions* are sets of common habits, norms, routines, established practices, rules, or laws that regulate the relations and interactions between individuals, groups and organizations' (ibid.).[3] Examples are the laws on intellectual property rights (patents, trademarks, etc.), habits of cooperation and competition between companies, collaboration practices between companies and universities, the rules that govern scientific research, innovation funding, etc.

Relations, finally, refers to the relationships that link the various components of the system. This aspect therefore regards the ties that are created between organisations within a specific institutional context. As previously touched upon, the NIS approach places a strong emphasis on the interactive dimension, taking into consideration both market and non-market relations between the actors involved.

Defining the boundaries of the system is crucial in order to identify which components and relationships are taken into account. NIS studies adopt a geopolitical criterion of definition, employing nation states as units of analysis. This is for two reasons. The first lies in the awareness that there exist marked economic, political, social and cultural differences at a national level that affect the institutional and organisational configuration of the various innovation systems: the resources that they invest in scientific research; the prevailing specialisations; the methods of innovation and the results that are achieved. The second is that the policies that support – directly or indirectly – the innovative capacity of companies and territories are to a significant extent determined at state level. This does not mean to exclude other aspects of analysis involving different spatial scales (local, regional, international and global) nor to deny that other regulatory bodies (international institutions, supranational and sub-national governments, multinationals, etc.) play a major role, all the more so in an era of increasing globalisation (Lundvall 1992a, 13; Nelson 1992, 367–9; Nelson and Rosenberg 1993, 19–20; Edquist 1999, 2005; Lundvall *et al.* 2002, 215).

In recent years, attention has also been devoted to the functions and activities of innovation systems. The main *function* of NIS is to 'develop, diffuse and use innovations' (Edquist 2005, 190). The *activities* are carried out by various organisations and represent their specific contribution to innovation. No univocal relationship exists, however, between organisations and activities. Organisations can, in fact, carry out more than one activity: universities, for example – as we shall see later in our discussions of the triple helix model – can perform activities regarding human capital training, R&D, and innovation and development at the local level. Conversely, the same activity can be carried out by different organisations: for example, the training of human capital can be performed by the school and university system but also by companies and other public and private institutions.

On the basis of the various contributions that appeared in the international literature, Edquist (ibid., 190–1) developed a list of the ten main activities carried out by NIS:

1   to produce new *knowledge* through R&D;
2   to build *skills* for human capital through the school-university education system, vocational training, etc.;
3   to establish new *markets* for products;
4   to define *qualitative requirements* for new products based on the needs of the demand;
5   to create and modify *organisations* necessary for the development of new fields of innovation;
6   to generate (market and non-market) *networks* to facilitate the circulation of knowledge;
7   to create and modify *institutions* that are able to provide useful ties and incentives for innovation;
8   to carry out *incubation activities* in support of new initiatives;
9   to ensure *funding* for innovation;
10 to provide qualified *consultancy services* (technology transfer, commercial and legal information, etc.).

Many of these activities take on a different significance depending on the regional and sectoral systems considered, and are only partially created in an intentional manner: innovation systems evolve over time with little in the way of organised planning.

In the NIS approach, institutions play an important role and this creates an interesting area of discussion with comparative political economy; that is, with sociological and political science approaches of an institutional kind. Indeed, in contrast to what is observed with the mainstream, neo-classical economy, which tends to accept only one rule of behaviour – a maximising and utilitarian rationale – the NIS approach views history and institutional contexts as important in order to understand the concrete modalities of behaviour, interaction and learning of economic actors (Johnson *et al.* 2003, 5). That said, it should also be noted that there is no shared definition of this concept. Some authors, in fact, following Douglas North's suggestion (1990), differentiate sharply between *organisations* and *institutions*. Others, such as Nelson and Rosenberg (1993, 5; Nelson 1993, 351), do not employ this distinction and interchangeably make use of the terms 'institutions' and 'institutional actors' to include all the organisations involved in innovation.[4] They believe, in fact, that it is difficult to draw a clear boundary between the first and second, as it is to make a distinction between the rules and principles that establish patterns of behaviour and the behaviour itself (Nelson 2008, 4).

Further differences exist in the NIS approach. A second difference concerns the more or less broad definition which is given to the object of analysis. Some scholars – especially those hailing from the American tradition of scientific and technological studies – tend to adopt a rather narrow analytical focus, concentrating on R&D and related policies to identify the specialisations of national scientific and innovation systems. Other scholars, in contrast – especially those in Europe – take a broader perspective, giving importance not only to more formalised research activity, but also to forms of tacit knowledge and modalities of learning based on productive routines and interaction (Lundvall and Maskell 2000, 362). The former, in other words, focus on the principal organisations (companies, universities, etc.) that promote and disseminate scientific knowledge and innovation; while the latter believe that these activities should be seen in a wider context, since economic, political and cultural factors influence the intensity and the results of innovative activities (Freeman 2002, 194).

A third difference relates to the degree of theorisation required within this field of study. Here the line of distinction lies between those who discern a deficit of theory and the need for greater rigour in the definition and operationalisation of concepts (e.g. Charles Edquist, Jan Fagerberg and Stanley Metcalfe), and those who instead consider the theoretical and analytical flexibility of this approach to be an advantage (e.g. Maureen McKelvey, Richard Nelson and Keith Smith) (Sharif 2006, 757–9). Substantial traces of these differing perspectives can already be seen in two major works that appeared in the early nineties: Nelson's book (1993), in fact, is based on a comparison of different national cases and deals mainly with actors in scientific-technological innovation; Lundvall (1992b), on the other hand, assumes a broader focus and is more theoretically oriented.[5]

The book edited by Richard Nelson is a study of 15 national economies and is aimed at highlighting the similarities and differences in the institutions and mechanisms that support innovation (Nelson and Rosenberg 1993, 3). The cases examined include the most industrialised economies (US, Japan, Germany, France, Italy and Great Britain), several small high-income states (Denmark,

Sweden, Canada and Australia) and some newly industrialised countries (South Korea, Taiwan, Argentina, Brazil and Israel). The case studies, although carried out in a different manner, pay particular attention to R&D and its funding, focusing on three main actors: companies, universities and governments. The contribution offered by these institutions and the different combinations present in the various countries – that is, the different institutional mix – define the distinctive features of the national innovation systems and condition their performance.

A good example of this approach is represented by the analysis carried out on the *US innovation system* (Mowery 1992, 1998; Mowery and Rosenberg 1993). What are its distinctive features, compared to those of other industrialised countries?

- The matter of scale – following World War Two, and for several decades, the volume of American investment in R&D far exceeded that of all other advanced economies.
- The prominent role of small start-ups in the commercialisation of new technologies, especially in high-tech areas: microelectronics, computers, software, robotics and biotechnology.
- Two other distinctive traits have to do with the policies promoted by the US government.
- The impact of the antitrust law on the innovative performance of companies.
- The high incidence of federal government spending on R&D activities, with particular reference to those related to defence programmes.

It is worthwhile to look at the latter two aspects in more detail. As noted in Chapter 2, in the second half of the nineteenth century the innovative system present in the US was largely based on a combination of mechanical skills and manufacturing firms that placed little reliance on scientific knowledge. Towards the end of the century the birth of large-scale industrial research redefined the profile of the American innovative system. This was a change linked to the introduction of antitrust laws, which prohibited cartel agreements between competing companies: those agreements, in other words, aimed at exerting collusive control over prices and markets. Starting in 1895, these norms generated a strong wave of mergers, with the emergence of giant corporations that in turn gave rise to the first large industrial research laboratories: the strategy was to beat the competition by focusing on innovative discoveries. Throughout the whole of the next century, the more or less stringent application of the antitrust laws profoundly affected the innovation behaviour of companies – in particular, the propensity to invest directly in in-house research activities or to monitor the external market to buy patents and technologies from other companies (Mowery 1992, 127–8).

In the early eighties, for example, the relaxing of antitrust restrictions – in relation to cooperation between companies on research and innovation – resulted in a massive proliferation of inter-company agreements. This factor, along with other 'politico-regulative' interventions (such as the Bayh-Dole law on university patents and more vigorous action at an international level for the protection of intellectual property rights), accompanied and facilitated structural change in the American innovation system. The large industrial laboratories were severely reduced in size and a process of research outsourcing saw the growth of inter-company partnerships and relationships with universities, and a trend towards R&D internationalisation.

Another item of great interest is the variable role played by public spending in American history. The American system of innovation was long dominated by private industry and in the first half of the twentieth century the great laboratories of the chemical, oil and electrical companies dominated industrial research. In 1946 these three industries provided employment for about 26,000 engineers and scientists – representing roughly 70 per cent of the total number of people working in the research laboratories of manufacturing firms (Mowery 1992, 130, Table 1). Federal government funding for R&D was rather limited: in the thirties it ranged between 12 per cent and 20 per cent of the national total. In contrast, the industrial sector contributed about two-thirds of the total expenditure. More-over, state (rather than federal) funding of universities – encouraging the latter's sense of responsibility towards local communities – fostered an early intertwining of relationships between universities and businesses at a regional level. This was something that did not take place in Europe. Already in the first half of the twentieth century, then, the contribution of American universities to industrial research – through courses of study tailored to the needs of regional economies – was particularly relevant, as was their contribution to the technological per-formance of companies. And this was all despite the fact that there were few sci-entific fields in which the US excelled over Europe. To sum up, the pre-war system of innovation was guided and dominated by large private companies.

The post-war system, however, underwent radical change as a result of the Cold War and America's new role as a world superpower. The federal govern-ment began to take a central position in the financing of research, both in indus-try and the universities. During the fifties and sixties the share of federal funding amounted on average to 62 per cent of national expenditure on R&D (Figure 5.2). Much of the research, although being conducted by non-governmental lab-oratories, was related to military spending and national defence programmes (Mowery 1992, 136, Table 3; Mowery and Rosenberg 1993, 42, Table 2.4). This massive public commitment swept the US to world leadership in basic scientific research – a position which, as we have seen, it did not previously hold. Mean-while, a 'by-product' of these huge military commissions was the development of new technologies for civilian use in strategic sectors such as aerospace, semi-conductors, computers and software (Mowery 1998, 640). Only in recent decades has there been a reduction in federal research funding, with a sharp decline especially towards the end of the eighties (Figure 5.2). This, however, is in line with what happened in other developed OECD countries.

As an idea of this contraction, it is enough to say that in the seventies US federal spending on R&D still accounted for 53 per cent of the national total. In the eighties this slipped to 46 per cent, and then in the following two decades plunged to 34 per cent and 28 per cent (based on National Science Foundation

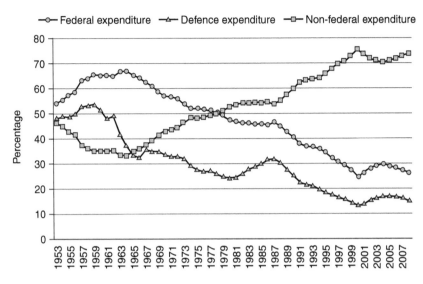

Figure 5.2 Share of federal public, non-federal and defence program expenditure in total US R&D funding (source: National Science Foundation, Division of Science Resources Statistics).

data). Much of this reduction was due to cuts in defence programmes. At the height of the Cold War, during the fifties, this sector alone funded more than 50 per cent of national research. This share progressively dwindled over the next few decades, to arrive at around 16 per cent in the twenty-first century.

The study carried out on the US clearly shows the analytical approach of the book edited by Nelson, heavily focused as it is on the contribution to R&D of the main actors in the system. This was not always intentional, as the example of the influence of the antitrust legislation shows. As we have seen, in some periods of American history this had the counterintuitive effect of stimulating the emergence of large corporations, which, through massive investment in research, managed to maintain a dominant position in the US innovation system for a long period of time. The comparison of national cases conducted by Richard Nelson and Nathan Rosenberg in the introduction to their book also prompts a reflection on the differences between the various national systems, which are stable over time and, above all, related to the role of government in the economy. The strength of innovation systems, in fact, reflects the conscious efforts made by the public sector to support the national economy. As seen above, in the case of the US a crucial role was played by policies dealing with defence.

According to the two scholars, however, the key ingredient to ensure NIS have a good performance is the innovative strength, competence and competitiveness of domestic firms. This does not mean that companies should necessarily be large and specialised in high-tech areas. Some of the cases studied, in fact, show that good innovative performance is possible even by national systems specialised in traditional industries and characterised by the presence of many small businesses. In all successful national cases, however, there is one common trait: companies were not protected against the market and were exposed to strong competitive pressures. But which conditions favoured the emergence and consolidation of a competitive economy, based on a dynamic entrepreneurial structure? Once again, the arrow points in the direction of the different forms of public regulation, and in particular the quality of the national education system and macroeconomic policies (fiscal, monetary and trade) aimed at stimulating exports. Interventions in favour of innovation also play an important role, but the results are rather variable depending on the measures taken. Support for scientific research has a significant impact on some sectors – the most science-based – especially if it is accompanied by specific measures designed to foster relations between universities and the business world. As regards direct financing of industrial research, the verdict is more controversial, however: national programmes are as highly differentiated as their outcomes.

Turning now to another book, edited by Lundvall (1992b), and published at the beginning of the nineties, it should first be noted that this does not contain a comparative study of national cases. Rather, it provides a theoretico-conceptual framework of innovation systems derived from research on economic development conducted by a team of economists from the Danish University of Aalborg. The starting point is represented by the statement that, in the new economic scenarios, the fundamental resources for competition are represented by *knowledge* and *learning processes*. A new stage in the development of capitalism has begun, one characterised by rapid economic change and driven by technology, and in which the success of companies, territories and nation states depends on their ability to learn – to create and/or acquire new knowledge. What can be defined, in other words, as a *learning economy* (Lundvall and Johnson 1994).

According to Lundvall, mainstream neo-classical economics, focused as it is on the static allocation of scarce resources, is not equipped with the wherewithal to explain these changes. In traditional theory, in fact, innovation is configured as an extraordinary exogenous event – one that removes the system from its state of equilibrium. In contrast, in modern capitalism, innovation is:

- *constitutive and ubiquitous* – it is spread throughout the economic fabric and involves continuous processes of learning;
- *gradual and cumulative* – it consists of 'new combinations' based on previously available knowledge, opportunities and components which are combined in a different way, introducing a variable level of radical discontinuity with the past;
- *processual* – it does not consist of a single event but a series of activities linked to, and influencing, each other, with a blurring of the classical distinctions between invention, innovation and diffusion;
- *interactive and collective* – learning is configured in relational terms (*interactive learning*) and knowledge is a common good that is shared within networks and organisations.

For all these reasons, Lundvall sustains the need for a new analytical model, an alternative to the neo-classical one with, at its centre, learning aimed at the acquisition and creation of knowledge useful for innovation. In this new approach, knowledge is more than the simple accumulation of information since it includes the ability to interpret and use it. *Learning,* therefore, is configured as a *process of skill-building* (Lundvall 1996, 3). There are four types of knowledge that are based on different kinds of skill: *know-what* and *know-why* relate to knowledge of facts (natural, social, etc.) and the principles that explain them, and rely on cognitive skills. *Know-how* refers to the practical knowledge and skills needed to perform specific tasks. And *know-who* refers to knowledge and social skills, to knowledge about people ('who knows what' and 'who knows how to do what') and the ability to build interpersonal relationships.

These kinds of knowledge are learned in different ways. The first two are more formalised and can be assimilated through study. The other two, however, present tacit aspects that are difficult to codify, and are acquired through practical experience and social relations. Their circulation, moreover, does not take place through ordinary market channels since the transmission of tacit knowledge and forms of learning mediated by interpersonal relationships are profoundly influenced by trust aspects. In other words, the *learning economy* requires a great deal of trust and social cohesion (ibid., 15–17). Precisely because of this socio-relational aspect, innovative processes cannot be understood without taking into account their specific cultural and institutional context: the national innovation system, in other words, which regulates the production, use and dissemination of new, economically useful knowledge. It is a *social* system, since these activities involve interaction between people, and *dynamic*, as it is driven by feedback that can either reinforce or hinder the growth and reproduction of its constituent elements.

Lundvall acknowledges a broad definition of NIS, one that focuses not only on the institutions and organisations that deal with scientific and technological research, but on all the components of the economic and institutional structure that influence learning processes. The latter are, in fact, embedded in routine activities that take place in the sphere of production, distribution and consumption and provide important stimuli for innovation. These 'ordinary' activities generate learning economies of three types: *learning by doing* produces improvements in the production process (Arrow 1962b); *learning by using* increases the efficiency of use of complex systems (Rosenberg 1982); *learning by interacting* introduces refinements and innovations that are derived from relationships with other subjects (e.g. between producers, suppliers and consumers) (Lundvall 1988, 1992a).

The Lundvall approach, too, combines economic and institutional analysis. The relationship between these two parts is a circular one. Production specialisations, in fact, influence national institutions and the latter, in turn, tend to attract and favour the most compatible businesses and industries. There is therefore a strong interdependence between economic structure and institutional context (Lundvall and Maskell 2000, 363). Institutions are understood as 'set of habits, routines, rules, norms and laws, which regulate the relations between people and shape human interaction' (Johnson 1992, 26). They are not necessarily the most efficient or most suitable solution and, in addition, they embody power relations. That said, institutions play a fundamental role in learning and innovation processes: they reduce risk, distribute incentives, mediate conflict and coordinate the use of knowledge. If, on the one hand, they provide the stability necessary for social reproduction, on the other hand they are also essential to facilitate change. In situations of uncertainty, such as those found in innovation processes, they provide a framework of certainty that actors find useful to stabilise – at least relatively speaking – their expectations. Institutions also organise the cognitive process through both the accumulation and transmission of knowledge that must be 'remembered'; and selecting what is to be forgotten and abandoned through the 'creative destruction' of knowledge. Both learning and 'creative forgetting' are essential for innovation processes, and these are governed through institutional channels (ibid., 29–30).

Institutions also shape four aspects that impact on the innovative orientations of economic actors: (1) the time horizons of the actors; (2) the role of trust; (3) the mix of rationales used; (4) the ways in which authority is exercised (Lundvall and Maskell 2000, 360–1; Lundvall *et al.* 2002, 220). For these reasons, the institutional, cultural and historical differences of various countries are reflected in the specificity of NIS through their influence on business structures, on firms' relationships, on the role of the public sector, on the structure of the financial sector, on the intensity of R&D, and on the organisations who deal with it (Lundvall 1992a, 13). Lundvall, for example, has applied this approach to the Danish case (DISKO, *Danish System of Innovation in a Comparative Perspective*), showing the importance of incremental innovation in an economy specialised in mature, low-tech industries. In recent years, moreover, he has sought to extend and adapt the NIS approach to developing countries, where greater attention must be paid to the overall system of the creation of socio-economic skills and not only those based on the science sector (Lundvall *et al.* 2002, 216). As can be seen, the analytical approach used by the Danish scholar is very close to themes and concepts of a sociological nature. But the same is true, more generally, for all the studies that fall within the NIS framework. The attention given to both the social networks of learning and to the institutional context builds interesting bridges towards the world of economic sociology. The first, more micro dimension pushes the dialogue in the direction of the new economic sociology; while the second, more macro dimension presses towards comparative political economy. As seen in Chapter 1, certain authors have already started – in a more systematic manner – to connect studies on the varieties of capitalism with studies regarding innovation. Another important trend, and one that we will look at in the next chapter, develops around the territorial aspects of innovation. First, however, other variants of the systemic approach must be introduced that do not – as their authors themselves recognise – offer an alternative to the study of national systems, but rather provide complementary perspectives.

5.4 Sectoral systems

So far we have focused on innovation systems defined on a geographical basis. Certain authors have proposed a different approach, based on production sectors. The assumption is that modalities of technological change and innovation depend on the specific characteristics of the various industries. There is a wide literature in economics on the industrial sectors – both theoretical and empirical – but the *sectoral innovation systems* (SIS) approach is one that stands apart from traditional perspectives. First, because, unlike industrial economics, it analyses the sectors in terms of their innovation processes and does not consider their boundaries as utterly static and fixed. Second, because it examines not only the companies but also other actors, analysing their interactions within institutionally shaped contexts (Malerba 2004a, 1; 2004c, 16).

Evolutionary economics provides the theoretical framework of this approach, furnishing some of the basic assumptions: (1) technological transformations are central to explaining economic change; (2) the actors involved in innovation processes are heterogeneous in terms of skills, experience and organisation, and act according to bounded rationality, within highly uncertain and continuously evolving scenarios; (3) company behaviour is shaped by context, and so their modalities of action and learning are constrained by technology, knowledge base and the institutional environment (Malerba 2002, 250). Starting from these premises, we can proceed to a first definition of SIS. A *sectoral system of innovation and production* 'is composed of a set of new and established products for specific uses, and a set of agents carrying out activities and market and non-market interactions for the creation, production and sale of those products' (Malerba 2004c, 16).

SIS have three main components.

1   *Knowledge and technology*. New knowledge is the foundation of technological change and each sector has its own knowledge base and specific learning processes.
2   *Agents and networks*. The main players in sectoral systems may be individuals (e.g. consumers, entrepreneurs or scientists) and/or organisations (companies, universities, research centres, government agencies, etc.). Analytical focus, as well as on agents, is also placed on their interactions, namely on the formal and informal ties of cooperation that unite them and which serve to integrate the complementarity of their knowledge, skills and specialisations (Malerba 2005).
3   *Institutions*. These include norms, routines, habits, practices, rules, laws and standards that shape the knowledge and behaviour of the actors (ibid., 385). These rules have different degrees of formality and cogency; some arise from interaction between agents (such as contracts), others impose rules and constraints from outside (such as laws). Institutions govern the interaction between the actors and their impact on technological change and the innovation activities of companies. Relevant institutions are both national (e.g.

patent laws, antitrust laws, a country's tax system, etc.) and sectoral (the specific characteristics of its labour market, training systems, funding methods, etc.). But the impact of national institutions is also differentiated at a sectoral level.

The first of the three factors mentioned above (knowledge and technology) represents the central and distinctive element of this approach. The idea is that each SIS has a different *technological regime* as its foundation. This concept, introduced by Nelson and Winter (1982) and redeveloped by Malerba and Orsenigo (1993; 1997; 2000) refers to the 'technological environment' in which companies operate. This differs in relation to the conditions in which technological change takes place (opportunity, appropriability, and degree of cumulativeness of technological progress) and the characteristics of the knowledge base.

Conditions of opportunity represent the 'likelihood of innovating for any given amount of money investend in research' (Malerba 2004c, 21). The presence of *high/low* opportunity defines a technological environment where there is *wide/narrow* potential for innovation and so *strong/weak* incentives are created to invest resources. *Conditions of appropriability* regard the possibility of protecting the results of innovation in order to achieve the relative economic benefits. A high *level of appropriability* means that through various *means* (patents, secrecy, continuous innovation, control of resources and complementary services) the company succeeds in protecting itself from imitation, thus translating its innovative activities into a source of profit. *Conditions of cumulativity* refer to the degree to which knowledge accumulated in the past is important for the production of new knowledge in the future: in other words, the extent to which the introduction of new technological solutions depends on those already previously introduced. Cumulativity can be connected to both the cognitive dimension (technological level) and to the sedimented experience and expertise in a specific productive organisation (company level), industry (sectoral level) or geographical area (local level). Finally, *knowledge base* refers to the necessary *know-how* for innovative activity, and differs according to its (more or less specific, tacit, complex and independent) *nature* and (formal/informal) *means of transmission.*[6]

The combination of these elements defines the technological regimes of the various sectors, with which various models of innovation are associated. Malerba and Orsenigo (2000, 231ff.) refer in particular to the two models proposed by Joseph Schumpeter, already mentioned in Chapter 1. The first is that of *creative destruction* – so-called *Schumpeter Mark I* – which is typical of markets with low entry barriers. These are markets characterised by the presence of many small- and medium-sized companies where innovation is generated by innovative entrepreneurs. The second is the *creative accumulation* model – *Schumpeter Mark II* – which is found in markets with high entry barriers, where innovative processes are dominated by the R&D labs of large companies (Nelson and Winter 1982; Kamien and Schwartz 1982; Fagerberg 2003). The two models imply different modes of technological change: Schumpeter Mark I is characterised by high innovation opportunities, low appropriability and low cumulativity (at company level). Schumpeter Mark II, on the other hand, features high appropriability and high cumulativity. But how can these models be linked to sectoral analysis? The study by Malerba and Orsenigo on patented innovations in the seventies and eighties in six advanced economies (Germany, France, Britain, Italy, the US and Japan) shows a remarkable *similarity between the countries* in sectoral models of innovation, and a remarkable *diversity between sectors* within the countries themselves. The first model (Schumpeter Mark I) tends to prevail in some traditional and mechanical sectors (clothing and footwear, furniture, machinery, industrial automation, etc.), while the second (Schumpeter Mark II) dominates in sectors that employ chemical and electronic technologies. To sum up: technological regimes influence the ways in which innovative activities are organised and produced in various industrial sectors (Malerba and Orsenigo 2000, 241–3).

Models of innovation are not static, however. They change over time, following the life cycle of a sector and the evolution of its technological regime. In the initial phase, when knowledge is still fluid, technological trajectory uncertain and entry barriers low, small, new companies are the mainspring of innovation. A Schumpeter Mark I model prevails, therefore. When the sector moves into a period of greater maturity and the technological trajectory stabilises, financial endowments and economies of scale instead begin to become more relevant. With the rise of market entry barriers, then, large companies take over and there emerges a Schumpeter Mark II model of innovation (Malerba 2005). This does not mean that we should imagine a linear type of evolution which inevitably leads all sectors to pass from a Mark I to a Mark II model. Trajectories may, in fact, also be of an opposite kind, since in the presence of strong discontinuities in the technological regime or market conditions, a sector characterised by large dominant companies (incumbent firms) may see the arrival of new firms (new entries) that are exploiting innovative technologies or meeting new demands. This represents a shift from a Mark II to a Mark I model, or even a hybrid of the two.

Some examples might be useful here to clarify this point. The evolution of the *pharmaceutical industry* has brought with it several structural rearrangements as a result of changes taking place in its technological regime (McKelvey *et al.* 2004).

- In its first phase of development (1850–1945) the pharmaceutical sector was part of the chemical industry and was mainly dominated by large German and Swiss companies (followed by British and North American companies), which started mass production of drugs without carrying out a great deal of research (at least up until the 1930s).
- During the second phase (1946–80) – the golden age of the pharmaceutical industry – the system changed. Large firms invested more in R&D, acquiring large laboratories that, employing random screening research methods,[7] discovered new molecules or active principles for potential therapeutic and pharmacological use. Many new drugs were launched by leading companies

in the industry – thanks to a growing demand on an international scale – due to the setting up of new national healthcare systems and public support for pharmaceutical research. At this stage the notable prominence of large firms in the field of innovation was due to the extensive R&D resources required for developing new drugs. The regulatory regime, moreover, also guaranteed the high levels of appropriability of the research results. In this area, in fact, patents were a particularly effective tool for the protection of intellectual property, making it easy to protect new discoveries from imitation by competitors. All of these sectoral characteristics, therefore, rendered the innovative core of the sector fairly stable, composed of large enterprises around which other minor actors operated following a mainly imitative kind of competitive strategy. At this stage, however, European supremacy in the pharmaceutical industry was challenged. The huge resources spent in the US on scientific research in the biomedical field, the building of relationships between businesses and universities, and a very strict regulatory regime for drug approval, laid the foundation of American leadership in the life sciences – which came to full fruition in the following period (ibid., 82ff.).

- During the third phase of development (from 1980 onwards), the scientific revolution represented by the development of molecular biology and recombinant DNA techniques created in the area a new system of learning that can be defined as *guided search* – a method that stands in contrast to the previous random screening regime which owed its existence to the lack of adequate knowledge regarding the biological basis of disease. By applying new theoretical discoveries in biology, new methods of drug discovery were launched that enabled a more focused and rational design of new compounds and drugs. All these developments modified the process of innovation and the organisational structure of the sector: relations between companies and universities grew far closer and university spin-offs[8] came dynamically to the fore, commercially exploiting the knowledge gained through scientific research. The new learning regime provided ample space for the so-called new biotechnology companies (NBC) – small firms with a high intensity of knowledge, often founded by star-scientists, and employing particularly productive and innovative researchers (Zucker and Darby 1996; Zucker *et al.* 1998, 292) who were able to come up with great, commercially viable discoveries.

The point to emphasise here is that the changes that occurred in this sector's technological regime reshaped the balance between the big sector leaders, the *incumbent* companies, and the *new entries* – the newly created small businesses that were taking their place in the market for the first time. The new technological regime, in fact – especially at the beginning – allowed a great deal of room for the innovations that the NBC brought to the table. It is worth adding, however, that, for the development and commercialisation of new discoveries, the NBC almost always made use of – or in some cases were even absorbed by – the large pharmaceutical companies. As time went on a collaborative co-existence was established between these two entities, thus creating a new division of innovative labour within the industry (Sharp and Senker 1999; McKelvey *et al.* 2004, 96). In phases of technological discontinuity, innovation is, in fact, not infrequently introduced by start-ups, passing through the establishment of small firms that bring new business ideas to market – or develop them in the early years of their existence (Bhide 2000) – working as trailblazers for subsequent exploitation on a larger scale.[9] There tends to prevail in these phases, in other words, a kind of innovation that approximates to the Schumpeter Mark I model – but this is not a foregone outcome. In the chemical industry, for example, where discontinuity occurred as radical as that which took place in the pharmaceutical sector, large incumbent firms never lost their central position within the SIS (Cesaroni *et al.* 2004).

Processes of sectoral change are far from linear, therefore, and mainly proceed through three types of evolutionary process:

1   the *creation of variety*, which increases the options available in terms of technology, product, business, organisation, institution, strategy and so on;
2   the *selection* of one or more of these options, which decreases variety in the economic system and reduces the inefficient use of resources;
3   the *reproduction* of the established solution, which, replicated, generates continuity and inertia.

These evolutionary mechanisms, however, never produce stable and long-lasting equilibriums and do not always select the best possible solutions since the trajectory of change also depends on the constraints derived from the actions previously carried out. The success and diffusion of certain initial solutions, the increasing profits associated with them, and the interdependence between the actors, can create situations of irreversibility in relation to the technological choices made in the early stages of development of an industry. This *path-dependency* can determine a *lock-in* effect – an 'entrapment' of the system within technological and structural configurations that are not always the very best available (Malerba 2004c, 98). A classic example of this is the 'QWERTY' keyboard, still in use today in our computer.

This type of keyboard is named after the sequence of letters placed on the left of the top row of keys. Why this strange layout? It was invented in 1873 by Christopher Sholes, a Milwaukee newspaper editor, with the intention of solving a problem related to frequent type-bar jamming in early versions of typewriters. Sholes' idea was to replace the keyboard's alphabetical order by separating the pairs of letters most commonly used in the English language so as to prevent the keys pertaining to these letters from being placed nearby and causing the type-bars to stick. Later, when this mechanical problem was solved in more advanced versions of the typewriter, other arrangements of the alphabetic keys were also tried out, which could speed writing up and make it easier. One example is the Dvorak Simplified Keyboard, patented in 1936 by

August Dvorak and William Dealey, which placed the most-used letters in the centre of the keyboard, facilitating the alternation of the two hands. But this alternative layout was never a success: the 'QWERTY' version had become the dominant standard and switching to other schemes, even more efficient ones, would have meant substantial learning and adaptation costs (David 1985, 334–5).

Returning to the evolution of SIS, it should be added that it depends not only on changes that occur in individual components (knowledge, technologies, actors and networks, institutions, etc.) but also on their *co-evolution* – the latter being defined as the joint and interdependent transformation of 'technology, demand, institutions and firm organizations and strategies' that takes place during the evolution of an industry (Malerba 2004c, 31).[10]

Another important aspect of SIS regards the technology flow between companies and sectors – the sources of innovation, that is, and the diffusion and utilisation processes of new technologies. This analytical perspective sheds light on a complex web of 'technology transactions' between various industries which occur not only through the purchase and sale of goods that incorporate the technology, but also through the exchange of information and expertise between the companies and product diversification in related sectors (suppliers and product users).

In relation to this, Keith Pavitt (1984) studied the models present in different industrial sectors, using information on 2,000 innovations introduced into Britain between 1945–79. Two main elements emerge from the analysis. The first is that companies explore new technical solutions based on the knowledge and skills available to them, implying that technological change at firm level is a cumulative process. The second concerns sectoral variety in the types of innovation (process or product) and in the sources of the technological process. In other words, recurrent models of technological change emerge that allow Pavitt to develop a *sectoral taxonomy* 'according to whether or not the sectors of production, of use, and the principal activity of the innovating firm, are the same' (ibid., 346). This classification – still the most widely accepted in Innovation Studies – is based on several aspects:

- *sectoral sources* of technology, to assess whether this is generated within a sector or comes from outside through the purchase of materials and means of production;
- *institutional sources* and the *nature* of the technology that is produced (in particular the sources of knowledge and innovation, which may be intramural or come from universities, research centres, etc.);
- *characteristics of innovative companies* (with reference to size, their primary activities and the degree of product diversification).

Using innovative companies and their technological trajectories as the unit of analysis, Pavitt develops the following classification: (1) supplier-dominated firms; (2) production-intensive firms, in turn divided into (a) scale-intensive firms and (b) specialised suppliers; and (3) science-based firms.[11]

Supplier-dominated firms prevail in traditional manufacturing sectors (textiles, footwear, etc.), agriculture, construction and services. They are usually small, carry out little research, and their competitive advantages are based on professional skills, product design, brands and advertising. Their technological trajectories are based mainly on cost reduction. They do not contribute, except to a limited extent, to the development of the technologies that they use: innovation comes mainly from the suppliers of materials or equipment, or from consumers, services or public research.

Scale-intensive firms operate in the production of materials (glass, steel, concrete, etc.), consumer durables and vehicles. They take advantage of the large size of the markets of reference to obtain economies of scale by implementing a strong division of labour internally, with standardisation and simplification of tasks and increasing mechanisation to make it possible to reduce production costs. Technological trajectories are mostly geared towards process innovation and, in certain cases, to improving product quality. These firms are typically medium to large in size and operate in productive sectors that can generate the technological innovations they use internally. Innovation sources come from the experience and skill gained by the production departments or from internal R&D activity, or from relationships with suppliers of specialised machinery. This last point brings us to the third class.

Specialised supplier firms operate in the field of industrial machines and in the production of machinery and equipment. Their technological trajectory is different from the previous one, oriented as it is towards product innovation designed to improve performance rather than towards process innovation to reduce costs. They are mostly small in size and produce innovation that is used by other companies and in other sectors. Innovation sources come from learning from experience (learning by doing) and interaction with users (learning by interacting), especially with large companies that can provide operational expertise, complementary design resources, and opportunities for innovation experimentation and testing.

Finally, *science-based companies* operate mainly in the chemical-pharmaceutical and electrical/electronics fields. In both cases, innovation sources come from company R&D activity – which tends to exploit knowledge produced by the scientific community. They often, therefore, maintain collaborative relationships with universities and other research centres. The high level of sophistication of knowledge required in the sectors in which they operate, and economies of learning related to internally carried out research, generate high barriers that hinder the entry of new actors. Firms are generally (though not always) medium to large in size – especially in the chemicals and electronics sectors – and produce much of the process and product innovation used in their respective fields, which are then employed in other productive sectors.

Before closing this section on SIS, a mention should be given to the studies of *technological innovation systems* (TIS). This approach, like that of sectoral systems, insists on the specificity of the cognitive and relational processes underlying technological change. While, on the one hand, it can be seen as restricting analytical focus – since it refers to specific technologies rather than to an entire industrial sector – on the other hand it also expands it, since it deals with generic technologies with less well defined sectoral and geographical boundaries, which can be applied to a plurality of industrial sectors and go beyond the regional and national level (Carlsson *et al.* 2002, 236). The starting point is provided by the *technological system* concept, understood as 'a network of agents interacting in the economic/industrial area under a particular institutional infrastructure and involved in the generation, diffusion, and utilization of technology' (Carlsson and Stankiewicz 1991, 94; 1995, 49). Technological systems are defined in terms of cognitive and experiential flows rather than of ordinary goods and services, and among their components – in addition to actors, organisations and institutions – there also appear physical or technological 'artefacts' such as turbo-generators, transformers and transmission lines in electric power systems and diagnostic techniques and drugs in biomedical systems (to give only a few examples related to artifacts that have actually been studied) (Carlsson *et al.* 2002, 234).[12]

5.5 The triple helix

The *triple helix (TH)* model also emphasises the systemic-interactional component of innovation processes. However, it stands partially apart from the literature on national systems of innovation, which TH scholars consider more appropriate for the study of innovation of an incremental kind since it treats companies as the main actors and focuses on the path-dependent features of institutional systems. The TH model, conversely, focuses mainly on radical innovation, which creates major structural discontinuities (Etzkowitz and Leydesdorff 2000, 109; Etzkowitz 2002, 2).

What is proposed is a spiral model of innovation which focuses on the interactions between three distinct institutional spheres – *universities, industry and government (UIG)* – considered to be the cornerstones for innovation and growth (Etzkowitz 2008, 1). In the new context of the knowledge economy a dense network of communications is created between these three spheres, modifying institutional structure and innovative dynamics and giving an increasingly central role to the university (Etzkowitz and Leydesdorff 1997). The TH – the spiral interaction, in other words, between universities, industry and government – evokes the image of the screw-type hydraulic pump, better known as Archimedes' screw: a mechanical device for raising liquids which in ancient Mesopotamia gave rise to an innovative hydraulic system for agriculture.[13]

This new model derives from the convergence of two different institutional structures: the *statist model*, under which the government controls both the university and the economy; and the liberal-style *laissez-faire model*, in which the spheres are independent and interact very weakly, separated as they are by rigid boundaries (Figure 5.3).

This of course means two opposing ideal-types in terms of governance: in the first, the government has the central role in promoting economic growth and

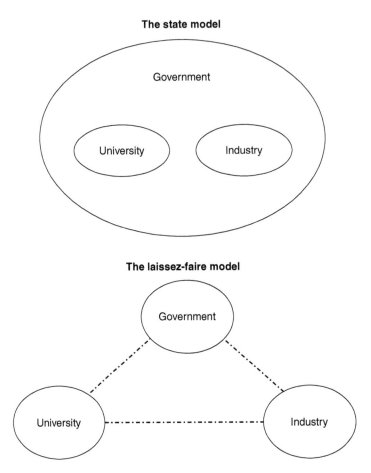

Figure 5.3 Models of relations between universities, industry and government (source: adapted from Etzkowitz (2002)).

social development; while in the second, this is the market's responsibility. In the new competitive scenarios, both of these models are unsuitable and are subject to growing pressures to change in the direction of institutional convergence. There are therefore two distinct pathways that lead towards the TH. The first – involving the statist model – is developed as a process of relative institutional *differentiation*, which gives greater autonomy to the university and industry, and then leads to a new point of equilibrium: here, there is interaction between the three institutional spheres, but on the basis of greater independence and equality. The second route – which regards the laissez-faire model – instead follows an opposite path, reducing the autonomy of the institutions and producing increasing integration between the institutional spheres. As a result of this convergence 'the common triple helix format supersedes variations in national innovation systems' (Etzkowitz 2008, 12).

In the TH model (Figure 5.4), unlike the previous two, a partial overlap of institutional spheres can be seen, which induces changes not only in their relationships but also within each of them: this does not, however, call their basic function into question. Each institution, in fact, tends to maintain its core identity, the loss of which would otherwise mean renouncing their autonomy.

The TH image is proposed in order to emphasise how innovation requires the contribution of all three institutional spheres. In addition, the change takes effect in all fields of society, albeit with slightly different modalities. While economic growth relies on technological innovation, social development requires institutional and organisational innovation. With regard to advanced economies, Etzkowitz refers to 'social inventions' – *hybrid organisations* that carry elements of TH inscribed in their very DNA, and which develop at the points of interconnection between the institutional spheres. These hybrid organisations are the result of a new configuration of relations between universities, industry and government, where the institutions increasingly assume each other's role. Universities carry out economic functions through the capitalisation of knowledge; companies shoulder responsibility for advanced training and research; and governments stimulate research, turning themselves into venture capitalists to finance innovation in order to sustain national competitiveness. This new configuration of relations triggers substantial changes in the institutional framework. At a first level, the transformations occur within each sphere – i.e. in each of the helixes – as a result of the hybridisation process of institutional logics. At a second level, there are changes related to the influence that each helix exerts upon the others. The typical example is represented by the Bayh–Dole Act passed by the US government in 1980.

This law meant that the ownership of patent rights arising from research funded by the public sector was granted to American universities, providing enormous stimulation for the commercialisation of scientific results and the development of entrepreneurial universities. And at a third level, there is 'the creation of a new overlay of trilateral networks and organizations from the interaction among the three helixes, formed for the purpose of coming up with new ideas and formats for high-tech development' (Etzkowitz and Leydesdorff 2000; Etzkowitz 2002, 2).

The triple helix model

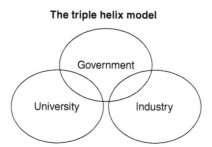

Figure 5.4 The triple helix (source: adapted from Etzkowitz (2002)).

The evolutionary spiral of TH is fed by circulation processes that occur at both micro and macro levels (Etzkowitz 2008, 21), with micro circulation taking place within each helix, and macro between the helixes, thus triggering inter-institutional fertilisation (through new ideas, collaborative projects and a better understanding between institutions). Both are fed by:

- the *circulation of individuals* among the occupational positions of the various institutions (or by simultaneous or alternating covering of roles);
- the *circulation of information* through innovative networks;
- *the circulation of results* achieved in various areas that – triggering dynamic imbalances – tend to strengthen innovative effort in complementary fields.

These various forms of 'horizontal' social mobility – transferring skills and experience from one institutional sphere to another – promote socio-organisational hybridisation and innovation processes. The 'functional contamination' associated with these horizontal interactions – with new actors dealing with tasks traditionally carried out by other institutions – results in the contribution of new ideas that improve both the performance of the system as a whole and that of individual institutions. For example, universities contribute to economic innovation through venture capital firms, incubators for the creation of start-ups and academic spin-offs.

But these phenomena also retroact on their two traditional missions (education and research), fostering the renewal of curricula and research programmes: 'Each institutional sphere is thus more likely to become a creative source of innovation and to support the emergence of creativity that arises in other spirals' (ibid., 9).

To sum up, the triple helix is a generative platform for institutions, creating new organisational formats for the promotion of innovation, as a synthesis of elements of the three helixes (ibid., 8). These developments take place primarily on a regional scale, whenever there is the intentional adoption of an innovative strategy based on the creation of new science-based companies – ones that make use of the knowledge generated by the scientific community. *TH regions* do not necessarily match the politico-administrative borders, and include three constitutive elements:

1   a source of knowledge (*knowledge space*);
2   a mechanism for achieving consensus (*consensus space*);
3   a project aimed at fostering innovation (*innovation space*).

As 'exemplary cases' of this particular development strategy, Etzkowitz indicates Silicon Valley (specialising in ICT) and the Boston area (specialising in biotechnology) in the United States; and the Linköping area in Sweden (specialising in the aerospace industry): all these areas feature a high concentration of innovative high-tech companies closely linked to universities and scientific research.

But how do these situations come about? The initial phase is often represented by the creation of a *knowledge space* – the territorial agglomeration of research activities focused on a specific theme – which can give rise to significant technological and commercial developments. In order for these knowledge resources to be put to good use, however, the relevant actors in the territory need to develop a shared strategy directed at their valorisation. A *consensus space* has to be created, in other words: a place where the major regional actors, hailing from different sectors and experiences, come together to develop a joint project, thus creating 'discussion networks' that go beyond the boundaries of institutional spheres. Examples of this are the New England Council in the Boston area during the twenties, or the Joint Venture Silicon Valley during the crisis of the early nineties. Finally, these projects must be actualised within an *innovation space*: a new hybrid organisation (business incubators, technology transfer offices, science parks, etc.) that promotes innovation on a regional scale, connecting TH resources, people and networks together in order to realise the goals articulated in the consensus space (Etzkowitz 2002, 7; 2008, 80). Not all TH institutions assume the same importance in promoting these 'regional projects'. One of them can take on the role of *regional innovation organiser*, operating as a leader in the planning and coordination of the other actors.

To take a concrete historical example one only has to look at the development of Route 128, a highly developed and innovative technology district in the Boston area (also discussed in Chapter 7). The genesis of an agglomeration of firms and universities with high innovative potential derives from a long incubation process made up of choices intentionally directed at the development of new knowledge and technologies with commercial value. A first step was the creation of the Massachusetts Institute of Technology in the mid-nineteenth century. William Barton Rogers, in fact, founded MIT with the precise idea of combining basic research and the development of new technologies, while gathering a pool of top-class researchers around the project (*knowledge space*). A second step was the establishment of the New England Council in the twenties and thirties, which brought together the area's academic, economic and political élite (*consensus space*). It was here that the then president of MIT, Karl Compton, relying on experience gained in the university in the creation of science-based companies, was able to launch a new project for the development of the region. The idea was to exploit comparative regional advantages related to the presence of a high endowment of academic resources, through a systematic strategy of start-up creation aimed at commercialising the results of scientific research. In 1946 this strategy also led to the creation of the first venture capital firm: the American Research and Development Corporation (*innovation space*). This was a hybrid organisation, which represented an early and informal version of the business incubators: in addition to funding firms, it also provided technical and entrepreneurial support, sometimes even allowing the location of new businesses directly inside the MIT campus.

Although the TH model places strong emphasis on the interaction and contribution of all three institutional spheres, Etzkowitz believes that universities represent the dynamic heart of the knowledge society: its 'generative principle' (Etzkowitz 2008, 1). In the scenarios of contemporary capitalism they are the equivalent of what coal mines and steel mills represented in the period of early industrialisation: formidable resources for social, economic and environmental transformation. According to Etzkowitz, there is under way in the universities of advanced countries – but with particular reference to the US – a major transformation, of a revolutionary kind. The 'primary mission' of medieval universities was originally the preservation and transmission of knowledge. A first revolution took place during the nineteenth century, inspired by the ideas of academic freedom and the unity of teaching and research propagated in Prussia in the early years of the century by the statesman and liberal philosopher Wilhelm von Humboldt. This new phase tended to emphasise the role of research as the universities' 'second mission', designed to complement – and integrate with – the first mission: the education and training of 'human capital'. A further revolution that affected the university began in the last decades of the twentieth century and introduced a third mission, which manifested itself as greater responsibility for the promotion of economic and social development.

This *third mission* involves a 'capitalisation of knowledge' and a greater openness to the outside world, linking teachers/researchers to the actual end-users of their thinking: creating, in other words, the *entrepreneurial university*. This rests on four pillars:

1 academic leadership capable of developing a strategic vision of its own role;
2 full control by the universities of their own resources (including tangible assets such as real estate and financial capitals, as well as intangible assets related to the intellectual property of research results etc.);
3 an organisational structure capable of activating technology transfer through patents, licences, incubators etc.;
4 the diffusion of an entrepreneurial *ethos* among administrators, teachers and students.

The process of capitalisation means that scientific knowledge is no longer only an epistemological enterprise: it also becomes an economically significant one. As we have seen, the creation of academic start-ups is not a recent development in the US, beginning as it did in the late nineteenth century in the Boston area, at Harvard and MIT, and then, later, after World War Two, moving out to the west coast, to Stanford University. That said, it is only in recent decades that the entrepreneurialisation of the academic world has really grown, with strong support and legitimacy provided by the Bayh–Dole Act – which allows universities to hold the intellectual property rights on the results of research funded by the federal government. In so doing, it has given a strong incentive to the commercial exploitation of academic research, offering a significant boost to the patenting of scientific discoveries.

According to Etzkowitz, the diffusion of the entrepreneurial model gives universities a leadership role in the emerging new mode of production of advanced countries 'based on continuing organizational and technological innovation' (Etzkowitz 2008, 1). Although TH scholars recognise some variability in this process (depending on previous national academic traditions and regional diversity), the strong hypothesis put forward is that of a convergence dictated by the functional requirements of the knowledge economy. In this perspective, the TH model is configured as a new system of innovation on a global scale, with the university becoming the predominant organisational format (ibid., 147). A progressive 'universalization of academic entrepreneurship' is, in other words, under way (ibid., 30–1).

Formulated in such a way, the thesis, however, appears a highly questionable one, tending to simplify processes that are in fact far more varied and complex, and most importantly, providing a functionalist explanation of the process of change, where the requirements of economic development determine the congruent institutional transformations. In reality, while it is true that universities are undergoing a process of institutional change that has reshaped internal governance and organisational models – in some cases pushing towards greater entrepreneurialisation and openness to the outside world – it is also true that the resulting model is a far from homogeneous one. Recent studies conducted on various European university systems show a wide difference in terms of the extension, pattern and speed of these changes – which can only be explained by taking into account regulatory and institutional frameworks and the specific relational dynamics of national systems (Regini 2011).

Box 5 Self-study prompts

1   Why are systemic study approaches to innovation so successful and what traits do they share?
2   What is a national innovation system and what are its main components?
3   Do differences exist within this particular strand of study?
4   What are the different types of skills and learning models illustrated by Lundvall?
5   What are sectoral innovation systems and what are their characteristics?
6   How can technological regimes be combined with the innovation models suggested by Schumpeter?
7   In Pavitt's taxonomy, what are the four main types of company?
8   What is the triple helix?
9   What are the constituent elements of triple helix regions?

Notes

1 The theme of industrial districts and local development will be addressed organically in Chapter 7. Suffice to say here that this concept – coined by Alfred Marshall and reintroduced to international debate by the Italian economist Giacomo Becattini – refers to systems of small- and medium-sized companies, *concentrated* in a specific area, *specialised* in a productive sector, and *integrated* into the production of certain

goods. Such systems generate a combination of cooperation and competition that rely on the social capital and networks of relationships that innervate the local communities. For an updated review of recent studies on industrial districts, including at an international level, see Becattini *et al.* (2009).

2 For some data regarding this growth, please refer to the Introduction.

3 In the original 1997 version, organisations were not mentioned in the definition of institutions. These were added by Edquist (2005, 188) in later versions of the same citation. I have decided to follow this use, given that it is more suitably congruent with the analytical distinction introduced by the authors.

4 More recently, however, Nelson has acknowledged that the 'evolutionary economists' under-theorised institutions and that the NIS 'is an institutional concept par excellence' (Nelson and Nelson 2002, 267). A definition of institutions was therefore proposed in terms of 'social technologies', which takes as its reference the routines, or more or less standardised procedures, that shape economic action and interaction. In other words, institutions are social technologies 'that have come to be regarded by the relevant social group as standard in the context' (Nelson and Sampat 2001, 40). As Nelson observed, this use of the concept – in terms of standard models of behaviour – is close to Veblen's, which defines institutions as widespread habits of action, or more precisely as 'settled habits of thought common to the generality of men' (1909, 626).

5 Lundvall, however, cannot be counted among those who support the need for greater theoretical abstraction as a necessary prerequisite for achieving a high level of 'scientific rigour'. The Danish scholar argued that the flexible and pragmatic nature of the concept of NIS – more so than its theoretical and formal rigour – was one of its major advantages. This has fostered its widespread application in policies as well as growing use in studies on economic development (Lundvall *et al.* 2002, 221; Johnson *et al.* 2003, 8).

6 For a more detailed look at the constitutive aspects of technological regimes, see Malerba and Orsenigo (2000, 236–40).

7 A research method that employs blanket testing of natural and chemically derived compounds.

8 In economics, the term *spin-off* refers to the birth of a new company that derives from organisational units or human resources which have become autonomous from the company/organisation of which they were originally a part. As regards universities, this means the creation of independent companies for the economic exploitation of discoveries and knowledge gained through scientific research.

9 With regard to software companies, for example, Torrisi (1996) observed a division of labour between firms that follows a dimensional logic. For the complex architecture that unites the various players in the software SIS in Europe, see Steinmueller (2004).

10 For examples of these co-evolution processes, see the detailed reports of six sectoral cases (pharmaceuticals and biotechnology, telecommunications, chemical, software, machine tools, services) in Malerba (2004b).

11 Pavitt later added another class to the taxonomy – information-intensive firms – deleting the category of supplier-dominated businesses. Information-intensive companies operate mainly in the banking, commerce and tourism sectors, and have advanced data processing as their main source of technological accumulation. The original taxonomy is, however, still the one generally referred to in IS. For a critical discussion of these changes, see Archibugi (2001).

12 The conceptual framework of technological systems has actually been applied to objects of study collocated at different levels of analysis: (1) to a technology, in the sense of a 'field of knowledge'; (2) to a product or artifact; (3) to a connected set of products or artifacts designed to satisfy a particular function. The first level is the study of technologies that can be applied to a plurality of products, such as the research conducted by Holmén (2002) on the microwave antennae that are used in

mobile phones, ovens, radar and automatic doors. At the second level, instead, specific 'technological products' are studied and these are what define the boundaries of the system in terms of the actors, networks and institutions involved. An example of this type is the study by Carlsson (1995) regarding numerical control machines and robots for industrial automation. And at the third level lies the study of a coordinated set of technological products and the relative 'skill blocks' that are necessary to meet the functional needs of complex systems, such as those in the healthcare field or the aviation industry (Eliasson 1998).

13 The invention of the hydraulic pump screw is attributed to the Greek scientist Archimedes, who lived in Syracuse in the third century BC, but its genesis is in fact a matter of some controversy. Some studies seem to indicate that Archimedes became aware of the mechanism – already known in the Middle East – during a period of study in Alexandria in Egypt. Its origins can therefore be back-dated to the seventh century BC. Stephanie Dalley (1993, 1994), for example, argues that the screw pump was already known during the reign of the Assyrian king, Sennacherib, and had been used to irrigate the gardens of the royal palace – the famous 'Hanging Gardens of Babylon', no less – which, however, were located in the city of Nineveh, also known as the 'old Babylon'. The controversy has been reconstructed and discussed in detail by Dalley and Oleson (supporters of the two opposing arguments), who came to the conclusion that, while the exact origin of the invention is still uncertain, Archimedes may at least be credited with its reinvention and diffusion throughout the Greco-Latin world – probably to solve the problem of irrigation in the Nile Delta (Dalley and Oleson 2003). For further development in this controversy, see also Simms and Dalley (2009).

6   The geography of innovation

This chapter addresses the issue of the geography of innovation. The first part analyses the distinctive features of knowledge as an 'economic good' and the role played by 'tacit knowledge' in the territorial agglomeration of innovation. This is followed by a discussion of several research contributions that examine the function of knowledge spillovers and star-scientists in the localisation of innovative processes. The chapter concludes with a review of the studies on learning regions and regional innovation systems.

6.1 The death of distance and the rediscovery of geography

In recent decades, the debate on globalisation and new information technologies has often raised the issue of the 'end of geography' (O'Brien 1992; Graham 1998; Greig 2002). The revolution that has occurred in means of communication and the reduction of regulatory and tariff barriers to the movement of goods and capital have led to speculation about the 'death of distance' (Cairncross 1997). This hypothesis is not a new one. At the beginning of the seventies, Alvin Toffler was already predicting a decline in the importance of place as a generator of socio-cultural diversity. According to Toffler (1970, 92), place is no longer a primary source of identity, and so differences between people are no longer *place-related*, i.e. linked to the geographical context in which they live.

On the economic front, the debates have alluded to the fact that technological change over the last few years has fundamentally altered the development model. On the one hand, the economy is increasingly based on the use of knowledge and intangible assets (such as creativity), while, on the other, a drastic spatial reorganisation of production is taking place that tends to relativise the influence of 'physical distance'. The British economist Richard O'Brien (1992, 1), studying international financial relations, launched the idea of the end of geography, describing it as 'a state of economic development where geographical location no longer matters'. Something very similar to the *flat world* that Thomas Friedman spoke of (2005), where geographical differences are flattened and socio-economic relations tend towards homogenisation.

Empirical evidence, however, suggests otherwise. Even today, in fact, the production of wealth and well-being does not just happen *anywhere in the world*.

Companies – especially industrial ones – are concentrated in specific locations where there are other companies like them, appropriate services and a skilled workforce. Some of these 'industrial locations' also have long-lasting productive traditions which tend to reproduce over time. No wonder, then, that during the same years in which there was talk of the end of geography and globalisation, other academics were rediscovering the importance of regions and local society, i.e. the spatial organisation of social and economic phenomena (Bagnasco 1999).

This rediscovery of territory is also the basis of the *geography of innovation* (Asheim and Gertler 2005). Innovation, in fact, does not happen everywhere: it tends to agglomerate in certain places, rich in resources strictly linked to the socio-institutional context (universities, research centres, advanced services, etc.). The spatial dimension is important for innovation for two main reasons.

1   The first is that the introduction of new products and production processes involves the interaction and exchange between a plurality of actors (companies, governments, research centres); it is configured as a joint process of creation and application of new knowledge, which is facilitated by spatial proximity.
2   The second reason relates to knowledge spillovers – the more or less voluntary circulation of information and knowledge produced in the activity of research and innovation. Spillovers produce positive externalities which also benefit actors who have not contributed to the production of the knowledge. As a result, the innovative performance of companies depends not only on the resources that they invest in research (within the company itself), but also from those invested by other companies in the same sector or related sectors, as well as by universities, research centres, etc. The appropriation of these spillovers is linked, however, to proximity to the source of new knowledge, and this proximity becomes even more relevant the more (non-codified) 'tacit knowledge' is also used in the innovation.

As we shall see in the next section, tacit knowledge (Polanyi 1966) is generated by experiences gained in specific contexts and is *embodied* (Pavitt 2002); that is, it is inextricably linked to the person who owns it and is transmitted through 'dense communication' based on personal relationships. The construction of these relationships takes time and trust, and is therefore facilitated by the proximity of the subjects involved (Gertler 2003). It is for these reasons that it is difficult for tacit knowledge to travel long distances: it is produced at a regional/local level and remains attached there; it is, as has been observed, *spatially sticky* (ibid.). This territorial expertise, rather than disappearing actually assumes particular importance against the backdrop of globalisation processes. The more codified knowledge circulates easily through global networks, the more tacit knowledge becomes a strategic asset, generating a competitive advantage that is difficult to imitate (Maskell and Malmberg 1999). In short, the production and dissemination of – economically significant – new knowledge often take place at a local level through the dynamics of learning through interacting (Lundvall and

Johnson 1994) – an interactive learning process embedded in territorial systems of innovation.

Various strands of the literature have contributed to the rediscovery of the importance of 'innovation places' and many of these contributions will be presented in the next chapter: (1) Krugman's new economic geography (1998a, 1998b); (2) studies on industrial districts by heterodox economists such as Giacomo Becattini; (3) research by Italian economic sociologists on the Third Italy and the social construction of the market; (4) the investigations into innovation processes at a local level brought together in the concept of *milieu innovateur* (innovative environment) developed by the *Groupe de recherche européen sur le milieu innovateurs* (GREMI) (Aydalot 1986; Camagni 1991), and; (5) reflections on learning regions (Florida 1995; Morgan 1997); and others.

All these studies share the idea that some territories provide specific location advantages that facilitate the processes of innovation and company competitiveness. Three elements in this literature are of particular interest.

1   The rediscovery of local and regional economies takes place with reference to the question of the accumulation and circulation of knowledge.[1]
2   This analytical venture is collocated in an interdisciplinary perspective, making use of the joint contribution of scholars belonging to different scientific fields (economists, geographers, sociologists, etc.) in the shared awareness that innovation takes the form of a complex and multifaceted process that requires a plurality of analytical skills.
3   Innovative activities are embedded within interpersonal and inter-organisational networks that involve a relationship of proximity. It is, as we shall see, first of all, a kind of geographical proximity.

And yet the importance of places does not mean that 'localistic closure' is beneficial to innovation processes, nor that the geographical aspect is the only one relevant to the processes of knowledge circulation. In recent years, in fact, the multi-dimensional nature of the concept of 'proximity' has been emphasised: the proximity relevant to the ends of innovation is not only physical, but also cognitive, organisational and socio-institutional.

In this chapter and the following one, only certain aspects of this complex debate will be addressed: the ones most relevant to a consideration of innovation in a territorial context. The next section will set out the conceptual premises that make it possible to explain the importance of tacit knowledge for innovation and its connections with territory. In the third section, the theme of knowledge spillover will be presented, and the fourth will offer some reflections on regional systems of innovation. Local innovation systems will, however, be discussed, in the next chapter.

6.2 Tacit knowledge and proximity

Tacit knowledge, often mentioned to explain the significance of territory in innovation processes, refers to a form of knowledge that, unlike the explicit kind, is difficult to translate into a written or codified form and to transmit to others. This aspect was highlighted by the philosopher Michael Polanyi – brother of sociologist and anthropologist Karl Polanyi – in his book *The Tacit Dimension* (1966, 4), in which he reminds us that 'we can know more than we can tell'. There are at least two reasons that make certain aspects of knowledge tacit (Gertler 2003, 77).

1 The first is related to subjective awareness: certain skills and competencies exist that are mastered without precise knowledge of the rules followed. The classic example given by Polanyi is the expert swimmer who cannot explain some of the elements that make his swimming performance so effective.
2 The second reason is related to the difficulty of communicating certain aspects of our skills through spoken or written language, so that their transmission to others is by means of exemplification and practical learning rather than through codification and study. The acquisition of such knowledge, then, benefits from the experience and example of those who are already experts in a particular field.

But what does tacit knowledge have to do with the territorial agglomeration of innovative phenomena? Two steps are required to explain this, bringing back into play certain salient characteristics of knowledge and linking it to the issue of economic development and (territorial) proximity between the subjects involved in its exchange. Let's consider the first step. Today it has become a cliché to say that knowledge – its production, diffusion and use for commercial purposes – is the basis of the competitiveness of advanced countries: it is a 'good', therefore, which possesses great economic value. However, knowledge has long been regarded by economists as a very special kind of 'economic good' – one for which it is difficult to organise a market and an efficient allocation of resources. The argumentative framework for this 'problem' was provided in a famous essay written in the early sixties by Kenneth Arrow (1962a). According to Arrow, market competition does not provide private companies with sufficient incentives to invest resources in research and invention – in the production of new knowledge, in other words. An emblematic case of 'market failure', then, which justifies the intervention of a centralised decision-maker: the public actor who invests in scientific research, particularly the basic kind.

Knowledge has, in fact, all the characteristics of a 'public good'. This type of good is characterised by two properties: (1) *non-rivalry in consumption*: their use by an actor does not limit the possibility of use by another actor as well, and; (2) *non-excludability of benefits*: it is difficult to exclude other people from using them (Cornes and Sandler 1986, 8–9). Typical examples are street lighting, public order, air quality, a beautiful sunset, etc. – all assets that cannot be subject to private appropriation.

Knowledge has similar traits, because, once a new idea has been created, it can be multiplied, disseminated and consumed by a plurality of actors without deterioration or damage in terms of quality. The low cost of the reproduction and circulation of information make it difficult to limit both the diffusion of new knowledge and its use by a more extensive public than the subjects involved in its production. The latter have, therefore, privately borne all the costs, but cannot fully appropriate all the benefits, since these have to be shared with others (sometimes, indeed, with their direct competitors). So there is a marked problem of *divergence between social benefits and private benefits*: the wide diffusion of new knowledge (high social utility) produces a lack of remuneration for the economic actors who have created it, and thus little incentive to invest resources (low private utility).

These arguments were developed by Arrow to show the difficulty of organising an efficient market for the production of knowledge due to its high level of portability (public) and low level of appropriability (private) of benefits.[2] Even with the presence of adequate legal protection of intellectual property, full private appropriation of the benefits of knowledge is difficult. Its use in the production of goods and services makes it public by exposing it to imitation by competitors, and staff mobility between different companies also tends to circulate information.

No legal protection, then, can transform an intangible asset such as knowledge/information into a commodity completely appropriable by individuals. Obstacles to the circulation of knowledge, meanwhile, on the one hand increase the private benefits of its possessor (who can commercially exploit a monopoly), but on the other decreases its social utility and reduces the overall efficiency of the production system (which is only ensured by the widest possible diffusion of new knowledge). Thus, ensuring the private profitability of invention leads to a 'nonoptimal allocation of resources', which reduces the social benefits (Arrow 1962a, 617). But this, in turn, creates a problem of drastic under-investment in research by private companies. Innovation is a risky activity in itself and its results – as we have said – can only be exploited by its producer to a very limited extent (ibid., 619). Two points arise from this set of considerations: (1) the importance attached to public funding of research, especially in fundamental areas, and; (2) the gradual discovery by development theorists of the crucial role of knowledge, and its externalities, in economic growth.

And now for the second step: explaining the importance of knowledge for development and for the territorial agglomeration of innovation. From the second half of the eighties, the new growth theories began to focus on knowledge stocks and spillovers in order to explain the different rates of productivity and development of various economies (Romer 1986; Grossman and Helpman 1991). In particular, new growth theory drew attention to technological progress, emphasising two aspects: (1) technological change is the result of conscious investment decisions by private enterprises and other actors; and (2) these investments produce significant externalities that generate increasing social returns (Griliches 1992, 1). The production output of individual firms, therefore, depends not only on internal production factors, but also on the knowledge available at a collective level (Romer 1986). Each private investment in research not only increases the knowledge stock of the individual company, but, through spillover, also increases the aggregate stock of public knowledge: for this reason, as indicated by Arrow, the social benefits of R&D investment are higher than the private benefits (Helpman, 2004).

To understand the significance of these new theories for the problem at hand – the territorial concentration of innovative processes – it is necessary to: (1) challenge the 'Arrow theorem', and in particular the assumption that no costs exist in the transfer and learning of knowledge by third parties, and; (2) introduce the idea that these transfer/learning costs are related to the proximity between the parties involved. The basic idea of the geography of innovation is the belief that this proximity is primarily a territorial one.

In the decades following Arrow's writing, the idea that knowledge is a public good with a very low cost of diffusion became a matter of discussion. New knowledge, in fact, presents both significant access barriers and information asymmetries. As we saw in Chapter 2, much *private knowledge* is *firm-specific*, linked to research tailored to the specific needs of a company, and this does not make it easily transferable. On the other hand, even the appropriation of *public knowledge* is not without cost and complication: it requires a significant investment in human capital within a company in order to deploy staff capable of searching outside the company for knowledge useful to it, assimilating it and applying it to the production process. In short, even to exploit knowledge produced by public actors (universities, research centres) private actors require a high *absorptive capacity* (Cohen and Levinthal, 1990).

For all these reasons, knowledge, rather than a public good, is more akin to a '*club good*' – an asset, that is shared privately by a limited number of subjects (a club) who may make exclusive use of it thanks to some 'mechanism of exclusion' – a mechanism that allows only those who are permitted to use a particular good (paying the related costs) to take advantage of its benefits, excluding all other consumers (Buchanan 1965).[3]

As we shall see, geography of innovation is based on the idea that territorial proximity represents one of these 'mechanisms of exclusion', allowing only the companies that operate in a given territory to benefit from the productive resources and collective assets located there. There is also the belief that knowledge transfer appears to be facilitated by relational proximity between the parties involved.

In this regard we can identify two main research strands which investigate the relationship between innovative activity and its location (Feldman 2000, 373–4). The first – which will be discussed in the next section – deals with 'knowledge spillovers', which analyse the geographic dimension of the diffusion of knowledge and its impact on the agglomeration of innovative companies. The second strand, instead, concerns the territorial structure of the economy and the differentiation of levels of development related to innovative activity and its 'spatial organisation'. It includes reflections on regional systems of innovation which will be considered in the fourth section, and those on local innovation systems which will be analysed in the next chapter.

6.3 Knowledge spillovers

One of the first scholars to raise the issue of the measurement of spillovers arising from R&D activity was the economist Zvi Griliches in an essay published in 1979 (Griliches 1998). The question he posed concerned the influence of external 'knowledge capital' on the productivity of a firm or industry. Productivity also depends on the reservoir of general knowledge that companies can access, and which can vary significantly between different sectors and geographical areas. Moreover, the ability to appropriate spillovers can vary depending on the technological and economic distance that separates them from the source of external knowledge (ibid., 30). In this perspective, a *pure knowledge spillover* is represented by 'ideas borrowed by the research teams of industry *i* from the research results of industry *j*' – i.e. the exchange of knowledge that firms in the same sector (or in a different one) derive from 'working on similar things and hence benefiting much from each other's research' (ibid., 31). The first empirical research on these issues by Adam Jaffe (1986) on two samples of more than 400 companies collected at two different times (1973 and 1979), indeed show that correlated research activities – that is, conducted in technological areas close to each other – make for significant increases in company performance: the estimate results show that if each firm increases the cost of R&D by 10 per cent then its productivity in terms of patents increases by 20 per cent, and that more than half of this increase is related to spillovers coming from research carried out by other companies (ibid., 994).[4]

A few years later Jaffe expanded his research, following one of the suggestions implicit, but not developed, in Griliches' observations: that the reservoir of general knowledge can vary not only in different technology areas but also in different territorial areas. Using the knowledge production function introduced by Griliches, but modified to take the spatial dimension into account, Jaffe (1989) explored the existence of *geographically mediated spillovers* in the US, especially those of academic origin. Using time-series data at state level (29 states for eight years) regarding the R&D expenditure and number of patents of companies and universities, Jaffe found that the latter exerted both a direct and an indirect influence on the commercial innovations of the former. University research, in fact, directly affected company patent activity, in particular in some technological macro-sectors (medical-pharmaceutical; electronic-optical-nuclear), while indirectly increasing industrial research and rendering it more productive (ibid., 968).

Jaffe thus demonstrated that universities have a positive effect on local innovation, not only through the graduates and services that they make available to the economy, but also through the diffusion of knowledge and information deriving from university research: in short, through geographically mediated knowledge spillovers (ibid., 957).

Other surveys conducted thereafter, using different indicators, confirmed these results. A database developed by the Small Business Administration of the United States regarding over 8,000 commercial innovations introduced in 1982

showed innovative activity's strong tendency to agglomerate in places characterised by a greater endowment of research activity and knowledge input (Acs *et al.*
1994; Feldman 1994; Feldman and Florida 1994). Audretsch and Feldman
(1996), for example, using a state concentration index of innovative activity,
show that the tendency to territorial agglomeration is stronger in industries that
use more new kinds of knowledge; that is, in sectors in which research and
human capital play a major role and where knowledge spillovers are more
present. According to these authors, the ability to receive and to capitalise on
knowledge spillovers is influenced by the distance from the source of knowledge
since the transfer costs of the latter rise with territorial distance. This gives rise
to the conclusion that the geographical location of production and innovative
activities is significant, as is, therefore, an analysis that takes territorial context
into account (ibid., 630).

These early studies, then, revealed the existence of '*geographically bounded*'
spillovers, but were based solely upon indirect evidence – that is, on statistical
correlations at a territorial level. They did not, however, examine the paths and
concrete mechanisms through which spillovers were actually produced (Feldman
2000, 379) and many doubts were raised regarding the possibility of direct analysis of this phenomenon. Paul Krugman, for example, launching the 'new economic geography', backed the opportunity to focus research on only some of the
territorial agglomeration factors suggested by Alfred Marshall[5] – visible and
measurable factors, such as the agglomeration of a specialised workforce and
intermediary producers of specialised goods – while neglecting industrial atmosphere and knowledge spillovers. The latter, in fact, leaving no 'paper trail' that
can be used for empirical measurement, are intangible and therefore, according
to Krugman (1991, 53), difficult to analyse. The research conducted by Adam
Jaffe, Manuel Trajtenberg and Rebecca Henderson (1993), on the other hand,
was dedicated to hunting down just this kind of '*paper trail*', examining the geographical distribution of *patents* and *patent citations* in order to show that knowledge spillovers are in fact 'geographically localized'.[6]

The citations contained in a patent are taken as evidence of subsequent
technological development that employs the knowledge of the patent cited (the
patent of origin): they are, in other words, visible traces of knowledge flow.
Given that patents provide indications regarding the geographical location of the
inventors, it is possible to analyse the territorial dimension of the spillovers and
their ability to travel across distances. The data used by Jaffe, Trajtenberg and
Henderson started with two cohorts of patents granted in 1975 and 1980. First of
all they collected the 'academic patents' of all American universities and then
built up two samples of 'entrepreneurial patents' that were similar in terms of
technological field and year of grant: on the one hand, those obtained from 200
American companies with the highest level of R&D spending (*top corporate*);
and, on the other, all the rest (*other corporate*). This collection of *patents of
origin* – around 2,400 – represented the source of potential spillovers. All the
subsequent patents containing citations referring to the original collection – the
citing patents – were then identified and, at the end of 1989, these amounted to

about 10,000 (ibid., 581).[7] The results of the analysis allowed the three scholars to demonstrate that:

- the citations came predominantly from the patents of American companies located in the same state and even in the same locality (metropolitan statistical area) as the patent of origin;
- the spillovers were stronger at a local level and in the first years following the grant of the patent, while the territorial effect tended to fade over the years as the knowledge became more widely diffused;
- local spillovers were not confined to the same technological sector but tended to travel beyond the various specialisations.

To sum up, the study showed two important things: first, that 'despite the invisibility of knowledge spillovers, they do leave a paper trail in the form of citations', and, second, that these traces indicate that knowledge spillovers are 'geographically localized' (ibid., 595).

This survey was subsequently subjected to a certain amount of criticism, mainly in relation to two aspects: on the one hand, the robustness of the results obtained at sub-national level, where more discriminating technological classifications might have been used for the compilation of the control group;[8] and, on the other, the reliability of the indicator employed. As regards the latter, it has been observed that a large proportion of the citations were entered by the patent office technicians who analysed the requests: this means it would have been a bureaucratic phenomenon, therefore, rather than an actual flow of knowledge between inventors. Research conducted by Alcacer and Gittelman (2004) estimated that, of the total number of citations, about 40 per cent were added by the examiners; and in 40 per cent of the patents analysed, all the citations were introduced through administrative channels (ibid., 10–11).[9] In light of this data, several scholars began to have doubts that the citations represented a reliable source of information regarding the inventors' 'state of knowledge' and territorial spillovers. That said, other research does show that actual flows of knowledge often exist behind the citations. A study conducted by Emmanuel Duguet and Megan MacGarvie (2005) shows that the patent citations of French companies match technology flows observed by European surveys on innovation. In addition, a survey carried out by Jaffe, Trajtenberg and Fogarty (2000) involving 380 inventors showed the existence of a good familiarity with the cited patents and also the existence of direct exchanges of communication. However, the researchers also pointed out that, in half the cases, the citations did not correspond to any communication or technological relationship between inventions. The conclusion to be drawn is that citations are indeed an indicator of knowledge flow, but of a *noisy* kind – a useful tool, anyway, albeit imperfect, to detect both knowledge spillovers and the importance attributed to the inventions.

Debatable as they are, studies on territorial spillover do represent an attempt to measure the significance of geographical proximity in relation to the exchange of knowledge and innovative activity. But they leave the specific mechanisms that enable these processes unexplored. This is an issue that has, however, been addressed by a team of Californian researchers studying the biotechnology field and the factors that lead it to operate in specific territories, focusing on the knowledge 'embodied' in human capital. This topic was introduced here in Chapter 3, discussing creative capital and the creative class. In that case, we saw territorial factors at work that attract creative actors to particular locations – actors who then go on to become the creators of development in that area. In the case study looked at in the next few pages, it is above all the human capital conveyed by *star-scientists* – particularly productive and innovative researchers – that represents the attractive factor of innovative companies.

These studies are mainly related to the work done by sociologist Lynne Zucker of the University of California. Research conducted together with other colleagues – primarily with economist Michael Darby – allowed Zucker to show that: (1) the initial creation of the commercial biotechnology sector is closely linked to the revolutionary cognitive contributions generated by universities, and; (2) the emergence and success of the new biotechnology companies are closely linked to the direct commitment of researchers located at the frontiers of this new scientific field. Zucker and her colleagues thus opened up the spillover black box, analysing the mechanisms that allow, at the micro level, the transfer of scientific knowledge from universities to the corporate sector. The focus in particular was on the initial stage of creation of the new biotechnology industry, following the 1973 discovery by Stanley Cohen and Herbert Boyer of the basic technique for DNA recombination. Over the next 15 years the biotechnology industry, virtually non-existent in the mid-seventies, saw the emergence of some 750 companies, over 500 of them start-ups. Zucker and Darby (1996) show that the growth and location of these new firms is linked to the presence in those areas of particularly innovative and productive researchers. Their intellectual capital plays a decisively attractive role, regardless of the prestige of the universities to which they belong and the number of research funds flowing in from public agencies.

The two Californians scholars identify a set of 327 particularly productive star-scientists at the cutting edge of the sector, having identified more than 40 genetic sequences before the routinisation and automation of these discoveries took place in the nineties. In a period of fundamental change – characterised by the 'invention of a method of inventing' (Griliches 1957, 502) – such researchers possess two special traits: they (1) are linked to a specific location (the university where they work), and; (2) have a 'naturally excludable' human capital due to the complexity and/or tacit character of the information necessary to carry out these innovations (Zucker, Darby and Brewer 1998, 291). In the initial phase of this scientific revolution, there were 'natural' obstacles to the circulation and rapid diffusion of the new knowledge, characterised – albeit only on a temporary basis – as tacit, scarce and of high economic value. It was, in fact, 'embodied' in the scientists working on the discoveries and had a high value because of its potential commercial applications. Until they were codified and routinised, therefore, these discovery procedures possessed features of 'natural excludability'.

Anyone wanting to know and learn these techniques had to gain direct experience by joining the research team that was discovering them (Zucker, Darby and Armstrong 1998, 70).

So, to transfer this knowledge to the companies, the mobility of human capital is required – one which must go beyond the boundaries of the university and access the commercial sector. These scientists, however – in the early stages – were territorially stable, with little desire to leave the universities and research teams in which they worked (Zucker, Darby and Brewer 1998, 292). They therefore determined the geographical location of the business, since the latter needed to use them directly to acquire the new knowledge. This is how '*localized effects of university research*' are created (Zucker, Darby and Armstrong 1998, 66).

The geographical location of the star-scientists was a key element in the explanation of when and where biotech companies began to proliferate (Zucker and Darby 1996). This took place in different forms. Existing companies became part of the new sector, signing contracts and launching collaborations with these important researchers, but more frequently the latter themselves founded start-ups or became involved with new firms that offered them participation in terms of equity and profits. Moreover, the degree of the scientists' direct involvement in company activity was a strong predictor of their commercial success. Contrary to what spillover literature sustained, this phenomenon does not seem to indicate that 'pure knowledge spillovers' were at work, but rather standard market mechanisms involving the exchange of private goods, featuring 'rivalry and excludability' in consumption (Zucker, Darby and Armstrong 1998, 80). Not all businesses operating in the area where star-scientists carried out research benefited from the results of their research and, in any case, not in equal measure: in the period between 1984–89, businesses that did not have direct links with star-scientists enjoyed modest average employment growth (82 units), whereas firms with direct collaborations grew over four times in size (366 units) and those with a high intensity of collaboration almost nine times (734 units) (ibid., 69). In turn, the scientists who became more involved in the process demonstrated greater productivity and scientific effectiveness than their colleagues who remained restricted to the universities. A virtuous circle exists, therefore, between scientific knowledge and commercial valorisation.

These phenomena were only typical of a transitional phase: the start-up of a new productive sector as a result of a radical scientific discovery 'embodied' in the intellectual capital of particular subjects. The same process took place in other high-tech sectors featuring wide-ranging 'technological opportunities' and *radical kinds of scientific discoveries*. Subsequent research, in fact, saw Zucker and Darby (2007) expanding the focus of their investigations. Following the career of more than 5,000 star-scientists operating in six science and technology macro-areas, and over a period of more than 20 years (1981–2004), they demonstrated that, keeping other factors under control, there was a correlation between the presence of these scientists and the creation of new companies. This occurred in a wide range of high-tech sectors both regionally, in the analyses of the US, and at a national level in the comparisons carried out among the most technologically advanced countries.

These studies show that knowledge spillovers are related to the quality of human capital and transfer of knowledge, *through market mechanisms*, to the corporate world. Later research also showed that the occupational mobility of human capital – for example, inventors with high patent performance – is one of the factors that explains the transfer of knowledge and innovative capacity between firms. This mobility, when confined prevalently to a specific area, tends to benefit the innovative capacity of local companies (Almeida and Kogut 1997, 1999).

It is not only market mechanisms that are involved, however. Research by Zucker and her colleagues shows that the companies with the closest relationships with star-scientists grow more than the others, taking on a leadership role. But they do not mention the fact that other companies still benefit from the context in which they operate, making use of the services and labour force provided by local schools and universities. Moreover, the regulatory structure and socio-institutional context count for a great deal in the virtuous circle set-up between universities and firms. And this produces effects at a variety of territorial levels.

In a comparative study of the US and Japan, Zucker and Darby once again underline the importance of star-scientists to explain the development of bio-technology companies. Scientists are an autonomous and additional factor both in relation to the resources allocated for university research and to local economic conditions. Yet this is truer in the case of the US than in Japan. As the authors themselves point out, in the latter case economic geography – that is, the significance of local context – exerts a greater role (Zucker and Darby 2007, 5). In Europe, moreover, the disconnection existing between universities and enterprise – in the formative period of biotechnology – prevented researchers from playing a significant role in the commercialisation of their discoveries. Despite the presence in Europe of 32 per cent of the world's star-scientists, the proportion of those who worked with biotech companies was just 9 per cent of the global total (ibid., 6). These differences show that socio-institutional context and legislative regulation significantly influence the modalities of circulation and economic exploitation of scientific knowledge, attributing variable importance to territorial aspects.

The importance of contextual factors and the various modes of local level regulation is also apparent from the analyses conducted by Zucker, together with other colleagues, on the field of nanoscience. The development of this sector in specific locations is connected to: (1) the breadth of the stock of pre-existing knowledge at a local level in various scientific fields; (2) the cooperation between organisations pertaining to different institutional fields (universities, companies, public research laboratories, etc.), and; (3) the amount of public funding poured into the area. This mix of elements focuses attention on factors – economic and otherwise – that are different from 'simple' market mechanisms: factors capable of generating geographically localised spillovers and, more generally, structuring a context conducive to radical scientific innovation. The latter, therefore, has its roots in a network of social structures and cooperation practices. As the authors conclude: 'The production of nanotechnology knowledge is embedded in the wider social context of institutional organizations, cross-institutional collaboration, and national structures of incentives and rewards' (Zucker *et al.* 2007, 862). It is a socio-institutional and cultural context which also ends up benefiting the companies marketing these scientific discoveries, as we have seen in the case of biotechnology. It is difficult, therefore, in the overall evaluation of the process of commercialisation of scientific discoveries, to separate the action of the market from the socio-institutional context.

The studies by Zucker and her colleagues, then, in the end come into alignment with those on the geographical localisation of spillovers and tacit knowledge. As we have seen, this latter element represents an important factor for the geography of innovation, produced as it is within specific contexts and only able to be shared through demonstration and practice. In comparison with interpretations that particularly emphasise the cognitive and experiential aspect of tacit knowledge, institutional economic sociology and economic geography (Gertler 2010) also tend to underline the socio-institutional infrastructure underpinning these processes.

The environment within which the production, appropriation and diffusion of tacit knowledge take place is strongly influenced by the institutional context that shapes both economic transactions and learning processes. It depends, in other words, on norms, conventions, values, expectations and shared routines which derive from the '*commonly experienced frameworks of institutions*' (Gertler 2003, 91). These institutional frameworks permeate the relationships of proximity within which the transmission not only of tacit, but also of codified knowledge, occurs.

Institutions exert their action at national, local and regional level. That said, the geography of innovation has focused primarily on sub-national areas, starting from the assumption that an institutional analysis is necessary of the origins of tacit knowledge and the exchanges of knowledge which occur mainly at these territorial levels (ibid., 90). This is also due to the growing awareness that learning processes are *socially organised*, based on interactions and knowledge flows that involve actors pertaining to different institutional spheres: companies, research organisations and public agencies (ibid., 79). As we will see in the remaining part of the book, a variety of contributions over the last several decades have explored this 'social construction of innovation' at different territorial levels – regional, as well as local. In the next section, we will analyse the former.

6.4 Regional systems

As we saw in Chapter 5, the basic assumption of the literature on national innovation systems (NIS) is that economic structure and institutions shape innovation processes. But is there only one system of innovation within a state? In the early nineties, several scholars began to question this statement, emphasising the importance of the regional dimension and its ability to generate new knowledge. At that point, *learning regions* (LR) became a topic for discussion (Florida 1995; Asheim 1996; Morgan 1997). These observations represent the first attempt to link innovation processes and territorial networks in the explanation of regional development. In the new competitive structures, in fact, knowledge becomes a strategic asset and innovation processes take on a network configuration, because – given their increasing complexity and uncertainty – no one company is able to master them alone (Rutten and Boekema 2012, 984). The LR literature suggests that regional economies are the most suitable in terms of responding to these changes.[10] It is divided into two main branches, one North American and one European (Rutten and Boekema 2007; Asheim 2012). The former tends to emphasise the role of socio-cognitive resources: the quality of knowledge infrastructures, universities, research centres and specialised workforces in high-tech sectors of the economy (Florida 1995). The latter focuses more on socio-normative resources: the role of social capital and trust in facilitating collaboration between companies and interactive learning processes (Asheim 1996; Morgan 1997).

The literature has not developed greatly since, mainly for two reasons: the tendency to confine networks and learning processes solely to regional space; and a strong mingling with innovation policies that – in contrast to systemic approaches – prevented its achieving full theoretical maturity (Rutten and Boekema 2012, 982–4). A strong holistic emphasis should also be added to these two elements, which tends to obscure the agency aspect, the intentional interventions made by regional actors: companies, collective organisations, government agencies, and so on.

That said, reflections on LR provided a seminal contribution that has since found its way into *regional innovation systems* (RIS). This line of research is placed in a complementary rather than an alternative position, with respect to studies on NIS. RIS, however, are not a simple projection of the latter on a regional scale, but must be thought of as systems in their own right, with special and differential characteristics. The concept was launched for the first time by Cooke (1992) in the early nineties.[11]

The RIS is configured as a geographical area in which, thanks to a favourable institutional and cultural context, cooperation for innovation is encouraged with the involvement of a number of organisations. The assumptions of this approach are:

- innovative companies are located within regional networks, where they interact and cooperate not only with suppliers, competitors and customers, but also with educational organisations, research centres, intermediary technological agencies, funding agencies and public bodies;
- the proximity of these organisations facilitates and fosters innovation processes;
- regional authorities can play an important part in supporting these processes, offering services and promoting interconnection between all the actors in the system.

But what precisely are the constituent factors of an RIS? According to Cooke, 'a regional innovation system consists of interacting knowledge generation and exploitation sub-systems linked to global, national and other regional systems for commercialising new knowledge' (Cooke 2004, 3). So there are two sides to the RIS: the offer, which includes all the organisations responsible for the production of knowledge and the training of human capital; and the demand, which includes businesses and other organisations that use and develop these resources (knowledge + human capital) to create and commercialise product and process innovation (Figure 6.1). Then there is a whole series of organisations that play an intermediary role in order to bridge the gap and facilitate relations between the two sides of the innovation system. Two constitutive dimensions of the RIS are also specified: territorial governance and economic innovation.

The *governance dimension* regards the public policies and knowledge infrastructure that support company innovation. The reference, in this case, is to the propensity for regional governments to build inclusive and interactive networks that facilitate the association and cooperation between local organisations, both

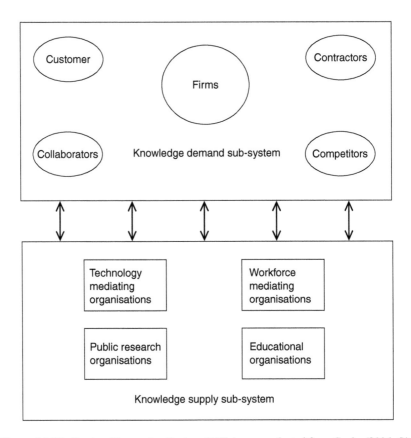

Figure 6.1 The Regional Innovation System (RIS) (source: adapted from Cooke (2006, 6)).

public and private (public agencies, interest associations, chambers of commerce, etc.).

The *company innovation dimension* concerns economic and industrial struc-ture, with particular reference to productive culture and company capacity for innovation. Contributing to this dimension are investment levels, resources devoted to R&D, company size, the presence of inter-company networks, and levels of collaboration with customers and suppliers. For each of these two dimensions, Cooke (ibid.) proposes a specific typology.

The systems of governance typology refers mainly to the modalities employed for 'technology transfer' – the services and initiatives set up to spread new knowledge and technology throughout local businesses. It is essentially based on five variables (see Table 6.1.): (1) initiative source; (2) funding source; (3) research skills; (4) degree of specialisation; and (5) degree of coordination.

Analysing regional governance according to these five dimensions produces three ideal-types of RIS.

1   The first type, the *grassroots system*, originates and develops through local initiatives in an urban or district area. Financial support for innovation is widespread and comes from households, the credit system and local institu-tions. Innovative stimuli derive from the market, and research skills are sparse and prevalently of the applicative kind. Technical specialisation is weak and directed at the resolution of problems that emerge from the pro-ductive area. The degree of coordination with supralocal institutions is low. The system also relies on social capital embedded in informal networks of collaboration rather than in formalised organisations, even though develop-ment agencies and local government play a central role in supporting innovation. Overall coordination, at a regional level, is limited. Although this model is applied in various national contexts, for Cooke the industrial districts of the Third Italy represent the most significant example.

2   The second type of governance is the *network system*. This is more formal-ised and integrated in comparison to the previous model. Institutional infra-structure involves various levels of government (local, regional and national) and innovation funding derives from agreements involving all rel-evant actors (banks and financial institutions, businesses and government

Table 6.1 Three systems of innovation governance

Characteristics of RIS	Grassroots	Network	Dirigiste
Initiative	Local	Multi-level	Central
Funding	Diffused	Guided	Determined
Research competence	Applications	Mixed	Basic
Coordination	Low	Potentially high	High
Specialisation	Weak	Flexible	Strong

Source: adapted from Cooke (1992, 370; 2006, 8).

agencies). Scientific skills are based on a mixture of theoretical and applicative knowledge, which allows for both basic research, wide-ranging and exploratory in nature, and operational and *near-market* research, directed by entrepreneurial requirements. Technico-scientific specialisation is flexible because requests come to the innovative system from a heterogeneous plurality of actors, ranging from companies that operate on a global scale to small, local businesses. The degree of system coordination may be high and tends to involve a large number of actors. It is a model that is not driven exclusively by the market, but neither is it planned by regional government. Rather, it configures as a network type of governance based on innovation partnerships, in which vertical power relationships are accompanied by horizontal cooperation relationships. One example of this model is provided by the Baden-Württemberg system, where the strength of the RIS was built up over time through long-term actions in a region previously characterised by considerable economic difficulty and migratory phenomena. The competitive advantages of this German *Land* – one of the richest and most highly developed areas in Europe – were intentionally established through interventions initiated in the second half of the nineteenth century. In 1868, in Esslingen near Stuttgart, Ferdinand von Steinbeis set up the first vocational education system specifically calibrated to the technological needs of the rail industry. He is considered the father of the German dual system, which combines scholastic education with professional training acquired through company apprenticeships. Steinbeis believed that the goal of the education system should be to turn out specialised industrial workers equipped with solid theoretical knowledge and practical skills acquired on the job. This represented an early example of the provision of collective public goods aimed at supporting the avant garde industry of the time (locomotive technology in the railway sector). The repetition of measures of this kind over time nourished the region's industrial vocation and engineering success, engendering a competitive advantage that also gave rise to the subsequent origins of leading companies in the automotive industry such as Porsche, Daimler and Bosch.

3   The third type is the *dirigiste system*. This model of governance derives its impetus mainly from the outside – from central government policies aimed at promoting innovation. Funding is therefore centralised and the various measures are implemented through regionalised public agencies. Levels of coordination and specialisation are high and technico-scientific skills are both basic and applicative, related to the needs of large public companies or, in any case, to requirements from outside the area. The Rhône-Alpes region of France, with its rich scientific-technological patrimony, is a good example of this type. France, during the seventies and eighties, was at the forefront of innovation policies, with a vigorous public planning project aimed at building centres of technological excellence. The idea of building *technopoles* – science parks with high-tech companies, research centres, universities, financial institutions and other agencies specialised in technological transfer

and intermediation gathered together in one place – was based on a model inspired by François Perroux,[12] involving development poles such as those established in Germany's Ruhr valley, where large steel plants were set up to feed industrial development. In the early nineties, thanks to the various measures adopted, many technology transfer and innovation centres were already active in the Rhône-Alpes area in sectors involving agribusiness, new materials, energy, chemistry and biotechnology. There were also decentralised offices of the Ministry of Research and Technology, private and public research centres, training institutions, large and small businesses, as well as substantial investment by the national fund for venture capital. Thanks to this series of measures the region assumed an innovation leadership role in energy, science and material engineering, as well as in the sectors of mechanical engineering and electronics. The point to emphasise is that the features of this model were distinctly *dirigiste*: all the basic infrastructure was designed and directed from outside the region, mainly from Paris (Cooke 2006, 11).

The ideal-typical models proposed by Cooke, however, should not be applied in too static a manner since the regions analysed can undergo transformations which fundamentally alter their character – something that can also occur because of changes within the national framework. For example, in the last few decades France has implemented a policy of decentralisation that has distanced the Rhône-Alpes region from the *dirigiste* model by bringing it closer to the network model (Cooke 2004, 13). Regional governments have been granted more autonomy and new powers, enabling the setting up of horizontal relationships with companies and universities along triple helix lines (see section 5, Chapter 5).

With regard to the second constitutive aspect of the RIS – firm innovation – Cooke presents another typology that takes into account the role of big business, the relationships between companies (and between companies and other local actors and the outside world) and their approach to innovation. In this case too, three ideal-types are proposed.

1   The first is the *localist system*. In this case, the role of large companies is very limited. The technico-scientific capacity and innovative performance of mainly small- and medium-sized companies is fairly limited. There is little funding and few public research institutions, although there may be private resources and centres (of limited size) working together with local businesses. The associative capacity of businesses and local governments can, however, be quite good.
2   The second type of company innovation is the *interactive system*. These regional economies are not dominated by either large or small-/medium-sized companies, but by a balanced mix of both, either local or external in origin. Company research ability and innovative performance operates on a regional scale, but, when necessary, can spread even further, on a national

or international scale, to acquire useful resources for innovation. On the research front, there is a combination of public and private centres, with a few large companies that have their headquarters in the region and regional governments that intervene to promote the economy of the area. There is a good associative level, both of a vertical kind – between the various levels of government – and, locally, of a horizontal type.

3   The third type, finally, is the *globalised system*. These RIS are dominated by large firms that operate on a global scale, often based on a value chain in which, at a local level, agglomerations of small- and medium-sized enterprises (SMEs) find some space. Research potential is, for the most part, concentrated within big corporations. It is therefore prevalently private in nature – although a public research infrastructure especially targeted towards the needs of SMEs may be present. The associative capacity of local businesses is also highly dependent on the role of big companies.

With these two typologies used as a basis, a taxonomy of cases was compiled, starting from a study of certain innovative regions located in different parts of the world (Table 6.2). Cooke is aware that the regions analysed approximate to the different types of RIS to a variable extent. In this regard, it must be remembered that the analytical framework proposes ideal-types that serve as a term of reference for the study of empirical reality. A possible antimony needs to be addressed. In 'conceptual terms' (theoretical level), in fact, the properties of systems have a dichotomous modality: a region either has an innovation system or it doesn't. In 'real terms' (empirical level), on the other hand, properties of territorial systems are continuous in nature: regions, in other words, possess traits that are more or less systemic. For this reason, Cooke proposes an analytical framework for the study of RIS that tries to hold together both the conceptual and the empirical dimension. The scheme consists of five interconnected concepts, defined as dichotomous polarities which make it possible to study and measure the concrete cases in terms of a combination of systemic indicators (Cooke 2001, 946, 953). The first of these five polar concepts is that of the

Table 6.2 Regional innovation systems: a taxonomy

Types of corporate innovation	Types of governance		
	Grassroots	*Network*	*Dirigiste*
Localist	Tuscany	Tampere Denmark	Slovenia Tohoku
Interactive	Catalonia	Baden-Württemberg	Gyeonggi
Globalised	Ontario	North Rhine-Westphalia Wales	Singapore

Source: adapted from Cooke (2004, 15).

region, understood as a meso-level politico-administrative unit, situated between the national/federal state and local government. A region may (or may not) have a homogeneous profile from a historico-cultural point of view, but it is essential for it to have powers of intervention in terms of economic policies. The second concept is that of *innovation*, understood as the capacity to commercialise new knowledge about products, processes and the organisation of production. The third concept is the *network*, and regards the presence of cooperative and trust relationships between the local/regional actors, making it possible to pursue common interests in terms of innovation. The fourth is *learning*: new knowledge, skills and abilities created or acquired at a regional level are spread, to be absorbed by companies and other innovative organisations, permeating their operational routines. The fifth concept, finally, is that of *interaction*, understood as a set of formal and informal networks of relations, meetings and communications regarding innovation, which enable local actors to join in learning activities of both individual and collective interest.

These five axes thus make it possible to define: (1) if, where regional governance is concerned, there is a good flow of knowledge between intermediary and entrepreneurial organisations; and (2) if, where company innovation is concerned, there exist partnerships and interactive learning networks between companies. To sum up, they make it possible to see whether or not a region has an innovation system and the degree to which this system is close to the ideal-type.

Good economic performance requires a sophisticated and prevalently market-driven system and that, in Cooke's opinion, is something that occurs more easily in the US than in Europe. In the old continent, in fact, RIS are mainly *institutional*, based on public institutions of the production and diffusion of knowledge such as research centres and laboratories, universities, technology transfer organisations, incubators, training and finance agencies and other intermediary organisations. In contrast, in the US *entrepreneurial* RIS are present, guided predominantly by private actors in sectors of the new economy (Cooke 2004, 4). This difference would explain the gap in innovative performance on the two sides of the Atlantic, since the second type of RIS, being in closer contact with market stimuli, is more dynamic and effective (Cooke 2001, 971).

More recently, however, Cooke's vision regarding the relative merits of market and policy has become more nuanced. Knowledge and innovative capacities at the regional level are seen as the possible result of a strategy intentionally aimed at creating relationships and mechanisms of intermediation between regional actors, both public and private. It is a question of producing *regional advantages* built up through 'platform policies': measures to increase knowledge flow and regional innovative capacity also through sectoral diversification strategies.[13] (Cooke 2007, 186–8; Asheim, Boschma and Cooke 2011).

Empirical research on RIS has multiplied over the last two decades, essentially producing two types of study. On the one hand, *case analyses* – the study of individual regions, held up as examples, which are examined in depth in terms of historical origins, evolutionary dynamics and innovation policies, with more or less explicit references to RIS literature. And on the other, *comparative ana-lyses*, conducted using the same analytical framework for the collection of data and interpretation of results: like the one presented in the preceding pages, made by Cooke and other academics.[14] With regard to the latter case, it is also worth mentioning the research carried out on certain regional production clusters in three Scandinavian countries: Denmark, Sweden and Norway (Asheim and Isaksen 2002; Asheim and Coenen 2005).

The term 'cluster' is used in the definition given by Porter[15] – a geographical concentration of interconnected companies and institutions pertaining to a par-ticular production sector. The cluster also includes, however, businesses and organisations in industries complementary to the particular sector of special-isation, which are important for the latter's competitiveness: for example, sup-pliers of components or equipment (Porter 1998, 78). The Scandinavian cluster can be classified into three different types of RIS, which resemble those already described by Cooke.

1   The first type can be defined as a *territorially embedded regional innovation network* in which companies innovate through localised learning processes, stimulated by socio-cultural and geographical proximity, but without a great deal of interaction with knowledge organisations.

2   The second type, instead, is a regional networked *innovation system* in which the local and interactive aspect of learning processes is still strong, but the system is more planned and systemic in character since specific pol-icies exist aimed at increasing the innovative capacity of companies, stimu-lating collaboration with research bodies and other institutions capable of providing advanced services at local and regional levels.

3   The third type is a *regionalised national innovation system* in which sectoral clusters and institutions are functionally integrated at a national and inter-national level so that innovation is prevalently realised through cooperation with actors outside the region. The knowledge necessary for innovation comes mostly from outside the regional system and is predominantly scient-ific in nature (Asheim and Isaksen 2002, 83–4).

This typology of regional systems was then interpolated with the knowledge used in the productive process, different in the high-tech and traditional fields, and not exclusively related to R&D activities. There are three types of know-ledge, based on a different combination of tacit and codified forms (Asheim and Gertler 2005, 295; Laestadius 1998).

First, the *synthetic knowledge base* is used in 'traditional' production sectors such as mechanical engineering, shipbuilding and so forth, in which notions are employed that are already available to create new productive combinations, in order to solve needs mostly arising from interaction with consumers or suppliers. In these sectors, innovation is mainly incremental and not greatly based on sci-entific research, especially the basic kind, while to a large extent making use of tacit knowledge.

Second, the *analytical knowledge base* is more present in economic activities, where scientific research plays a major role (sectors related to genetics, biotechnology, information technology, and so on). Codified knowledge, then, assumes greater importance and innovation processes can be radical in nature. In these areas, relationships with sources of scientific knowledge (universities and research centres), as well as spending on intramural research, are more significant (Asheim and Coenen 2005, 1176–7).

Third, the *symbolic knowledge base* refers to the creation of meanings, desires and aesthetic attributes for cultural types of goods and their economic valorisation (Asheim, Boschma and Cooke 2011, 897). This type of knowledge is used in the fields of media, advertising, fashion and design, where there is a shift of importance from the use value of the products to the sign value of the brands. The knowledge applied in the innovation process in this case is embedded and transmitted through symbols, images, sounds and narrations with a strong cultural content. The input is mainly aesthetic rather than cognitive, with a high component of tacit knowledge, linked to specific social groups and contexts.

Each of these knowledge bases shapes in a different way the modalities of innovation present in the various productive sectors and territories, since the different knowledge mix employed renders them more or less sensitive to geographical distance. Spatial proximity is less significant for the learning processes centred on analytical knowledge, and more important for those based on synthetic and symbolic knowledge. In the latter case there is an added social proximity based on class and gender cultures as well as the sharing of particular lifestyles (ibid., 897–8).

Box 6 Self-study prompts

1 How valid is it to talk about the 'end of geography' and the 'death of distance'?

2 What basic elements are shared by the studies on the geography of innovation?

3 Is knowledge a 'public good' or a 'club good'? What are the differences between these two types of goods?

4 What is tacit knowledge and what role does it play in the territorial agglomeration of innovation?

5 What are 'knowledge spillovers'? Why do some scholars argue that they are 'geographically bounded'?

6 How did star-scientists contribute to the development of the commercial sector of biotechnology?

7 What are learning regions?

8 What are the key elements in regional innovation systems (RIS)? What are the main types of RIS described in the literature?

9 What are the differences between a synthetic, analytical and symbolic knowledge base?

To conclude: scholars who deal with RIS recognise a variety of innovative systems in which learning networks are developed on different territorial levels. That said, in this literature the most important dimension is the regional one. In the next chapter we'll discuss contributions that address the same theme at the sub-regional level to understand how external economies and socio-institutional factors present at a local level foster innovative activities. In recent decades this type of analysis, originally created in the context of studies on 'traditional industrial districts', has also been applied to 'technological districts'.

Notes

1 At two levels: (1) *diachronic*, since the sedimentation of knowledge in certain places and the skills transmitted from one generation to another create evolutionary path-dependent dynamics, and; (2) *synchronic*, since the social networks that innervate the territories facilitate the diffusion of information and innovation.

2 For Arrow, in situations of uncertainty, knowledge/information is transformed into a commodity that can have an economic value. It is an indivisible good: at first, in fact, it is possessed only by the person who produced it. The producer behaves like a monopolist, seeking to take advantage of this condition of lack of competition. However, without adequate legal protection of his rights over the knowledge/information produced (e.g. using patents, licence fees, etc.), he will not be able to enjoy the resulting benefits – for example, selling the information, or products that contain it, on the open market. The costs of reproduction and transmission of information are, in fact, practically nil, so it only takes a single buyer who decides to pass the information on to others for the monopoly to quickly shatter.

3 In so-called 'club theory', a club is defined as 'a voluntary group deriving mutual benefit from sharing one or more of the following: production costs, the members' characteristics, or a good characterized by excludable benefits' (Sandler and Tschirhart 1997, 335). Club goods also take this form because they are subject to congestion/crowding, so that any eventual overuse by one person reduces the benefits or the quality for the other users.

4 Jaffe (1986, 998) found confirmation of spillover influence through various indicators of success: for example, with the same expenditure on research, companies operating in technology areas with more R&D obtain better results in terms of patents, profits and market value.

5 These agglomeration factors will be analysed in detail in the next chapter.

6 A patent is a legal instrument that gives the owner of a new invention, which may be susceptible to industrial application, the exclusive right to its use in the context of a specific area and for a fixed period of time (in Italy, for example, 20 years). A patent prevents third parties from using the invention without permission. In exchange, the owner of the invention is required to publicly disclose (via the documentation requested by the patent application) a detailed description of the invention's contents, specifying the way in which it is innovative compared to the knowledge already present in the technology sector. Citations referring to earlier patents show the knowledge 'debts' contracted by the inventor, defining the innovations presented by the new invention in relation to the preceding state of the art.

7 Jaffe, Trajtenberg and Henderson also compiled a control group of patents, similar in terms of year of grant and technological class to the citing patents, but with no direct connection to the patents of origin. This second group of patents made it possible to analyse the impact of the geographical concentration of the various sectors of technology: patents having the same location (co-localisation of citing patents and patents of origin) could simply have been due to the fact that firms specialising in certain

technologies are highly agglomerated in certain geographical areas. In this case, this would have been a sectoral more than a territorial effect. If, however, the co-localisation was superior in the sample studied to those registered in the control group, this would demonstrate that the spillovers had a territorial origin rather than a sectoral one (Jaffe *et al.* 1993, 581–3). And this was an event that – depending on the patent cohorts and actors considered – always occurred: co-localised citations in the sample studied were from two to seven times higher than those of the control sample (ibid., 590, Table III).

8 On this point, see the remarks put forward by Peter Thompson and Melanie Fox-Kean (2005), and the answers given by Rebecca Henderson, Adam Jaffe and Manuel Trajtenberg (2005).

9 The two scholars analysed 16,000 citations generated by a random sample of 1,500 patents granted between 2001–03.

10 Florida (1995, 534), for example, emphasises the presence of a plurality of elements of great importance at this territorial level: a manufacturing infrastructure based on networks of collaboration between enterprises; a human infrastructure of knowledge workers oriented towards ongoing learning; a physical and communication infrastructure that facilitates the sharing of information and the timely exchange of goods and services; a flexible and decentralised financial and industrial governance infrastructure, making for an efficient allocation of capital and providing advanced services.

11 For a reconstruction of the various contributions that make up the studies of regional innovation systems, see Asheim, Lawton Smith and Oughton (2011) and Miceli (2010, 25–36). For the characteristics that distinguish the regional innovation system from certain contiguous concepts (*milieux innovateurs*, districts, etc.), see Doloreux (2002, 253–6).

12 A French economist (1903–1987) who worked on regional development.

13 As will be seen in the next chapter, the aim is to generate 'related variety' – sectoral diversification that enables the exchange of complementary knowledge in areas that are technologically similar and capable of interactive learning.

14 Concise reviews of these studies and the relative typologies can be found in Doloreux and Parto (2005), and Doloreux (2002).

15 A scholar we will come back to in the next chapter.

7   Innovation and local development

This chapter addresses the issue of innovation at a local level. The basic idea shared by the contributions examined in this chapter is that the local agglomeration of companies creates competitive advantages. First, we will discuss the differences between localisation and urbanisation economies. This is followed by an outline of Marshall's observations on external economies and by the presentation of the analysis of the 'Italian school of industrial districts and local development' on the diffuse and collective nature of innovation in traditional sectors. Next, we examine the contributions of the 'Californian school of external economies' and of the school of the innovative 'milieu'. The second part of the chapter presents studies on technological districts, emphasising the need for an integrated approach to innovation, combining ecological, individual and relational analysis.

7.1 Agglomeration economies

The study of local innovation processes starts from the assumption that the territorial agglomeration of firms within specific areas creates special competitive advantages. What are the reasons for this phenomenon? Why do companies tend to choose locations close to each other? What benefits do they derive? Over the past few decades these questions have raised a heated debate among geographers, sociologists and economists. We will focus on one particular aspect of this debate here, showing how localisational advantages are connected to innovation processes.

A first definition to begin with: with the term *agglomeration economies*, economists mean the economic benefits that companies derive from the fact of being geographically localised close to one other. In economic literature, two different types are identified: *localisation economies*, resulting from the co-location of firms in the same sector, and *urbanisation economies*, related to the urban dimension – population volume, population density and the variety of activities and services available in the city (Feldman 2000, 383). This distinction is connected to the kind of external economies which can benefit businesses. In the first case, *Marshall-Arrow-Romer externalities* occur (Glaeser *et al.* 1992), due to sectoral specialisation, while in the second *Jacobs externalities* take place, related to sectoral diversification and the exchange of complementary knowledge. Let's have a more detailed look at these two concepts, starting with the latter.

Jacobs' idea (1969) is that, in urban areas, population density, proximity and interaction make exchange of information and contact between different ideas more fluid, thus facilitating innovation. The variety that circulates through social and economic relations makes it possible for individuals and businesses to acquire new knowledge that can be useful, allowing them to experiment with combinations never previously attempted. For example, technological solutions used in one economic activity may be applied experimentally to other activities; or the conjunction of knowledge or applications deriving from different sectors may generate innovative combinations. It follows then that the fostering of innovation has not so much to do with the concentration of firms in the same sector and the high level of specialisation, as with the variety and diversity of economic activities located in the same geographical area. The emphasis, in other words, is placed on the 'variety of resources' and the cross-fertilisation that occurs between firms pertaining to different sectors.

This idea has been tested on the largest cities in the US by Glaeser and his colleagues. The research set out to explain the development that took place over a period of 30 years (1956–87) in 170 cities, using the degree of sectoral specialisation/concentration present in local industry as the explanatory variable (Glaeser *et al.* 1992). The study's authors found that companies pertaining to a particular industry (for example, shoe companies, textile firms, etc.) registered higher employment growth in cities with certain specific features, where: (1) there is less specialisation in that particular sector of activity (i.e. where there are fewer shoe companies, textile firms etc.); (2) there are smaller companies and therefore more competition; (3) there is also a low concentration of other industrial sectors (other than shoes, textiles, etc.).

In other words, judging by the results of this research, an excess of sectoral specialisation slows down employment growth in industrial enterprises, while competition and diversification stimulate it. Economic exchanges, collaborations and knowledge spillovers within the same sector, therefore, are less important than those between different sectors.[1]

The idea of diversity as a factor in economic dynamism has also recently been reclaimed in regional and local innovation studies through the concept of *related variety*. The basic idea is Jacobs', but with a significant qualification. The hypothesis put forward is that neither sectoral diversity itself (which could involve excessive cognitive distance), nor sectoral specialisation (which could imply an excess of cognitive proximity), creates competitive advantage in certain territorial areas. It is, rather, the presence in the territory of a plurality of productive specialisations in *technologically related sectors* that facilitates interactive learning and regional innovation (Asheim, Boschma and Cooke 2011, 895). A study conducted in the Netherlands, for example, tested the effects on economic growth of the 'related varieties' of productive specialisations present at a local level (Frenken *et al.* 2007). This study confirmed the hypothesis: diversification tends to create Jacobs externalities, thus fostering product innovation and more radical innovation that generates greater employment growth (ibid., 687, 696).[2] But it is not simple variety that stimulates innovation and growth – as the study by Glaeser and his colleagues indicated – but rather the presence of multi-specialisation in *adjacent technology sectors*, or at least sectors with compatible knowledge bases. The 'cognitive proximity' between these areas, in fact, results in a higher *absorptive capacity*, facilitating the reception and use of their respective kinds of knowledge and therefore their cross-fertilisation.

7.2 The 'Italian school'

Localised externalities related to production specialisation, on the other hand, refer to classical economist Alfred Marshall's writings about the industrial districts of small- and medium-size companies present in late nineteenth century England. The concept of the *industrial district* (ID) was then rediscovered and relaunched into international debate by the Italian economist Giacomo Becattini, who defines it as

> a socio-territorial entity characterised by the active coexistence, in a natural-istically and historically determined, circumscribed land area, of a com-munity of people and a population of industrial enterprises. In the district, as opposed to what happens in other environments (e.g. manufacturing cities) community and companies tend, so to speak, to interpenetrate one other.
>
> (Becattini 1990; 2000, 58–9)

As can be seen, this is a definition that combines aspects that are both socio-territorial (the local community) and economic (the companies). The main characteristic of the *community of people* is the fact that they incorporate a homogeneous system of values 'expressed in terms of an ethic of work, activity, family, reciprocity and change' (ibid., 59). This also requires an institutional and regulatory system that supports those values and ensures their inter-generational reproduction. The district's continuity over time requires that there remains – against the backdrop of productive and technological change taking place in the world – an unsimple congruence between the socio-cultural and economic com-ponents (ibid., 76). It involves, that is, a 'complete production process', which also includes the reproduction of human factors and the preservation of its col-lective identity. As regards the ID's productive infrastructure, the *population of industrial companies* is composed of small- and medium-sized independent enterprises (SMEs), pertaining to the same productive sector – in a broad sense – linked together by a specialised division of labour. This sub-division of produc-tion enables SMEs to achieve a high level of efficiency and competitiveness in each of the phases that comprise the productive process typical of the district. Marshall, in fact, believed that the 'economies of scale' – the benefits associated with large production volumes, which reduce the average unit costs of goods – were not the exclusive preserve of large enterprises. In the case of products for which it is possible to break the production process up into different phases, an alternative is the concentration, within the same ID, of a large number of small companies, which specialise in a single part of the processing. These specialised producers are able to carry out the work very cheaply and with high quality standards (Whitaker 1975, 196).

Marshall conceives the ID's field of specialisation, however, in a particularly broad sense, including not only the main productive activity (e.g. textiles, foot-wear, furniture, etc.), but also the 'subsidiary industries' that provide equipment, materials, complementary products and specialised services. Indeed, the pres-ence of a plurality of complementary sectors ensures better stability over time for the industrial district, both by modernising the original industry and by creat-ing new productive specialisations (Becattini 2000, 55; Bellandi 1987, 64–5).[3]

But why does the localisation of a number of SMEs within the same ID create a competitive advantage? Marshall distinguishes *internal economies*, which depend on the organisational efficiency and resources specific to individual com-panies, from *external economies*, which depend on the general development of the industry to which those companies pertain. Speaking of the ID, he is prim-arily referring to external economies, which create three types of competitive advantage for SMEs (ibid., 52).[4]

1   The first advantage is related to the so-called *economies of specialisation* arising from the presence of a large number of qualified suppliers and 'sub-sidiary industries': manufacturers specialising in the construction of machinery specifically designed for each production phase of a particular activity; companies specialising in the supply of materials, in product mar-keting, etc. (Becattini 2000, 53). This makes it possible for SMEs to take advantage of high quality, reasonably priced machinery, products and ser-vices.

2   The second advantage is connected to a *qualified and skilled labour market*, which provides SMEs with a high level of human capital thanks to the pro-ductive traditions historically sedimented in the local community. The socialisation processes that take place in the family, in schools, workshops and businesses, and the strong specialisation in that particular sector, create a special aptitude for industrial work that has cognitive components (know-ledge and expertise), normative components (the work ethic) and social components (personal knowledge and social skills). In short, there exists an '*industrial atmosphere*' in these areas, so that 'the mysteries of the trade become no mysteries; but are as it were in the air, and children learn many of them unconsciously' (Marshall 1890, Chapter 10).

3   Finally, the third advantage involves two distinct aspects: *circulation of information* and *knowledge spillovers*. The first, information flow, is related to the ease of obtaining information crucial for trade: for example, regarding product quality, pricing, reliability of suppliers, etc. These are elements that significantly lower the transaction costs of economic activities and reduce the possibility of 'opportunistic behaviour' – receiving a nasty surprise, in

other words (due to deception) in economic transactions. The second aspect (knowledge spillovers) is related to the presence of a stock of specific knowledge and specialist skills, linked to the local context, which facilitate the production of new ideas and their diffusion amongst SMEs. This *contextual knowledge* is mostly tacit and informal, and can only be acquired through long processes of socialisation which require a sharing of experience at a local level (Becattini and Rullani 2000, 105).

That said, contextual knowledge is not enough in itself to preserve the competitiveness of the ID over time. To ensure continuous renewal, companies and other district actors must also draw on the codified knowledge that circulates in the global networks and in particular on more formalised scientific and technological knowledge. It is therefore a matter of maintaining a process of *versatile integration* active between two cognitive spheres: the first related specifically to local context, the second to external contexts and more formalised codes (ibid., 105–6). This interchange involves an activity of knowledge encoding/decoding: on the one hand, a partial formalisation of contextual knowledge and, on the other, an adaptation of abstract and formalised knowledge to specific local needs.

The ID represents a particularly favourable environment for innovation, for a number of reasons. First, *economic reasons* related to competition and specialist division of labour. Second, *normative reasons* related to work ethic, professional reputation and to the particular appreciation that innovative ideas receive. Third, *social reasons* related to the relational networks that innervate the local economy and that facilitate both the cross-fertilisation of ideas and the spread of imitative innovation. In the district, in fact, the introduction of *technological innovation assumes a collective and diffuse characterisation*. Configured as a social process that takes place gradually and involves both companies and the entire population, it brings into play the very identity of the local producers, whose values also include pride at being technologically up to date (Becattini 2000, 72).

Marshall recognised the advantages of large companies in terms of innovation, but believed that small entrepreneurs as well, especially if collocated in industrial districts, could make a contribution to technological progress (Bellandi 1987, 61). The strong specialist division of labour, in fact, encourages innovation focused on individual stages of production, in a way very similar to what Adam Smith had already pointed out (Robertson *et al.* 2009, 271).[5] In addition, innovative processes enjoy two advantages in ID: (1) on the one hand, they can make use of the *individual creativity* and absolute dedication typical of independent producers, who work for themselves and know how to draw immediate competitive benefit from their discoveries; (2) on the other, they can take advantage of the *collective creativity* that involves the whole local community.

In fact, in the ID, many manufacturers and economic actors are faced simultaneously with the same problems, try out new paths, propose solutions that are discussed locally and subjected to the critical scrutiny of experts and the market. Information circulates both through economic transactions – in relations with suppliers, customers and competitors – and in social relations that innervate the local community through relationships of kinship, friendship and neighbourship. Errors and failures, as well as successful solutions, swiftly become shared patrimony, breathing new life into the testing of further technological and organisational solutions:

> Good work is rightly appreciated, inventions and improvements in machinery, in processes and the general organization of the business have their merits promptly discussed: if one man starts a new idea, it is taken up by others and combined with suggestions of their own; and thus it becomes the source of further new ideas.
>
> (Marshall 1890, Chapter 10)

What has been defined as a *diffuse innovative capacity* permeates the district, referring as it does to the decentralised nature of the production of new knowledge. This mainly involves forms of learning by experience which exploit the practical knowledge gained operationally by producers (*learning by doing*) and users (*learning by using*), or arising from their relationships (*learning by interacting*). This 'distributed knowledge' makes it possible to introduce incremental improvements to products and production processes, continuously improving the overall innovative capacity of the ID (Bellandi 1989, 150).

While the mix of competition and cooperation that characterises the district's 'community market' continually stimulates the search for new technological solutions to beat the competition, it also facilitates collaboration, because the fractioned nature of skills leads to the search for a plurality of contributions, often giving rise to a phenomenon of genuine *collective innovation* (Dei Ottati 1987, 134).

> when the total number of men interested in the matter is very large there are to be found among them many who, by their intellect and temper, are fitted to originate new ideas. Each new idea is canvassed and improved upon by many minds; each new accidental experience and each deliberate experiment will afford food for reflection and for new suggestions, not to a few persons but to many.
>
> (Whitaker 1975, 198)

The motivations that provide the impetus for innovation are not only economic. In addition to competition and financial incentives, there is also the desire to establish or consolidate professional reputation and social prestige (Bellandi 1987, 64). Economic and non-economic motives deeply pervade the history and daily life of these local communities.

It is therefore no coincidence that Italian economic sociologists have actively contributed to the study of these productive zones, highlighting the social and institutional roots of ID in the regions of the so-called 'Third Italy' (Triveneto, Emilia-Romagna, Tuscany, Marche and Umbria): areas that have combined vibrant industrial growth based on small- and medium-sized enterprises with solid social integration (Bagnasco 1977; Paci 1980; Crouch *et al.* 1986). Research on the Third Italy and 'diffuse development' – one that is not concentrated in large urban agglomerations and huge productive units – has seen a fruitful convergence between a variety of disciplines transform into a combined, interpretative effort regarding the modality of the *social construction of the market* (Bagnasco 1986; Pyke and Sengenberger 1991, 1992).

The contribution of sociology – but not sociology alone – has made it possible to shed more light on the social and territorial logics that have supported and nurtured this development model. This brought out the importance of 'non-economic' factors such as the history and socio-institutional structure of these regions, which in turn led to focusing on the role played by variables such as pre-industrialisation agricultural structures, patterns of urbanisation, artisanal traditions, the *economic functions* of the extended family, the role of familial and parental relations in the ownership of companies and in the relationships between these companies, the importance of territorial political sub-cultures and models of regulation of the economy, and the more or less interventionist approach of municipal and regional governments depending on preceding political traditions (Trigilia 1990; Ramella 2000, 2005a). To sum up, studies on the Third Italy have favoured an interpretative effort involving a convergence between economic sociologists and 'heterodox' economists that has given rise to *an Italian school of industrial districts and local development*, which, as will be seen later, also investigated innovation in technological districts.

7.3 Worlds of production and innovative 'milieux'

A very similar approach to that of the 'Italian school' is found in certain works by Michael Storper, in which he talks about technological districts based on SMEs. Here, too, the basic idea is that innovation derives benefit from the geographical and cultural proximity that facilitates the exchange of information and knowledge (Storper 1993). The so-called '*Californian school of external economies*' – which started in the US in the early eighties and which Storper helped found – stresses that the division of labour between firms is a response to the uncertainty caused by market and technological change, which tends to increase the costs of economic transactions. Territorial agglomeration allows companies to reduce these costs and to take advantage of external economies that increase competitive capacity (Storper 1995, 198). Regions and localities, in fact, generate a variety of *untraded interdependencies* – a set of relations, conventions, informal rules and customs that are able to facilitate the coordination of economic actors under conditions of uncertainty (Storper 1997, 5). 'Relational goods', in other words, which – in the context of a *learning economy* – make it possible for some areas to learn better and faster than others, turning this knowledge into a competitive advantage difficult to imitate. Similar contextual knowledge can, in fact, only be reproduced very slowly and with great difficulty.

Storper defines these territorial agglomerations as 'regional worlds of production': 'the interlinkage of people, organizations, objects and ideas, with a certain indivisibility and wholeness' (ibid., 112). Fundamental to these agglomerative tendencies is one of proximity's key advantages: the possibility of establishing *personal, face-to-face contact* (Storper and Venables 2004). This type of relationship is particularly relevant when information is imperfect, subject to rapid change and not easily codifiable, as often happens in innovative and creative activities. In such situations, co-presence greatly facilitates interaction between economic actors and the possibility of reaching an agreement.

Face-to-face relationships, in fact, represent an effective mechanism of economic coordination thanks to four characteristics: (1) efficient communication technology, allowing control of both verbal and non-verbal dimensions; (2) stimulation of reciprocal trust and collaborative behaviour; (3) facilitation of screening and socialisation, learning and mutual monitoring processes: personal networks lead to shared norms and codes of communication, the circulation of reliable opinions and information regarding people's competence and professionalism, and, therefore, facilitate reputational screening; and (4) provision of appropriate psychological motivations to carry out personal 'good performance', stimulating imitation and competition.

At a territorial level, this set of factors determines a specific *buzz effect*, which facilitates the communication of thoughts and complex concepts and the cross-fertilisation of ideas rendering the companies operating in these areas more productive and innovative. Cities, above all – especially those exposed to transnational flows – create this kind effect. As Storper and Venables write, 'the most globalized cities also seem to have the most localized buzz' (ibid., 366).

An equally strong emphasis on learning processes and on the local dimension is found among scholars belonging to the *Groupe de recherche européen sur les milieux innovateurs* (GREMI). The *innovative milieu* (innovative environment) can be defined as a 'complex network of mainly informal social relationships on a limited geographical area, often determining a specific external "image" and a specific internal "representation" and sense of belonging, which enhance the local innovative capability through synergetic and collective learning processes' (Camagni 1991, 3). This approach, the development of which began in the eighties, shares the same concepts as the Italian school of districts and local development, focusing in particular on innovative processes that take place in SME areas – the *milieux innovateurs* (Aydalot 1986). Cognitive and interactional dimensions play a central role in this study approach: the territory is conceived as a relational space that stimulates collective learning processes, incorporated in the milieu and the local labour market, reducing uncertainty related to technological change (Camagni and Capello 2002, 11).[6] Collective learning is defined as 'the growth of knowledge within a technological trajectory incorporated in a local context' (ibid., 16). Spatial proximity creates three types of learning channel:

1 stable, long-term relationships with local suppliers and customers;
2 a labour market with high worker mobility;
3 spin-off mechanisms from local businesses.

The local dimension of these processes does not, however, rule out strategic partnerships with actors external to the innovative milieu. These extra-local collaborations are essential in order to convey new knowledge and avoid the risk of *lock-in*,[7] which reduces the ability to perceive and cope with emerging challenges. As already noted, the *milieux* are designed to have the SMEs as a reference, but they are not limited to them, nor to the traditional sectors or to smaller urban contexts. Aydalot (1986, 1988), for example, identifies three modalities of innovation, which also involve different territorial processes. The first refers to the restructuring taking place in traditional industrial regions, through technological change implemented by local companies, with the work of those directly involved in the production cycle (engineers, skilled workers). The second concerns the restructuring/innovation of large companies, which makes the most of in-house R&D activities, especially when these are directed towards new productive sectors related to emerging markets. This innovation modality may be associated with the process of territorial reconversion thanks to the external attraction of large companies that make it possible to renew the local economy, distancing it from pre-existing specialisations. Finally, the third modality is related to more radical innovations and connects to scientific production and entrepreneurial activities pertaining to the world of research and academia (as in the case of biotechnology analysed in Chapter 6).

As can be seen, both the Californian school of external economies and GREMI's innovative *milieux* hark back to a large extent to the guidelines and mechanisms already analysed by the Italian school of districts while, however, setting out certain considerations regarding innovation in non-traditional sectors and in technological districts which then went on to generate further developments over the following years.

7.4 High-tech districts

In recent decades, studies on local innovation systems have more systematically addressed the contexts of high technology, with Silicon Valley (SV) – already mentioned in some of the earlier chapters – as a starting point. One well-known study dedicated to this particular case is AnnaLee Saxenian's (1994), which compares the famous Californian technology region and Route 128 in the Boston area (R128).[8] In the early eighties both of these productive systems – world leaders in electronics in the previous decade – experienced radical challenges due to increased international competition: the SV chip manufacturers were threatened by Japanese competition in the market for semiconductor memories, while R128 minicomputer manufacturers had to cope with the advance of new companies producing workstations and personal computers. In responding to these radical challenges the two areas followed divergent developmental trajectories, and by the end of the decade the Boston area had ceded leadership in computer production to SV. According to Saxenian, this different response capacity depended on the economic structure of the two areas. Companies are not isolated from their geographical context, they are inserted in a social and institutional environment that shapes them, and it is shaped by their strategies and structures (ibid.). The local productive system[9] consists of three elements:

1 local culture and institutions;
2 productive structure;
3 the internal organisation of companies.

SV is an example of an industrial system based on horizontal, inter-company networks, while R128 is a typical system based on vertically integrated, independent companies. The first system – similar to the one present in the Italian industrial districts – can stimulate collective learning and adaptive flexibility because it is based on a mix of enterprises that cooperate with each other, share work and specialise in related products and technologies.

High-tech companies are highly internationalised and operate in global markets, and yet for SV firms strategic relationships are at the local level since face-to-face relations and rapidity of trade play a crucial role in the development of their products. The proliferation of social relations, an open and mobile labour market, the continuous arrival on the scene of new entrepreneurs, and, above all, competition between companies, ensure SV's continual renewal. Learning and innovation benefit from worker mobility and an organisational structure within companies based on working teams characterised by 'weak ties' and little hierarchy, which facilitates communication between the various business units, as well as with customers and suppliers. Corporate boundaries are also permeable to the outside, both to other companies and to local organisations and institutions such as universities, public agencies and trade associations (ibid.).

In contrast, the R128 production system hinges on a few large, integrated, independent companies, who carry out most of their activities in-house. Corporate boundaries are well defined, the organisation is hierarchical, and information mainly descends from the company's higher echelons. Secrecy and corporate loyalty govern relationships with employees, as they also do in relationships with suppliers and customers: the kind of link that hinders circulation of information in the economy, remaining as it does segregated within corporate circuits that are isolated from each other.

SV's network productive system, therefore, guarantee it a crucial competitive advantage by supporting its companies' innovative and adaptive capacity. It is a decentralised system wholly suitable for a rapidly changing technological environment: it stimulates the exploration of a variety of technological paths and the boundaries between large and small firms and between different sectors are rendered porous. On the other hand, a system based on independent businesses, like R128, is suitable for a more stable technological context and market, which make it possible to benefit from strong economies of scale. When this scenario changed, however, local businesses ran into serious difficulties in terms of renewal.

In Saxenian's view, Marshallian external economies cannot account for the different evolution of the two areas: the explanation cannot be based on spatial proximity and economies of agglomeration since in both cases production activities are concentrated in geographically bounded areas. A network approach to the analysis of productive systems is required, such as the one used to explain SV's great adaptive capacity (Saxenian 2001, 357–61).

Actually, in light of what we have seen in previous sections, we know that the dynamics described by Saxenian are typical of collective learning and 'diffuse innovation', previously highlighted by the Italian school of districts and local development, with the difference that Italian scholars had mainly focused on traditional sectors (e.g. textiles, leather goods, furniture, tiles) and modern sectors (e.g. mechanical engineering). Saxenian's study is interesting because it applies the same analytical categories to analyse what can be defined as 'high-tech districts' – areas, that is, specialised in productive sectors employing new technologies related to scientific advances, such as the fields of chemistry and pharmaceuticals, biotechnology, aerospace, information and communication (ICT) and others.

The question that arises, then, is this: why should the phenomena of agglomeration, which in the past proved to be so important in traditional manufacturing sectors, also turn out to be of great importance for high technology sectors and the most innovative companies? The research carried out by some Italian economic sociologists has tried to come up with a suitable answer. Carlo Trigilia (2005), for example, highlights how the reasons are connected to the evolution of productive models and competitive scenarios. In the operating conditions of the contemporary economy, the social and relational dimension of innovation tends to become increasingly more important compared to the strictly corporate one, as well as augmenting the local embeddedness of innovation processes. Innovation has a crucial interactive and dialogical component; it involves 'conversations', as Lester and Piore (2004) called it, between a number of subjects with different experiences that enhance learning and discovery. To function, however, these conversations require – as we have seen – an informal and directly interactive component that brings territorial proximity into play.

Thus, *local innovation systems* or high-tech districts take form, with a concentration of SMEs – or even large companies in some cases – that collaborate with one other. Of course, not all high-tech production assumes a district configuration. For this to happen, three conditions have to be realised:

1   the production process must be broken down into different phases or components;
2   the uncertainty of technological trajectories must stimulate the sharing of risks and costs of innovation;
3   market variability must demand a high degree of relational and organisational flexibility, and stimulate the continuous search for new productive solutions (Trigilia 2005, 54–5).

In such circumstances, economies external to individual firms, but within a specific territorial area, acquire great importance – as is the case with the traditional

ID. According to Trigilia, external economies are the product of *local collective competition goods*, which create benefits for the companies because they both lower production costs and increase innovative capacity (Crouch *et al.* 2001, 215; Crouch *et al.* 2005). These externalities can be either tangible or intangible: the former include infrastructure and local services; the latter, both cognitive and regulatory resources, such as tacit, contextualised knowledge, conventions, norms of reciprocity, and local social capital (Le Galès and Voelzkow 2001, 3). SMEs are not able to produce these competitive advantages by themselves: these are instead generated and supplied within the local production system as typical collective or club goods.

Based on research carried out on certain local production systems of high-tech SMEs in Italy and Europe, Trigilia also highlights some specificities with respect to traditional districts.[10] In addition to the external economies that characterise all the ID, there are some that assume a specific connotation in high-tech areas. First of all, it is necessary to consider access to research and the possibility of linking up with scientific structures and universities. The importance of this type of collective goods, for companies specialising in high-technology sectors, is clear: for this reason, innovation is closely connected to the possibility of incorporating continuous progress made in the field of scientific research.

A second type of externality is the availability of specialised suppliers of goods and advanced services, specific to high-tech companies: for example, financial services, especially in the form of venture capital, support services for start-ups, consultancy services for patenting, etc.

A third type of externality is related to context. The availability of suitably equipped areas or technology parks, as well as adequate communication infrastructure, is obviously important for businesses. But the socio-cultural and environmental quality of the local system is also a vital factor for high-tech productive systems, influencing as it does the ability to attract – and retain – skilled and highly educated specialists and their families.[11] Context quality, therefore, affects the possibility of forming innovative professional communities, which are particularly relevant in technological districts.

The relationship with the territory is also different in high-tech districts. The activities of these sectors permeate the economy in a less totalising way, which means that a lower level of identification with the local community is created: so the sense of territorial belonging becomes less important and the fact of belonging to the professional community assumes greater significance. That said, one must also mention the other socio-economic factors that mark the diversity of technological districts.

- The role of family and kinship networks is less crucial than in traditional districts. High-tech companies are, in fact, not 'family-firms', as often happens in ID, but rather 'partner-firms', formed by people who meet during their studies or professional career.
- The training of entrepreneurs is more formalised and based on longer periods of education.

- The social capital on which the entrepreneurs can rely is different, based less on community and parental networks with respect to traditional sectors (Ramella 2005).
- The modalities of generation of public goods and local governance are based less on what is inherited from the history of the local communities and more on intentional processes of cooperation between public and private actors. Their origin is to a greater extent dependent on specific policies – at national, regional and local levels – as well as on intermediation organisations that play an effective role of interfacing and reciprocal openness between the production centres of new knowledge and local companies.

Like traditional districts, however, high-tech areas are also based on 'a *social construction of innovation* that is locally embedded' (Trigilia 2005, 61). Some recent investigations have made it possible to investigate these issues in more detail, showing that a strong territorial agglomeration of innovative activity is also registered in Italy. Research on high and medium-high technology sectors[12] analysed these phenomena at a sub-regional level – that of local labour systems[13] – using patent applications filed by Italian firms between 1995 and 2004 at the European organisation for the protection of intellectual property rights (European Patent Office, EPO) as an indicator. Patents are a well-established indicator in the scientific literature (especially in the economic field) that studies innovative output.[14] The results of the survey revealed several findings of interest (Ramella and Trigilia 2010a).

First of all, the strong relevance of sectors of high and medium-high technology in patenting activity, which represent, respectively, 24 per cent and 50 per cent of the national total. Second, the geographical concentration of EPO patents in the more developed Italian regions, in large metropolitan cities and in the medium-sized cities of the Third Italy. Third, the marked local agglomeration. The macro data, in fact, risks overshadowing the clustering of patent activities in more circumscribed territorial systems. Although they correspond to a small portion of the local labour systems (just over 6 per cent), *innovation leading systems* in mechanical engineering (the leading medium-high technology sector) and high technology represent the vast majority of EPO patents: 76 per cent in mechanical engineering and 84 per cent in high technology.

The socio-territorial profile of the leading systems, however, is significantly different in the two sectors. High technology is characterised by an urban connotation, an embeddedness in large cities, with a large number of university and college graduates, and where the larger firms and advanced service industry play an important role. The quality of life and the presence of local collective goods appears high. The mechanical engineering leading systems also show a fairly high quality in terms of the socio-institutional context, with a provision of infrastructure above the national average. In this case, however, a relatively greater agglomeration is to be found in the regions and manufacturing productive systems of the Third Italy, with a significant presence of medium-sized enterprises. The urban dimension plays an important role, but – in contrast to the high technology systems – the endowment of advanced services, universities and college graduates is less common.

What makes the innovation leading systems in the sectors of mechanical engineering and high-tech stand out? Compared to other local economic systems (control group) – endowed with good entrepreneurial and productive resources in the two sectors but with a far lower patenting capacity – what differentiates most leading systems is the quality of the local collective goods (Biagiotti 2010).[15] In fact, in order to develop a highly innovative local system, in addition to an adequate economic and entrepreneurial base, the support of a strong institutional structure is also necessary; the latter comprises a good endowment of human capital and university centres, a developed infrastructure network, qualified services and a high quality of life.

What do these results tell us? That an analysis conducted at a national level alone is not sufficient to exhaustively define the characteristic features of a country's innovation system. For example, Italy's experience in the most technologically advanced sectors, like that of the rest of continental Europe, is characterised more by *incremental*, rather than *radical*, innovation (Hall and Soskice 2001). The continental systems, in fact, have problems in dealing with the rapid reconversion of financial and human resources which in the Anglo-Saxon models foster radical innovation based on the speedy introduction of completely new products or processes.

In the Italian case, however, the analysis carried out on EPO patents indicates strong territorial and sectoral variability. In other words, there emerges a national model with two prevailing specialisations featuring different geographical locations and socio-economic characteristics. In short, *two distinct sectoral and territorial innovation systems*: (1) the *mechanical engineering system* (in particular the machinery and equipment industry), more embedded in the Third Italy cities, and; (2) the *high-tech system*, more present in the north-west, in large metropolitan cities, especially in Milan, but also in Rome and in other smaller cities of the Third Italy.

The territorial differentiation in the Italian innovation system is also confirmed by the ('micro-level') analysis of collaboration networks that emerge from the patent documents. These collaborative networks show, on the one hand, the strong importance of a local dimension – short networks of collaboration – and, on the other hand, the presence of long, extra-regional networks, especially in high-tech sectors (Caloffi 2010a). In particular, an examination of the partnerships between the teams of inventors registered in the patents highlights the existence of *regional models* of innovative activity (Figure 7.1). Two configurations emerge in the centre-north: on the one hand, polycentric structures are found in the Third Italy regions, with collaborations more self-contained within the local and regional context; the north-west, on the other hand, is characterised by the predominance of a few large urban centres (including Milan and Turin), with radiating networks that extend both within and outside the regional area.

In the centre-south, instead, we have the 'Lazio model', where Rome, a pole of the first magnitude, centralises the set of relationships, connecting almost

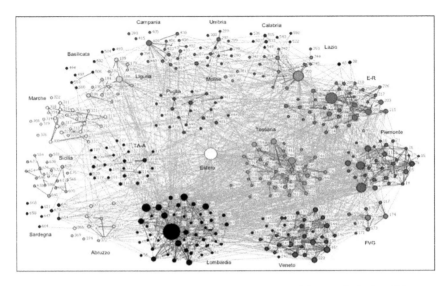

Figure 7.1 Territorial networks of inventors (source: adapted from Caloffi (2010b)).

exclusively to other large urban extra-regional centres; while the southern regions of Italy are present in the analysed networks to a far lesser degree than other geographical areas (Caloffi 2010b; Ramella and Trigilia 2010b).

Besides local systems (ecological analysis) and patent collaborations (relational analysis), the study on EPO patents also examined in depth 400 EPO companies in the mechanical engineering and high-tech sectors (individual analysis). What are the distinctive features that differentiate the EPO firms from other companies? First of all, these are solid companies operating in highly competitive markets (Ramella 2011). In the majority of cases, they are small-medium or large enterprises that have worked for many years in environments characterised by strong uncertainty: partly due to the competition they face, partly due to rapid technological change, partly due to instability of demand. Second, they are *highly innovative* – research-intensive companies that introduce many innovations to the market. Third, they are *deeply embedded at both a social and territorial level*. The uncertainty of the competitive environments is, in fact, dealt with through the social embeddedness of their activities.

One of the elements that most distinguishes EPO companies is their *innovative partnerships*: external collaborations (with other companies, universities, research centres) for research and innovation activities. Such partnerships are fairly generalised in these companies, with 70 per cent making use of them. As a point of comparison, it is worth noting that nationally only 11 per cent of other industrial innovative companies have signed cooperation agreements on innovation: a figure that places Italy last in Europe (the EU average is 26 per cent; Cis 2010).

Innovation, as we have seen, also has a clear territorial embeddedness. Most companies with European patents hail from the leading innovative systems in mechanical engineering and high technology; that is, they operate in local contexts that are highly qualified in both economic and socio-institutional terms. That said, their innovative partnerships are not confined exclusively to a local level. The companies with the best innovative performance, in fact, manage to combine the advantages of short networks (local and regional) with those of long networks (extra-regional). But even the latter are socially embedded. The majority of innovative partnerships, in fact, do not respond to purely economic and market logic, but are based on collaborations in which social ties play a major role.

The literature has often pointed out that innovation, especially in high technology areas, requires a 'project-led' organisation, with the establishment of ad hoc teams configured as 'temporary systems' of relations (Goodman 1981). In other respects, however, this specific form of organisation – founded on close interaction and interdependence within the working groups – is also based on the reputations for competence and reliability that the various partners have earned over time. These 'temporary collaborations', in other words, have their roots in the recurring practices of inter-firm cooperation (Grabher 2002). The Italian research clearly shows the predominant role of strong ties in structuring innovative partnerships, both local and extra-local; and this relational architecture occurs among both mechanical engineering and high-tech companies. The importance of tacit knowledge, but also the risks of opportunism associated with the use of more codified knowledge, makes trust an extremely significant resource for this type of transaction.

The last element that distinguishes EPO firms is their *high economic performance*. These are companies with high levels of turnover, productivity and exporting, maintaining a discreet dynamism even during the most difficult years of the international economic crisis. However, the link between innovation and economic performance is not automatic: even among EPO firms, revenue demonstrates a high level of heterogeneity. This heterogeneity depends on variable manufacturing, managerial and market expertise, which is not necessarily associated with the technico-scientific skills and innovative capacity present within a company. In particular, positive results in terms of turnover require a strong *strategic integration*: a good endowment of human capital and organisational practices that valorise company flexibility and cohesion.

It is this *internal organisational strategy* that augments the effectiveness of *external innovative partnerships*. In addition to the importance of the organisational dimension, this makes it possible to emphasise the close relationship that unites the cognitive and fiduciary aspects in innovation processes. The socio-normative component is often neglected in innovation studies, especially those from an economic perspective. However, the generation of new knowledge and its economic valorisation depends on the social capital that the company may have internally, as well as in its external relations.

In conclusion, the research on companies with European patents confirms the importance of the social and territorial embeddedness of innovation, but also the importance of the strategic choices that companies make. Crucial to their success is the ability to use different skills, in terms of type and origin, balancing *resources of cohesion and resources of variety*. Innovation and economic performance require a mix of resources collocated both inside and outside the company. If on the one hand external resources increase the *requisite variety* of knowledge, on the other, internal resources are important to potentiate the *capacity of productive use* of such knowledge. Successful company strategies, therefore, are those which exploit the *embedded complementarity of innovative resources*, deploying socially and territorially structured learning mechanisms for economic purposes.

To sum up, the investigation carried out into Italian leading innovative systems in high and medium-high technology sectors brings up several points.

- First, even limiting the analysis to sectors with greater use of 'codified knowledge', at least two different sectoral and regional innovation systems are found at the national level – mechanical engineering and high technology – which have distinct innovation methods and socio-territorial roots.
- It is therefore important to conduct an analysis on different territorial levels.
- The study of innovation systems still requires microfoundations (micro-level analyses) relating to the strategies of the actors and their relationships.

The emphasis placed on the systemic nature of innovation should not lead to the role of *agency* and relational networks being overlooked: it is, in fact, necessary to take account of the actors' intentional strategies and the constraints and opportunities arising from the relationships that they establish at various territorial levels.

The crucial role of agency regards not only companies but also territories – a point brought out by another survey conducted on Italian cities of innovation (Burroni and Trigilia 2011). The study identified 34 high-tech urban centres, which were grouped into three distinct types: (1) *metropolitan cities*; (2) *medium-sized university cities*; and (3) *small towns*. These 34 poles encompass the vast majority of Italian high-tech activity: while representing only 5 per cent of the local labour systems, with 32 per cent of the Italian population, they include more than 60 per cent of high-tech workers and 75 per cent of the European patents granted to Italian companies (ibid., 43–7).

With regard to the *generative mechanisms* that create these high-tech specialised local systems, two types of factors stand out: *context* (historical and natural endowments, external economies, etc.), to which the authors refer in terms of the '*system-city*'; and *agency*, linked chiefly to entrepreneurial action (economic, scientific and political) and the intentional intervention of public and private actors, which delineate the profile of the '*actor-city*'. High-tech urban centres arise from the intersection of the 'system-city' and the 'actor-city': new high technology activities are produced by the encounter between certain innovative actors and the contextual factors they activate and valorise.

One general feature of particular importance which affects Italian cities[16] is the centrality of autonomous entrepreneurial action; something which is not – or only slightly – influenced by the actions of other public actors. Autonomous entrepreneurial action – an agency factor – is linked to historically formed context elements, and often to the transformation or reorganisation processes of pre-existing large firms. This means that it is the city as a system of rich and complex endowments and relationships, as well as of pre-existing skills, that above all promotes high-tech growth. But it is a factor – related to historically formed external economies – that does not necessarily bring about the triggering effect. There are urban areas – especially among medium-sized and small cities – with contexts that provide this sort of potential but where the high-tech phenomenon does not take root or is marginal. Agency factors are therefore the ones that make a difference: the presence, that is, of specific and autonomous entrepreneurial action that valorises the resources of the context.

7.5 Territorial and relational proximity

It is time to draw some more general conclusions from the contributions analysed in this chapter. What are the common factors in this set of approaches to the theme of innovation?

The first element is the importance of the geographical aspect. Innovative activities tend to be geographically concentrated, and their spatial dislocation is not random. The spatial dimension becomes important both for traditional, and more modern sectors of production, in low-tech and medium-tech industries as well as in high-tech industries.

The second element is the centrality of knowledge and human capital – in the new global productive scenarios, the creation of new ideas has in fact become crucial.

The third element is the importance given to the socio-institutional context and the presence of local collective goods capable of generating external economies, both tangible and intangible, which increase companies' innovative capacity. It is important to stress that the economic endowments of territories and individual companies, as well as their investments in R&D activity, are not enough by themselves to explain innovation agglomeration.

Finally, *the fourth element* is the systemic and network dimension of innovation. The contributions we reviewed particularly emphasised the relational aspect, involving relationships between different institutional spheres, between individual and collective actors, and between public and private subjects. Innovation actors (be they entrepreneurs, researchers, research centres, etc.) make use of personal and relational ties (weak and strong) for their activity – ties that convey *cognitive resources of variety*, as well as *normative resources of cohesion and trust*.

Two core beliefs lie behind these elements. First, the idea that *tacit knowledge*, of a personal and contextual kind, plays an important role in innovation and that this knowledge is sticky and therefore difficult to circulate. The second is that innovation pivot points are to be found at a regional and local level, since knowledge, networks and crucial competitive advantages develop more easily at this territorial level.

In recent years, however, both of these assumptions have been called into question by the intensification of phenomena that represent seemingly radical challenges to territorial approaches to innovation. On the one hand there is the growing importance of scientific and more formalised knowledge; on the other hand there are the globalisation processes – the proliferation of innovative partnerships with actors collocated externally to the territory of reference and often operating on a global scale (i.e. multinationals) (Becattini *et al.* 2009, xxiii). The first challenge especially concerns the traditional industrial districts, which see their usual innovation modality, based mostly on incremental improvements and learning by doing, called into question. The second, however, also involves technological districts and high-tech companies which, as we have seen, have a relationship that is less tied to their home territory.

Even if they change the modus operandi and the relational architecture of local economies, these challenges do not really question the agglomeration of innovative activities which, with clear empirical evidence, continue to occur (Crescenzi *et al.* 2007; Crescenzi and Rodríguez-Pose, 2011; Usai 2008). Even companies operating in international markets, in fact, are not indifferent to the territories and the resources that these offer, just as local economies are not all equally able to take advantage of opportunities arising from the global expansion of markets.

Such challenges, therefore, do not indicate a loss of importance for the territorial aspect of innovation, but suggest rather that geographic locations should not be reified, and not be considered important in themselves regardless of the opportunities and benefits they offer. As has been said, *territory should be understood as a relational context in which the social construction of innovation takes place.* This does not mean that the relationships that take place externally to it are irrelevant. On the contrary – and especially in Europe – in the most dynamic and innovative local systems there exists a plurality of actors and institutions (universities, individual teachers, companies, as well as public agencies, etc.) that function as relational hubs towards the outside: portals, of a kind, which connect local actors with the global dimension. Moreover, not all the actors relevant to the competitiveness of companies and territory are local. Partnerships with extra-regional businesses or universities, national policies and the activities of *global players* (e.g. multinational corporations) can have a great importance for territories. In other words, the following statements should not be considered as contradictory to one other.

- The study of the geography of innovation is still relevant today because the resources generated at local and regional level continue to be important for the economic actors operating there.
- Territorial dimension assumes a different configuration and greater or lesser importance depending on the country.

- Studying territories does not mean a static and self-contained analysis of their endowments of resources and collective goods.
- The more informed territorial studies – the ones analysed in this chapter – apply in fact a processual and dynamic approach to innovation, integrating a plurality of explanatory levels that are geographical (from local to global), sectoral and analytical in nature.

First, an *ecological analysis* of the 'contextual factors' – that is, of the institutional and regulatory arrangements to see the endowments of public goods and economic resources present in a territorial area and productive sectors. These can derive both from history and local productive traditions and from the intentional interventions of various public or private actors. Second, the *individual analysis* of 'agency factors' – that is, of the strategies and actions deployed by actors, whether individual or collective, local or extra-local. This analysis is important in order to understand the generative mechanisms of innovation at both the company level and in local governance. For example, not all businesses enjoy the same benefits or exploit the opportunities offered by the socio-territorial context and the market (local, national and global). Third, the *relational analysis* of interpersonal and inter-organisational relationships. As we have repeatedly pointed out, the socio-economic networks and relational architectures that actors and territories create, and in which they operate, exercise an autonomous influence, partially independent from the effect of contextual elements and individual strategies.

Contextual factors, agency factors and relational factors must therefore be integrated in the analysis of innovation processes, without it being taken for granted that the geographical dimension (both local and regional) is always crucial with regard to innovation. Its relevance, rather than being presupposed, must be inferred from specific empirical research and from what emerges from the behaviour and (social and economic) relationships of the innovation actors. This makes it possible to reconstruct how far their innovative resources depend on the local/regional context and how much on relationships and non-geographical forms of proximity.

Not coincidentally, economic geography is witnessing a gradual 'relativisation' of the concepts of distance and proximity and their transformation in relational terms (Rodríguez-Pose 2011; Rutten and Boekema 2012). Recent considerations have attempted to make these categories less static and more processual, transforming them into a continuum of multi-level relations – relations, in other words, that take place on different territorial levels. In this way, *distance* is *socialised*: different types of relationship between the actors render territorial proximity more or less important – *proximity* thus becomes a *multi-dimensional concept*.

Ron Boschma (2005), for example, identifies five different dimensions:

1 *cognitive proximity*, related to the different knowledge bases possessed by economic actors;

2　*organisational proximity*, related to the different solutions developed for the collaboration and exchange of knowledge within one or more organisations;
3　*social proximity*, related to ties and interpersonal relationships;
4　*institutional proximity*, related to the institutions that define values and standards of behaviour at a macro level;
5　*geographical proximity*, related to the spatial distance between the actors.

In Boschma's view there exists an inverted-U relationship between proximity and innovation. Both too much, as well as too little, proximity may hinder rather than encourage innovation: in the former case, because of the creation of blocking effects (lock-in), since an excess of similarity creates a deficit of variety in the cognitive resources that does not stimulate innovation; in the latter, because too little proximity fails to generate resources of cohesion and trust between the actors, thus hindering interaction and reciprocal knowledge learning. The most significant point of this analysis, however, is that territorial proximity is shown as *only one* of the possible ways of solving the problem of coordination between the actors. Geographical proximity is therefore not a necessary, nor a sufficient condition for innovation, although it may facilitate it by triggering the various dimensions of proximity and reinforcing their action.[17]

In conclusion, the economic geographers' thinking highlights a 'relational stretching' of the distance/proximity dyad, with the result that these concepts lose their exclusive anchorage to the dimension of geographical space. It follows, then, that the relations of proximity between innovation actors are not limited to those that occur in situations of territorial proximity and even physical co-presence. In addition, the requirements of co-presence, which facilitate collaboration, do not necessarily imply the co-localisation of companies, given that new communication technologies and the speed of modern transportation make it possible to solve the need for temporary face-to-face relations between partners (using videoconferencing, for example, or business trips for personal meetings) (Torre and Rallet 2005).

These ideas are based on both theoretical sociological contributions and the results of empirical research. The former include, for example, Anthony Giddens' observations (1990) on modernity as a process of increasing abstraction, standardisation and separation of space-time coordinates, which are then recombined at different levels.[18] The latter include a substantial amount of research that highlights how the most innovative companies and regional and local systems are those able to integrate internal and external resources, short and long networks, tacit and codified knowledge – those, in other words, able to combine and exploit the *complementarity of innovative resources*. This leads to an increase in remote social relations and greater interconnection between spatially distant locations. In this sense, globalisation can be defined as 'the intensification of worldwide social relations which link distant localities in such a way that local happenings are shaped by events occurring many miles away and vice versa' (ibid., p. 64). Social relations, therefore, disembed: they are detached from local contexts of interaction and from the constraints of physical co-presence, and restructured on more abstract levels.

All this should help to complicate territorial analysis and render it richer and more sophisticated, but it should not obscure the central message of the analytical contributions discussed in this chapter: the *continuing importance of the geography of innovation and its regional and local dimensions.* The 'variable geometries' of innovative partnerships should not hide the fact that today innovative companies and activities still tend to be concentrated in specific territories (Rodríguez-Pose and Crescenzi 2008; Healy and Morgan 2012). Globalisation, in fact, also means greater interpenetration between the global and the local dimensions; so, together with the processes of disembedding of social relationships, there also occur processes of re-embedding. There takes place, in other words, the 'reappropriation or recasting of disembedded social relations so as to pin them down (however partially or transitory) to local conditions of time and place' (ibid., 79–80).

In this respect, today's innovation territories constitute privileged environments of connection between the 'space of place and the space of flux' (Bagnasco 2003, 111) – points of intersection where the identities and (social, cultural and economic) resources of different locations encounter people, goods, capital and information arriving from the outside. This is the 'global flux' that penetrates into local societies and calls boundaries into question, generating uncertainty and imbalance; while at the same time creating new opportunities for innovation, putting different people in touch with one another.

In conclusion, it is this complexity that necessitates an integrated analytical approach to innovation – one capable of merging contributions from a plurality of disciplines and (analytical, territorial and sectoral) levels of explanation.[19] It is this very need for integration that should make us aware of the relative, and at

---

Box 7 Self-study prompts

1 What are the economies of agglomeration and what are the main types?
2 What is an industrial district?
3 What external economies, according to Marshall, are characteristic of an ID?
4 In an ID, why does the innovation process assume diffuse and collective features?
5 What does the expression 'buzz effect' mean?
6 What traits characterise an innovative milieu?
7 Why was Silicon Valley better able than Route 128 to cope with the challenges of the eighties?
8 What traits distinguish high-tech from traditional districts?
9 With reference to Italy, why is it possible to talk about two distinct sectoral and territorial innovation systems?
10 What is meant by the 'embedded complementarity of innovative resources'?
11 What are the differences between ecological, individual and relational analyses? Can these types of analyses be integrated with each other?
12 Why do some scholars define 'proximity' as a multi-dimensional concept?

the same time complementary, nature of most of the approaches analysed in this book. They should, following Lundvall's suggestion, be regarded as *focusing devices*, which make it possible to explore the various components of economic innovation in greater depth.

Notes

1 These results were then confirmed by Feldman and Audretsch (1999), who – with reference to metropolitan urban areas in the US – tested the impact of sectoral diversification on innovative activities. In this case too, no effect deriving from productive specialisation was found. Other research carried out in Europe, however, gave different results, showing the positive impact of sectoral specialisation – for a review of these studies see Usai (2008). In addition, certain recent studies show the opposite, with the effect of Jacobs' externalities on innovation greater in Europe than in the US (Crescenzi *et al.* 2007). The debate on the relative merits of sectoral specialisation or diversification is still very open, also with reference to innovation. The apparent contradiction of the results, in fact, highlights the importance of regulatory aspects and not only those related to the sectoral specialisation/diversification of productive activities. It is becoming increasingly evident, in fact, that the geographical distribution of innovative activity, the presence of sectoral specialisation or diversification and its effects, also depend on the characteristics of innovation systems at various territorial levels (supranational, national, regional and local). In other words, there is no sectoral effect which can be isolated from the socio-institutional and regulatory context within which it operates.

2 As regards Italy, with reference to the different development trajectories present in two regions of the Third Italy – Veneto and Tuscany – see the observations put forward by Luigi Burroni (2001) on the influence exerted by different models of productive organisation and socio-institutional regulation on the performance of the two economies.

3 This, incidentally, tends to blur the rather clear-cut distinction that is found in the literature between Marshallian external economies (based on sectoral specialisation) and those of Jacobs (based on sectoral diversification).

4 Paul Krugman (1991; 2011, 5) defined these advantages (jokingly) as the 'Marshallian trinity'.

5 As regards this particular aspect, please refer to the section dedicated to Smith's work in Chapter 1.

6 The *milieu* supports the innovative capacity of firms through: inter-generational transfer of knowledge; imitation of successful organisational and technological solutions; face-to-face personal relationships; formal and informal collaborations between companies and between public and private actors; the circulation of technological and economic information, and so forth. In a cognitive context, the *milieu* performs three main functions: it reduces uncertainty, as spatial and cultural proximity between the various actors make it possible to predict the probable consequences of their choices; it facilitates the development of conventions, standards of behaviour and shared codes of social inclusion and exclusion that foster cooperation; it reduces the risk of opportunism on the part of the other actors with the monitoring carried out through networks of interpersonal relationships.

7 To remain trapped, in other words, in solutions that have proved successful in the past.

8 For a comparison between Route 128 and Turin, on the other hand, see Perulli (1989).

9 Saxenian uses the term 'regional productive system', but refers to land areas that do not coincide with a specific county (administrative region), and so the definition *local* (albeit large in size) is preferred here, to differentiate them from the regional systems analysed in the previous chapter.

10 The media system in Cologne in Germany, high-tech in Grenoble, software and computer systems in Italy and biotechnology in Britain, were studied in particular (Crouch *et al.* 2004; Ramella 2005; Ramella and Trigilia 2006).

11 As seen in Chapter 3, sociologist Richard Florida drew a lot of attention to this aspect (2002; 2005a).

12 The Eurostat-OECD classification was used to identify the productive sectors – this classification subdivides manufacturing activities according to a decreasing order of technological intensity. High-tech manufacturing activity includes companies pertaining to the following sectors: aerospace, pharmaceutical, information technology, telecommunications and medical, and scientific precision equipment. Medium-high technology manufacturing activity includes the production of machines and mechanical and electrical equipment, chemical products, motor vehicles and other means of transportation.

13 This refers to the division of Italian territory into local labour markets carried out by the National Institute of Statistics on census data. Local labour systems classify the municipalities on the basis of 'home-work commuting', identifying the areas in which there is a high level of 'self-containment' in relation to the population's daily commuting.

14 The analytical potential, as well as the limitations, of this indicator have been pointed out. The main defect is that of particularly highlighting more radical and formalised innovation while concealing the different patent propensity in productive sectors. In other words, it does not make it possible to adequately register the type of incremental innovation prevalent in more traditional sectors and in smaller-sized companies. The research in question, however, intended to study the innovative dynamics of major relevance in the high and medium-high technology sectors – hence the decision to use the patent indicator for inventions protected at European level. One of the advantages of this tool lies in the availability of homogeneous quantitative information that makes it possible to carry out comparative analyses between different contexts through indicators that show 'patent intensity' at territorial and sectoral levels.

15 The local systems pertaining to the control group (those with few patents) are severely undersized in terms of telecommunication networks and economic and social infrastructure and services, not only with respect to the innovation leading systems but also to the national average. In short, the weak quality of the socio-institutional context inhibits the innovative potential of these local economic systems.

16 Some European cities are also analysed in the study for comparative purposes.

17 As we have seen in the discussion regarding innovation systems, this type of analysis should not neglect the impact of the production sector and the type of knowledge transmitted. A recent study, for example, shows how social proximity is particularly important for the transmission of knowledge of intermediate complexity. Simpler knowledge, in fact, tends to spread easily, while very complex knowledge circulates with difficulty (Sorenson *et al.* 2006).

18 In Giddens' view, social relations in pre-modern societies were strongly bound to place: space and time were closely interconnected. Modernity, however, involves a process of abstraction that detaches time and space references from one another and from social relations. The measurement of time is detached from place and becomes more uniform; space is also detached from place – from the geographically defined, physical context of social relations. Pre-modern societies, where the space and place of social relations coincided, were related to situations of co-presence and reciprocal knowledge. With modernity, relations may become anonymous and not tied to physical co-presence: they may take place between the absent and spatially remote. Place becomes influenced by geographically remote social relations and space becomes autonomous from any specific location. In other words, space, like time, becomes standardised and can be recombined in order to connect the global and the local.

19 See, for example, the interesting attempt by Crescenzi and Rodríguez-Pose (2011) to integrate into a single analytical approach three different strands of literature and three distinct interpretative models: (1) the linear model of innovation (which links scientific research directly and linearly to innovation and growth); (2) the model of innovation systems, especially at a local level; and (3) that of knowledge spillovers, which questions the phenomena of assimilation and diffusion of innovation (ibid., 9–10). According to the two authors, to explain the geography of innovation all three of these analytical strands must be taken into account, because (1) the resources invested in research and innovation are important (even if there is a threshold effect); (2) socio-institutional structures are also significant, (3) as are knowledge spillovers. These latter factors, in fact, render the various territories more or less able to translate the resources invested in the production of new knowledge into innovation and economic growth.

Bibliography

Acemoglu, D. and Robinson, J.A. (2012), *Why Nations Fail. The Origins of Power, Prosperity and Poverty*, New York: Crown Publishers.

Acs, Z.J. and Audretsch, D.B. (1988), 'Innovation in Large and Small Firms: An Empirical Analysis' in *The American Economic Review*, vol. 78, no. 4, pp. 678–90.

Acs, Z.J., Audretsch, D.B. and Feldman, M.P. (1994), 'R&D Spillovers and Recipient Firm Size' in *Review of Economics and Statistics*, vol. 76, no. 2, pp. 336–40.

Addario, N. (2009), *Sociologia dell'economia e dell'innovazione*, Bologna: Archetipo Libri-Gedit Edizioni.

Ahuja, G. (2000), 'Collaboration Networks, Structural Holes, and Innovation: A Longitudinal Study' in *Administrative Science Quarterly*, vol. 45, no. 3, pp. 425–55.

Albert, M. (1991), *Capitalisme contre capitalisme*, Paris: Édition du Seuil.

Albert, R., Jeong, H. and Barabási, A.L. (1999), 'Diameter of the World-Wide Web' in *Nature*, vol. 401, 9 September, pp. 130–1.

Alcacer, J. and Gittelman, M. (2004), *How do I Know what you Know? Patent Examiners and the Generation of Patent Citations*, Social Science Research Network, available at: http://ssrn.com/abstract=548003.

Allen, R.C. (1983), 'Collective Invention' in *Journal of Economic Behavior and Organization*, vol. 4, no. 1, pp. 1–24.

Almeida, P. and Kogut, B. (1997), 'The Exploration of Technological Diversity and the Geographic Localisation of Innovation' in *Small Business Economics*, vol. 9, no. 1, pp. 21–31.

Almeida, P. and Kogut, B. (1999), 'Localization of Knowledge and the Mobility of Engineers in Regional Networks' in *Management Science*, vol. 45, no. 7, pp. 905–17.

Amabile, T.M. (1983), 'The Social Psychology of Creativity: A Componential Conceptualization' in *Journal of Personality and Social Psychology*, vol. 45, no. 2, pp. 357–76.

Amabile, T.M. (1996), *Creativity in Context*, Boulder, CO: Westview.

Amable, B. and Petit, P. (2001), *The Diversity of Social Systems of Innovation and Production during the 1990s*, Cepremap Working Papers, no. 0115, pp. 1–33.

Amesse, F. and Desranleau, C. (1991), 'The Individual Inventor and the Role of Entrepreneurship: A Survey of the Canadian Evidence' in *Research Policy*, vol. 20, no. 1, pp. 13–27.

Amsden, A.H. (1989), *Asia's Next Giant: South Korea and Late Industrialization*, New York and Oxford: Oxford University Press.

Anand, N. and Daft, R.L. (2007), 'What is the Right Organization Design?' in *Organizational Dynamics*, vol. 36, no. 4, pp. 329–44.

Archibugi, D. (2001), 'Pavitt's Taxonomy Sixteen Years On: A Review Article' in *Economics of Innovation and New Technology*, vol. 10, no. 5, pp. 415–25.

Aron, R. (1965), *Main Currents in Sociological Thought*, New York: Basic Books.

Arrow, K.J. (1962a), 'Economic Welfare and the Allocation of Resources for Invention' in R.R. Nelson (ed.), *The Rate and Direction of Inventive Activity. Economic and Social Factors*, Princeton: Princeton University Press, pp. 609–25.

Arrow, K.J. (1962b), 'The Economic Implications of Learning by Doing' in *The Review of Economic Studies*, vol. 29, no. 3, pp. 155–73.

Ashby, W.R. (1956), *Introduction to Cybernetics*, London: Chapman & Hall.

Asheim, B.T. (1996), 'Industrial Districts as "Learning Regions": A Condition for Prosperity?' in *European Planning Studies*, vol. 4, no. 4, pp. 379–400.

Asheim, B.T. (2012), 'The Changing Role of Learning Regions in the Globalizing Knowledge Economy: A Theoretical Re-examination' in *Regional Studies*, vol. 46, no. 8, pp. 993–1004.

Asheim, B.T. and Coenen, L. (2005), 'Knowledge Bases and Regional Innovation Systems: Comparing Nordic Clusters' in *Research Policy*, vol. 34, no. 8, pp. 1173–90.

Asheim, B.T. and Gertler, M.S. (2005), 'The Geography of Innovation: Regional Innovation Systems' in J. Fagerberg, D.C. Mowery and R.R. Nelson, (eds), *The Oxford Handbook of Innovation*, pp. 291–317, New York: Oxford University Press.

Asheim, B.T. and Isaksen, A. (2002), 'Regional Innovation Systems: The Integration of Local "Sticky" and Global "Ubiquitous" Knowledge' in *Journal of Technology Transfer*, vol. 27, no.1, pp. 77–86.

Asheim, B.T., Boschma, R. and Cooke, P. (2011), 'Constructing Regional Advantage: Platform Policies Based on Related Variety and Differentiated Knowledge Bases' in *Regional Studies*, vol. 45, no. 7, pp. 893–904.

Asheim, B.T., Lawton Smith, H. and Oughton, C. (2011), 'Regional Innovation Systems: Theory, Empirics and Policy' in *Regional Studies*, vol. 45, no. 7, pp. 875–89.

Asso, P.F. and Trigilia, C. (eds) (2010), *Remare contro corrente. Imprese e territori dell'innovazione in Sicilia*, Roma: Meridiana Libri, Donzelli.

Audretsch, D.B. and Feldman, M.P. (1996), 'R&D Spillovers and the Geography of Innovation and Production' in *The American Economic Review*, vol. 86, no. 3, pp. 630–40.

Aydalot, P. (1986), *Milieux Innovateurs in Europe*, Paris: Gremi.

Aydalot, P. (1988), 'Technological Trajectories and Regional Innovation in Europe' in P. Aydalot and D. Keeble (eds), *High Technology Industry and Innovative Environments: The European Experience*, London: Routledge.

Baer, J. (2008), 'Commentary: Divergent Thinking Tests Have Problems, but This Is Not the Solution' in *Psychology of Aesthetics, Creativity, and the Arts*, vol. 2, no. 2, pp. 89–92.

Bagnasco, A. (1977), *Tre Italie. La problematica territoriale dello sviluppo italiano*, Bologna: Il Mulino.

Bagnasco, A. (1988), *La costruzione sociale del mercato*, Bologna: Il Mulino.

Bagnasco, A. (1999), *Tracce di comunità*, Bologna: Il Mulino.

Bagnasco, A. (2003), *Società fuori squadra. Come cambia l'organizzazione sociale*, Bologna: Il Mulino.

Balconi, M., Breschi, S. and Lissoni, F. (2004), 'Networks of Inventors and the Role of Academia: An Exploration of Italian Patent Data' in *Research Policy*, vol. 33, no. 1, pp. 127–45.

Baldini N., Grimaldi, R. and Sobrero, M., (2007), 'To Patent or not to Patent? A Survey of Italian Inventors on Motivations, Incentives, and Obstacles to University Patenting' in *Scientometrics*, vol. 70, no. 2, pp. 333–54.

Ballarino, G. and Regini, M. (2008), 'Convergent Perspectives in Economic Sociology: An Italian View of Contemporary Developments in Western Europe and North America' in *Socio-Economic Review*, vol. 6, no. 2, pp. 337–63.

Barabási, A.L. (2002), *Linked: The New Science of Networks*, Cambridge, MA: Perseus Press.

Barabási, A.L. and Albert, R. (1999), 'Emergence of Scaling in Random Networks' in *Science*, vol. 286, 15 Ottobre, pp. 509–12.

Barbera, F. (2004), *Meccanismi sociali. Elementi di una sociologia analitica*, Bologna: Il Mulino.

Barbera, F. and Negri, N. (2008), *Mercati, reti sociali, istituzioni. Una mappa per la sociologia economica*, Bologna: Il Mulino.

Barron, F. and Harrington, D.M. (1981), 'Creativity, Intelligence, and Personality' in *Annual Review of Psychology*, vol. 32, pp. 439–76.

Barry, A. and Thrift, N. (2007), 'Gabriel Tarde: Imitation, Invention and Economy' in *Economy and Society*, vol. 36, no. 4, pp. 509–25.

Basberg, B. (1987), 'Patents and the Measurement of Technological Change: A Survey of the Literature' in *Research Policy*, vol. 16, nn. 2–4, pp. 131–41.

Baum, J.A.C., Calabrese, T. and Silverman, B.S. (2000), 'Don't Go it Alone: Alliance Network Composition and Startups' Performance in Canadian Biotechnology' in *Strategic Management Journal*, vol. 21, no. 3, pp. 267–94.

Baum, J.A.C., Shipilov, A.V. and Rowley, T.J. (2003), 'Where Do Small Worlds Come From?' in *Industrial and Corporate Change*, vol. 12, no. 4, pp. 697–725.

Baumol, W.J. (2002), *The Free Market Innovation Machine: Analyzing the Growth Miracle of Capitalism*, Princeton: Princeton University Press.

Baumol, W.J. (2004), *Education for Innovation: Entrepreneurial Breakthroughs Vs. Corporate Incremental Improvements*, NBER Working Paper Series, Working Paper 10578, available at: www.nber.org/papers/w10578.

Becattini, G. (ed.) (1975), *Lo sviluppo economico della Toscana*, Firenze: Le Monnier.

Becattini, G. (1990), 'The Marshallian Industrial District as a Socio-economic Notion' in F. Pyke, G. Becattini and W. Sengenberger (eds), *Industrial District and Inter-firm Cooperation in Italy*, Geneva, IILS, ILO, pp. 37–51.

Becattini, G. (2000), *Il distretto industriale*, Torino: Rosenberg & Sellier.

Becattini, G. and Rullani, E. (2000), 'Sistema locale e mercato globale' in G. Becattini (ed.), *Il distretto industriale*, pp. 93–116, Torino: Rosenberg & Sellier.

Becattini, G., Bellandi, M. and De Propris, L. (2009), 'Critical Nodes and Contemporary Reflections on Industrial Districts: An Introduction' in G. Becattini, M. Bellandi and L. De Propris (eds), *A Handbook of Industrial Districts*, pp. xv–xxxv, Cheltenham, UK, and Northampton, USA: Edward Elgar.

Becker, M.H. (1970), 'Sociometric Location and Innovativeness: Reformulation and Extension of the Diffusion Model' in *American Sociological Review*, vol. 35, no. 2, pp. 267–82.

Beckert, J. and Zafirovski M. (eds) (2006), *International Encyclopedia of Economic Sociology*, London and New York: Routledge.

Bellandi, M. (1987), 'La formulazione originaria' in G. Becattini (ed.), *Mercato e forze locali: il distrretto industriale*, pp. 49–67, Bologna: Il Mulino.

Bellandi, M. (1989), 'Capacità innovativa diffusa e sistemi locali di imprese' in G. Becattini (ed.), *Modelli locali di sviluppo*, pp. 149–72, Bologna, Il Mulino.

Bergek, A., Jacobsson, S., Carlsson, B., Lindmarki, S. and Rickne, A. (2005), 'Analyzing the Dynamics and Functionality of Sectoral Innovation Systems – A Manual' in

DRUID Tenth Anniversary Summer Conference 2005 on Dynamics of Industry and Innovation: Organizations, Networks and Systems, Copenhagen, Danimarca, 27–29 June, pp. 1–34.

Berger, S. (2005), *How We Compete*, New York: Currency/Doubleday.

Berger, S. (2013), *Making in America*, Cambridge: The MIT Press.

Bertoni, F. and Randone, P.A. (2006), 'The Small-World of Italian Finance: Owenership Interconnections and Board Interlocks amongst Italian Listed Companies', available at: www.ssrn.com.

Bhide, A.V. (2000), *The Origin and Evolution of New Business*, Oxford: Oxford University Press.

Biagiotti, A. (2009), 'I brevetti e il radicamento sociale e territoriale dell'economia della conoscenza' in *Stato e Mercato*, no. 1, pp. 129–55.

Biagiotti A. (2010), 'I sistemi locali leader nei brevetti' in F. Ramella and C. Trigilia (eds), *Imprese e territori dell'Alta Tecnologia in Italia*, pp. 75–97. Bologna: Il Mulino.

Biagiotti, A., Burroni, L., Faraoni, N. and Gherardini, A. (2011), 'I sistemi locali dell'alta tecnologia in Italia' in L. Burroni and C. Trigilia (eds), *Le città dell'innovazione. Dove e perchè cresce l'alta tecnologia in Italia*, pp. 41–59, Bologna: Il Mulino.

Bijker W. (1987), 'The Social Construction of Bakelite: Toward a Theory of Invention' in W. Bijker, T.P Hughes and T.J Pinch (eds), *The Social Construction of Technological Systems. New Directions in the Sociology and History of Technology*, pp. 159–87, Cambridge, MA: The MIT Press.

Bijker, W. (1995), *Of Bicycles, Bakelites, and Bulbs: Toward a Theory of Sociotechnical Change*, Cambridge, MA: MIT Press.

Bijker, W.E., Hughes, T.P. and Pinch, T.J. (eds) (1987), *The Social Construction of Technological Systems. New Directions in the Sociology and History of Technology*, Cambridge, MA: The MIT Press.

Block, F. (2011), 'Introduction: Innovation and the Invisible Hand of Government' in F. Block and M.R. Keller (eds), *State of Innovation: The US Government's Role in Technology Development*, Boulder: Paradigm.

Block, F. and Evans, P. (2005), 'The State and the Economy' in N.J. Smelser and R. Swedberg (eds), *The Handbook of Economic Sociology*, Princeton: Princeton University Press, pp. 505–26,

Block, F. and Keller, M.R. (2009), 'Where Do Innovations Come From? Transformations in the US Economy, 1970–2006' in *Socio-Economic Review*, vol. 7, no. 3, pp. 459–83.

Block F. and Keller, M.R. (eds) (2011), *State of Innovation. The U.S. Government's Role in Technology Development*, Boulder: Paradigm.

Boschma R.A. (2005), 'Proximity and Innovation: A Critical Assessment' in *Regional Studies*, vol. 39, no. 1, pp. 61–74.

Boudon, R. (1984), *La place du désordre. Chritique des théories du changement social*, Paris: Presses Universitaires de France.

Breschi, S. and Lissoni F. (2006), 'Mobility of Inventors and the Geography of Knowledge Spillovers' in *New Evidence On US Data*, CESPRI, WP no. 184, October.

Breznitz, D. (2007), *Innovation and the State. Political Choice and Strategies for Growth in Israel, Taiwan and Ireland*, New Haven and London: Yale University Press.

Brown, J.S. and Duguid, P. (1991), 'Organizational Learning and Communities-of-Practice: Toward a Unified View of Working, Learning, and Innovation' in *Organization Science*, vol. 2, no. 1, pp. 40–57.

Brown, J.S. and Duguid, P. (2001), 'Knowledge and Organization: A Social-Practice Perspective' in *Organization Science*, vol. 12, no. 2, pp. 198–213.

Bucchi, M. (2010), *Scienza e società*, Milano: Raffaello Cortina Editore.

Buchanan, J.M. (1965), 'An Economic Theory of Clubs' in *Economica*, vol. 32, no. 1, pp. 1–14.

Burns, T. and Stalker, G.M. (1961), *The Management of Innovation*, London: Tavistock.

Burroni, L. (2001), *Allontanarsi crescendo. Politica e sviluppo locale in Veneto e Toscana*, Torino: Rosenberg & Sellier.

Burroni, L. and Trigilia, C. (eds) (2011), *Le città dell'innovazione. Dove e perché cresce l'alta tecnologia in Italia*, Bologna: Il Mulino.

Burt, R.S. (1979), 'A Structural Theory of Interlocking Corporate Directorates' in *Social Network*, vol. 1, no. 4, pp.415–35.

Burt, R.S. (1983), *Corporate Profits and Cooptation: Networks of Market Constraints and Directorate Ties in the American Economy*, New York: Academic Press.

Burt, R.S. (1987), 'Social Contagion and Innovation: Cohesion versus Structural Equivalence' in *American Journal of Sociology*, vol. 92, no. 6, pp. 1287–1335.

Burt, R.S. (1992), *Structural Holes: The Social Structure of Competition*, Cambridge, MA: Harvard University Press.

Burt, R.S. (2005), *Brokerage and Closure*, Oxford: Oxford University Press.

Butera, F., Bagnara, S., Cesaria, R. and Di Guardo, S. (eds) (2008), *Knowledge Working. Lavoro, lavoratori, società della conoscenza*, Milano: Mondadori.

Cairncross, F. (1997), *The Death of Distance*, Cambridge, MA: Harvard Business School Press.

Caloffi, A. (2010a), 'I brevetti 'multiproprietari': reti locali e multi-territoriali' in F. Ramella and C. Trigilia (eds), *Imprese e territori dell'Alta Tecnologia in Italia*, pp. 99–123, Bologna, Il Mulino.

Caloffi, A. (2010b), 'Inventori isolati e gruppi di ricerca: le reti professionali e territoriali' in F. Ramella and C. Trigilia (eds), *Invenzioni, inventori e territori in Italia*, pp. 181–208, Bologna, Il Mulino.

Camagni, R. (1991), 'Introduction: from the Local 'Milieu' to Innovation through ICL Cooperation Networks' in R. Camagni (ed.), *Innovation Networks: Spatial Perspectives*, pp. 1–9, London: Belhaven Press.

Camagni, R. and Capello, R. (2002), 'Apprendimento collettivo, innovazione and contesto locale' in R. Camagni and R. Capello (eds), *Apprendimento collettivo e competitività territoriale*, pp. 11–26, Milano: Angeli.

Campbell, J.L. (2010), 'Institutional Reproduction and Change' in G. Morgan, J.L. Campbell, C. Crouch, O.K. Pedersen and R. Whitley (eds), *The Oxford Handbook of Comparative Institutional Analysis*, pp. 87–115, Oxford and New York: Oxford University Press.

Carlsson, B. (ed.) (1995), *Technological Systems and Economic Performance: The Case of Factory Automation*, Dordrecht: Kluwer Academic Publishers.

Carlsson, B. and Eliasson, G. (1994), 'The Nature and Importance of Economic Competence' in *Industrial and Corporate Change*, vol. 3, no. 1, pp. 687–711.

Carlsson, B. and Stankiewicz, R. (1991), 'On the Nature, Function and Composition of Technological Systems' in *Journal of Evolutionary Economics*, vol. 1, no. 2, pp. 93–118.

Carlsson, B. and Stankiewicz, R. (1995), 'On the Nature, Function and Composition of Technological Systems' in B. Carlsson, *Technological Systems and Economic Performance: The Case of Factory Automation*, pp. 21–56, Dordrecht: Kluwer Academic Publishers.

Carlsson, B., Jacobsson, S., Holmén, M. and Rickne, A. (2002), 'Innovation Systems: Analytical and Methodological Issues' in *Research Policy*, vol. 31, no. 2, pp. 233–45.

Carr, L.J. (1932), 'The Patenting Performance of 1,000 Inventors During Ten Years' in *The American Journal of Sociology*, vol. 37, no. 4, pp. 569–80.

Casper, S. (2006), 'Exporting the Silicon Valley to Europe: How Useful is Comparative Institutional Theory?' in J. Hage and M. Meeus (eds), *Innovation, Science, and Institutional Change. A Research Handbook*, pp. 483–504, Oxford: Oxford University Press.

Casper, S. (2010), 'The Comparative Institutional Analysis of Innovation: From Industrial Policy to the Knowledge Economy' in G. Morgan, J.L. Campbell, C. Crouch, O.K. Pedersen and R. Whitley (eds), *The Oxford Handbook of Comparative Institutional Analysis*, pp. 335–362, Oxford and New York: Oxford University Press.

Casper, S. and Soskice, D. (2004), 'Sectoral Systems of Innovation and Varieties of Capitalism: Explaining the Development of High-Technology Entrepreneurship in Europe' in F. Malerba (ed.), *Sectoral Systems of Innovation*, pp. 348–87, New York; Cambridge University Press.

Casper, S. and Whitley, R. (2004), 'Managing Competences in Entrepreneurial Technology Firms: A Comparative Institutional Analysis of Germany, Sweden and the UK' in *Research Policy*, vol. 33, no. 1, pp. 89–106.

Castells, M. (2010), *The Rise of the Network Society*, Malden, USA, and Oxford, UK: Wiley-Blackwell.

Catino, M. (2012), *Capire le organizzazioni*, Bologa: Il Mulino.

Cavalli, A. (1967), 'Introduzione' in W. Sombart (1916), *Der Moderne Kapitalismus*, seconda edizione, Berlino: Duncker & Humblot (It. trans. (1967), *Il capitalismo moderno*, pp. 9–49, Torino: Utet).

Cavalli, L. (1970), *Il mutamento sociale*, Bologna: Il Mulino.

Cavalli, L. (1981a), *Il capo carismatico*, Bologna: Il Mulino.

Cavalli, L. (1981b), 'Il carisma come potenza rivoluzionaria' in P. Rossi (ed.), *Max Weber e l'analisi del mondo moderno*, pp. 161–88, Torino: Einaudi.

Cesaroni, F., Gambardella, A., Garcia-Fontes, W. and Mariani, M. (2004), 'The Chemical Sector System: Firms, Markets, Institutions and the Processes of Knowledge Creation and Diffusion' in F. Malerba, *Sectoral Systems of Innovation*, pp. 121–54, New York: Cambridge University Press.

Chesbrough, H.W. (2003), *Open Innovation: The New Imperative for Creating and Profiting from Technology*, Boston (MA): Harvard Business School Press.

Chesbrough, H.W. (2006), 'Open Innovation: A New Paradigm for Understanding Industrial Innovation' in H.W. Chesbrough, W. Vanhaverbeke and J. West (eds), *Open Innovation: Researching a New Paradigm*, pp. 1–12, Oxford: Oxford University.

Chiesi, A.M. (1978), 'I legami personali tra i consigli di amministrazione in Italia' in *Studi Organizzativi*, no. 10, pp. 25–72.

Chiesi, A.M. (1982), 'L'élite finanziaria italiana' in *Rassegna Italiana di Sociologia*, no. 23, pp. 571–95.

Chiesi, A.M. (1999), *L'analisi dei reticoli*, Milano: Angeli.

Christensen, C.M. (1997), *The Innovator's Dilemma: When New Technologies Cause Great Firms to Fail*, Boston: Harvard Business School Press.

CIS (2010), 'Types of co-operation partner for product and process innovation', Community Innovation Survey 2010, available at: http://epp.eurostat.ec.europa.eu/portal/page/portal/science_technology_innovation/data/database

Clark, T.N. (2010), 'Introduction' in G. Tarde (ed.), *On Communication & Social Influence. Selected Papers*, pp. 1–70, Chicago: The University of Chicago Press.

Cohen, W. and Levinthal, D. (1990), 'Absorptive Capacity: A New Perspective on Learning and Innovation' in *Administration Science Quarterly*, vol. 35, no. 1, pp. 123–33.

Coile, R.C. (1977), 'Lotka's Frequency Distribution of Scientific Productivity' in *Journal of the American Society for Information Science*, vol. 28, no. 6, pp. 366–70.

Coleman, J., Katz, E. and Menzel, H. (1957), 'The Diffusion of an Innovation Among Physicians' in *Sociometry*, vol. 20, no. 4, pp. 253–70.

Coleman J., Katz E. and Menzel H. (1966), *Medical Innovation: A Diffusion Study*, New York: Bobbs-Merrill.

Collins R. (1985), *Three Sociological Traditions*, New York: Oxford University Press.

Conti, R., Gambardella, A. and Mariani, M. (2010), *Learning to Be Edison? Individual Inventive Experience and Breakthrough Inventions*, Paper presented to summer conference 2010, 'Opening Up Innovation: Strategy, Organization and Technology', Imperial College, London Business School, June 16–18.

Cooke, P. (1992), 'Regional Innovation Systems: Competitive Regulation in the New Europe' in *Geoforum*, vol. 23, no. 3, pp. 365–82.

Cooke, P. (2001), 'Regional Innovation Systems, Clusters, and the Knowledge Economy' in *Industrial and Corporate Change*, vol. 10, no. 4, pp. 945–74.

Cooke, P. (2004), 'Introduction. Regional Innovation Systems – an Evolutionary Approach' in P. Cooke, M. Heidenreich and H. Braczyk (eds), *Regional Innovation Systems. The Role of Governance in a Globalized World*, second edition, pp. 1–18, London and New York: Routledge.

Cooke, P. (2006), *Regional Innovation Systems as Public Goods*, United Nations Industrial Development Organization (UNIDO), Vienna.

Cooke, P. (2007), 'To Construct Regional Advantage from Innovation Systems First Build Policy Platforms' in *European Planning Studies*, vol. 15, no. 2, pp. 179–94.

Cornes, R. and Sandler T. (1986), *The Theory of Externalities, Public Goods and Club Goods*, New York: Cambridge University Press.

Cowan, R. and Jonard, N. (2003), 'The Dynamics of Collective Invention' in *Journal of Economic Behavior & Organization*, vol. 52, no. 4, pp. 513–32.

Crescenzi, R. and Rodríguez-Pose, A. (2011), *Innovation and Regional Growth in the European Union*, Berlin: Springer.

Crescenzi, R., Rodríguez-Pose, A. and Storper, M. (2007), 'The Territorial Dynamics of Innovation: A Europe–United States Comparative Analysis' in *Journal of Economic Geography*, vol. 7, no. 6, pp. 673–709.

Crouch, C. (2010), 'Complementarity' in G. Morgan, J.L. Campbell, C. Crouch, O.K. Pedersen and R. Whitley, (eds), *The Oxford Handbook of Comparative Institutional Analysis*, pp. 117–37, Oxford and New York: Oxford University Press.

Crouch, C., Le Galès, P., Trigilia, C. and Voelzkow, H. (2001), *Local Production Systems in Europe. Rise or Demise?* Oxford: Oxford University Press.

Crouch, C., Le Galès, P., Trigilia, C. and Voelzkow, H. (2004), *Changing Governance of Local Economies. Responses of European Local Production Systems*, Oxford: Oxford University Press.

Crouch C., Schröder, M. and Voelzkow, H. (2009), 'Regional and Sectoral Varieties of Capitalism' in *Economy and Society*, vol. 38, no. 4, pp. 654–78.

Csikszentmihalyi, M. (1988), 'Society, Culture, and Person: A Systems View of Creativity' in R.J. Sternberg (ed.), *The Nature of Creativity: Contemporary Psychological Perspectives*, pp. 325–39, New York: Cambridge University Press.

Csikszentmihalyi, M. (1996), *Creativity*, New York: Harper Collins.

Csikszentmihalyi, M. (1999), 'Implications of a Systems Perspective for the Study of Creativity' in R.J. Sternberg (ed.), *Handbook of Creativity*, pp. 313–38, Cambridge, New York: Cambridge University Press.

Csikszentmihalyi, M. and Sawyer, R.K. (1995), 'Creative Insight: The Social Dimension of a Solitary Moment' in R.J. Sternberg and J.E. Davidson (eds), *The Nature of Insight*, pp. 329–63. Cambridge, MA: The MIT Press.

Dahlin, B.K. and Behrens, D.M. (2005), 'When Is an Invention Really Radical? Defining and Measuring Technological Radicalness' in *Research Policy*, vol. 34, no. 5, pp. 717–37.

Dahlin, B.K., Taylor, M. and Fichman, M. (2004), 'Today's Edisons or Weekend Hobbyists: Technical Merit and Success of Inventions by Independent Inventors' in *Research Policy*, vol. 33, no. 8, pp. 1167–83.

Dalley, S. (1993), 'Ancient Mesopotamian Gardens and the Identification of the Hanging Gardens of Babylon Resolved' in *Garden History*, vol. 21, no. 1, pp. 1–13.

Dalley, S. (1994), 'Nineveh, Babylon and the Hanging Gardens: Cuneiform and Classical Sources Reconciled' in *Iraq*, vol. 56, January, pp. 45–58.

Dalley, S. and Oleson, J.P. (2003), 'Sennacherib, Archimedes, and the Water Screw: The Context of Invention in the Ancient World' in *Technology and Culture*, vol. 44, no. 1, pp. 1–26.

Damanpour, F. (1991), 'Organizational Innovation: A Meta-Analysis of Effects of Determinants and Moderators' in *Academy of Management Journal*, vol. 34, no. 3, pp. 555–90.

Dasgupta, P. and David, P.A. (1994), 'Toward a New Economics of Science' in *Research Policy*, vol. 23, no. 5, pp. 487–532.

David, P.A. (1985), 'Clio and the Economics of QWERTY' in *The American Economic Review*, vol. 75, no. 2, pp. 332–37.

Davis, G.F, Yoo, M. and Baker, W.E (2003), 'The Small World of the America Corporate Elite, 1982–2001' in *Strategic Organization*, vol. 1, no. 3, pp. 301–26.

De Backer, K, López-Bassols, V. and Martinez, C. (2008), 'Open Innovation in a Global Perspective: What Do Existing Data Tell Us?' in *OECD, Technology and Industry Working Papers*, 2008/4, pp. 1–36.

Dei Ottati, G. (1987), 'Il mercato comunitario' in G. Becattini (ed.), *Mercato e forze locali: il distrretto industriale*, pp. 117–41, Bologna: Il Mulino.

Del Sesto, S.L. (1983), 'Technology and Social Change. William Fielding Ogburn Revisited' in *Technological Forecasting and Social Change*, vol. 24, no. 3, pp. 183–96.

Della Malva, A., Breschi, S., Lissoni, F. and Montobbio, F. (2007), 'L'attività brevettuale dei docenti universitari: L'Italia in un confronto internazionale' in *Economia e Politica Industriale*, vol. 34, no. 2, pp. 43–70.

De Vaan M., Stark, D. and Vedres, B. (2014), 'Game changer: topologia della creatività' in *Stato e Mercato*, no. 3, pp. 307–40.

Dewar R.D. and Dutton, J.E. (1986), 'The Adoption of Radical and Incremental Innovations: An Empirical Analysis' in *Management Science*, vol. 32, no. 11, pp. 1422–33.

DiMaggio, P.J. and Powell, W. (1983), 'The Iron Cage Revisited: Institutional Isomorphism and Collective Rationality in Organizational Fields' in *American Sociological Review*, vol. 48, no. 2, pp. 147–60.

Ding, W.W., Murray, F. and Stuart, E.T. (2006), 'Gender Differences in Patenting in the Academic Life Sciences' in *Science*, vol. 313, 4 August, pp. 665–7.

Dodds, P.S., Muhamad, R. and Watts, J.D. (2003), 'An Experimental Study of Search in Global Social Networks' in *Science*, vol. 301, August, pp. 827–9.

Dodds, P.S., Watts, J.D. and Sabel, C.F. (2003), 'Information Exchange and the Robustness of Organizational Networks' in *PNAS*, vol. 100, no. 21, pp. 12516–21.

Doloreux, D. (2002), What We Should Know about Regional Systems of Innovation' in *Technology in Society*, vol. 24, no. 3, pp. 243–63.

Doloreux, D. and Parto, S. (2005), 'Regional Innovation Systems: Current Discourse and Unresolved Issues' in *Technology in Society*, vol. 27, no. 2, pp. 133–53.

Donegan, M., Drucker, J., Goldstein, H., Lowe, N. and Malizia, E. (2008), 'Which Indicators Explain Metropolitan Economic Performance Best? Traditional or Creative Class' in *Journal of the American Planning Association*, vol. 74, no. 2, pp. 180–95.

Dore, R. (1987), *Taking Japan Seriously. A Confucian Perspective on Leading Economic Issues*, London: The Athlone Press.

Dore, R. (2000), *Stock Market Capitalism: Welfare Capitalism: Japan and Germany versus the Anglo-Saxons*, Oxford: Oxford University Press.

Dosi, G., Freeman, C., Nelson, R., Silverberg, G. and Soete (1988), *Technical Change and Economic Theory*, Londra and New York: Pinter.

Dosi, G., Orsenigo, L. and Sylos Labini, M. (2005), 'Technology and the Economy' in N.J. Smelser and R. Swedberg (eds), *The Handbook of Economic Sociology*, pp. 678–702, Princeton: Princeton University Press.

Duguet, E. and MacGarvie, M. (2005), 'How Well do Patent Citations Measure Flows of Technology? Evidence from French Innovation Surveys' in *Economics of Innovation and New Technology*, vol. 14, no. 5, pp. 375–93.

Dunbar, K. (1995), 'How Scientists Really Reason: Scientific Reasoning in Real-World Laboratories' in R.J. Sternberg and J.E. Davidson (eds), *The Nature of Insight*, pp. 365–95, Cambridge (MA): The MIT Press.

Durkheim, E. (1897), *Le formes élémentaires de la vie réligieuse*, Paris: Alcan. (Eng. trans. (1965), *The Elementary Forms of the Religious Life*, New York: Free Press.)

Durkheim, E. (1902), *De la division du travail social*, Paris: Alcan. (Eng. trans. (1947), *The Division of Labor in Society*, Glencoe: The Free Press.)

Dutton, H.I. (1984), *The Patent System and Inventive Activity during the Industrial Revolution, 1750–1852*, Manchester: Manchester University Press.

Edquist C. (1997), 'Systems of Innovation Approaches – their Emergence and Characteristics' in C. Edquist (ed.), *Systems of Innovation: Technologies, Institutions and Organizations*, pp. 1–35, London: Pinter.

Edquist, C. (2005), 'Systems of Innovation' in J. Fagerberg, D.C. Mowery and R.R. Nelson, (eds), *The Oxford Handbook of Innovation*, pp. 181–208, New York: Oxford University Press.

Edquist, C. and Hommen, L. (eds) (2008), *Small Country Innovation Systems: Globalisation, Change and Policy in Asia and Europe*, Cheltenham: Edward Elgar.

Edquist, C. and Johnson, B. (1997), *Institutions and Organisations in Systems of Innovation*, in C. Edquist (ed.), *Systems of Innovation: Technologies, Institutions and Organizations*, pp. 41–63, London: Pinter.

Elias, N. (1991), *Mozart. Zur Soziologie eines* Genies, Frankfurt: Suhrkamp Verlag. (Eng. trans. (2010), *Mozart and other Essys on Courtly Art*, Dublin: University College Dublin Press.)

Eliasson, G. (1998), 'Competence Blocs and Industrial Policy in the Knowledge Based Economy' in *STI-Science Technology, Industry Review*, OECD, no. 22, pp. 209–41.

Erickson, B.H. (1979), 'Some Problems of Inference from Chain Data' in *Sociological Methodology*, vol. 10, no. 1, pp. 276–302.

Ernst H., Leptien, C. and Vitt, J. (2000), 'Inventors are not Alike: The Distribution of Patenting Output among Industrial R&D Personnel' in *IEEE Transactions on Engineering Management*, vol. 47, no. 2, pp. 184–99.

Ettlie, J.E., Bridges, W.P. and O'Keefe, R.D. (1984), 'Organization Strategy and Structural Differences for Radical Versus Incremental Innovation' in *Management Science*, vol. 30, no. 6, pp. 682–95.

Etzkowitz, H. (2002), *The Triple Helix of University–Industry–Government. Implications for Policy and Evaluation*, Working paper 2002/11, SISTER, Stockholm, available at: www.sister.nu/pdf/wp_11.pdf

Etzkowitz, H. (2008), *The Triple Helix. University–Industry–Government. Innovation in Action*, New York and London: Routledge.

Etzkowitz, H. and Leydesdorff, L. (eds) (1997), *Universities in the Global Knowledge Economy: A Triple Helix of University–Industry–Government Relations*, London: Cassell.

Etzkowitz, H. and Leydesdorff, L. (2000), 'The Dynamics of Innovation: From National Systems and "Mode2" to a Triple Helix of University–Industry–Government Relations' in *Research Policy*, vol. 29, no. 2, pp. 109–23.

Evans P. (1995), *Embedded Autonomy: States and Industrial Transformation*, Princeton: Princeton University Press.

Evans, P. (2005), 'The Challenges of the "Institutional Turn": New Interdisciplinary Opportunities in Development Theory' in V. Nee and R. Swedberg (eds), *The Economic Sociology of Capitalism*, Princeton: Princeton University Press.

Fagerberg, J. (2003), 'Schumpeter and the Revival of Evolutionary Economics: An Appraisal of the Literature' in *Journal of Evolutionary Economics*, vol. 13, no. 2, pp. 125–59.

Fagerberg, J. (2005), 'Innovation: A Guide to the Literature' in Fagerberg, J., Mowery, D.C. and Nelson, R.R. (eds) *The Oxford Handbook of Innovation*, pp. 1–26, New York: Oxford University Press.

Fagerberg, J., Martin, B.R. and Andersen E.S., (eds) (2013), *Innovation Studies. Evolution and Future Changes*, Oxford: Oxford University Press.

Fagerberg and Sapprasert (2010), *Innovation: Exploring the Knowledge Base*, Tik Working Papers on Innovation Studies, No. 20100616, Centre for Technology, Innovation and Culture, Blindern, Oslo, Norway.

Fagerberg J. and Verspagen B. (2009), 'Innovation Studies—The Emerging Structure of a New Scientific Field' in *Research Policy*, vol. 38, no. 2, pp. 218–33.

Fagerberg, J., Mowery, D.C. and Nelson, R.R. (eds) (2005), *The Oxford Handbook of Innovation*, New York: Oxford University Press.

Feldman, M.P. (1994), *The Geography of Innovation*, Boston: Kluwer Academic Publishers.

Feldman, M.P. (2000), 'Location and Innovation: The New Economic Geography of Innovation, Spillovers, and Agglomeration' in G.L. Clark, M.P. Feldman and M.S. Gertler (eds), *The Oxford Handbook of Economic Geography*, pp. 372–94, New York: Oxford Univesity Press.

Feldman M.P. and D.B. Audretsch (1999), 'Innovation in Cities: Science-based Diversity, Specialization and Localized Competition' in *European Economic Review*, vol. 43, no. 2, pp. 409–29.

Feldman, M.P. and Florida R. (1994), 'The Geographic Sources of Innovation: Technological Infrastructure and Product Innovation in the United States' in *Annals of the Association of American Geographers*, vol. 84, no. 2, pp. 210–29.

Fenton, E.M. and Pettigrew, A.M. (2000), 'Theoretical Perspecitves on New Forms of Organizing' in A.M. Pettigrew and E.M. Fenton (eds), *The Innovating Organization*, pp. 372–94, London: Sage.

Ferrarotti, F. (1985), *Max Weber e il destino della ragione*, Roma-Bari: Laterza.

Ferrarotti, F. (1986), *Manuale di sociologia*, Roma-Bari: Laterza.

Ferrarotti, F. (2002), *Lineamenti di storia del pensiero sociolgico*, Roma: Donzelli.

Ferrary, M. and Granovetter, M. (2009), 'The Role of Venture Capital Firms in Silicon Valley's Complex Innovation Network' in *Economy and Society*, vol. 38, no. 2, pp. 326–59.

Fleming, L. (2001), 'Recombinant Uncertainty in Technological Search' in *Management Science*, vol 47, no. 1, pp. 117–32.

Fleming, L. and Marx, M. (2006), 'Managing Creativity in Small Worlds in *California Management Review*, vol. 48, no. 4, pp. 6–27.

Fleming, L. and Sorenson, O. (2001), 'Technology as a Complex Adaptive System: Evidence from Patent Data' in *Research Policy*, vol. 30, no. 7, pp. 1019–39.

Fleming, L. and Waguespack, M. (2007), 'Brokerage, Boundary Spanning, and Leadership in Open Innovation Communities' in *Organization Science*, vol. 18, no. 2, pp. 165–80.

Fleming, L., King, C. and Juda, A.I. (2007), 'Small Worlds and Regional Innovation' in *Organization Science*, vol. 18, no. 6, pp. 938–54.

Fleming, L, Mingo, S. and Chen, D. (2007), 'Collaborative Brokerage, Generative Creativity, and Creative Success' in *Administrative Science Quarterly*, vol. 52, no. 3, pp. 443–75.

Fleming, L., Colfer, L., Marin, A. and McPhie, J. (2004), 'Why the Valley Went First: Agglomeration and Emergence in Regional Inventor Network', available at: https://www.funginstitute.berkeley.edu/sites/default/files/Why%20the%20Valley%20Went%20First.pdf

Florida, R. (1995), 'Toward the Learning Region' in *Futures*, vol. 27, no. 5, pp. 527–36.

Florida, R. (2002), *The Rise of the Creative Class*, New York: Basic Books.

Florida, R. (2005a), *Cities and the Creative Class*, New York: Routledge.

Florida, R. (2005b), *The Flight of the Creative Class*, New York: Harper Collins.

Freeman, C. (1974) *The Economics of Industrial Innovation*, London: Penguin Books.

Freeman, C. (1987), *Technology Policy and Economic Performance: Lessons from Japan*, London: Pinter.

Freeman, C. (1991), 'Networks of Innovators: A Synthesis of Research Issues' in *Research Policy*, vol. 20, no. 5, pp. 499–514.

Freeman, C. (1994), 'Innovazioni tecnologiche e organizzative' in *Enciclopedia delle Scienze Sociali*, vol. IV, pp. 731–746, Roma: Treccani.

Freeman, C. (2002), 'Continental, National and Sub-National Innovation Systems – Complementarity and Economic Growth' in *Research Policy*, vol. 31, no. 2, pp. 191–211.

Frenken, K., Van Oort, F. and Verburg, T. (2007), 'Related Variety, Unrelated Variety and Regional Economic Growth' in *Regional Studies*, vol. 41, no. 5, pp. 685–97.

Freud, S. (1910), 'Un ricordo d'infanzia di Leonardo da Vinci' in S. Freud, *Opere*, Torino: Bollati Boringhieri.

Friedman, T. (2005), *The World is Flat: A Brief History of the Twenty-First Century*, New York: Farrar Straus and Giroux.

Furfey, P.H. (1944), 'Steam Power: A Study in the Sociology of Invention' in *The American Catholic Sociological Review*, vol. 5, no. 3, pp. 143–53.

Gambardella, A. and Malerba, F. (eds) (1999), *The Organization of Economic Innovation in Europe*, Cambridge: Cambridge University Press.

Gardener, H. (1993), 'Seven Creators of the Modern Era' in J. Brockman (ed.), *Creativity*, pp. 28–48, New York: Simon & Schuster.

Gertler, M.S. (2003), 'Tacit Knowledge and the Economic Geography of Context, or the Undefinable Tacitness of Being (There)' in *Journal of Economic Geography*, vol. 3, no. 1, pp. 75–99.

234   *Bibliography*

Gertler, M.S. (2010), 'Rules of the Game: The Place of Institutions in Regional Economic Change' in *Regional Studies*, vol. 44, no. 1, pp. 1–15.

Gherardi, S. (2010), 'L'innovazione come processo continuo' in *RA. Rivista dell'Ais*, no. 1, pp. 15–29.

Gibbons, M., Limoges, C., Nowotny, H., Schwartzman, S., Scott, P. and Trow, M. (1994), *The New Production of Knowledge. The Dynamics of Science and Research in Contemporary Societies*, London: Sage.

Giddens, A. (1978), *Durkheim*, New York: Harper Collins.

Giddens, A. (1990), *The Consequences of Modernity*, Cambridge: Polity.

Gilfillan, S.C. (1935), *The Sociology of Invention*, Cambridge: MIT Press.

Giovannini, P. (1987), *Tra conflitto e solidarietà. Teorie sociologiche sulla divisione del lavoro*, Padova: Cedam.

Giuri, P., Mariani, M., Brusoni, S., Crespi, G., Francoz, D., Gambardella, A., Garcia-Fontes, W., Geuna, A., Gonzales, R., Harhoff, D., Hoisl, K., Le Bas, C., Luzzi, A., Magazzini, L., Nesta, L., Nomaler, O., Palomeras, N., Patel, P., Romanelli, M. and Verspagen, B. (2007), 'Inventors and Invention Processes in Europe: Results from the Patval-EU Survey' in *Research Policy*, vol. 36, no. 8, pp. 1107–27.

Glaeser, E.L., Kallal, H., Scheinkman, J. and Shleifer, A. (1992), 'Growth in Cities' in *Journal of Political Economy*, vol. 100, no. 6, pp. 1126–52.

Godin, B. (2005), *The Linear Model of Innovation: The Historical Construction of an Analytical Framework*, Project on the History and Sociology of S&T Statistics, Working Paper no. 30.

Godin, B. (2008), *Innovation: The History of a Category*, Project on the History and Sociology of S&T Statistics, Working Paper no. 1.

Goel, S., Muhamad, R. and Watts, D. (2009), 'Social Search in 'Small-World' Experiments', World Wide Web Conference Committee, 20–24 April, Madrid, Spain.

Goodman, R.A (1981), *Temporary Systems*, New York: Praeger.

Göktepe, D. (2006), *Identification of University Inventors and University Patenting Patterns at Lund University: Conceptual-Methodological & Empirical Findings*, Munich Personal RePEc Archive, Paper no. 1628, pp. 1–35

Göktepe, D. (2008a), *A Theoretical Framework for Understanding University Inventors and Patenting*, Jena Economic Research Papers, no. 2008–031, pp. 1–43.

Göktepe, D. (2008b), *Why and How Do Scientists Commercialize Their Research? Towards a Typology of Inventors*, Jena Economic Research Papers, no. 2008–071, pp. 1–22.

Göktepe, D. and Edquist, C. (2006), 'A Comparative Study Of University Scientists' Motivations For Patenting: A Typology Of University Inventors', SPRU 40th Anniversary Conference, University of Sussex, UK, 11–13 September.

Göktepe, D. and Mahagaonkar, P. (2008), *What do Scientists Want: Money or Fame?* Jena Economic Research Papers, no. 2008–032.

Goyal S., van der Leij, M.J. and Moraga-González, J.L. (2006), 'Economics: An Emerging Small World' in *Journal of Political Economy*, vol. 114, no. 2, pp. 403–12.

Grabher, G. (2002), 'Cool Projects, Boring Institutions: Temporary Collaboration in Social Context' in *Regional Studies*, vol. 36, no. 3, pp. 205–14.

Graham, S. (1998), 'The End of Geography or The Explosion of Place: Conceptualizing Space, Place and Information Technology' in *Progress in Human Geography*, vol. 22, no. 2, pp. 165–85.

Granovetter, M. (1973), 'The Strength of the Weak Ties' in *American Journal of Sociology*, vol. 78, no. 6, pp. 1360–80.

Granovetter, M. (1974), *Getting a Job*, Cambridge: Harvard University Press.

Granovetter, M. (1985), 'Economic Action and Social Structure: The Problem of Embeddedness' in *American Journal of Sociology*, vol. 91, no. 3, pp. 481–510.

Granovetter, M. (2004), 'The Impact of Social Structure on Economic Outcomes' in *Journal of Economic Perspectives*, vol. 19, no. 3, pp. 33–50.

Granovetter, M. and P. McGuire (1998), 'The Making of an Industry: Electricity in the United States' in M. Callon (ed.), *The Laws of the Market*, pp. 147–73, Oxford: Blackwell.

Greig, J.M. (2002), 'The End of Geography?: Globalization, Communications, and Culture in the International System' in *The Journal of Conflict Resolution*, vol. 46, no. 2, pp. 225–43.

Griliches, Z. (1957), 'Hybrid Corn: An Exploration in the Economics of Technological Change' in *Econometrica*, vol. 25, no. 4, pp. 501–22.

Griliches, Z. (1992), *The Search for R&D Spillovers*, NBER Working Paper No. 3768, pp. 1–18.

Griliches, Z. (1998), 'Issues in Assessing the Contribution of Research and Development to Productivity Growth' in Z. Griliches, *R&D and Productivity: The Econometric Evidence*, pp. 17–45, Chicago: University of Chicago Press.

Grossman, G.M. and Helpman. E. (1991), *Innovation and Growth in the Global Economy*, Cambridge: MIT Press.

Guare, J. (1994), *Six Degrees of Separation*, New York: Vintage Books.

Guilford, J.P. (1950), 'Creativity' in *American Psychologist*, vol. 5, no. 8, pp. 444–54.

Guilford, J.P. (1967), *The Nature of Human Intelligence*, New York: McGraw-Hill.

Guiot, J.M. (1976), 'A Modification of Milgram's Small World Method' in *European Journal of Social Psychology*, vol. 6, no. 4, pp. 503–7.

Gulati, R. (1998), 'Alliances and Networks' in *Strategic Management Journal*, vol. 19, no. 4, pp. 293–317.

Gurevich, M. (1961), *The Social Structure of Acquaintanceship Networks*, Cambridge, MA: The MIT Press.

Haas, P.M. (1992), 'Introduction: Epistemic Communities and International Policy Coordination' in *International Organization*, vol. 46, no. 1, pp. 1–35.

Hage, J. and Meeus, M. (eds) (2006), *Innovation, Science, and Institutional Change: A Research Handbook*, Oxford: Oxford University Press.

Hall, B.H. (2005), *Innovation and Diffusion*, in J. Fagerberg, D.C. Mowery and R.R. Nelson, (eds), *The Oxford Handbook of Innovation*, pp. 459–84, New York: Oxford University Press.

Hall, P.A. and Soskice D. (eds) (2001), *Varieties of Capitalism. The Institutional Foundations of Comparative Advantage*, Oxford: Oxford University Press.

Hagedoorn, J. (2002), 'Inter-firm R&D Partnerships: An Overview of Major Trends and Patterns since 1960' in *Research Policy*, vol. 31, no. 4, pp. 477–92.

Hancké, B. (ed.) (2009), *Debating Varieties of Capitalism*, Oxford: Oxford University Press.

Hansen, M.T. (1999), 'The Search-Transfer Problem: The Role of Weak Ties in Sharing Knowledge across Organization Subunits' in *Administrative Science Quarterly*, vol. 44, no. 1, pp. 82–111.

Healy, A. and Morgan, K. (2012), 'Spaces of Innovation: Learning, Proximity and the Ecological Turn' in *Regional Studies*, vol. 46, no. 8, pp. 1041–53.

Hedström, P. and Swedberg, R. (1998), *Social Mechanisms*, Cambridge: Cambridge University Press.

Helpman, E. (2004), *The Mystery of Economic Growth*, Cambridge: The Belknap Press of Harvard University Press.

Henderson, R.M. and Clark, K.B. (1990), 'Architectural Innovation: The Reconfiguration of Existing Product Technologies and the Failure of Established Firms' in *Administrative Science Quarterly*, vol. 35, no. 1, pp. 9–30.

Henderson, R., Jaffe, A. and Trajtenberg, M. (2005), 'Patent Citations and the Geography of Knowledge Spillovers: A Reassessment: Comment' in *The American Economic Review*, vol. 95, no. 1, pp. 461–4.

Hennessey, B.A. (2003), 'The Social Psychology of Creativity' in *Scandinavian Journal of Educational Research*, vol. 47, no. 3, pp. 253–71.

Hennessey, B.A. and Amabile, T.M. (2010), 'Creativity' in *Annual Review of Psychology*, vol. 61, no. 1, pp. 569–98.

Hodgson, G.M. (2006), 'What Are Institutions?' in *Journal of Economic Issues*, vol. XL, no. 1, pp. 1–25.

Hoegl, M. and Proserpio, L. (2004), 'Team Member Proximity and Teamwork in Innovative Projects' in *Research Policy*, vol. 33, no. 8, pp. 1153–65.

Hoisl, K. (2007), 'Tracing Mobile Inventors – The Causality Between Inventor Mobility and Inventor Productivity Research' in *Research Policy*, vol. 36, no. 5, pp. 619–36.

Hollingsworth, J.R. and Boyer, R. (1997), *Contemporary Capitalism. The Embeddedness of Institutions*, Cambridge: Cambridge University Press.

Hollingsworth, J.R., Schmitter, P.C. and Streeck, W. (1994), *Governing Capitalist Economies. Performance and Control of Economic Sectors*, Oxford: Oxford University Press.

Hollingsworth, R. (2006), 'A Path Dependent Perspective on Institutional and Organizational Factors Shaping Major Scientific Discoveries' in J. Hage and M. Meeus (eds), *Innovation, Science, and Institutional Change: A Research Handbook*, pp. 423–42, Oxford: Oxford University Press.

Hollingsworth, R., Hollingsworth, E.J. and Hage, J. (2008), *Fostering Scientific Excellence: Organizations, Institutions, and Major Discoveries in Biomedical Science*, New York: Cambridge University Press.

Holmén, M. (1998), 'Regional Industrial Renewal: The Growth of "Antenna Technology" in West Sweden' in *Technology Analysis and Strategic Management*, vol. 14, no. 1, pp. 87–106.

Hoyman, M. and Faricy, M. (2009), 'It Takes a Village. A Test of the Creative Class, Social Capital, and Human Capital Theories' in *Urban Affairs Review*, vol. 44, no. 3, pp. 311–33.

Hughes, E. (1961), 'Tarde's Psychologie Economique: An Unknown Classic by a Forgotten Sociologist' in *The American Journal of Sociology*, vol. LXVI, no. 6, pp. 553–9.

Hughes, T. (2004), *American Genesis: A Century of Invention and Technological Enthusiasm, 1870–1970*, Chicago: Chicago University Press.

Jacobs, J. (1969), *The Economy of Cities*, New York: Vintage.

Jackson, G. (2010), *Actors and Institutions*, in G. Morgan, J.L. Campbell, C. Crouch. O.K. Pedersen and R. Whitley (eds), *The Oxford Handbook of Comparative Institutional Analysis*, pp. 63–86, Oxford and New York: Oxford University Press.

Jaffe, A.B. (1986), 'Technological Opportunity and Spillovers of R&D: Evidence from Firms' Patents, Profits, and Market Value' in *The American Economic Review*, vol. 76, no. 5, pp. 984–1001.

Jaffe, A.B. (1989), 'Real Effects of Academic Research' in *The American Economic Review*, vol. 79, no. 5, pp. 957–70.

Jaffe, A.B., Trajtenberg, M. and Fogarty, M.S. (2000), *The Meaning of Patent Citations: Report on the NBER/Case-Western Reserve Survey of Patentees*, NBER Working Paper No. 7631.

Jaffe, A., Trajtenberg, M. and Henderson, R. (1993), 'Geographic Localization of Knowledge Spillovers as Evidenced by Patent Citations' in *Quarterly Journal of Economics*, vol. 108, no. 3, pp. 577–98.

Janis, I.L. (1972), *Victims of Groupthink*, Boston: Houghton Mifflin Company.

John-Steiner, V. (2000), *Creative Collaboration*, New York: Oxford University Press.

Johnson, A. and Jacobsson, S. (2003), *The Emergence of a Growth Industry: A Comparative Analysis of the German, Dutch and Swedish Wind Turbine Industries*, in S. Metcalfe and U. Cantner (eds), *Transformation and Development: Schumpeterian Perspectives*, pp. 197–227, Heidelberg: Physical/Springer.

Johnson, B. (1992), 'Institutional Learning' in Lundvall, B.-Å. (ed.), *National Systems of Innovation: Towards a Theory of Innovation and Interactive Learning*, pp. 21–45, London: Pinter.

Johnson, B., Edquist, C. and Lundvall, B.-Å. (2003), *Economic Development and the National System of Innovation Approach*, Paper presented to the First Globelics Conference, Rio de Janeiro, 3–6 November.

Johnson, C. (1982), *MITI and the Japanese Miracle*, Stanford: Stanford University Press.

Jolivet, E. and Maurice, M. (2006), 'How Markets Matter: Radical Innovation, Societal Acceptance, and the Case of Genetically Engineered Food' in J. Hage and M. Meeus (eds), *Innovation, Science, and Institutional Change: A Research Handbook*, pp. 334–68, Oxford: Oxford University Press.

Jones, F.B. (2005a), *Age and Great Invention*, NBER Working Paper No. 11359.

Jones, F.B. (2005b), *The Burden of Knowledge and the 'Death of the Renaissance Man': Is Innovation Getting Harder?*, NBER Working Paper No. 7631.

Kamien, M. and Schwartz, N. (1982), *Market Structure and Innovation*, Cambridge: Cambridge University Press.

Karinthy, F. (2006), 'Chain-Links' in M. Newman, A.L. Barabási and D.J. Watts, *The Structure and Dynamics of Networks*, pp. 21–6, Princeton, NJ: Princeton University Press.

Katzenstein, P.J. and Nelson, S.C. (2014), 'Uncertainty, Risk, and the Financial Crisis of 2008' in *International Organization*, vol. 68, no. 2, pp. 361–92.

Keller, M.R. and Block, F. (2013), 'Explaining the Transformation in the US Innovation System: The Impact of a Small Government Program' in *Socio-Economic Review*, vol. 11, no. 4, pp. 629–56.

Kemp, R.G.M., Folkeringa, M., de Jong, J.P.J. and Wubben, E.F.M. (2003), *Innovation and Firm Performance*, Research Report H200207, Zoetermer, SCALES.

Khan, B.Z. and Sokoloff, K.L. (1993), 'Schemes of Practical Utility' in *Journal of Economic History*, vol. 53, June, pp. 289–307.

Khan, B.Z. and Sokoloff, K.L. (1998), 'Two Paths to Industrial Development and Technological Change' in M. Berg and K. Bruland (eds), *Technological Revolutions in Europe, 1760–1860*, pp. 292–313, Cheltenham: Edward Elgar.

Khan, B.Z. and Sokoloff, K.L. (2004), 'Institutions and Technological Innovation During Early Economic Growth: Evidence from the Great Inventors of the United States, 1790–1930' in T. Eicher and C. Penalosa Garcia (eds), *Institutions and Growth*, pp. 123–58, Cambridge, MA: The MIT Press.

Killworth, P.D., McCarty, C., Bernard, H.R. and House, M. (2006), 'Social Networks: the Accuracy of Small World Chains in Social Networks' in *Social Networks*, vol. 28, no. 1, pp. 85–96.

Kim J., Lee, J.S. and Marschke, G. (2007) *Research Scientist Productivity and Firm Size: Evidence from Panel Data on Inventors*, Institute of Economic Research, Korea University, Discussion Paper Series no. 0708.

Kimberly, J.R. and Evanisko, M.J. (1981), 'Organizational Innovation: The Influence of Individual, Organizational, and Contextual Factors on Hospital Adoption of Technological and Administrative Innovations' in *The Academy of Management Journal*, vol. 24, no. 4, pp. 689–713.

King, N. and Anderson, N. (2002), *Managing Innovation and Change: A Critical Guide for Organizations*, London: Thompson.

Kinnunen J. (1996), 'Gabriel Tarde as a Founding Father of Innovation Diffusion Research' in *Acta Sociologica*, vol. 39, no. 4, pp. 431–42.

Klein, H.K. and Kleinman, D.L. (2002), 'The Social Construction of Technology: Structural Considerations' in *Science, Technology, & Human Values*, vol. 27, no. 1, pp. 28–52.

Kleinberg, J.M. (2000a), 'Navigation in a Small World' in *Nature*, vol. 406, 24 August, p. 845.

Kleinberg, J.M. (2000b), *The Small World Phenomenon: An Algorithmic Perspective*, Proceedings of the 32nd Annual ACM Symposium on the Theory of Computing, Association of Computing Machinery, New York, pp. 163–70.

Kleinfeld, J.S. (2002), 'The Small World Problem' in *Social Science & Public Policy*, vol. 39, no. 2, pp. 61–6.

Kline, S.J. and Rosenberg, N. (1986), *An Overview of Innovation*, in R. Landau and N. Rosenberg (eds), *The Positive Sum Game*, pp. 275–305, Washington, DC: National Academy Press.

Knight, F. (1921), *Risk, Uncertainty and Profit*, Boston: Hart, Schaffner & Marx.

Kochen, M. (1989), 'Preface' in M. Kochen (ed.), *The Small World*, pp. vii–xiv, Norwood, NJ: Ablex.

Kogut, B. and Walker, G. (2001), 'The Small World of Germany and the Durability of National Networks' in *American Sociological Review*, vol. 66, no. 3, pp. 317–35.

Korte, C. and Milgram, S. (1970), 'Acquaintance Networks Between Racial Groups: Application of the Small World Method' in *Journal of Personality and Social Psychology*, vol. 15, no. 2, pp. 101–8.

Kossinets, G. and Watts, D.J. (2009), 'Origins of Homophily in an Evolving Social Network' in *American Journal of Sociology*, vol. 115, no. 2, pp. 405–50.

Krugman, P. (1991), *Geography and Trade*, Cambridge: MIT Press.

Krugman P. (1998), 'What's New about the New Economic Geography?' in *Oxford Review of Economic Policy*, vol. 14, no. 2, pp. 7–17.

Krugman, P. (2011), 'The New Economic Geography, Now Middle-aged' in *Regional Studies*, vol. 45, no. 1, pp. 1–7.

Laestadius S. (1998), 'Technology Level, Knowledge Formation and Industrial Competence in Paper Manufacturing' in G. Eliasson, C. Green and C. McCann (eds), *Microfoundations of Economic Growth*, pp. 212–16, Ann Arbor, MI: University of Michigan Press.

Lam A. (2005), 'Organizational Innovation' in J. Fagerberg, D.C. Mowery and R.R. Nelson (eds), *The Oxford Handbook of Innovation*, pp. 153–82, New York: Oxford University Press.

Lamoreaux, N.R. and Sokoloff, K.L (1997), *Inventors, Firms, and the Market for Technology: U.S. Manufacturing in the Late Nineteenth and Early Twentieth Centuries*, NBER Working Paper Series, Historical Paper 98.

Lamoreaux, N.R. and Sokoloff, K.L (2005), *The Decline of the Independent Inventor: A Schumpeterian Story*, NBER Working Paper Series, Working Paper 11654, available at: www.nber.org/papers/w11654

Lamoreaux, N.R. and Sokoloff, K.L (2007), 'Introduction: The Organization and Finance of Innovation in American History' in N.R. Lamoreaux and K.L Sokoloff (eds), *Financing Innovation in the United States, 1870 to the Present*, pp. 1–37, Cambridge, MA: The MIT Press.

Landes, D. (1969), *The Unbound Prometheus. Technological Change and Industrial Development in Western Europe from 1750 to the Present*, Cambridge: Cambridge University Press.

Lave J. and Wenger E. (1991), *Situated Learning: Legitimate Peripheral Participation*, New York: Cambridge University Press.

Lazarsfeld, P.F. and Merton, R.K. (1954), 'Friendship as a Social Process: A Substantive and Methodological Analysis' in M. Berger (eds), *Freedom and Control in Modern Society*, pp. 18–66, New York: Van Nostrand.

Lazonick, W. (2005), 'The Innovative Firm' in J. Fagerberg, D.C. Mowery and R.R. Nelson (eds), *The Oxford Handbook of Innovation*, pp. 29–55, New York: Oxford University Press.

Le Galès, P. and Voelzkow, H. (2001), 'Introduction: The Governance of Local Economies' in C. Crouch, P. Le Galès, C. Trigilia and H. Voelzkow (eds), *Local Production Systems in Europe. Rise or Demise?*, pp. 1–24, Oxford: Oxford University Press.

Lepinay, V.-A. (2007), 'Economy of the Germ: Captial, Accumulation and Vibration' in *Economy and Society*, vol. 36, no. 4, pp. 526–48.

Leskovec, J. and Horvitz, E. (2007) *Planetary-Scale Views on an Instant-Messaging Network*, Microsoft Research Technical Report, June, no. 186, available at: http://research.microsoft.com/en-us/um/people/horvitz/leskovec_horvitz_worldwide_buzz.pdf

Lester, R.K. and Piore, M.J. (2004), *Innovation. The Missing Dimension*, Cambridge, MA: Harvard University Press.

Lettl, C. (2005) 'Users as Inventors and Developers of Radical Innovation' in *Journal of Customer Behaviour*, vol. 4, no. 2, pp. 277–97.

Lettl, C., Rost, K. and von Wartburg, I. (2009), 'Why Are some Independent Inventors "Heroes" and Others "Hobbyists"? The Moderating Role of Technological Diversity and Specialization' in *Research Policy*, vol. 38, no. 2, pp. 243–54.

Leydesdorff, L. and Fritsch, M. (2006), 'Measuring the Knowledge Base of Regional Innovation Systems in Germany in Terms of a Triple Helix Dynamic' in *Research Policy*, vol. 35, no. 10, pp. 1538–53.

Leydesdorff, L. and Meyer, M. (2006), 'Triple Helix Indicators of Knowledge-based Innovation Systems. Introduction to the Special Issue' in *Research Policy*, vol. 35, no. 10, pp. 1441–9.

Leydesdorff, L., Dolfsma, W. and Van der Panne, G. (2006), 'Measuring the Knowledge Base of an Economy in Terms of Triple-Helix Relations among "Technology, Organization, and Territory"' in *Research Policy*, vol. 35, no. 2, pp. 181–99.

Lin, N., Dayton, P.W. and Greenwald, P. (1977), 'The Urban Communication Network and Social Stratification: A "Small World" Experiment' in B.D. Ruben (ed.), *Communication Yearbook I*, pp. 107–19, New Brunswick, NJ: Transaction.

Lissoni, F. (ed.) (2011), *L'imprenditorialità accademica. Un'analisi multidisciplinare*, Roma: Carocci.

Liu, X. and White, S. (2001), 'Comparing Innovation Systems: A Framework and Application to China's Transitional Context' in *Research Policy*, vol. 30, no. 7, pp. 1091–114.

Locke, R.M. and Wellhausen, R.L. (2014), *Production in the Innovation Economy*, Cambridge: The MIT Press.

Lotka, A.J. (1926), 'The Frequency Distribution of Scientific Productivity' in *Journal of the Washington Academy of Science*, vol. 16, no. 12, pp. 317–23.

Lubart, T.I. (2001), 'Models of the Creative Process: Past, Present and Future' in *Creativity Research Journal*, vol. 13, no. 3, pp. 295–308.

Lundberg, P.P. (1975), 'Patterns of Acquaintanceship in Society and Complex Organization: A Comparative Study of the Small World Problem' in *The Pacific Sociological Review*, no. 18, pp. 206–22.

Lundvall, B.-Å. (1985), *Product Innovation and User–Producer Interaction*, Aalborg: Aalborg University Press.

Lundvall, B.-Å. (1988), 'Innovation as an Interactive Process: From User–Producer Interaction to the National Innovation Systems' in G. Dosi, C. Freeman, R.R. Nelson, G. Silverberg and L. Soete (eds), *Technical Change and Economic Theory*, pp. 349–69, London: Pinter.

Lundvall, B.-Å. (1992a), 'Introduction' in Lundvall, B.-Å. (ed.), *National Systems of Innovation: Towards a Theory of Innovation and Interactive Learning*, pp. 1–19, London: Pinter.

Lundvall, B.-Å. (ed.) (1992b), *National Systems of Innovation: Towards a Theory of Innovation and Interactive Learning*, London: Pinter.

Lundvall, B-Å. (1996), *The Social Dimension of The Learning Economy*, Druid Working Paper no. 96–1.

Lundvall, B.-Å. (2001), *Innovation, Growth and Social Cohesion: The Danish Model*, London: Edward Elgar.

Lundvall, B.-Å. and Johnson, B. (1994), 'The Learning Economy' in *Journal of Industry Studies*, vol. 1, no. 2, pp. 23–42.

Lundvall, B-Å. and Maskell, P. (2000), 'Nation States and Economic Development: From National Systems of Production to National Systems of Knowledge Creation and Learning' in G.L. Clark, M.P. Feldman and M.S. Gertler (eds), *The Oxford Handbook of Economic Geography*, pp. 353–72, Oxford: Oxford University Press.

Lundvall, B.-Å., Johnson, B., Andersen, E.S. and Dalum, B. (2002), 'National Systems of Production, Innovation and Competence Building' in *Research Policy*, vol. 31, no. 2, pp. 213–31.

MacKenzie, D. (1984), 'Marx and the Machine' in *Technology and Culture*, vol. 25, no. 3, pp. 473–502.

MacKenzie, D. and Millo, Y. (2003), 'Constructing a Market, Performing a Theory: The Historical Sociology of a Financial Derivatives Exchange' in *American Journal of Sociology*, vol. 109, no. 1, pp. 107–45.

MacLeod, C. (1988), *Inventing the Industriul Revolution: The English Patent System, 1660–1800*, Cambridge: Cambridge University Press.

MacLeod, C. (1999), 'Negotiating the Rewards of Invention: The Shop-Floor Inventor in Victorian Britain' in *Business History*, vol. 41, no. 2, pp. 17—36.

MacLeod, C. (2007), *Heroes of Invention: Technology, Liberalism and British Identity, 1750–1914*, Cambridge: Cambridge University Press.

Malerba, F. (ed.) (2000), *Economia dell'innovazione*, Roma: Carocci.

Malerba, F. (2002), 'Sectoral Systems of Innovation and Production' in *Research Policy*, vol. 31, no. 2, pp. 247–64.

Malerba, F. (2004a), 'Introduction' in Malerba, F. (ed.), *Sectoral Systems of Innovation*, pp. 1–5, New York: Cambridge University Press.

Malerba, F. (ed.) (2004b), *Sectoral Systems of Innovation*, New York: Cambridge University Press.

Malerba, F. (2004c), 'Sectoral Systems of Innovation: Basic Concepts' in F. Malerba (ed.), *Sectoral Systems of Innovation*, pp. 9–41, New York: Cambridge University Press.

Malerba, F. (2005), 'Sectoral Systems: How and Why Innovation Differs across Sectors' in J. Fagerberg, D.C. Mowery and R.R. Nelson (eds), *The Oxford Handbook of Innovation*, pp. 380–406, New York: Oxford University Press.

Malerba, F. and Orsenigo, L. (1993), 'Technological Regimes and Firm Behavior' in *Industrial and Corporate Change*, vol. 2, no. 1, pp. 45–74.

Malerba, F. and Orsenigo, L. (1997), 'Technological Regimes and Sectoral Patterns of Innovative Activities' in *Industrial and Corporate Change*, vol. 6, no. 1, pp. 83–117.

Malerba, F. and Orsenigo, L. (2000), 'Regimi tecnologici e pattern settoriali di innovazione' in Malerba, F. (ed.), *Economia dell'innovazione*, pp. 231–53, Roma: Carocci.

Mariani, M. and Giuri, M. (2007), *Appropriability, Proximity, Routines and Innovation*, Paper presented to the DRUID summer conference, Copenhagen, 18–20 June.

Mariani, M. and Romanelli, M. (2007), ' "Stacking" and "Picking" Inventions: The Patenting Behavior of European Inventors' in *Research Policy*, vol. 36, no. 8, pp. 1128–42.

Marshall, A. (1890 [1920]), *Principles of Economics*, 8th edition, London: Macmillan.

Marshall. A. (1981), *Antologia di scritti economici*, Bologna: Il Mulino.

Martin, B.R. (2012), 'The Evolution of Science Policy and Innovation Studies' in *Research Policy*, vol. 41, no. 7, pp. 1219–39.

Marx, K (1847), *Misère de la philosophie*, Paris-Bruxelles: Frank. (Eng. trans. (1892), *The Poverty of Philosophy*, Moscow: Progress Publishers.)

Marx, K (1859), *Zur Kritik der Politischen Ökonomie*, Berlin: Franz Duncher. (Eng. trans. (1904), *A Contribution to the Critique of Political Economy*, Chicago: Charles H. Kerr.)

Marx, K (1867), *Das Kapital*, vol. I, Hamburg: O. Meissner. (Eng. trans. (1887), *Capital*, Vol. I, Moscow: Progress Publishers.)

Marx, K. and Engels, F. (1848), *Manifest der kommunistischen Partei*. (Eng. trans. (1969), *Manifesto of the Communist Party*, in K. Marx and F. Engels, *Selected Works*, vol. 1, pp. 231–53, Moscow: Progress Publishers, Marxiste Internet Archive.)

Maskell, P. and Malmberg, A. (1999), 'Localised Learning and Industrial Competitiveness' in *Cambridge Journal of Economics*, vol. 23, no. 2, pp. 167–86.

Maucourant, J. and Plociniczak, S. (2013), 'The Institution, the Economy and the Market: Karl Polanyi's Institutional Thought for Economists' in *Review of Political Economy*, vol. 25, no. 3, pp. 512–31.

Mayer, R.E. (1995), 'The Search for Insight: Grappling with Gestalt Psychology's Unanswered Questions' in R.J. Sternberg and J.E. Davidson (eds), *The Nature of Insight*, pp. 3–32, Cambridge, MA: The MIT Press.

Mayer, R.E. (1999), 'Fifty Years of Creativity Research' in R.J. Sternberg (ed.), *Handbook of Creativity*, pp. 449–60, Cambridge: Cambridge University Press.

Mazzucato. M. (2013), *The Entrepreneurial State. Debunking Public Vs. Private Sector Myths*, London-New York: Anthem Press.

McCraw, T.K. (2007), *Prophet of Innovation: Joseph Schumpeter and Creative Destruction*, Cambridge: Harvard University Press.

McEvily B. and Zaheer A. (1999), 'Bridging Ties: A Source of Firm Heterogeneity in Competitive Capabilities' in *Strategic Management Journal*, vol. 20, no. 12, pp. 1133–56.

McKelvey, M., Orsenigo, L. and Pammolli, F. (2004), 'Pharmaceuticals Analyzed through the Lens of a Sectoral Innovation System' in Malerba, F. (ed.), *Sectoral Systems of Innovation*, pp. 73–120, New York: Cambridge University Press.

McGee, D. (1995), 'Making up Mind: The Early Sociology of Invention' in *Technology and Culture*, vol. 36, no. 4, pp. 773–801.

McPherson, J.M. and Smith-Lovin, L. (1987), 'Homophily in Voluntary Organizations: Status Distance and the Composition of Face-to-Face Groups' in *American Sociological Review*, vol. 52, no. 3, pp. 370–9.

McPherson, J.M., Smith-Lovin, L. and Cook J.M. (2001), 'Birds of a Feather: Homophily in Social Networks' in *Annual Review of Sociology*, vol. 27, no. 3, pp. 415–44.

Meeus, M.T.H. and Faber, J. (2006), 'Interorganizational Relations and Innovation: A Review and a Theoretical Extension' in Hage, J. and Meeus, M. (eds), *Innovation, Science, and Institutional Change: A Research Handbook*, pp. 67–87, Oxford: Oxford University Press.

Merton, R.K. (1965), *On the Shoulders of Giants*, New York; The Free Press.

Merton, R.K. (2000), *Teoria e struttura sociale III. Sociologia della conoscenza e della scienza*, Bologna: Il Mulino.

Merton, R.K (2006), 'Afterword: Autobiographical Reflections on the The Travels and Aventures of Serendipity' in R.K. Merton and E.G. Barber, *The Travels and Aventures of Serendipity: A Study in Sociological Semantics and the Sociology of Science*, pp. 230–98, Princeton, Princeton University Press.

Merton, R.K. and Barber, E.G. (2006), *The Travels and Aventures of Serendipity: A Study in Sociological Semantics and the Sociology of Science*, Princeton: Princeton University Press.

Miceli, V. (2010), *Distretti tecnologici e sistemi regionali di innovazione. Il caso italiano*, Bologna: Il Mulino.

Milgram, S. (1967), 'The Small World Problem' in *Psychology Today*, vol. 1, no. 1, pp. 61–7.

Mintz, B. and Schwartz, M. (1985) *The Power Structure of American Business*, Chicago: University of Chicago Press.

Mizruchi, M.S. (1982), *The American Corporate Network: 1904–1974*, Beverly Hills, CA: Sage.

Mizruchi, M.S. (1996), 'What Do Interlocks Do? An Analysis, Critique, and Assessment of Research on Interlocking Directorates' in *Annual Review of Sociology*, vol. 22, no. 1, pp. 271–98.

Moiso, V. (2011), 'I fenomeni finanziari nella letteratura sociologica contemporanea: l'emergenza di nuove prospettive' in *Stato e Mercato*, no. 2, pp. 313–42.

Mokyr, J. (1990), *The Lever of Riches. Technological Creativity and Economic Progress*, New York: Oxford University Press.

Moon, C.I. and Prasad, R. (1994), 'Beyond the Developmental State: Networks, Politics, and Institutions' in *Governance: An International Journal of Policy and Administration*, vol. 7, no. 4, pp. 360–86.

Moretti, E. (2012), *The New Geography of Jobs*, New York: Houghton Mifflin Harcourt.

Morgan, G., Campbell, J.L., Crouch, C., Pedersen, O.K. and Whitley, R. (eds) (2010), *The Oxford Handbook of Comparative Institutional Analysis*, Oxford and New York: Oxford University Press.

Morgan, K. (1997), 'The Learning Region: Institutions, Innovation and Regional Renewal' in *Regional Studies*, vol. 31, no. 5, pp. 491–503.

Mowery, D.C. (1983), 'The Relationship Between Intrafirm and Contractual Forms of Industrial Research in American Manufacturing, 1900–1940' in *Explorations in Economic History*, vol. 20, no. 4, pp. 351–74.

Mowery, D.C. (1992), 'The U.S. National Innovation System: Origins and Prospects for Change' in *Research Policy*, vol. 21, no. 2, pp. 125–44.

Mowery, D.C. (1998), 'The Changing Structure of the U.S. National Innovation System: Implications for International Conflict and Cooperation in R&D Policy' in *Research Policy*, vol. 27, no. 6, pp. 639–54.

Mowery, D.C. and Rosenberg, N. (1993), *The U.S. National Innovation System*, in Nelson, R.R. (ed.), *National Innovation Systems: A Comparative Analysis*, pp. 29–75, New York: Oxford University Press.

Mumford, M.D. (2001), 'Something Old, Something New: Revisiting Guilford's Conception of Creative Problem Solving' in *Creativity Research Journal*, vol. 13, no. 3, pp. 267—76.

Mumford, M.D., Vessey, W.B. and Barrett, J.D. (2008), 'Commentary. Measuring Divergent Thinking: Is There Really One Solution to the Problem?' in *Psychology of Aesthetics, Creativity, and the Arts*, vol. 2, no. 2, pp. 86–8.

Murphy, L.J. (1973), 'Lotka's Law in the Humanities?' in *Journal of the American Society for Information Science*, vol. 24, no. 6, pp. 461–2.

Murray, F. (2004), 'The Role of Academic Inventors in Entrepreneurial Firms: Sharing the Laboratory Life' in *Research Policy*, vol. 33, no. 4, pp. 643–59.

Mutti, A. (2009), 'Produzione di reputazione tramite regolazione' in *Sistemi Intelligenti*, no. 2, pp. 261–72.

Narin, F. and Breitzman, A. (1995), 'Inventive Productivity' in *Research Policy*, vol. 24, no. 4, pp. 507–19.

Narin, F., Hamilton, K.S. and Olivastro, D. (1997), 'The Increasing Linkage Between US Technology Policy and Public Science' in *Research Policy*, vol. 26, no. 3, pp. 317–30.

NBER (1962), *The Rate and Direction of Inventive Activity: Economic and Social Factors*, Princeton: Princeton University Press.

Nee, V., Kang, J.-H. and Opper, S. (2010), 'A Theory of Innovation: Market Transition, Property Rights, and Innovative Activity' in *Journal of Institutional and Theoretical Economics*, vol. 166, no. 3, pp. 397–425.

Nelson, R.R. (1959), 'The Simple Economics of Basic Scientific Research' in *Journal of Political Economy*, vol. 67, no. 2, pp. 297–306.

Nelson, R.R. (1987), *The Rate and Direction of Inventive Activity*, Princeton: Princeton University Press.

Nelson, R.R. (1992), 'National Innovation Systems: A Retrospective on a Study' in *Industrial and Corporate Change*, vol. 1, no. 2, 1992, pp. 347–74.

Nelson, R.R. (ed.) (1993), *National Innovation Systems: A Comparative Analysis*, New York: Oxford University Press.

Nelson, R.R. (1998), 'The Agenda for Growth Theory: A Different Point of View' in *Cambridge Journal of Economics*, vol. 22, no. 4, pp. 497–520.

Nelson, R.R. (2008), 'What Enables Rapid Economic Progress: What Are the Needed Institutions?' in *Research Policy*, vol. 37, no. 1, pp. 1–11.

Nelson, R.R. and Nelson, K. (2002), 'Technology, Institutions, and Innovation Systems' in *Research Policy*, vol. 31, nn. 8–9, pp. 265–72.

Nelson, R.R. and Rosenberg, N. (1993), *Technical Innovation and National Systems*, in Nelson, R.R. (ed.) (1993), *National Innovation Systems: A Comparative Analysis*, pp. 3–21, New York: Oxford University Press.

Nelson, R.R. and Sampat, B. (2001), 'Making Sense of Institutions as a Factor Shaping Economic Performance' in *Journal of Economic Behavior and Organization*, vol. 44, no. 1, pp. 31–54.

Nelson, R.R. and Winter, S.G. (1982), *An Evolutionary Theory of Economic Change*. Cambridge, MA: Harvard University Press.

Newman, M.E.J. (2001a), 'Scientific Collaboration Network: I. Network Construction and Fundamental Results' in *Physical Review E*, vol. 64, no. 1, pp. 016131–1/8.

Newman, M.E.J. (2001b), 'Scientific Collaboration Network: II. Shortest Paths, Weighted Networks, and Centrality' in *Physical Review E*, vol. 64, no. 1, pp. 016132–1/7.

Newman, M.E.J. (2001c), 'The Structure of Scientific Collaboration Network' in *Proceedings of the National Academy of Sciences*, vol. 98, no. 2, pp. 404–9.

Newman, M.E.J., Barabási, A.L. and Watts, D.J. (2006*), The Structure and Dynamics of Networks*, Princeton: Princeton University Press.

Newman, M.E.J., Strogatz, S. and Watts, D. (2001), 'Random Graphs with Arbitrary Degree Distributions and Their Applications' in *Physical Review*, vol. 64, no. 2, pp. 1–17.

North, D.C. (1990), *Institutions, Institutional Change and Economic Performance*, Cambridge: Cambridge University Press.

O'Brien, R. (1992), *Global Financial Integration: The End of Geography*, London: Royal Institute of International Affairs.

OECD (1999), *Managing national Innovation Systems*, Paris: OECD.

OECD (2005), *Governance of Innovation Systems. Volume 1: Synthesis Report*, Paris: OECD.

OECD (2008), *Open Innovation in Global Networks*, Paris: OECD.

OECD (2010), *The OECD Innovation Strategy*, Paris: OECD.

OECD/Eurostat (2005), *Oslo Manual. Guidelines for Collecting and Interpreting Innovation Data*, Paris: OECD.

Ogburn, W.F. (1922), *Social Change, with Respect to Culture and Original Nature*, New York: Viking Press.

Ogburn, W.F. (1926), 'The Great Man versus Social Forces' in *Social Forces*, vol. 5, no. 2, pp. 225–31.

Önis, Z. (1991), 'The Logic of the Developmentalist State' in *Comparative Politics*, vol. 24, no. 1, pp. 109–21.

Ó Riain, S.P. (2004), 'The Flexible Developmental State: Globalization, Information Technology, and the "Celtic Tiger"', in *Politics & Society*, vol. 28, no. 2, pp. 157–93.

Ó Riain, S.P. (2004), *The Politics of High-Tech Growth: Developmental Network States in the Global Economy*, Cambridge: Cambridge University Press.

O' Riain, S.P. (2014), *The Rise and the Fall of Ireland's Celtic Tiger. Liberalism, Boom and Bust*, Cambridge and New York, Cambridge University Press.

Osterloh, M. and Rota, S. (2007), 'Open Source Software Development – Just Another Case of Collective Invention?' in *Research Policy*, vol. 36, no. 2, pp. 157–71.

Paci, M. (ed.) (1980), *Famiglia e mercato del lavoro in un'economia periferica*, Milano: Angeli.

Padgett, J.F. and Powell, W.W. (2012), *The Emergence of Organizations and Markets*, Princeton & Oxford: Princeton University Press.

Parini, E.G. and Pellegrino, G. (eds) (2009), *S come scienza T come tecnica e riflessione sociologica*, Napoli: Liguori.

PatVal-EU (2005), *The Value of the European Patents. Evidence from a Survey of European Inventors. Final Report of The PatVal Eu Project*, DG Science & Technology, European Commission, Contract no. HPV2-CT-2001–00013, Brussels.

Paulus, P.B. and Nijstad, B.A. (eds) (2003), *Group Creativity. Innovation Through Collaboration*, New York: Oxford University Press.

Pavitt, K. (1984), 'Sectoral Patterns of Technical Change: Towards a Taxonomy and a Theory' in *Research Policy*, vol. 13, no. 6, pp. 343–73.

Pavitt, K. (2002), *Knowledge about Knowledge since Nelson & Winter: A Mixed Record*, electronic working paper, series paper no. 83, SPRU, University of Sussex, June, pp. 1–21.

Pavitt, K. (2005), *Innovation Processes*, in J. Fagerberg, D.C. Mowery and R.R. Nelson (eds), *The Oxford Handbook of Innovation*, pp. 86–114, New York: Oxford University Press.

Perulli, P. (1989), *Società e innovazione*, Bologna: Il Mulino.

Pettigrew, A.M. and Fenton, E.M. (2000), *The Innovating Organization*, London: Sage.

Pettigrew, A.M. and Massini, S. (2003), 'Innovative Forms of Organizing: Trends in Europe, Japan and the USA in 1990' in A.M. Pettigrew, R. Whittington, L. Melin, C. Sanchez-Runde, F. Van den Bosch, W. Ruigrok and T. Numagami (eds) (2003), *Innovative Forms of Organizing: International Perspectives*, London: Sage.

Pinch, T. and Bijker, W. (1987), 'The Social Construction of Facts and Artifacts: Or How the Sociology of Science and the Sociology of Technology Might Benefit Each Other' in W.E. Bijker, T.P. Hughes and T.J. Pinch (eds), *The Social Construction of Technological Systems. New Directions in the Sociology and History of Technology*, pp. 17–50, Cambridge, MA: The MIT Press.

Piore, M.J. and Sabel, C.F. (1984), *The Second Industrial Divide*, New York: Basic Books.

Podolny, J.M. and Page, K.L. (1998), 'Network Forms of Organization' in *Annual Review of Sociology*, vol. 24, no. 1, pp. 57–76.

Polanyi, M. (1966), *The Tacit Dimension*, New York: Anchor Books.

Polanyi, K. (1968), *Primitive, Archaic and Modern Economies*, New York: Doubleday & Company.

Polanyi K. (1977), *The Livelihood of Man*, New York: Academic Press.

Pool, I.D.S. and Kochen, M. (1978), 'Contacts and Influence' in *Social Networks*, vol. 31, no. 1, pp. 5–51.

Porter, M. (1998), 'Clusters and the New Economics of Competition' in *Harvard Business Review*, vol. 76, no. 6, pp. 77–90.

Powell, W.W. and Grodal, S. (2005), 'Networks of Innovators' in J. Fagerberg, D.C. Mowery and R.R. Nelson (eds), *The Oxford Handbook of Innovation*, pp. 56–85, New York: Oxford University Press.

Powell, W.W. and Owen-Smith, J. (1999), 'Network Position and Firm Performance' in S. Andrews and D. Knoke (eds), *Research in the Sociology of Organizations*, pp. 129–59, Greenwich, CN: JAI Press.

Powell, W.W. and Snellman, K. (2004), 'The Knowledge Economy' in *Annual Review of Sociology*, vol. 30, no. 1, pp. 199–220.

Powell, W.W., Koput, K.W. and Smith-Doerr, L. (1996), 'Interorganizational Collaboration and the Locus of Innovation: Networks of Learning in Biotechnology' in *Administrative Science Quarterly*, vol. 41, no. 1, pp. 116–45.

Powell, W.W., Koput, K.W., Bowie, J.I. and Smith-Doerr, L. (2002), 'The Spatial Clustering of Science and Capital: Accounting for Biotech Firm-Venture Capital Relationships' in *Regional Studies*, vol. 36, no. 3, pp. 291–305.

Pyke, F. and Sengenberger, W. (1991), 'Introduzione' in F. Pyke, G. Becattini and W. Sengenberger (1991), 'Distretti industriali e cooperazione fra imprese in Italia' in *Studi e Informazioni*, pp. 15–34, Quaderni 34, Banca Toscana.

Pyke, F. and Sengenberger, W. (1992), 'Industrial Districts and Local Economic Regeneration: Research and Policy Issues' in F. Pyke and W. Sengenberger, *Industrial Districts and Local Economic Regeneration*, Geneva: International Institute for Labour Studies.

Pyke, F., Becattini G. and Sengenberger, W. (1991), 'Distretti industriali e cooperazione fra imprese in Italia' in *Studi e Informazioni*, Quaderni 34, Banca Toscana.

Ramella, F. (2000), 'Still a "Red Subculture"? Continuity and Change in Central Italy' in *South European Society and Politics*, vol. 5, no. 1, pp. 1–24.

Ramella, F. (2005a), *Cuore rosso? Viaggio politico nell'Italia di mezzo*, Roma: Donzelli.

Ramella, F. (2005b), 'Reti sociali e performance economiche nelle imprese ICT' in *Stato e Mercato*, no. 3, pp. 355–90.

Ramella, F. (2007), *Political Economy*, in G. Ritzer (ed.), *The Blackwell Encyclopedia of Sociology*, pp. 3433–6, Oxford: Blackwell.

Ramella, F. (2011), 'L'impresa dell'innovazione' in *Sociologia del lavoro*, no. 122, pp. 57–68.

Ramella, F. and Trigilia, C. (eds) (2006), *Reti sociali e innovazione. I sistemi locali dell'informatica*, Firenze: Firenze University Press.

Ramella, F. and Trigilia, C. (eds) (2010a), *Imprese e territori dell'Alta Tecnologia in Italia*, Bologna: Il Mulino.

Ramella, F. and Trigilia, C. (eds) (2010b), *Invenzioni, inventori e territori in Italia*, Bologna: Il Mulino.

Regini, M. (2006a), 'Political Economy' in J. Beckert and M. Zafirovski (eds), *International Encyclopedia of Economic Sociology*, pp. 517–22, London and New York: Routledge.

Regini, M. (2006b), *Uncertain Boundaries. The Social and Political Construction of European Economies*, New York: Cambridge University Press.

Regini, M. (ed.) (2007), *La sociologia economica contemporanea*, Roma-Bari: Laterza.

Regini, M. (2011), *European Universities and the Challenge of the Market. A Comprarative Analysis*, Cheltenham, UK, and Northampton, USA: Edward Elgar.

Robertson, P.L., Jacobson, D. and Langlois, R.N. (2009), 'Innovation Processes and Industrial Districts' in G. Becattini, M. Bellandi and L. De Propris (eds), *A Handobook of Industrial Districts*, pp. 269–98, Cheltenham, UK, and Northampton, USA: Edward Elgar.

Rodríguez-Pose, A. (2011), 'Economists as Geographers and Geographers as Something Else: On the Changing Conception of Distance in Geography and Economics' in *Journal of Economic Geography*, vol. 11, no. 2, pp. 347–56.

Rodríguez-Pose, A. and Crescenzi, R. (2011), 'Mountains in a Flat World: Why Proximity Still Matters for the Location of Economic Activity' in *Cambridge Journal of Regions, Economy and Society*, vol. 1, no. 3, pp. 371–88.

Rodrik, D. (2007), *One Economics. Many Recipes. Globalization, Institutions and Economic Growth*, Princeton: Princeton University Press.

Rogers, E.M. (2003), *Diffusion of Innovations*, New York: Free Press.

Romer, P.M. (1986), 'Increasing Returns and Long-Run Growth' in *Journal of Political Economy*, vol. 94, no. 5, pp. 1002–37.

Rosenberg, N. (1974), 'Karl Marx on the Economic Role of Science' in *Journal of Political Economy*, vol. 82, no. 4, pp. 713–28.

Rosenberg, N. (1982), *Inside the Black Box: Technology and Economics*, Cambridge: Cambridge University Press.

Rosenberg, N. (2007), 'Endogenous Forces in Twentieth-Century America' in E. Sheshinski, R.J. Strom and W.J Baumol (eds), *Entrepreneurship, Innovation, and the Growth*

Mechanism of the Free-Enterprise Economies, pp. 80–99, Princeton: Princeton University Press.

Rossi, P. (1981), 'L'analisi sociologica delle "religioni universali"' in P. Rossi (ed.), *Max Weber and l'analisi del mondo moderno*, pp. 127–59, Torino: Einaudi.

Rossi, S. and Travaglini, R. (1997), *Progettare la creatività. Teorie psicologiche e analisi dei casi*, Milano: Guerin.

Rothwell, R. (1977), 'The Characteristics of Successful Innovators and Technically Progressive Firms' in *R&D Management*, vol. 7, no. 3, pp. 191–206.

Ruef M. (2002), 'Strong Ties, Weak Ties and Islands: Structural and Cultural Predictors of Organizational Innovation' in *Industrial and Corporate Change*, vol. 11, no. 3, pp. 427–49.

Rullani, E. (2004), *Economia della conoscenza. Creatività e valore nel capitalismo delle reti*, Roma: Carocci.

Runco, M.A. (2004), 'Creativity' in *Annual Review of Psychology*, vol. 55, pp. 657–87.

Rusconi, G.E. (1981), 'Razionalità, razionalizzazione e burocratizzazione' in P. Rossi, (ed.), *Max Weber e l'analisi del mondo moderno*, pp. 189–214, Torino: Einaudi.

Rutten, R. and Boekema, F. (eds) (2007), *The Learning Region. Foundations, State of the Art, Future*, Cheltenham: Edward Elgar.

Rutten, R. and Boekema, F. (2012), 'From Learning Region to Learning in a Socio-spatial Context' in *Regional Studies*, vol. 46, no. 8, pp. 981–92.

Sandler, T. and Tschirhart J. (1997), 'Club Theory: Thirty Years Later' in *Public Choice*, vol. 93, nn. 3–4, pp. 335–55.

Sauermann, H. and Cohen, W.M. (2010), 'What Makes Them Tick? Employee Motives and Firm Innovation' in *Mangement Science*, vol. 56, no. 12, pp. 2134–53.

Sawyer, R.K. (2003), *Group Creativity*, Mahwah, NJ: Lawrence Erlbaum Associates.

Sawyer, R.K. (2006), *Explaining Creativity. The Science of Human Innovation*, New York: Oxford University Press.

Saxenian, A. (1994), *Regional Advantage: Culture and Competition in Silicon Valley and Route 128*, Cambridge, MA: Harvard University Press.

Saxenian, A. (2001), 'Inside-Out: Regional Networks and Industrial Adaptation in Silicon Valley and Route 128' in M. Granovetter and R. Swedberg (eds), *The Sociology of Economic Life*, pp. 357–74, Boulder, CO: Westview Press.

Saxenian, A. (2007), *The New Argonauts. Regional Advantage in a Global Economy*, Cambridge, MA: Harvard University Press.

Schilling, M.A. and Phelps, C.C. (2007), 'Interfirm Collaboration Networks: The Impact of Large-Scale Network Structure on Firm Innovation' in *Management Science*, vol. 53, no. 7, pp. 1113–26.

Schmookler, J. (1957), 'Inventors Past and Present' in *The Review of Economics and Statistics*, vol. 39, no. 3, pp. 321–33.

Schnettler, S. (2009a), 'A Small World on Feet of Clay? A Comparison of Empirical Small-World Studies Against Best-Practice Criteria' in *Social Network*, vol. 31, no. 3, pp. 179–89.

Schnettler, S. (2009b), 'A Structured Overview of 50 Years of Small World Research' in *Social Network*, vol. 31, no. 3, pp. 165–78.

Schrank, A. and Whitford, J. (2011), 'The Anatomy of Network Failure' in *Sociological Theory*, vol. 29, no. 3, pp. 151–77.

Schumpeter, J.A. (1912) *Theorie der wirtschaftlichen Entwicklung*, Leipzig: Duncker & Humblot. (Eng. trans. (1980), *The Theory of Economic Development*, London: Oxford University Press.)

Schumpeter, J.A. (1939), *Business Cycles. A Theoretical, Historical and Statistical*

Analysis of the Capitalist Process, 2 vols, New York, Toronto and London: McGraw-Hill Book Company.

Schumpeter, J.A. (1942 [2003]), *Capitalism, Socialism and Democracy*, London and New York: Routledge.

Schumpeter, J.A. (1947), 'The Creative Response in Economic History' in *The Journal of Economic History*, vol. 7, no. 2, pp. 149–59.

Scott, J. (1986), *Capitalist Property and Financial Property*, Brighton: Wheatsheaf.

Scott, J. (1991), *Social Network Analysis. A Handbook*, London: Sage.

Sharif, N. (2006), 'Emergence and Development of the National Innovation Systems Concept' in *Research Policy*, vol. 35, no. 5, pp. 745–66.

Sharp, M. and Senker, J. (1999), *European Biotechnology: Learning and Catching-up*, in A. Gambardella and F. Malerba (eds), *The Organization of Economic Innovation in Europe*, pp. 269–302, Cambridge: Cambridge University Press.

Simms, D.L. and Dalley, S. (2093), 'The Archimedean Screw' in *Technology and Culture*, vol. 50, no. 3, pp. 730–5.

Simmel, G. (1907), *Philosophie des Geldes*, Leipzig: Duncker & Humblot. (Eng. trans. (2004), *The Philosophy of Money*, London: Routledge.)

Simmel, G. (1908), *Soziologie*, Leipzig: Duncker & Humblot. (Eng. trans. (1950) *The Sociology of Georg Simmel*, New York: The Free Press.)

Simonton, D.K. (1992), 'The Social Context of Career Success and Course for 2,026 Scientists and Inventors' in *Personality and Social Psychology Bulletin*, vol. 18, no. 4, pp. 452–63.

Simonton, D.K. (1999), 'Creativity from a Historiometric Perspective' in R.J. Sternberg (ed.), *Handbook of Creativity*, pp. 116–34, Cambridge: Cambridge University Press.

Singh, J. and Fleming, L. (2010), 'Lone Inventors as Sources of Breakthroughs: Myth or Reality?' in *Management Science*, vol. 56, no. 1, pp. 41–56.

Sismondo, S. (2007), *An Introduction to Science and Technology Studies*, Malden, USA, and Oxford, UK: Wiley-Blackwell.

Smelser, N.J. and Swedberg, R. (eds) (1994), *The Handbook of Economic Sociology*, Princeton: Princeton University Press.

Smelser, N.J. and Swedberg, R. (eds) (2005), *The Handbook of Economic Sociology*, Princeton: Princeton University Press.

Smith A. (1776 [2005]) *An Inquiry into the Nature and Causes of the Wealth of Nations*, The Pennsylvania State University, available at: http://www2.hn.psu.edu/faculty/jmanis/adam-smith/wealth-nations.pdf

Smith A. (1763), 'An Early Draft of Part of The Wealth Of Nations' in W.R. Scott (1937) *Adam Smith as Student and Professor*, pp. 317–56, Glasgow: Jackson, Son & Company.

Smith, D.K. and Alexander, R.C. (1988) *Fumbling the Future: How Xerox Invented, and Then Ignored, the First Personal Computer*, New York: Morrow.

Smith-Doerr, L. and Powell, W.W. (2005), 'Networks and Economic Life' in Smelser, N.J. and Swedberg, R. (eds), *The Handbook of Economic Sociology*, pp. 379–402, Princeton: Princeton University Press.

Solow R. (1987), 'We'd Better Watch Out' in *New York Times Book Review*, July 12, p. 36.

Sombart, W. (1916), *Der Moderne Kapitalismus*, Berlin: Duncker & Humblot, 2nd edition. (It. trans. (1967), *Il capitalism moderno*, Torino: Utet.)

Sorenson, O., Rivkin, W.J. and Fleming, L. (2006), 'Complexity, Networks and Knowledge Flow' in *Research Policy*, vol. 35, no. 7, pp. 994–1017.

Soskice, D. (1999), 'Divergent Production Regimes: Coordinated and Uncoordinated Market Economies in the 1980s and 1990s' in H. Kitschelt, P. Lange, G. Marks and J.D. Stephens (eds), *Continuity and Change in Contemporary Capitalism*, Cambridge: Cambridge University Press.

Stark, D. (2009), *The Sense of Dissonance*, Princeton: Princeton University Press,

Steinmueller, W.E. (2004), 'The European Software Sectoral System of Innovation' in Malerba, F. (ed.), *Sectoral Systems of Innovation*, pp. 193–242, New York: Cambridge University Press.

Sternberg, R.J. and Lubart, T.I. (1999), 'The Concept of Creativity: Prospects and Paradigms' in R.J. Sternberg (ed.), *Handbook of Creativity*, pp. 3–15, Cambridge: Cambridge University Press.

Storper, M. (1993), 'Regional "Worlds" of Production: Learning and Innovation in the Technology Districts of France, Italy and the USA' in *Regional Studies*, vol. 27, no. 5, pp. 433–55.

Storper, M. (1995), 'The Resurgence of Regional Economies, Ten Years Later: The Region as a Nexus of Untraded Interdependencies' in *European Urban and Regional Studies*, vol. 2, no. 3, pp. 191–221.

Storper, M. (1997), *The Regional World: Territorial Development in a Global Economy*, New York: The Guilford Press.

Storper, M. and Scott, A.J. (2009), 'Rethinking Human Capital, Creativity and Urban Growth' in *Journal of Economic Geography*, vol. 9, no. 2, pp. 147–67.

Storper, M. and Venables A.J. (2004), 'Buzz: Face-to-Face Contact and the Urban Economy' in *Journal of Economic Geography*, vol. 4, no. 4, pp. 351–70.

Streeck, W. (2009), *Re-Forming Capitalism. Institutional Change in the German Political Economy*, Oxford: Oxford University Press.

Streeck, W. (2010), *E Pluribus Unum? Varieties and Commonalities of Capitalism*, MPIfG discussion paper 10/12, Max Planck Institute for the Study of Societies, Cologne, October.

Swedberg, R. (1994), *Schumpeter. A Biography*, Princeton: Princeton University Press.

Tarde, G. (1890), *Les lois de l'imitation*, Paris, Félix Alcan. (Eng. trans. (1903), *The Laws of Imitation*, New York: Henry Holt and Company.)

Tarde, G. (1895), *La logique sociale*, Paris: Félix Alcan.

Tarde, G. (1898), 'La sociologie' in G. Tarde, *Etudes de psychologie sociale*, pp. 1–62, Paris: Félix Alcan. (Eng. trans. (2010), *On Communication & Social Influence. Selected Papers*, pp. 73–105, Chicago: The University of Chicago Press.)

Tarde, G. (1902a), 'L'Invention, Moteur de l'Evolution Sociale' in *Revue Internationale de Sociologie*, vol. 7, pp. 561–74.

Tarde, G. (1902b), *Psychologie économique*, Paris: Félix Alcan. (Partial Eng. trans. *On Communication & Social Influence Selected Papers* (2010), pp. 149–64, Chicago: The University of Chicago Press.)

Tarde, G. (2010), *On Communication & Social Influence. Selected Papers*, Chicago: The University of Chicago Press.

Taymans, A.C. (1950), 'Tarde and Schumpeter: A Similar Vision' in *The Quarterly Journal of Economics*, vol. 64, no. 4, pp. 611–22.

Toffler, A. (1970), *Future Shock*, New York: Random House.

Thelen, K. (2010), 'Beyond Comparative Statics: Historical Institutional Approaches to Stability and Change in the Political Economy of Labor?' in G. Morgan, J.L. Campbell, C. Crouch, O.K. Pedersen and R. Whitley (eds), *The Oxford Handbook of Comparative Institutional Analysis*, pp. 41–61, Oxford and New York: Oxford University Press.

Thompson, P. and Fox-Kean, M. (2005), 'Patent Citations and the Geography of Knowledge Spillovers: A Reassessment' in *The American Economic Review*, vol. 95, no. 1, pp. 450–60.

Torre, A. and Ralle, A. (2005), 'Proximity and Localization' in *Regional Studies*, vol. 39, no. 1, pp. 61–74.

Torrisi, S. (1999), 'Firm Specialization and Growth: A Study of the European Software Industry' in A. Gambardella and F. Malerba (eds), *The Organization of Economic Innovation in Europe*, pp. 239–68, Cambridge: Cambridge University Press.

Trajtenberg, M. (1987), *Patents, Citations and Innovations. Tracing the Links*, Cambridge, MA: National Bureau of Economic Research.

Travers, J. and Milgram, S. (1969), 'An Experimental Study of the Small World Problem' in *Sociometry*, vol. 32, no. 4, pp. 425–43.

Trigilia, C. (1986), *Grandi partiti e piccole imprese. Comunisti e democristiani nelle regioni a economia diffusa*, Bologna: Il Mulino.

Trigilia, C. (1990), 'Work and Politics in the Third Italy's Industrial District' in F. Pyke, G. Becattini and W. Sengenberger (eds), *Industrial District and Inter-firm Cooperation in Italy*, pp. 160–84, Geneva: IILS, ILO.

Trigilia, C. (2005), *Sviluppo locale. Un progetto per l'Italia*, Roma-Bari: Laterza.

Trigilia, C. (2006), 'Economic Sociology' in Beckert, J. and Zafirovski M. (eds), *International Encyclopedia of Economic Sociology*, pp. 192–206, London and New York: Routledge.

Trigilia, C. (2007a), 'Crescita squilibrata: perché la sociologia economica ha più successo nella teoria che nelle politiche?' in *Stato e Mercato*, no. 1, pp. 11–29.

Trigilia, C. (2007b), 'La costruzione sociale dell'innovazione. Economia società e territorio' in *Quaderni della Biblioteca del Polo Universitario Città di Prato*, no. 4, pp. 1–56, Firenze: Firenze University Press.

Trigilia, C. (2009), *Sociologia economica II. Temi e percorsi contemporanei*, Bologna: Il Mulino.

Usai, S. (2008), 'The Geography of Inventive Activities in OECD Regions' in *OECD Science, Technology and Industry Working Papers*, 2008/3, OECD Publishing. doi: 10.1787/230083500260, pp. 1–63.

Uzzi, B. (1997), 'Social Structure and Competition in Interfirm Networks: The Paradox of Embeddedness' in *Administrative Science Quarterly*, vol. 42, no. 1, pp. 35–67.

Uzzi, B. (1999), 'Embeddedness in the Making of Financial Capital: How Social Relations and Networks Benefit Firms Seeking Financing' in *American Sociological Review*, vol. 64, no. 4, pp. 481–505.

Uzzi, B. and Spiro, J. (2005), 'Collaboration and Creativity: The Small World Problem' in *American Journal of Sociology*, vol. 111, no. 2, pp. 447–504.

Van Vijk, R., Van Den Bosch, F.A.J. and Volberda, H.W. (2003), 'Knowledge and Networks' in M. Easterby-Smith and M.A. Lyles (eds), *Blackwell Handbook of Organizational Learning and Knowledge Management*, pp. 428–53, Oxford: Blackwell.

Veblen, T.B. (1899), *The Theory of the Leisure Class: An Economic Study in the Evolution of Institutions*, New York: Macmillan.

Veblen, T.B. (1909), 'The Limitations of Marginal Utility in *Journal of Political Economy*, vol. 17, no. 9, pp. 620–36.

Verspagen, B. and Duysters, G. (2004), 'The Small Worlds of Strategic Technology Alliances' in *Technovation*, vol. 24, no. 7, pp. 563–71.

Von Hippel, E. (1988), *The Sources of Innovation*, New York and Oxford: Oxford University Press.

Von Hippel, E. (2005), *Democratizing Innovation*, Cambridge, MA: The MIT Press.

Von Hippel, E. and Von Krogh, G. (2003), 'Open Source Software and the "Private-Collective" Model: Issues for Organization Science' in *Organization Science*, vol. 14, no. 2, pp. 209–23.

Wade, R. (1990), *Governing the Market: Economic Theory and the Role of Government in East Asian Industrialization*, Princeton: Princeton University Press.

Waller, W.T. Jr. (1994), 'The Evolution of the Veblenian Dichotomy: Veblen, Hamilton, Ayres, and Foster' in *Journal of Economic Issues*, vol. 16, no. 3, pp. 757–71.

Wasserman, S. and Faust, K. (1994), *Social Network Analysis. Methods and Applications*, Cambridge, MA: Cambridge University Press.

Watts, D.J. (1999), 'Networks, Dynamics and the Small-World Phenomenon' in *American Journal of Sociology*, vol. 105, no. 2, pp. 493–527.

Watts, D.J. (2004a), *Six Degrees. The Science of a Connected Age*, London: Vintage Books.

Watts, D.J. (2004b), 'The "New" Science of Networks' in *Annual Review of Sociology*, vol. 30, August, pp. 243–70.

Watts, D.J. and Strogatz, S.H. (1998), 'Collective Dynamics of "Small World" Networks' in *Nature*, vol. 393, 4 June, pp. 440–2.

Watts, D.J., Dodds, P.S. and Newman, M.E.J. (2002), 'Identity and Search in Social Networks' in *Science*, vol. 296, no. 5571, pp. 1302–5.

Weber, M. (1922a), *Die protestantische Ethik und der Geist des Kapitalismus*, Tübingen: Mohr. (Eng. trans. (2005), *The Protestant Ethic and the Spirit of Capitalism*, London and New York: Routledge.)

Weber, M. (1922b), *Wirtschaft und Gesellschaft*, Tübingen: Mohr. (Eng. trans. (1947), *Max Weber: The Theory of Social and Economic Organization*, New York: Oxford University Press.)

Weber, M. (1958), *Wirtschaftsgeschichte: Abriß der universalen Sozial und Wirtschaftsgeschichte*, Berlin: Duncker & Humblot. (Eng. trans. (2003), *General Economic History*, New York: Greenberg.)

Weber, M. (2008), *Max Weber's Complete Writings on Academic and Political Vocations*, New York: Algora.

Weber, M. (2005), 'Remarks on Technology and Culture' in *Theory, Culture & Society*, vol. 22, no. 4, pp. 23–38.

Weimann, G. (1983), 'The Not-So-Small World of Ethnicity and Acquaintance Networks in Israel' in *Social Networks*, vol. 5, no. 3, pp. 289–302.

Weisberg, R. W. (1993), *Creativity: Beyond the Myth of Genius*, New York: Freeman.

Wenger, E. (1998), *Communities of Practice. Learning, Meaning and Identity*, Cambridge: Cambridge University Press.

West, A.M. (2003), 'Innovation Implementation in Work Teams' in P.B. Paulus and B.A. Nijstad (eds), *Group Creativity. Innovation Through Collaboration*, pp. 245–68, New York: Oxford University Press.

Whitaker, J.K. (1975), *The Early Economic Writings of Alfred Marshall, 1867–1890*, vol. II, London: Macmillan.

White, H.C. (1970), 'Search Parameters for the Small World Problem' in *Social Forces*, vol. 49, no. 2, pp. 259–64.

Williams, R. and Edge, D. (1996), 'The Social Shaping of Technology' in *Research Policy*, vol. 25, no. 6, pp. 865–99.

Winter, S.G. (1984), 'Schumpeterian Competition in Alternative Technological Regimes' in *Journal of Economic Behavior and Organization*, vol. 5, nn. 3–4, pp. 287–320.

Woodward, J. (1965), *Industrial Organization: Theory and Practice*, New York: Oxford University Press.

Zucker, L.G. and Darby, M.R. (1996), 'Star Scientists and Institutional Transformation: Patterns of Invention and Innovation in the Formation of the Biotechnology Industry' in *Proceedings of the National Academy of Sciences*, vol. 93, no. 23, pp. 12709–16.

Zucker, L.G. and Darby, M.R. (2007), *Star Scientists, Innovation and Regional and National Immigration*, NBER Working Paper Series, no. 13547, pp. 1–41.

Zucker, L.G., Darby, M.R. and Armstrong, J. (1998), 'Geographically Localized Knowledge: Spillovers or Markets?' in *Economic Inquiry*, vol. XXXVI, January, pp. 65–86.

Zucker, L.G., Darby, M.R. and Brewer, M.B (1998), 'Intellectual Human Capital and the Birth of U.S. Biotechnology Enterprises' in *The American Economic Review*, vol. 88, no. 1, pp. 290–306.

Zucker, L.G., Darby, M.R., Furner, J., Liu, R.C. and Ma, H. (2007), 'Minerva Unbound: Knowledge Stocks, Knowledge Flows and New Knowledge Production' in *Research Policy*, vol. 36, no. 6, pp. 850–63.

Index

For Product Safety Concerns and Information please contact our EU
representative GPSR@taylorandfrancis.com
Taylor & Francis Verlag GmbH, Kaufingerstraße 24, 80331 München, Germany

www.ingramcontent.com/pod-product-compliance
Ingram Content Group UK Ltd.
Pitfield, Milton Keynes, MK11 3LW, UK
UKHW021618240425
457818UK00018B/622